Rural Poverty Alleviation in Brazil

Toward an Integrated Strategy

THE WORLD BANK
Washington, D.C.

ISBN: 0-8213-5206-7
eISBN: 0-8213-5207-5
ISSN: 0253-2123

Library of Congress Cataloging-in-Publication Data

Rural poverty alleviation in Brazil: toward an integrated strategy.
      p. cm. -- (World Bank country study)
   Includes bibliographical references (p.).
   ISBN 0-8213-5206-7
    1. Poverty--Brazil. 2. rural poor--Brazil. 3. Economic assistance--Brazil. I. World Bank. II. Series.

HC 190.P6 R87 2003
339.4'6'0981091734--dc21

2002032186

CONTENTS

ABSTRACT

The objective of this report is to design an integrated strategy for rural poverty reduction in Brazil. It contains an updated and detailed profile of the rural poor in the northeast and southeast regions of Brazil; identifies key determinants of rural poverty in these regions; and proposes a five-pronged strategic framework and a tentative set of policy options. The latter were identified via an analysis of rural poverty determinants complemented with an evaluation of relevant current public programs and six in-depth thematic studies: (a) the dynamics of the Brazilian small farm sector, (b) rural labor markets, (c) rural land markets, (d) rural non-farm employment, (e) rural education, and (f) rural pensions.

PREFACE

This study was prepared by Alberto Valdés (Task Manager) and Johan A. Mistiaen (Consultant). We gladly acknowledge the helpful observations by the peer reviewers Malcolm Bale (Sector manager, EASRD) and Robert Thompson (Director, RDV) and the constructive comments by Gobind Nankani (Former Country Director, LCC5C), Joachim von Amsberg (Lead Economist, LCC5C), Norman Hicks (Sector Manager, LCSPP), Indermit Gill (Lead Economist, LCSHD), and Mark Roland Thomas (Economist, LCC5A).

Drafts of this report have been discussed with many institutions and individuals of the Brazilian Government, and their comments have been taken into account. However, the views expressed in this report are exclusively those of the World Bank.

> Vice President: David de Ferranti
> Country Director: Vinod Thomas
> Sector Director: Ernesto May
> Sector Manager: Norman L. Hicks
> Task Manager: Alberto Valdés

ABBREVIATIONS AND ACRONYMS

FUMAC	Municipal Fund for Community Support (*Fundo Municipal de Apoio Comunitário*)
FUMAC-P	Pilot Municipal Fund for Community Support (*Fundo Municipal de Apoio Comunitário—Piloto*)
FUNRURAL	Rural Pension System
H$_d$	hectares
IBGE	Brazilian Institute of Statistics and Geography (*Instituto Brasileiro de Geografia e Estatística*)
INCRA	National Land Reform Institute
LSMS	Living Standard Measurement Survey
NE	Northeast Region
NGO	Non-Governmental Organization
NRDP	Northeast Rural Development Program
PNAD	*Pesquisa Nacional por Amostra de Domicilios*
PPV	Living Standard Measurement Survey (*Pesquisa sobre Padrões da Vida*)
PROCERA	Family Farm Credit for Land Reform Beneficiaries, now replaced by PRONAF
PRONAF	Family Farm Credit
RGPS	Public Pensions System for Private Sector Workers
RNF	Rural Non-Farm
R-NRDP	Reformulated Northeast Rural Development Program
RPAP	Rural Poverty Alleviation Program
SE	Southeast Region
TA	Technical Assistance

Currency Equivalents

Currency Unit—Real (R$)
December 1999: R$1.79/US$
December 2000: R$ 1.95/US$
December 2001: R$ 2.40/US$

Weights And Measures
The Metric System is used throughout the report.

Fiscal Year
January 1 to December 31

EXECUTIVE SUMMARY

T his constitutes a step towards the objective of designing an integrated strategy for rural poverty reduction in Brazil. The report contains an updated and more detailed profile of the rural poor in the northeast (NE) and southeast (SE) regions of Brazil; identifies key determinants of rural poverty in these regions; and proposes a five-pronged strategic framework in which to couch a set of integrated policies that could effectively help to reduce rural poverty in Brazil. This tentative set of policy options was identified via an analysis of rural poverty determinants complemented with an evaluation of relevant current public programs and six in-depth thematic studies that bear on critical components of the proposed integrated policy approach aimed at reducing rural poverty in the NE and SE of Brazil: (a) the dynamics of the Brazilian small farm sector, (b) rural labor markets, (c) rural land markets, (d) RNF employment, (e) rural education, and (f) rural pensions.

While this study emphasizes primarily microeconomic events—such as the impact of schooling, income transfers, and access to land and credit—poverty reduction requires both economic growth (macro-level) and specific anti-poverty policies (micro-level). Especially in Brazil, where agriculture represents less than 10 percent of GDP and about 23 percent of employment, fast-growing employment in urban areas and expansion in domestic demand for farm products that would result from fast growth in the overall economy—particularly for small farmers producers of non-tradables—could go a long way in reducing rural poverty, even if the agricultural economy does not grow very fast. Essentially, achieving a significant reduction in rural poverty without rapid overall economic growth would be quite difficult in Brazil. Note also that this report covers only the NE and the SE regions of Brazil due to household level data constraints. Thus, while the bulk of the rural poor live in the latter regions, the issues addressed and the tentative strategic framework for rural poverty reduction might need to be somewhat adapted in other regions. Some of the potentially important issues in a poverty reduction context that could not be covered include: (i) the impact of commercial agricultural policies, (b) the effect of overall government programs in rural areas that are not poverty focused per se (for example, the substantial spending by the Ministry of Agriculture and overall credit programs), and (c) the often complex and important environment-poverty inter-linkages.

I

The bottom-line in terms of strategy recommendations is the need for a set of integrated policies that channels the rural poor into multiple poverty exit paths. The rationale underlying this conclusion emerges from a synthesis of several key issues identified in this report. First, the poverty profile indicates that the rural poor in the NE and SE of Brazil is not only large—about 9.8 million people—but also very heterogeneous in terms of income sources, quantity and quality of human- and physical-capital endowments, and location. This is suggestive of multiple possible poverty exit paths and this should be reflected in a set of integrated policies that is tailored to capitalize on the heterogeneous living conditions of the rural poor. The need for an integrated approach is further underscored by synergetic effects among policy relevant determinants of rural poverty in farm households. A key finding in this context is that returns to farmland are highly dependent on the levels of complementary productive factors (such as, purchased inputs, machinery) and demographic factors (for example, age of operator, education). Consequently, for land to have a large productivity and revenue increasing impact in farming, it appears necessary to simultaneously improve the levels of other factors such as purchased inputs and machinery.

A Profile of Rural Poverty: Updated Facts and New Findings

Designing effective rural poverty reduction programs in a large and diverse country such as Brazil is difficult in a vacuum with respect to knowledge of a disaggregated rural poverty profile.

- Poverty continues to disproportionately affect the rural NE where the poverty incidence is estimated to be about 49 percent (compared to 24 percent in the rural SE).
- Rural poverty reduction in Brazil remains a substantial challenge: approximately 43 percent of the poor in the northeast (NE) and southeast (SE) of Brazil are rural (9.8 million people).

The importance of poverty estimates lies not *per se* in specific numbers, but rather in the identification of the most deprived groups. This is borne out by previously unavailable estimates for Brazil via disaggregation over both detailed geographical and income-group categories:

- Rural poverty disproportionately affects the northeastern states of Brazil, particularly Maranhão, Piauí, Ceará, Alagoas, and Bahia. Even within the NE, the overall impression is one of considerable geographical (and presumably agro-climatic, though this level of disaggregation is presently not feasible due to data constraints) diversity regarding the incidence of poverty.
- The bulk of the total estimated poor in the rural NE and SE, 83.6 percent (about 6.7 million people) and 90.3 percent (about 1.6 million people) respectively, are found to be farm households located in remote, isolated, sparsely populated and low productivity areas, for whom income from farming and agricultural labor represents approximately 70 percent of their total household income. Regardless of region, those that receive their main income via farming or farm labor are consistently the poorest group, whilst non-agricultural workers comprise the relatively better off group. Public pensions are the main source of non-labor income.
- Location matters. Poverty incidence is lower in rural areas directly adjacent to, but not formally incorporated into the urban perimeter of municipalities. Similarly, the share of Rural Non-Farm (RNF) income increases in these areas. However, given the geographically biased distribution of poverty towards remote rural areas, for the bulk of the rural poor RNF income represents only a small fraction of income.

Compared to their urban counterparts, the rural poor in the NE and SE of Brazil are worse off in terms of demographics, educational achievement, access to and quality of services. For instance:

- In 1996, only 43 percent of households in the lowest income quintile from the rural NE had access to electricity;
- Of the latter group, an average of 75 percent of the household heads are illiterate;

- In the rural NE, 27 percent of teachers have not completed their primary education and only 15 percent of children are enrolled past the fourth grade; and
- Only 2 percent of poor farms received some form of technical assistance.

Aging small farmers and the relatively high proportion of female-headed rural households emerge as particular groups to consider in the context of safety net policies:

- The average age of the head of household in small farms is high and there appears to be a strong relationship between aging, productivity and poverty in small farms.
- Female-headed households represent an approximate 15 percent of all rural households in the NE (12 percent in SE) and this proportion reaches up to 30 percent among rural households whose main income source is non-agricultural (20 percent in the SE). In these households where husbands migrated or died, income is found to be significantly increased by pension payments.

Finally, In contrast to urban areas, rural poverty analysis in Brazil continues to be greatly constrained by the scarceness of adequate data (*miseria estadistica*). Particularly constraining is the scarceness of adequate household income data in rural areas. For instance, the absence of comparable inter-temporal data (unlike some countries in the region) currently precludes an analysis of how the poverty profile and determinants have changed over time. Moreover, data limitations precluded computing estimates of the number of rural poor that could be assisted via each of the five strategies—this should be a priority in follow-up work. This report draws primarily on two household survey data sets fielded in 1996: the *Pesquisa Nacional por Amostra de Domicílios* (PNAD) data and the *Pesquisa sobre Padrões de Vida* (PPV) survey implemented by the *Instituto Brasileiro de Geografia e Estatística* (IBGE) based on the World Bank's LSMS survey design. Both data sets suffer from strengths and weaknesses. Consequently, the preliminary expenditure based spatially disaggregated poverty profile presented in this report could be produced only by employing very recently developed small-to-large survey imputation techniques.

A Five-Prong Strategic Framework for Rural Poverty Reduction

The main findings emerging out of this new and more detailed rural poverty profile essentially reveal an overall pattern of pronounced heterogeneity in welfare indicators and income sources among the rural poor in Brazil. Consequently, *the proposed rural poverty reduction strategy is framed in terms of an integrated set of policies that provide multiple paths out of poverty tailored to the heterogeneous cross-section of poor rural household groups.* A five-prong poverty exit paths approach is envisaged:

1. Agricultural Intensification of the Small Farm Sector

Agricultural policy geared towards small-scale low productivity farms should be viewed primarily as part of a poverty reduction strategy as opposed to an agricultural growth program per se. In the NE, there are opportunities for developing viable full-time small-farm activities, typically comprising a combination of subsistence and market production. The crucial policy areas are rural land and finance market reform, increasing R&D and technological transfers, supplying public goods, and building up social capital. A key finding in the context of this potential poverty exit path is that returns to farmland are highly dependent on the levels of complementary productive (for example, purchased inputs, machinery, etc.) and demographic factors (for example, age of operator, education). Consequently, for land to have a large productivity and revenue increasing impact in farming, it appears necessary to simultaneously improve the levels of other factors such as purchased inputs and machinery. This reinforces the need for an integrated policy framework that recognizes these synergies and brings them into play.

Approximately 85 percent of the total estimated poor in the rural NE and SE (about 8.3 million people) are found among farm households located in remote, isolated, sparsely populated and low productivity areas, for whom income from farming and agricultural labor represents approximately

70 percent of their total household income. What must be further examined at this stage is how big the subset of this target group is that could effectively pursue this poverty exit path.

2. A More Dynamic Commercial Agricultural Sector

A revitalized commercial agriculture sector could increase employment and reduce rural poverty directly by absorbing wage labor and indirectly via growth of the downstream processing industry. For example, efficient, market-driven expansion of irrigated areas in the Northeast can create new opportunities. Critical for growth and increased employment in the sector are improvements in the workings of the factor markets, labor, water, land, and capital. From the perspective of the poor, better education levels and reform of the labor code will increase the chances of finding employment in the commercial agriculture sector. Finally, given that the commercial agricultural sector is produces the bulk of Brazil's export crops, avoiding real exchange rate appreciations, sharp interest rate fluctuations, and a trade policy regime that moves towards relatively low tariffs on importables (of both inputs and final products) could significantly improve the sectors international competitiveness which would in turn lead to greater real wages rates and increased employment opportunities—both on-farm and downstream processing and transport.

3. Stimulating Rural Non-Farm (RNF) Sector Growth

An expanding RNF sector could increase rural employment, especially in the food processing and service sectors, and thus reduce poverty. However, this strategy is likely not to be feasible for the bulk of the poor who live in remote, low density, and poorer rural areas. Overall, the evidence for Brazil and other countries in the region suggests that greater RNF is found in areas that are better served by roads, electricity and communications. In other words, RNF is concentrated in areas where factor and product markets work better and transaction costs are lower. This typically implies that they develop in proximity to urban areas. Furthermore, evidence was found suggesting that: more schooling and access to such infrastructure significantly increases the likelihood of high-return versus low-return RNF employment; RNF employment is less important in the rural NE compared to the SE; and that while women are particularly highly represented in the RNF sector, they are typically employed in the low-return activities (for example, domestic services). The critical ingredients to stimulate the development of a vibrant rural non-farm economy are better education levels, good basic infrastructure, building up social capital, and well functioning labor and credit markets.

4. Migration of the Young

While analytical work on the migration process per se (for example, on the determinants of migration) and the consequences of migration for the rural population in Brazil were beyond the scope of the current study, migration into urban areas and rural towns seems inevitable and even desirable, considering the high incidence of rural poverty, the extremely large absolute number of very small farms combined with the rather largish average household size, and the relatively low agricultural growth potential in the vast areas of dry and semi-dry non-irrigated farmland in the Northeast. The findings in the current study suggest that the determinants of migration in Brazil need to be better understood and analyzed by explicitly incorporating the heterogeneity among the poor rural households (for example, in terms of age, education, gender, liquid capital and the distance to promising job opportunities). The lack of a time series data set with reliable income and household characteristics data is a major limiting factor explaining the scarcity of such empirical analysis in Brazil. Despite the current scarcity of empirical analysis of migration determinants in Brazil, both descriptive findings in Brazil and the experiences in other countries provide some pointers for further research and the policy agenda.

Income differentials are the single largest driving force explaining migration rates. Wage differentials and labor productivity ratios typically suffice to explain the majority of migration rates among landless agricultural workers. However, the bulk of the rural poor in the NE are small farmers and to analyze the migration process for this group one must account for other income sources (for example, returns to capital), which is more often than not difficult because of data availability and reliability constraints. There are certain income sources, land for instance, that are not fully transferable when migrating. This raises the possibility of strong interactions between the land market and the migration process. Potential migrants, especially poor ones, generally want to take all of their capital along. In the case of farmers this would require the sale of agricultural specific physical capital and land. The lack of land titles and a well functioning land market would impede selling land at a price that reflects its economic value to the operators.

A second factor constraining migration is the agricultural-specific human capital (for example, skills and experience in farming generally acquired on a learning-by-doing basis) that is not valued at comparable returns outside the agricultural sector. This is especially problematic for older potential migrants since not much can be done to relax this constraint. This underscores the importance of investing in the education of the currently young rural generation and endeavoring to endow them with basic levels of non-sector specific human capital. More training and educational opportunities for the rural poor appear to be the most critical policy variable for facilitating this absorption into other sectors of the economy. Migration will benefit not only the migrant but in many cases also household members who stayed in rural areas via remittances.

5. Safety Net Provision for those "Trapped" in Poverty
There is a group of rural poor that will not be able to benefit from opportunities in commercial agriculture, from small-scale intensification, or from migration. Members of this group are typically older, often widows, and occasionally farm workers in poorly endowed areas. This group is "trapped" in extreme poverty with no viable future in agriculture beyond subsistence. Members of this group face considerable barriers in finding off-farm employment. For this group, a social safety net, for instance in the form of pensions, is critical to ensure a basic decent living standard. A key design challenge of safety net programs lies in also making them administratively accessible for the rural poor living in remote, low population density areas characterized by high rates of illiteracy.

In addition to recognizing the multi-dimensionality of potential poverty exit paths and policy options, the strategic framework for action should also recognize intergenerational facet of rural poverty. Hence, parallel efforts to reach the young (especially in the poorest households and in those that are heavily dependent on safety net provisions) via education is critical to provide them with the opportunity of breaking out of the vicious cycle in which their elders are trapped.

A Tentative Portfolio of Integrated Rural Poverty Reduction Policies
Canalizing a large and heterogeneous group of rural poor into the poverty exit path suitable to each is challenging task that requires the design and implementation of an integrated policy portfolio. The matrix below summarizes the tentative set of policy options identified in this report and serves to highlight core policies, the cross-cutting nature of several policies (for example, important in the context of multiple poverty exit paths), and the synergistic nature of certain policies (for example, policies that are mutually reinforcing when implemented simultaneously). The overview chapter contains a more detailed description of these policy options and how these are interwoven into the five-prong poverty exit paths strategy.

A Strategic Framework for Action: A Tentative Set of Integrated Policy Options					
Poverty Exit Path Policy Typology	Increase incomes via small farm sector intensification	Improve farm employment opportunities in dynamic commercial agriculture	Stimulate growth of the RNF sector	Migration of the young	Safety net provision for those "trapped" in poverty
Improving human capital endowments	. Moderate long- · run effect on · returns from · farming	. Moderate effect on · returns from · farming (for · example, . managerial skills) · but limited for wage · laborers.	Critical to facilitate employment, especially in high-return activities and/or entrepreneurial activities	Essential to enable opportunity-driven migration via education and investing in non-farm specific human capital	Reduces the number that are dependent on safety net income

Rural land market reform	· Crucial for
	  increasing small
	  farms beyond
	. poverty threshold
	  and enable rentals
			Limited direct impact	Potentially important impact for farmers.	

Increasing R&D and transfer of technology	· Significant
	  positive effects on
	  returns from
	· farming
		Significant positive effects on returns from farming	Limited role for public policy role	Limited direct impact	

Rural finance market reform	· Crucial to relax currently binding · credit constraints	Crucial to relax credit constraints	Crucial to relax potential credit constraints	Limited direct impact	
Rural labor market reform	Little or no direct impact	Important for farm workers	Important for RNF employment	Improves the integration between the rural and urban labor market	
Supply of public goods and building of social capital	· Important to improve · productivity and · market access	Critical to improve productivity and market access	Important to improve RNF growth, productivity and market access	Important to improve integration between rural and urban areas	Little or no direct impact
Price and trade policy	Impact depends on level of tradables (inputs and output) and typically this sector produces non-tradables.	Avoiding real exchange rate appreciation and sharp interest rate fluctuations are critical policy elements that will contribute to strengthen the competitiveness of the agricultural tradable sector (outputs and inputs); both on-farm and in downstream off-farm sectors. Together with relatively low tariffs on importables (inputs and final products) this should enhance the export orientation of the sector.		Limited direct impact	Limited direct impact
Transfer programs	Limited direct impact	Limited direct impact	Limited direct impact	Limited direct impact	Crucial for groups (for example, the elderly) "trapped" in poverty and are not benefiting from other policies

Synergistic Policies   : . . . . :   Core Policies   [   ]

OVERVIEW

Introduction

This report constitutes a step towards the objective of designing an integrated strategy for rural poverty reduction in Brazil. The report contains an updated and more detailed profile of the rural poor in the northeast (NE) and southeast (SE) of Brazil; identifies key determinants of rural poverty in these regions; and proposes a strategic framework in which to couch a set of integrated policies that could effectively help to reduce rural poverty in Brazil. The need for an integrated set of policies arises foremost because of the heterogeneous nature of the rural poor in Brazil. No single simple remedy for rural poverty reduction in Brazil could be identified and consequently, an integrated policy approach that provides multiple paths out of rural poverty tailored to key characteristics distinguishing various household groups emerges as more effective alternative.

Designing effective rural poverty reduction programs in a large and diverse country such as Brazil is difficult in a vacuum with respect to knowledge of a disaggregated rural poverty profile. Accordingly, a first key objective of this project was to update and improve data pertaining to the state of rural poverty in the northeast (NE) and southeast (SE) of Brazil. This new rural poverty profile disaggregates across two principal dimensions: household income sources and geographical location. One the one hand, rural poverty estimates where disaggregated according to three key income categories: farmers, landless agricultural workers, and Rural Non-Farm (RNF) workers. On the other hand, poverty estimates where spatially disaggregated to cover the regional (for example, NE versus SE) and state levels, and according to the degree of urbanization over a spectrum ranging from metropolitan to remote rural areas. In addition to providing new and disaggregated facts regarding rural poverty in the NE and SE of Brazil, this exercise has also identified remaining data and knowledge gaps.

We start with an overview of the main findings and present the proposed strategic framework for rural poverty reduction in the NE and SE of Brazil that emerged from this project. A 5-pronged rural poverty exit paths approach is introduced followed by a discussion of the envisioned policy portfolio. This policy portfolio is interwoven with the five poverty exit paths and synthesized in a strategy matrix. Finally, the methodology and results from a preliminary policy portfolio selection analysis are presented. The proposals in this report emerge from an analysis of rural poverty determinants and an

7

examination of these from a policy vantage point. This study was complemented by seven in-dept thematic studies that bear on critical components to move towards the formulation of an integrated rural poverty alleviation strategy: (i) the dynamics of the Brazilian small farm sector, (ii) rural labor markets, (iii) rural land markets, (iv) RNF employment, (v) rural education, and (vi) rural pensions. This analysis, together with an evaluation of relevant current public programs, underlies the proposed strategic framework of policy options aimed at reducing rural poverty in the NE and SE of Brazil.

A Profile of Rural Poverty: Updated Facts and New Findings

Rural poverty reduction in Brazil remains a substantial challenge. Contrary to popular opinion, poverty in Brazil is currently not an overwhelmingly urban phenomenon. In fact, despite migration trends and the considerable larger urban population, poverty remains so widespread in rural areas that a preliminary conservative estimate suggests approximately 43 percent of the poor population in the NE and SE of Brazil is rural (Table A), that is, *the standard of living of some 9.8 million people in the rural NE and SE is estimated to be below the poverty line.* Moreover, poverty is also found to be typically deeper in rural areas.

TABLE A: RURAL AND URBAN POVERTY INCIDENCE IN BRAZIL (NE AND SE)

	Rural	Urban	Total	percent Rural
Population	23,931,137	88,797,554	112,728,690	21.2 percent
Population in poverty	9,812,557	12,844,435	22,656,992	43.3 percent
Poor as percent of population	41.0 percent	14.5 percent	20.1 percent	

Source: Preliminary estimates from Lanjouw, Chapter 7, Volume II.

The incidence of rural poverty is highest in the northeast of Brazil. Our findings confirm that, as reported in previous studies (World Bank, 1995), poverty continues to disproportionately affect the northeast (NE). The headcount index is estimated to be about 49 percent in the rural NE versus 24 percent in the southeast (SE). While the regional difference between the NE and SE was previously known, the overall magnitude of rural poverty in Brazil remains larger than commonly thought. Moreover, urban poverty in the northeast is also disproportionately higher. None withstanding these results, the importance of poverty estimates lies not *per se* in specific numbers, but rather in the identification of the most deprived groups. This is borne out by previously unavailable estimates via further desegregation over both detailed geographical and income-group categories.[1]

TABLE B: DISAGGREGATED RURAL AND URBAN POVERTY INCIDENCE IN NE AND SE BRAZIL

	NE		SE	
	Rural	Urban	Rural	Urban
Population	16,335,965	29,318,906	7,595,172	59,478,648
Population in poverty	8,002,241	9,022,559	1,810,316	3,821,876
Poor as percent of population	49.0	30.8	23.8	6.4

Source: Preliminary estimates from Lanjouw, Chapter 7, Volume II.

---

1. A poverty profile at the levels of disaggregation presented in this report was previously unavailable. Details regarding the estimation procedures are presented in Volume II by Romano (Chapter 1) and Lanjouw (Chapter 7), and are summarized in the background studies section in this Volume.

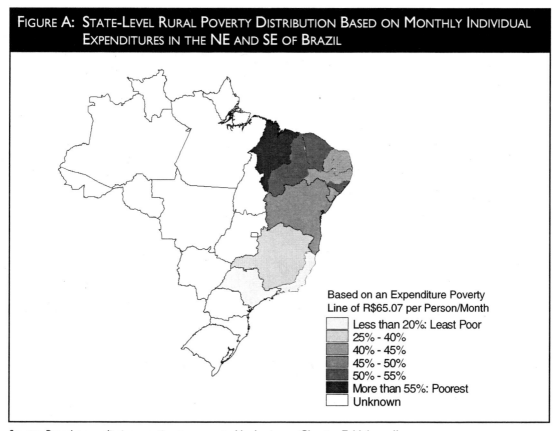

FIGURE A: STATE-LEVEL RURAL POVERTY DISTRIBUTION BASED ON MONTHLY INDIVIDUAL EXPENDITURES IN THE NE AND SE OF BRAZIL

Based on an Expenditure Poverty Line of R$65.07 per Person/Month

- Less than 20%: Least Poor
- 25% - 40%
- 40% - 45%
- 45% - 50%
- 50% - 55%
- More than 55%: Poorest
- Unknown

Source: Based on preliminary estimates reported by Lanjouw, Chapter 7, Volume II.

Rural poverty disproportionally affects the northeastern states of Brazil. This is revealed by state-level poverty estimates (Figure A). The incidence of poverty rises over 45 percent in the northeastern states of Maranhão, Piauí, Ceará, Alagoas, and Bahia versus less than 20 percent in the southeastern states (with the exception of Minas Gerais). Moreover, even within the northeast, the overall impression is one of considerable geographical (and presumably agro-climatic, though this level of desegregation was not feasible due to current data constraints) diversity regarding the incidence of poverty.

Rural poverty is essentially concentrated among farm households located in remote areas. This finding emerges from a previously unexplored geographical desegregation of the preliminary poverty estimates across a more detailed locational spectrum ranging over seven categories from densely populated metropolitan urban areas on one extreme to remote and sparsely populated rural areas on the other (Table C). Of the total estimated number of rural poor in the NE and SE, about 83.6 percent and 90.3 percent respectively reside in remote, isolated, sparsely populated and low productivity areas referred to as "rural exclusive" areas (defined as areas that do not meet any of the criteria defining a rural agglomeration—little or no infrastructure, few permanent structures, and low population density).[2] *This group of approximately 8.3 million poor people represents about 85 percent of all rural poor in the NE and SE of Brazil emerges rather clearly as a primary concern from a rural poverty reduction policy perspective.* Preliminary estimates further suggest that for these households, income from farm related activities (farm and agricultural labor) represents

---

2. For further background, definitions and results, see Lanjouw, Chapter 7, Volume II.

TABLE C: LOCATIONALLY DISAGGREGATED POVERTY INCIDENCE IN NE AND SE BRAZIL

	NE			SE		
	Poor as percent of pop.	Population in poverty	Population	Poor as percent of pop.	Population in poverty	Population
Urban	30.8	9,022,559	29,318,906	6.4	3,821,876	59,478,648
metropolitan area	18.6	1,575,835	8,472,231	4.9	1,461,739	29,831,408
área urbanizada	35.7	7,375,228	20,658,902	7.9	2,311,735	29,262,468
área não urbanizada	36.9	52,993	143,612	18.2	28,156	154,703
área isolada	41.9	18,503	44,160	8.8	20,246	230,068
Rural	49.0	8,002,241	16,335,965	23.8	1,810,316	7,595,172
extensão urbana	15.9	114,061	717,365	9.6	40,703	423,990
Povoado	46.0	1,167,745	2,538,576	24.4	135,750	556,352
Núcleo	31.8	25,468	80,088	n/a	n/a	n/a
Exclusive	51.5	6,694,967	12,999,936	24.7	1,633,863	6,614,830
Total	37.3	17,024,800	45,654,870	8.4	5,632,192	67,073,820

Source: Preliminary estimates from Lanjouw, Chapter 7, Volume II.

no less than two thirds of total household income from all sources and that their principal income source is generated via small-scale farming and/or farm work.

Regardless of region, non-agricultural workers comprise the relatively better-off group. This revealing facet of rural poverty in Brazil becomes evident from a classification of the rural population into three groups—*farmers, agricultural workers, and non-agricultural workers*—according to their main income source. On the one hand, farm workers have the highest extreme headcount poverty measures (59 percent in the NE and 27 percent in SE). On the other hand, rural non-farm workers are characterized by extreme poverty measures of about half this magnitude (25 percent in NE and 15 percent in SE). Regardless of region, those that receive their main income via farming or farm labor are consistently the poorest group, whilst non-agricultural workers comprise the better off group (see Chapter 1).

Poorer rural households are more dependent on agricultural wages and labor markets. For the poorest 20 percent of families in the rural NE, labor income represents 23.6 percent of their total household income (22.2 percent in SE), compared to only 3.8 percent for high-income families (17.4 percent in the SE). Income from farming is more important as a source of household income in the NE, where it reaches almost 50 percent of total income (see Chapter 1). For rural households that are poor in the NE, income from farming and from agricultural labor represents approximately 70 percent of total household income (53.4 percent and 16 percent respectively). In the SE this figure is 62.3 percent.

The bulk of the rural poor in the NE are small farmers. About 50 percent of all farms in Brazil are smaller than 10 hectares (IBGE, 1996). In the NE, farmers in the lowest income tercile group live in extreme poverty (annually below R$781 per capita) and operate plots of 5.1 hectares on average. Even northeastern farmers in the mid-income tercile group still live in poverty (annually less than R$1,562 per capita) and operate on average plot sizes of 7.9 hectares. In the SE, while farmers in the lowest income tercile group operate plots of 16.3 hectares on average, their income remains substantially below the extreme poverty line (see Chapter 1). In total numbers in the NE, small farmers constitute the largest poorest group followed by farm workers.

Rural Non-Farm (RNF) employment is growing, but is still relatively unimportant for the rural poor because location matters. RNF employment in Brazil is growing faster than agricultural employment (3.6 percent versus—2.4 percent between 1992–98).[3] However, RNF income continues to represent only a small fraction of household income for the poorest families. For the majority of the rural poor in the NE, rural non-farm income contributes only 14.7 percent (16 percent in the SE) to total household income. The share of income from RNF activities increases with income in both the NE and SE, indicating that better-off households are more dependent on RNF income sources. Head-count poverty estimates are lower in rural areas directly adjacent to, but not formally incorporated into the urban perimeter of municipalities; in fact, in the NE poverty in these adjacent areas is lower than in urban areas. RNF income is concentrated in the relatively more urbanized areas, it is less important in the NE compared to the SE, and within the NE its incidence is higher in certain states including Bahia, Maranhão, Rio Grande de Norte.[4] Because the bulk of the rural poor (85 percent) live in "rural exclusive" areas, the possibilities to increase income via local RNF employment appear limited.

Public pensions are the main source of non-labor income. Public pensions are by far the main source of non-labor income (about 95 percent) with an average proportion of total income from public pensions of 15 percent in the SE and 18 percent in the NE. The mid-income quintiles have the highest proportion of families receiving pensions, as well as the highest proportion of pensions in total household income. Pension income represents a higher proportion of income for household headed by women (the average age of which is quite high, at around 41 years), on average reaching 50 percent in the NE, while agricultural workers receive a strikingly low proportion of income from public pension (12 percent in the NE and 4 percent in the SE). It should be noted though that pension income in the PPV data above includes pension income from all sources, not just from the Previdência Social in rural areas. The latter provides one minimum wage per month per beneficiary, regardless of income status, and thus it is well targeted considering that it contributes with a relatively higher proportion of household income for the poorest families.

The rural poor in Brazil are worse off in terms of demographics, access to and quality of services. Vis-à-vis poor households in urban areas, the rural poor tend to have less access to services (for example, electricity, safe water, and health care), more children, and worse health indicators. Overall, the trends are quite similar for the NE and SE. In terms of demographic characteristics, average family size is higher among the poor and is greatest in the NE, especially among farmers. Larger families seem to perpetuate poverty, since school attendance is typically negatively correlated with family size. Access to services is limited especially in the NE. For instance among the lowest income quintile group, only about 43 percent in the NE have access to electricity (63 percent in the SE). Moreover, only 2 percent of poor farms received some form of technical assistance, compared to 31 percent of non-poor farmers and subsidized credit follows a similar pattern, with small farmers receiving practically none.

The rural poor in Brazil are also worse off in terms of educational achievement, access and quality. Illiteracy in the NE is strikingly high, and higher than in other lower income countries in the region. Among the poorest 20 percent of households in the NE, 75 percent of the household heads are illiterate, 62 percent of all household heads and 51 percent of all family members above 10 years old are illiterate. Agricultural workers, the group characterized by the highest poverty incidence, have an exceptionally high rate of illiteracy (81 percent among households heads). Younger generations appear to have enjoyed somewhat better access to education, however the NE lags considerably behind the SE in this respect. Regarding quality of education, consider that in the rural NE, 27 percent of teachers have incomplete primary education and 26 percent of schools do not have sanitation infrastructure. Furthermore, rural education essentially continues to be a 1st to 4th grade affair. The first four grades accounted for 85 percent of enrolled rural children in 1998, as opposed to 50 percent

---

3. Graziano da Silva (2000), based on PNAD data presented in the Workshop "Desafios da Pobreza Rural no Brasil" sponsored jointly by IPEA, The World Bank, NEAD and the Ministério do Desenvolvimento Agrário, Rio de Janeiro, August 30–September 1.

4. Adding another dimension, at the recent IPEA workshop in Rio, Jose Eli de Veiga argued that areas dominated by family-size farms experienced higher RNF employment growth compared to those where larger scale farming ("agricultura patronal") is predominant.

for Brazil as a whole. Repetition rates are higher in the NE and rural students from the region also perform the worst in terms of standardized test scores. A key emerging question is whether the 400,000 children in the rural NE that were not enrolled come mainly from those poor semi-subsistence farming households with access problems or whether these were simply children that were tired of repeating and dropped out of school. There is a major knowledge gap regarding the appropriate mix of demand-side programs such as Bolsa Escola, universal programs such as FUNDEF, and specific rural education programs to bring rural education up to at least the urban area levels.

Aging of small farmers and the relatively high proportion of female-headed rural households are important factors to consider in the context of safety net policies. The average age of the head of household in small farms is high and there appears to be a strong relationship between aging, productivity and poverty in small farms. For the subset of poor small-scale farmers that are old, this raises a number of policy issues, such as the viability of exiting poverty via farming, and it reinforces the importance of providing social safety nets such as the Previdência Social. Women household heads represent an approximate 15 percent of all rural households in the NE (12 percent in SE) and this proportion increases to the strikingly high level of 30 percent among all non-agricultural rural households (20 percent in the SE). It was found that in households where husbands migrated or died, income is significantly increased by pension payments.

The rural-urban migration trend from the NE will continue. The study identifies five different major trends in rural-urban migration indicators for Brazil during the 1950–1990s. Major waves of rural-urban migration took place from the NE region during the 1950s–70s in response to wage differentials. During the 1990s a new pattern emerged with the stabilization of migration trends and the appearance of RNF employment opportunities, particularly in the South. Projecting towards the next 15 years, recent research in projecting future rural-urban migration flows suggests that a stabilization of urbanization rates will take place in the South, SE and Center West, but the North and NE will continue to be the main source of rural migrants. Improvements in the provision of education and a selective revision of the labor code should increase the prospects of formal employment both in urban and in rural areas.

In contrast to urban areas, rural poverty analysis in Brazil continues to be greatly constrained by the scarceness of adequate data ("miseria estadistica"). Particularly constraining is the scarceness of adequate household income data in rural areas. For instance, the absence of comparable inter-temporal data (unlike some countries in the region) currently precludes an analysis of how the poverty profile and determinants have changed over time. This report draws primarily on two household survey data sets fielded in 1996: the *Pesquisa Nacional por Amostra de Domicílios* (PNAD) data and the *Pesquisa sobre Padrões de Vida* (PPV) survey implemented by the *Instituto Brasileiro de Geografia e Estatística* (IBGE) based on the World Bank's LSMS survey design. Both data sets suffer from strengths and weaknesses. While, the PPV reports quite detailed consumption expenditure data and permits the construction of price indices to account for spatial price variables, the sample size is not large enough to be representative at levels of spatial disaggregation much below the regional and large metropolitan area level. The PNAD sample is substantially larger than the PPV and is representative at the state level; but, alas, the PNAD does not report expenditure data and the income measures in rural areas are rather unreliable. Consequently, the preliminary expenditure based spatially disaggregated poverty profile presented in this report could be produced only by employing very recently developed small-to-large survey imputation techniques (see Chapter 7).

A Strategic Framework for Rural Poverty Reduction

The main findings emerging out of this new and more detailed rural poverty profile reveal an overall pattern of pronounced heterogeneity in welfare indicators and income sources among the rural poor in Brazil. Consequently, *the proposed rural poverty reduction strategy is framed in terms of an integrated set of policies that provide multiple paths out of poverty tailored to the heterogeneous cross-section of poor rural household groups.* A five-prong poverty exit paths approach is envisaged: (a) intensification of the small farm sector to increase income from farming; (b) a dynamic commercial agricultural sector that provides increased farm employment opportunities; (c) stimulating growth of the

Rural Non-Farm (RNF) sector; (d) migration of the young, especially those from remote, low density, and low productivity rural areas; and (e) provision of a safety net for those "trapped" in poverty. This study has identified a tentative set of integrated policy instruments that could be implemented to facilitate one or more of these five poverty exit paths.

This tentative set of policy options was identified via an analysis of rural policy determinants. Measuring poverty and assessing where the problem is greatest is a crucial first step, but designing an effective anti-poverty policy also requires uncovering the determinants of poverty. This analysis was further complemented with an evaluation of relevant current public programs and six in-depth thematic studies that bear on critical components of the proposed integrated policy approach aimed at reducing rural poverty in the NE and SE of Brazil: (a) the dynamics of the Brazilian small farm sector, (b) rural labor markets, (c) rural land markets, (d) RNF employment, (e) rural education, and (f) rural pensions. Before turning to a discussion of the five exit strategies, the analytical findings, and the proposed set of integrated policy instruments, a note regarding the macroeconomic environment in Brazil is warranted.

While this study emphasizes primarily microeconomic events—such as the impact of schooling, income transfers, and access to land and credit—poverty reduction requires both economic growth (macro-level) and specific anti-poverty policies (micro-level). In Latin America, overall economic growth has proven important for poverty reduction. An increasing body of empirical evidence shows that under faster overall growth (5 percent or more) the incomes of the poor have risen significantly.[5] Specifically in Brazil, where agriculture represents less than 10 percent of GDP and about 23 percent of employment, fast-growing employment in urban areas and expansion in domestic demand for farm products that would result from fast growth in the overall economy—particularly for small farmers producers of non-tradables—can go a long way in reducing rural poverty, even if the agricultural economy does not grow very fast. Essentially, achieving a significant, sustained, and politically viable reduction in rural poverty without rapid overall economic growth would be quite difficult in Brazil.

Finally, primarily because of data and time constraints, the coverage of this report is not exhaustive. Some of the potentially important issues in a poverty reduction context that could not be covered include: (i) the impact of commercial agricultural policies, (b) the effect of overall government programs in rural areas that are not poverty focused per se (for example, programs such as PRONAF of which about 25 percent of beneficiaries were rural poor), and (c) the often complex and important environment-poverty inter-linkages. Also, by way of reiterating, due to household level data constraints, this report covers only the NE and the SE regions of Brazil. Thus, while the bulk of the rural poor live in the latter regions, the issues addressed and the tentative strategic framework for rural poverty reduction might need to be somewhat adapted in other regions.

Rural Poverty Exit Paths: A Five-Prong Approach

Agricultural Intensification of the Small Farm Sector

A large proportion of poverty in Brazil is confined to rural areas and a large segment of these rural poor are small farmers. Thus, if we can understand the major economic trends that are affecting the small farm sector in Brazil, then we should understand a great deal about the economic trends that are affecting many of the poor in Brazil. Market developments and government policies since the late 1980s appear to have reinforced the sector's disposition towards technologically advanced producers and against low technology, small and semi-subsistence farmers.[6]

---

5. See for instance Morley (1995) for Latin America and, for a larger sample of developing countries, see the recent work by Dollar and Kraay (2000).

6. In their recent study, S. Helfand and G. Castro de Rezende (2000) also conclude that combined effect of the various reforms, including the currency appreciation, have had a differential impact related to farm size. Their study documents the dramatic adverse price effect for producers of some products, such as wheat and milk, in contrast to positive price effects on exportables. Most of the gains were concentrated in the Center-West, while most of the difficulties occurred in the South.

Openness to trade, deregulation of domestic marketing, the reduction in subsidized credit programs, a new production technology with more intensive use of purchased inputs, the restructuring of the agri-food processing and marketing industries (vertical integration) are all factors that have favored the technologically more advanced commercial producers better able to cope with price and yield variability, and with the more demanding requirements from agro-processors (higher volume and quality standards). Trade liberalization and deregulation had a major impact on the output mix and intensification of agriculture. Simultaneously with a decline in the domestic price of import-competing products, lower trade barriers induced a significant decline in the domestic price of purchased inputs. However, the low technology and subsistence farmers, now also exposed to the lower output prices, could not benefit as much from the lower price of inputs. From an intra-regional perspective, market liberalization has triggered major geographic shifts in the location of production, reallocation of resources away from the southeast region into more capital-intensive and larger scale agriculture in the center-western region.

How to assist small farmers with potential to survive without quasi-permanent subsidies in the more competitive policy environment of today—quite different from that in the 1960s through most of the 1980s—is a major issue in Brazil today. From the vantage point of poverty reduction, the most difficult challenge arises in the semi-arid regions of the Northeast. As emphasized before, the bulk of the rural poor live in low density, remote areas and continue to depend on agriculture as their main source of income—either via farming or labor. Unfortunately, it is precisely in these areas where agriculture is contracting. In this context, two main thrusts that could drive agricultural public programs would include:

- ■ Reducing the gap in productivity and returns by investing in technologies tailored to the needs of those poor small-scale farmers with productive potential; and
- ■ Reducing the transaction costs in agricultural markets by improving for instance, transport infrastructure, technical assistance, access to credit, and farmer organizations.

Agricultural policy geared towards small-scale low productivity farms should be viewed primarily as part of a poverty reduction strategy as opposed to an agricultural growth program per se. In the Northeast, there are some opportunities for viable full-time small-farm activities, typically comprising a combination of subsistence and market production. Capitalization, physical investments, and services for family farmers can increase labor productivity and incomes and reduce migration pressures. These programs include intensification through, for instance, improved technical assistance, community-based land reform, and small infrastructure investments such as access roads. Where such investments are efficient and where the underlying economic activity is viable, they should be supported. However, this strategy applies only to a subset of the small farm sector. For instance, this strategy would be very difficult and expensive to implement in the remote arid and semi-arid regions of the NE where, alas, a significant proportion of rural poor live. Given current data constraints, what remains unclear at this stage is exactly how big this subset is.

A critical issue emerging from the analysis in this report is that the returns to assets (including land) are highly dependent on the levels of other complementary assets, including human capital. Consequently, returns differ significantly depending on the size of farms, and some underlying constraints—but not all—can be resolved by public policies. A key message from this analysis is the importance of a "package" approach—policies that accounts for the synergies between access to the various assets.

More Dynamic Commercial Agriculture

A revitalized commercial agriculture sector could increase employment and reduce rural poverty directly by absorbing wage labor and indirectly via growth of the downstream processing industry. For example, efficient, market-driven expansion of irrigated areas in the Northeast will create new opportunities. Critical for growth and increased employment in the sector are improvements in the workings of the factor markets, labor, water, land, and capital. From the perspective of the poor, better education levels and reform of the labor code will increase the chances of finding employment in the commercial agriculture sector. Finally, given that the commercial agricultural sector produces the bulk of Brazil's export crops, avoiding real exchange rate appreciations, sharp interest rate fluctuations, and a trade policy regime that moves towards relatively low tariffs on importables (of both inputs and final products) could significantly improve the sectors international competitiveness which would in turn lead to greater real wages rates and increased employment opportunities— both on-farm and downstream processing and transport.

When analyzing the trends in the structure of Brazilian agriculture it also useful to draw on the possible relevance of the discussion concerning small farming in the US agricultural sector just a few years ago.[7] The trend in Brazil in light of developments in US and elsewhere suggest that overall agricultural output growth will be driven primarily by the commercial farmers and not by the small-scale farm sector in low productivity areas such as the NE. Thus, this further highlights the dilemma that arises because of the fact that while agricultural income is critical for these small-scale low productivity farms, they are not critical to Brazil's agricultural sector growth as a whole.

Rural Non-Farm Employment

Rural non-farm activities are promising to increase rural employment, especially in the food processing and service sectors, and thus reduce poverty. However, this strategy is not feasible for those who live in more remote, low density, and poorer rural areas. Overall, the evidence for Brazil and other countries in the region also suggest that greater RNF is found in areas that are better served by roads, electricity and communications. In other words, RNF is concentrated in areas where factor and product markets work better and transaction costs are lower. In most cases, this implies that they develop in proximity to urban areas. In this study, evidence was found suggesting that more schooling and access to such infrastructure significantly increase the likelihood of a home-based enterprise. RNF employment is less important in the rural NE compared to the SE. The evidence for Brazil also indicates that women are particularly highly represented in the RNF sector— particularly in education and domestic services. The critical ingredients to stimulate the development of a vibrant rural non-farm economy are better education levels and good basic infrastructure.

Migration of the Young

While analytical work on the determinants of migration and the consequences of migration for the rural population in Brazil were beyond the scope of the current study, migration into urban areas and rural towns seems inevitable and even desirable, considering the high incidence of rural poverty, the extremely large absolute number of very small farms combined with the rather largish average household size, and the relatively low agricultural growth potential in the vast areas of dry and semi-dry non-irrigated farmland in the Northeast. Though descriptive analysis of the principal inter-regional migration trends in Brazil since the 1950s are available (for example, see Carneiro, Nov. 2000), the findings in the current study suggest the need to go further by estimating for instance migration functions that incorporate the heterogeneity among the poor rural households

---

7. A few years ago the USDA positioned itself among those worried about the possible untenable position of smaller family farms. During a period of remarkable record of productivity growth in US agriculture, technological change in pursuit of trade competitiveness was inducing ownership and control over agricultural assets in fewer and fewer hands. In fact, the largest 25 percent of farms that accounted for 50 percent of farm sales in 1940 account for 90 percent of sales today. However, as shown very recently by Gardner (2000), the economic situation of smaller farms in the US as not worsened. Indeed, considering both farm and off-farm sources, household income of people in smaller farms has improved consistently through time. The story behind this success is one of a rising importance of off-farm income and migration, which highlights the key role of a well-articulated labor market for a better integration between farm and non-farm activities. The analysis finds no evidence that agricultural policies have contributed to the growth of farm household income of small farmers and most relevant for our analysis for Brazil, no evidence that farm productivity and farm size had any effect on the growth or level of farm household income.

(for example, in terms of age, education, gender, liquid capital and the distance to promising job opportunities). The lack of a time series data set with reliable income and household characteristics data is a major limiting factor explaining the scarcity of such empirical analysis in Brazil. Despite the current scarcity of empirical analysis of migration determinants in Brazil, both descriptive findings in Brazil and the experiences in other countries provide some pointers for further research and the policy agenda. Historically, rural-urban migration has been a major factor explaining the reduction rural poverty during the 1990s in most of Latin America.[8] Consequently, as will be expanded on shortly, the need to improve educational levels in rural areas to prepare migrants for a successful absorption in urban and RNF employment (with higher paying jobs) should be viewed as a fundamental component of Brazil's rural poverty alleviation strategy.

Income differentials are the single largest driving force explaining migration rates. Wage differentials and labor productivity ratios typically suffice to explain the majority of migration rates among landless agricultural workers. However, the bulk of the rural poor in the NE are small farmers and to analyze the migration process for this group one must account for other income sources (such as returns to capital), which is more often than not difficult because of data availability and reliability constraints. There are certain income sources, land for instance, that are not fully transferable when migrating. This raises the possibility of strong interactions between the land market and the migration process. Potential migrants, especially poor ones, generally want to take all of their capital along. In the case of farmers this would require the sale of agricultural specific physical capital and land. The lack of land titles and a well functioning land market would impede selling land at a price that reflects its economic value to the operators.

A second factor constraining migration is the agricultural-specific human capital (for example, skills and experience in farming generally acquired on a learning-by-doing basis) that is not valued at comparable returns outside the agricultural sector. This is especially problematic for older potential migrants since not much can be done to relax this constraint. This underscores the importance of investing in the education of the currently young rural generation and endeavoring to endow them with basic levels of non-sector specific human capital. More training and educational opportunities for the rural poor appear to be the most critical policy variable for facilitating this absorption into other sectors of the economy. Migration will benefit not only the migrant but in many cases also household members who stayed in rural areas via remittances. Essentially, policy-wise the issue is not one of encouraging an exodus of the rural young nor is it one of artificially keeping people in rural areas. Rather the issue is one of giving the rural young a chance at opportunity-driven migration. In other words, provide them with the ability to respond to potentially better economic opportunities in urban areas or the non-farm sector.

A Safety Net for Those "Trapped" in Poverty

There is a group of rural poor that will not be able to benefit from opportunities in commercial agriculture, from small-scale intensification, or from migration. Members of this group are typically older, often widows, and occasionally farm workers in poorly endowed areas. This group is "trapped" in extreme poverty with no viable future in agriculture beyond subsistence. Members of this group face considerable barriers in finding off-farm employment. For this group, a social safety net, for instance in the form of pensions, is critical to ensure a basic decent living standard. A key design challenge of safety net programs lies in also making them administratively accessible for the rural poor living in remote, low population density areas characterized by high rates of illiteracy. In addition to recognizing the multi-dimensionality of potential poverty exit paths and policy options,

---

8. In their analysis using CEPAL data for nine countries in Latin America, de Janvry and Sadoulet (2000) conclude that the observed reduction in the number of rural poor relative to the number of urban poor in the region was not the result of successful rural development; it was driven by out-migration. They estimate that approximately 68 percent of the observed reduction in rural poverty during 1990–97 is attributed to rural-urban migration. A recent study by Paes de Barros (2000) examines the relation between the observed fall in rural poverty and conditions in rural labor markets in Brazil.

FIGURE B: STRATEGIC FRAMEWORK FOR ACTION: A TENTATIVE SET OF INTEGRATED POLICY OPTIONS

Poverty Exit Path / Policy Typology	Increase incomes via small farm sector intensification	Improve farm employment opportunities in dynamic commercial agriculture	Stimulate growth of the RNF sector	Migration of the young	Safety net provision for those "trapped" in poverty
Improving human capital endowments	Moderate long-run effect on returns from farming	Moderate effect on returns from farming (for example, managerial skills) but limited for wage laborers.	Critical to facilitate employment, especially in high-return activities and/or entrepreneurial activities	Essential to enable opportunity-driven migration via education and investing in non-farm specific human capital	Reduces the number that are dependent on safety net income
Rural land market reform	Crucial for increasing small farms beyond poverty threshold and enable rentals		Limited direct impact	Potentially important impact for farmers.	
Increasing R&D and transfer of technology	Significant positive effects on returns from farming	Significant positive effects on returns from farming	Limited role for public policy role	Limited direct impact	
Rural finance market reform	Crucial to relax currently binding credit constraints	Crucial to relax credit constraints	Crucial to relax potential credit constraints	Limited direct impact	
Rural labor market reform	Little or no direct impact	Important for farm workers	Important for RNF employment	Improves the integration between the rural and urban labor market	
Supply of public goods and building of social capital	Important to improve productivity and market access	Critical to improve productivity and market access	Important to improve RNF growth, productivity and market access	Important to improve integration between rural and urban areas	Little or no direct impact
Price and trade policy	Impact depends on level of tradables (inputs and output) and typically this sector produces non-tradables.	Avoiding real exchange rate appreciation and sharp interest rate fluctuations are critical policy elements that will contribute to strengthen the competitiveness of the agricultural tradable sector (outputs and inputs); both on-farm and in downstream off-farm sectors. Together with relatively low tariffs on importables (inputs and final products) this should enhance the export orientation of the sector.		Limited direct impact	Limited direct impact
Transfer programs	Limited direct impact	Limited direct impact	Limited direct impact	Limited direct impact	Crucial for groups (for example, the elderly) "trapped" in poverty and are not benefiting from other policies

Synergistic Policies · · · · · · · · · · · · · ·   Core Policies

the strategic framework for action should also recognize intergenerational facet of rural poverty. Hence, parallel efforts to reach the young (especially in the poorest households and in those that are heavily dependent on safety net provisions) via education is critical to provide them with the opportunity of breaking out of the vicious cycle in which their elders are trapped.

An Integrated Policy Portfolio For Rural Poverty Reduction

Canalizing the rural poor towards their respective applicable poverty exit paths and paving the latter requires implementing an integrated policy portfolio. This section discusses how various current policies fit within the proposed five-prong rural poverty reduction strategy and proposes additional complementing policy efforts towards building a more comprehensive framework.

Improving Human Capital Endowments

More and better education for the rural population should be considered a top priority. Better education will not only increase employment opportunities but will also facilitate opportunity-driven migration—and the latter should be viewed as a pivotal rural poverty reduction path both in the shorter and longer term. Education-based policies should be viewed as a grassroots strategy to provide the young members in rural poor households with the opportunity of breaking out of the vicious poverty cycle in which their elders are trapped. The degree to which human capital endowments of the rural poor working age population can be improved are limited largely to retraining initiatives. Moreover, the opportunity cost of investing in human capital (the income that could be generated if working) is typically much greater for them vis-à-vis their children. Investing in education to endow the younger generations with nonagricultural-specific human capital is key. As the discussion below indicates, the findings on education suggest that the policy challenge is to find an appropriate mix of demand-side programs such as *Bolsa Escola*, universal programs such as FUNDEF, and specific rural education programs to bring rural education up to at least urban levels.

Soares *et. al.* (Chapter 7) report a number salient facts regarding rural education. About 10 percent of rural school age children are not enrolled and this corresponds to 400,000 kids in the rural NE and 300,000 in the rural SE.[9] Between 1991–98, net enrolment rates increased from 91 percent to 96 percent in urban areas and from 75 percent to 91 percent in rural areas. While this is an indication of substantial improvement, especially in rural areas, there is also still a lot of room for improvement. In 1998, about 85 percent of rural children were enrolled in the 1st to 4th grade as opposed to 50 percent for Brazil as a whole, while rural secondary education continues to be virtually non-existent. In 1998, only 6 percent of 5th to 8th graders in Brazil were rural children and, representing a mere 1 percent of total enrollment. The evidence suggests that repetition of grades remains a critical issue in Brazilian education. While the increase in 1st to 4th grade rural enrollment rates reflects improved access to schooling, we are also interested in gauging the progress and achievement once these children are attending classes. Regarding progress, the evidence suggests that repetition of grades remains a critical issue in Brazilian education, especially in rural areas were it is not uncommon for children to repeat the same grade several times.[10] Similarly, test score comparisons indicate a significant gap between urban and rural students.

Eighteen percent of rural teachers in Brazil are individuals with incomplete primary education (0 percent in urban areas) and only 5 percent have completed higher education (28 percent in urban areas). The rural-urban differences in educational resources are striking. The same gap that exists in teacher qualification also exists in physical (bathrooms and sanitation) and pedagogical (library, computers and audiovisual equipment) school infrastructure. For example, in contrast to practically all urban schools, about 30 percent of rural schools have no sanitation infrastructure. The under-equipment of rural schools is even more striking in terms of pedagogical facilities con-

---

9. See Soares *et. al.*, Chapter 7, Volume II.

10. Note in this context, that using 'years of education' as a dependent variable in analysis would be problematic.

sidering that for instance only 3 percent have computers (44 percent in urban) and 7 percent a library (58 percent in urban).

Regional comparisons of rural education indicators reveal that the NE is consistently worse off. While differences in terms of net enrollment have become negligible in recent years, 90 percent of these children in the NE are enrolled in the 1st to 4th grades compared to only 68 percent in the South. Grade repetition is substantially more frequent in the North and Northeast and rural students from these regions also perform the worst in terms of standardized test scores. Likewise, 27 percent of teachers in the rural NE have not completed their primary education versus only 4 percent in the South and similar differences also emerge when comparing physical and pedagogical school infrastructure.

While non-attendance is an issue in both the rural NE and south, quality of education for those who attend in the rural south is not only much better compared to the rural North and Northeast but, in addition, school results in the rural South are not that different from their urban counterparts. For instance, in the South there is practically no difference in the rate of grade repetition between rural and urban schools; likewise with regard to physical school infrastructure. This observed heterogeneity raises a number of important questions in the context of education and its role in the context of a rural poverty alleviation strategy.

The key demand-side issue is dealing with non-attendance in rural areas. Essentially, the 10 percent non-attendance level and the high extent of repetition in rural schools raises the question: To what degree are these explained by the household opportunity costs of child labor? To this extent, programs such as *Bolsa Escola, PETI* (a child labor eradication programs), *PNAE* (a school lunch program), and *PNTE* (a school transportation program) could be very relevant by compensating households for this opportunity cost.[11] While *Bolsa Escola* is often thought of as a single federal program that monetarily compensates households for school attendance, there are actually also a wide variety of various "*Bolsa Escola*" programs at the state level.

A preliminary evaluation of the Bolsa Escola in Brasilia indicates that the program has been almost 100 percent effective at keeping kids in school. Unfortunately, a comprehensive review of these programs is not yet available—we recommend that this is undertaken—and thus far the scale at which these programs are currently implemented is still very modest and not widespread. Likewise, *PETI* despite being very effective is still a very small program. Given the apparent success of these programs, we recommend that, in the context of possibly expanding these programs, a study be undertaken to understand the household characteristics and determinants associated with non-attendance in rural areas. The key supply-side issue is improving the low quality and assets (teachers and infrastructure) of rural schools. The question this raises is whether this requires just increases in funding or also institutional reform.

Rural Land Market Reform

Brazilian agriculture is characterized by a historical pattern of land concentration in which the lion share of the land is owned by relatively small number of large estates (*agricultura "patronal"*) that coexist with a much larger number of small farms (*familiar*). In 1996, almost 50 percent of agricultural establishments were smaller than 10 hectares, these comprised only about 2.25 percent of the total area farmed and 12 percent of gross farm output in Brazil. By contrast, less than 11 percent of farms were larger than 100 hectares, but this group accounted for 80 percent of the total area farmed. During the decade spanning the 1985 and 1996 agricultural census, the number of small farms declined by approximately 700,000 units (total farm land declined by 5.6 percent during the same period). Management by owner is the predominant tenancy (74 percent of all farm units) and it is worth highlighting that tenant farmers (share and cash lease) represents a low and declining share, reaching only 11 percent of all farm units in 1995–96. The remaining 14 percent are squatters (710,000 in 1995–96).

---

11. Soares et al. (Chapter 8, Volume II) provide a description of the various programs.

A salient feature in the NE, is the predominance of farms that are simply too small to generate an income level sufficient to lift them above poverty, regardless of how efficiently they produce. For a large proportion of small farmers current farm income is very low. This is not an issue of relative efficiency in resource allocation among small farmers (such as value added per hectare). It is primarily a issue of farming in an environment which is collectively too constrained by size, lack of working capital, distance to markets, lack of access to credit and extension, high risks in production and prices. The latter arise in the context of a far more open economy than was the tradition in Brazil in the past, and continues today in Japan, Taiwan, and Europe. Some estimates suggest that farm returns for approximately 70 percent of family farms in Brazil are below the minimum wage per worker.[12] For example, just in the State of Ceará there are about 245,000 farms below 10 hectares and this, in the absence of irrigation and of off-farm income, is widely considered to be well below the minimum size necessary for farmers to generate sufficient income to be able to exit poverty.[13]

For their analysis of farm revenue determinants, López and Romano (Chapter 6) classified farmers in NE and SE into four groups: minifundia (up to 2 ha), small farmers (2.1 to 10 ha), medium size farmers (10.1 to 50 ha) and large farms (50.1 to 2000 ha). They find that the effect of per capita land on per capita farm revenues varies dramatically between these farm size categories. The marginal revenue effect of increasing land is practically negligible for small farms while it becomes greater and significant for medium and large farms. While this finding by itself might be counterintuitive at first sight, because it is a partial elasticity result it is in fact highly informative. In other words, the finding reflects the marginal contribution of land to farm revenues *given* the level of all other productive factors (for example, purchased inputs, machinery) and demographic characteristics (such as, age of operator, education). Thus, there is a synergy between land and the other productive factors that mutually reinforces their productivity and returns. While this result is economically intuitive, it is often overlooked and is another key finding underscoring the importance of pursuing a rural poverty reduction strategy consisting of an integrated policy set. For land to have a large productivity and revenue increasing impact in farming, it appears necessary to simultaneously improve the levels of other factors such as purchased inputs and machinery.

The recently designed and implemented community-based approach to land reform is one program concept with flexibility to be tailored in ways that account for these synergies: beneficiary groups negotiate directly with potential sellers of suitable properties, and then obtain financing for the purchase of the land and complementary subprojects and receive technical assistance. Two pilot projects (the Ceará Rural Poverty Alleviation Project and the Cédula da Terra) designed along these lines have been evaluated as successful in terms of speed, cost per family, participation of beneficiaries and anticipated impact (World Bank, 2000). Together these projects have redistributed a total of approximately 640,000 hectares to benefit some 23,700 households—for example, about 100,000 individuals and an average farm size of 27 hectares—at an average estimated cost of R$10,000 per family (World Bank, 2000). This is a significant achievement and there appears to be considerable scope for further action along these lines. However, in the bigger context of the estimated 9.8 million rural poor in the NE and SE of Brazil, these pilot community-based land reform programs have currently reached only about 1 percent of the rural poor. Hence, community-based land reform should not be thought of as the panacea for rural poverty reduction but rather as a critical component in a wider set of integrated policies.

Essentially, rural poverty can no longer be explained solely according to the land ownership pattern. The declining share of land in the value of production also reflects this. For instance, Brandão et al. (Chapter 4) report dramatic reductions in ratio's of the value of agricultural production to the sale and rental values of the corresponding land stock. These trends are manifestations of the overall trend, especially of the commercial agricultural sector, towards more production methods that require larger proportions of technology, renewable capital and purchased inputs.

---

12. IPEA/World Bank/Ministério do Desenvolvimento Agrário, Rio, August 2000.
13. World Bank (2000), Brazil Poverty Reduction, Growth, and Fiscal Stability in the State of Ceará.

Is the decline in farmland prices since 1994 permanent or cyclical? The analysis on the evolution of farm land prices distinguishes several episodes since the early 1970s: an increase in real land prices up to 1975, fairly constant prices during 1975–83, unstable and falling prices during 1984–94, and a significant decline since 1994.[14] The decline since 1994, particularly in the south, is attributed to several quasi-permanent factors, namely a consequence of Mercosur with cheaper land in Argentina, Uruguay and Paraguay (land prices in the South are three to four times higher than in neighboring countries), low rates of inflation, higher interest rates, changes in land taxation, all factors that took away some of the attractiveness of holding land as an investment. What is unclear is the extent to which lower profitability in farming was another influential factor explaining this decline until 1996. Some recovery in land prices after the 1998 devaluation of the Real would be consistent with the profitability argument, but which could not be examined due to lack of data. Lower farmland prices provide a most favorable price environment for the acquisition of land under the current land reform program in the NE. On the other hand, the income potential of the beneficiaries of the land reform would of course be reduced if the reduction in land prices reflects a decline in farm profitability, a variable that should be monitored.

Overall, it is somewhat surprising that a country with the level of development of Brazil would be so far behind the modernization of its rural land market. Brazil is characterized by substantial numbers of by and large unprotected sharecroppers and tenants. This is essentially a result of current provisions of the Land Statute, under which tenants (even informal sharecropping arrangements) can claim rights to the land (in some cases even expropriate the farm) when certain conditions are met. In particular, when perennial crops are planted or investments are made. Consequently, landowners typically accept rental or other arrangements on a highly precarious basis providing annual crops are planted and under which there is no legal protection of tenants. The current Land Statute thus constrains the farm sector—especially poor rural landless farmers—by inhibiting more flexible and secure tenancy arrangements. This issue deserves special attention. Agriculture in Brazil, as in most middle-income countries, is becoming more capital intensive and more exposed to foreign markets; hence the critical role of flexible tenancy arrangements that facilitate farm restructuring, the entry and the exit of farmers.

Land rentals should be seen as an important complement to the land reform program currently being implemented. The land reform program alone will inevitably not resolve the question of land access for a large fraction of the potential beneficiaries. There is a need to open more opportunities through the land market for small and medium scale labor-intensive farming. The focus of the program recommended in this report could take the form of consolidating property rights by the revision of the land legislation so as to secure longer-term tenancy arrangements, resolution of disputes regarding interpretation and enforcement of land rental arrangements. In addition, the impact of such program would be greatly enhanced by simultaneous adjustments of the labor code and in the land tax system. Labor laws have had an anti-sharecropping bias. In this context, the experience with the Rural Leasing Exchange in the Triângulo Mineiro contains useful lessons. Although not oriented towards social goals, this program has been successful and it represents an approach that should be examined further.

Increasing R&D and Transfer of Technology

López and Romano (Chapter 5) find that in 1996 only about 2 percent of minifundia and small farmers received some form of technical assistance; rising to 8 percent and 31 percent for medium size and large farms respectively. Econometrically estimated income and revenue functions are a powerful tool to capture the interactions between various determinants (such as human and physical capital, the policy framework, etc) as well as to reveal to relative impact of changes in the various factors on household income.

---

14. See Brandão, Bastos and Brandão, Chapter 4, Volume II.

López and Romano (Chapter 5) estimated farm revenue functions and report that policies that increase access to technical assistance would benefit poor and non-poor farmers alike. The potential for increasing farm revenues of small farmers via increased technical assistance is quite significant. Farmers with access to technical assistance have between 7 percent and 11 percent more revenues, ceteris paribus, than those that do not. This increase, while significant, does not however guarantee that the income of these small farmers will necessarily surpass the poverty line. Considering that for instance in the NE, 57 percent of farmers live in extreme poverty and up to 82 percent live in poverty; this further underscores the need for a policy approach that is integrated and tailored to accommodate for policy synergies.

Rural Finance Market Reform
López and Romano (Chapter 6) report that of the minifundia (up to 2 ha) and small farms (2.1–10 ha) in the rural NE and SE, on average only 2 percent received government subsidized credit in 1996. For farms sized between 10.1 and 50 hectares, this proportion rises only to a mere 8 percent, while on average some 31 percent of farms that are larger receive government subsidized credit. These descriptive findings are reflective of the degree of access-to-credit problems that were faced by small and poorer farmers in the rural NE and SE. Since 1996, programs such as PRONAF have been expanded substantially and the situation is likely to have improved but updated figures were not available.

The need to improve rural finance market functioning is further borne out via the farm revenue determinants analysis by López and Romano (Chapter 6). Most notably, for small farmers, the elasticity of purchased inputs is considerably larger than the observed input shares.[15] In other words, the marginal revenue of purchased inputs is higher than their marginal cost in production and this reflects their credit constrained induced sub-optimal allocation of purchased inputs. In the context of the synergy findings between land and other factors of production, this further reinforces the need for an integrated strategy that focuses not only land but also recognizes policy synergies involving other rural factor markets to increase revenues from farming.

Low liquidity is thus a very influential constraint for small farmers and without complementary assets (for example, purchased inputs, machinery, education), the value of land, by itself is very small. For land to have a large impact on income (revenue) it is necessary that the liquidity constraints faced by small farmers are reduced and this in turn enables the purchase of inputs and more capital for on-farm investments. Relaxing these constraints is within the scope of agricultural policy initiatives. However, note that this does not resolve the consequences of low human capital endowments and the possible output price effect induced by the non-tradability. This implies that for a subset of small-scale poor farmers we might have to consider alternative poverty reduction measures in the form of direct income transfers such as Brazil's *previdência rural* and carefully evaluate the potential for programs a la Mexico's *Pro Campo*.

Rural Labor Market Reform
Labor markets can play a vital role, both directly and indirectly, for rural poverty reduction. In a very direct sense, labor market functioning is key because poor rural households are much more dependent on wage earnings. For example, on average in the rural NE, for poor households labor wages account for 30.6 percent of total income compared to only 12.6 percent for the non-poor (see Chapter 7). Flexible, efficient and well-functioning labor markets can also play an important indirect role by facilitating labor reallocation across skills, types of employment, and geographical locations. In the context of the proposed integrated policy framework, labor market functioning is crucial for three of the five poverty exit strategies.

---

15. This corresponds to the analysis by de January et al. (1991) whom find that market failures, including lack of access to the credit market, are typically reflected in the elasticities of the responses of small poor farmers to various factors of production.

Reviewing the Labor Code

Labor contract legislation is critical because to a large extend it determines the degree of market flexibility. Agriculture is a special and somewhat difficult case. Agriculture activities are typically beset by considerable variability in both production and prices—and thus parallel fluctuations in labor demand—and are generally further constrained by the need to harvest and process production in a short period of time. Moreover, the sector is characterized by high monitoring costs and seasonal production patterns under typically very heterogeneous employment conditions, even within the same geographic region. Consequently, a labor code that establishes overly restrictive or too many regulations can result in two reinforcing effects: limiting the use of contracts that induce cooperation between workers and employers, and therefore lower total factor productivity levels (López and Valdés, 2000).

Both farm and rural non-farm employment are particularly sensitive to labor regulations, particularly when these impede the flexibility to tailor the contracts to accommodate for firm and labor characteristics. Current labor regulations appear to be restricting rural employment opportunities. Earlier studies have raised the concern that the Brazilian labor code as it applies to agriculture was contributing to reducing salaried work and thereby encouraging excessive substitution from labor- to capital-intensive farming. Carneiro (Chapter 3) finds that this concern continues to apply today. In the NE, the share of salaried workers in agriculture fell from 41 percent in 1981 to 32 percent in 1997, while during the same period there was a significant increase in "unpaid" (family) workers from 22 percent to 30 percent. Throughout the 1980s and 1990s, only 28 percent of the agricultural labor force was engaged in formal employment and earning a regular wage. This small proportion combined with the high share of aggregate output from medium and large commercial farms is illustrative of substantively lower labor productivity in the "unpaid" family farming sector. The evidence presented by Carneiro (Chapter 3, Volume II) is consistent with a strong anti-employment bias, showing: (a) the complexity and rigidity introduced by the labor code and the pro-labor bias in its enforcement, and (b) the high labor tax that is raising the total cost of hiring formal work to 102 percent of the basic salary. However, "hard" evidence on the magnitude in question would require a quantitative approach that captures the interactions among the various determinants of employment and this is currently not available for Brazil.

Two types of arrangements, cooperatives and "condomínios", offer advantages for hiring temporary workers, but do not address the issue of hiring under longer term contracts. The rapid proliferation of indirect hiring through cooperatives and "condomínios" for hiring temporary workers in agriculture was largely a market response induced by the rigidity in rural labor markets in Brazil. Cooperatives act as contractors and thus there is no formal link between workers and farmers as employers. While cash wages are about 30 percent higher than cash wages under traditional arrangements, workers forego several benefits such as severance payment, paid vacations, weekly rest, and the 13th salary. Condomínios are employers associations and workers do have access to benefits extended in the formal sector, although cash wages are lower than under cooperatives. The number of claims against cooperatives has increased substantially, creating an atmosphere of conflict and tension in agricultural labor markets.

The fact that income per person among farm workers in the NE is generally extremely low underscores the importance of removing institutional and policy constraints that inhibit the growth of higher paid formal rural employment. The Brazilian government has already submitted to Congress a package of reforms of the labor code, aimed at increasing flexibility and reducing the incentives to switch to informal arrangements. According to the analysis by Carneiro (see Chapter 3), the most critical changes for improvement in the working of labor markets for temporary workers—meaning those that would favor more employment and higher labor income for the poor in rural areas, are:

▪ Reductions in the value and number of taxes that employers have to pay as social contributions when hiring temporary labor.
▪ Reductions in FGTS deposits and exemption of the 40 percent fine upon termination of contract, in the case of temporary employment.

■ Encourage the organization of employer's condominiums, extending all labor rights to temporary workers and avoiding future labor claims.

■ Reduce pro-labor bias in conflict resolution by ending the legal power of the Labor Courts while retaining their standing to engage in voluntary arbitration in collective economic conflicts, at the request of the parties.

RNF Issues

Non-farm employment in rural areas is growing in Brazil. This mirrors recent trends throughout Latin America where RNF currently represents over one-third of total rural employment and generates 40 percent of rural incomes (Berdegue et al., 2000). There is consensus that RNF employment is desirable because it represents a critical component of a rural poverty alleviation strategy. Then the question is what is required and who pays to make rural areas more attractive for the creation of RNF employment. Moreover, RNF represent a variety of very diverse employment activities (including down- and up-stream farm activities as well as the industry and service sectors) rather than constituting an economic sector per se, and thus part of the challenge is to identify which activities are likely to be most dynamic in employment generation and their spatial distribution.

Overall, the study suggests that location matters in the context of developing RNF employment opportunities. This is a consequence of the spatially heterogeneity with regard to areas where agriculture is more prosperous, which have better access to infrastructure and education. In the NE, is RNF is concentrated in the states of Bahia, Maranhão, and Rio Grande do Norte. However, The RNF sector does not provide a vehicle for addressing poverty in the less dynamic, more remote and poorer agricultural regions. This is a concern in those regions characterized by low levels of infrastructure and where agricultural incomes are low and highly variable, as for instance in the semi-arid areas of the NE.

Supply of Public Goods and Building of Social Capital

Due to the heterogeneous nature of rural poverty and its constraints (for example, differences with respect to access to assets, household characteristics, institutional gaps, regional specificity) exit paths out of rural poverty are equally diverse. This would suggest that rural development programs and rural poverty alleviation strategies should be demand driven and tailored to meet these heterogeneous local needs. In this context, in addition to abstracting from community level heterogeneity, the failure of numerous rural development projects since the 1970s can be partially linked to inadequate community participation and local capacity, as well as the excessive centralization of decision making—a common source of politically induced resource misallocation (van Zyl et al., 2000). This warrants going beyond merely considering the heterogeneity of the poor and to actually encourage the poor to actively share in the identification of their needs and organize themselves so they can press effectively for their fulfillment (Lipton and van der Gaag, 1993). In other words, a key objective in a poverty reduction strategy should be to encourage poor people within communities to build up the social "grassroots" capital that simultaneously gives them a collective political voice and provides them the basis for involvement in the management of their own local development efforts.

Recent experience from an increasing number of developing countries suggests that properly decentralized development programs that are accompanied by parallel efforts to promote greater involvement and autonomy in decision making for local communities can offer genuine opportunities to improve rural development outcomes.[16] These redesigned community based programs can be particularly effective with respect to the provision of a wide variety of public good infrastructure. For instance, a recent comprehensive evaluation (van Zyl et al., 2000) of the so-called Rural

---

16. Past approaches such as the so-called Integrated Rural Development Projects (IRDPs) while premised on the need for more localized operations, failed both to properly involve local poor people in a participatory process and to build local social capital (van Zyl et al., 2000).

Poverty Alleviation Projects (RPAPs) introduced with cooperation by the World Bank in eight states in the northeast of Brazil, concluded that these have achieved the objectives and, to a large extend, the targets established at the start of the projects in 1995.

Among the public goods infrastructure sub-projects, rural electrification and water supply dominated the profile of community demands but the wide range of other infrastructure demanded (road improvements, small bridges, and public telephones) are reflective of the anticipated heterogeneity in development priorities across different communities. Many of the productive sub-projects (meaning those requiring direct investment into production or processing of agricultural and non-agricultural goods) that are typically demanded after communities infrastructure needs are met, were found to be successful depending on the complexity of the productive process (simple projects included "casas de farinha's," small irrigation schemes, and agricultural mechanization) and the extend to which the activity was exposed to market risks. More complex undertakings (such as clothing, ceramic and community brick factories) had some success but required a significantly greater provision of technical support.

Price and Trade Policy

The analysis by López and Romano (Chapter 5) revealed that larger farms tend to produce more tradable crops while smaller farms produce more non-tradable crops and, on the consumption side, small farmers spend a relatively higher share of income on food. These differences in the structure of production and consumption implies that:

- Trade liberalization that raises the relative price of exportables improves the revenues of non-poor farmers to a larger extent in comparison to poor (smaller) farmers;
- The marginal effect of a reduction in import tariffs on farm revenue is small and negative across farm sizes; and
- Devaluation is not likely to play an important role in increasing the incomes of the poorest farmers.

The output mix concentration on non-tradables of small farmers is also somewhat disquieting considering that factor returns are quite dependent on output prices. A significant expansion in their output could reduce their output price. By contrast, tradables in Brazil are practically "price-takers" and thus an output expansion would have no significant effect on their prices. For example, a rise of 10 percent in export prices (such as a result of a devaluation) increases the marginal returns to labor by 10 percent.

Avoiding real exchange rate appreciations and sharp interest rate fluctuations emerge as critical macroeconomic policy elements that will contribute to strengthen the competitiveness of the agricultural tradable sector (outputs and inputs); both on-farm and in downstream off-farm sectors. The latter would be very complementary with a trade policy regime that moves towards relatively low tariffs on importables (inputs and final products) because this should significantly enhance the export orientation of the sector. Together these macroeconomic policies can also have an important positive impact in the agricultural labor market. Under a reformed more flexible regulatory framework in rural labor markets, an exchange rate devaluation and trade liberalization are likely to have an important positive impact in the agricultural labor market by inducing higher real wages. This will help to revitalize the commercial agricultural sector and thus benefit landless agricultural workers and small farmers engaged in off-farm employment to complement their income.

Transfer Programs

Since 1991, there has been a substantial increase in the coverage of social security for rural workers in Brazil. Social security benefits paid to rural households as income support for workers in old age, for the surviving spouses and children of deceased workers, for the temporarily injured and the permanent disabled, have steadily increased. In addition to contributory pensions, the Previdência

Rural currently pays a non-contributory social assistance pension for old age and disability to poor workers without a documented work/contribution history. Rural workers are allowed to receive an old age pension five years earlier than workers in urban areas. Under the Previdência Rural, all beneficiaries who qualify receive the equivalent on one minimum salary, regardless of their previous salary. A critical feature of the new program is the de facto combination of social insurance and social assistance for the elderly under a single regime. The former program is exclusive—requiring that beneficiaries contribute to qualify for benefits—while the latter is universally available to any worker who reaches the age of 70.

Recent evidence by Delgado (2000) report that the Previdência Rural: (i) constitutes an increasing share of household income among the rural poor, and (ii) has lead to a lower incidence of poverty in rural areas. However, the findings do not provide a clear answer as to whether the positive impact of rural pensions can be attributed to the successful implementation of contributory social insurance for rural workers, or to the expansion and increased generosity of non-contributory social assistance transfers.

The current actuarial and fiscal imbalance raises questions regarding the sustainability of the current program. This raises the question as to whether the current scheme should be maintained, or restructured into two separate programs: one based on earmarked payroll taxes (social security) and the other (social assistance) financed with a more broadly based source of finance, namely from the general government budget (see Chapter 8). The current scheme is laying the burden of income redistribution to rural households on the shoulders of workers and employers in the private sector. The net impact on income distribution is ambiguous, because due to lack of the necessary information, the incidence of contributory and non-contributory social insurance cannot be analyzed separately.

A Preliminary Policy Portfolio Selection Analysis

Does Brazil currently have the right arsenal of policies and programs to combat rural poverty? An effective rural poverty strategy requires complementary programs and instruments that capture the heterogeneity in asset positions and household characteristics among the rural poor and thereby paved multiple poverty exit paths. A preliminary portfolio of potential policy directions was identified in the previous section. Given the realities of government budget constraints, the next step consists of prioritizing and selecting an "optimal" policy portfolio. While a comprehensive assessment was beyond the scope of this report, the overriding objective was to provide a strategic framework and policy suggestions, this section provides a methodological that permits a quantitative comparison of various government programs in terms of three criteria, namely their coverage, targeting, and cost-effectiveness (see Chapter 9).

The approach ranks programs by their effectiveness to transfer resources to the poor. However, some programs may have additional objectives that need to be considered in a more comprehensive evaluation The approach focuses on the benefits received by the proportion of the population that falls in the bottom national expenditure quintiles, and the analysis compares eleven programs, namely land reform (Cédula da Terra), the Rural Poverty Alleviation Projects (RPAP), drought relief, school lunch program, basic health, PRONAF loans, access to electricity, children in primary and in secondary school, access to piped water, and pension recipients. The analysis requires several rather strong assumptions to fill data gaps and make programs comparable, and thus the results should serve as a practical departure point for further in-depth analysis, rather than a mechanistic and premature policy conclusions. Some programs are universal (basic health, education, and school lunches) and thus their low targeting does not mean that they should be abandoned. With some programs, non-monetary benefits for the poor are difficult to measure.

Overall, rural social spending is very progressive compared to total social spending in Brazil. Simply because the poverty rate is so much higher in rural areas, a less intensive targeting effort is necessary for bringing a larger share of the benefits to the poor. Rural social spending has a larger poverty reducing effect than social spending overall. This would suggest, on the margin, that increasing rural social spending more than urban social spending would have a greater effect on poverty reduction. The analysis conclude that approximately 30 percent of the total social expenditure in rural areas is captured by the poorest families (first quintile), which is relatively high compared to social programs overall. To some extent the extent of targeting reflects that some of the programs apply primarily to the Northeast, by far the poorest region in Brazil. Moreover, one would also expect that rural social spending would also be significantly more cost-effective in the NE, considering its higher incidence of poverty.

Several programs are well targeted but reach a small share of the poor (such as land reform) and, on the other extreme, some programs are poorly targeted and do not reach many of the poor (for example, secondary education, urban services, and credit PRONAF). Regarding pensions, a caveat applies because income figures from pensions include both the Providence Rural and the traditional social security program. Hence, the analysis underestimates the targeting effectiveness of the Previdência Rural program.

Finally, there are social programs that are both well targeted and reach a large share of the poor. The two programs that apply only to the Northeast—the Drought relief and the Rural Alleviation Projects (RPAPs) come close to this criterion. The analysis also suggests some tradeoffs between targeting and coverage, and between benefit size and coverage. With higher coverage programs it is more difficult to control leakages, a challenge in up-scaling small and well-targeted programs. On the latter, more expensive programs but which provide significantly higher income streams such as land reform, reach only a small proportion of the poor, while cheaper programs such as RPAP can afford larger coverage.

TABLE D: GOVERNMENT PROGRAMS: TOTAL EXPENDITURE, NUMBER OF BENEFICIARIES, COVERAGE AND TARGETING RATIOS

Program/Area	Total spending 1998 in R$ bn	Beneficiary Households (million)	Coverage Ratio	Targeting Ratio
PRONAF	1.65	0.72	6 percent	25 percent
Rural Electrification	0.04	5.10	40 percent	18 percent
Land Reform	1.90	0.37	11 percent	85 percent
NE Drought Workfare	0.56	1.20	56 percent	75 percent
Food Distribution	0.22	3.00	66 percent	41 percent
Piped Water Supply	0.41	3.40	7 percent	15 percent
Health Services	1.98	6.60	75 percent	31 percent
Ensino Fundamental	2.08	6.60	60 percent	45 percent
Ensino Médio	0.09	0.62	3 percent	17 percent
Rural Pensions	10.80	6.30	28 percent	13 percent
RPAPs	0.21	1.30	57 percent	70 percent
Total of Listed Programs	19.92			

Source: von Amsberg, Chapter 9, Volume II.

Given the realities of government budgetary constraints, coverage and targeting criteria should be complemented by a rigorous cost-effectiveness of the various programs. In other words, how many Reais from the budget does it take to transfer one Real of benefits to the poor through the various programs as currently structured? A preliminary analysis is presented in the report, but—given the severe data constraints faced at this stage—should be interpreted as highly tentative. From a broader government (federal and state) budgeting perspective, however, an equally challenging budgeting issue emerges: how to allocate rural spending between 'general' regional development programs (for example, infrastructure, development of commercial activities, etc.) and those specifically targeted at the rural poor.

References

Alves, E., M. Lopes, and E. Contini. 1999. "Como esta pobre nossa agricultura." mimeo, Brasilia.

Carneiro, F. G., and A. Henley. 2000. "Real Wages and the Lucas Critique: Can the Government Tax Policy Influence Wage Growth in Brazil?," *Revista de Econometria*, forthcoming.

Carter, C., and P. Olinto. 2000. "Getting Institutions Right for Whom? The wealth-differentiated impact of property rights reform on investment and income in rural Paraguay." in Byerlee and Valdes (2000).

de Janvry, A., and E. Sadoulet. 1999. "Rural poverty and the design of effective rural development strategies." presented in Bahia, Brazil, at the Junta Interamericana de Agricultura.

de Janvry, A., and I. Sadoulet. 2000. "Making investment in the rural poor into good business: new perspectives for rural development in Latin America." presented in New Orleans at the Annual Meetings of the Inter-American Development Bank.

Delgado, G. 2000. "A Universalização de Direitos Sociais no Brazil: a Previdencia Rural nos anos 90."

Dollar, D., and A. Kraay. 2000. "Growth is good for the poor." World Bank, Development Economics Research Group.

Ferreira, F., P. Lanjouw, and M. Neri. 1998. "The Urban Poor in Brazil in 1996: a new poverty profile using PPV, PNAD and Census data." mimeo, Rio de Janeiro.

Helfand, S. M., and G. Castro de Rezende. 2000. "Brazilian agriculture in the 1990s: impact of the policy reforms." presented at the XXIV Int'l Conference of Agricultural Economists (IAAE), Berlin, August.

Lopez, R. 1998. "Land Titles and Farm Productivity in Honduras" in Byerlee and Valdes (2000).

Lopez, R., and A. Valdes eds. 2000. "Rural Poverty in Latin America." Macmillan Press (UK) and St Marin's Press, New York.

Morley, S. 1995. "Poverty and Inequality in Latin America: the impact of adjustment and recovery." Baltimore, The J. Hopkins University Press.

Paez de Barros, R. 2000. "Considerations about the rural labor market in Brazil." presented at the IPEA workshop on rural development, Rio, July 2000.

Reordan T., and Berdegue J. 2002. "World Development." Special issue on rural non-farm employment in Latin America.

Schultz, T. W. 1993. "The Economics of Being Poor." Blackwell.

Van Zyl, J. L. Sonn, and A. Costa. 2000. "Decentralized rural development, enhanced community participation and local government performance: evidence from Northeast Brazil." Washington DC, The World Bank.

World Bank 2000. "Brazil poverty reduction, growth and fiscal stability in the State of Ceará." Washington DC.

World Bank. 2000. "Brazil—Pernambuco State Economic Memorandum." ch. by Valdés and Mistiaen., Washington DC.

CHAPTER I

POVERTY PROFILE IN BRAZIL

Introduction[17]

This section provides a descriptive analysis of the rural population in Brazil, based on data from a survey applied to the Northeast and Southeast regions of the country in the period between 1996 and 1997. It focuses on comparisons of income and farm production, education, access to services and demographic characteristics, as well as poverty levels across different population segments and across income levels of the rural population, identifying the key characteristics associated with rural poverty.

Given the fact that rural areas are characterized increasingly by a diversity of economic activities, including the non-agricultural sector, it seems appropriate to analyze their social and economic characteristics by disaggregating the population into groups according to the main economic activity of the households. This type of disaggregation allows us to determine what the differences, if any, in economic and social characteristics are for the different groups as well as the differences in poverty incidence. In this study, the rural population is separated into three groups: farmers, comprising those households where at least one family member operates land for agricultural production (not necessarily owned land); non-farmers whose main economic activity is related to agriculture, that is, those non-farm households whose largest share of total labor income comes from work in the agricultural sector as employees; and non-farmers whose principal economic activity is in the non-agricultural sector.

The next section describes the data used in this study, its strengths and weaknesses, as well as some of the assumptions made in the definition of variables. The third section provides a detailed description of the characteristics of the rural population by income level, followed by an analysis according to the type of main economic activity. The fifth section presents the poverty estimates for the rural population as a whole and for different groups.

---

17. This paper on Rural Poverty in Brazil (1996/97) is a comparative analysis based on the PPV and was prepared by Claudia B. Romano.

The Data

The data comes from the 1996/97 *Pesquisa sobre Padrões de Vida* (PPV) survey, implemented by the Brazilian Statistical Agency (IBGE, standing for *Instituto Brasileiro de Geografia e Estatística*). Its design is based on the World Bank's *Living Standards Measurement Survey* (LSMS). The sample covers two out of the five administrative national regions, namely the Northeast (NE) Southeast (SE), with approximately 5,000 households, of which about 1,100 are rural. Although not representative on a national basis, the PPV covers about 73 percent of Brazil's population and is representative at the regional level.

The survey includes information on a wide range of demographic characteristics, income and expenditure, agricultural and non-agricultural activities, access to services, health, and education. Expenditure data is very detailed and comprehensive, with information on the expenses of food, manufactured goods, and other services such as education, health, housing, as well as the estimated value of food and other goods produced and consumed by the family. Questions related to income are also detailed. Income can be calculated from a disaggregated set of responses that include earnings from the main and secondary jobs, in-kind payments, benefits, consumption of own-produced goods, pension, donations, remittances, etc.[18] Moreover, in the case of farmers and fishermen, it is possible to obtain the net income using information on costs of production and on prices and quantities produced. The use of detailed questions in the calculation of income produces much better estimates than is usually obtained from most surveys that generally have only one question that inquires about the total income without any breakdown. Answers to single questions about net income are known to result in income underreporting, as has been confirmed for urban areas in Brazil in a study that compared the PPV calculated income values with single-answer values.[19]

However, one should be aware of some weaknesses in the available income data from the PPV and consequently, in the income values calculated in this study. In the case of farmers, it was not possible to obtain the value of sales from cattle or other animal raising activities.[20] Although the PPV has detailed information on the number of animals raised and sold, it does not have the prices or the total money value received for sold products. Additionally, income from forestry activities, collected forest products, and processed products from either cattle or crops are also missing because information on prices or total value sold was not collected. Therefore, we can assume that farm income values used in this study are under-estimations. Another problem with the farm income values is the level of aggregation of prices of agricultural products. Price information was obtained by IBGE from a community questionnaire applied in the same period as the survey, but not all villages or municipalities were interviewed. Therefore, the variation in the prices that agricultural producers receive was not captured completely and, thus, is not reflected in the farm income values. Prices, averaged across each state, were used to calculate farm income, thus, probably underestimating farm revenue for farmers located closer to markets and overestimating revenue for farmers with more difficult access to markets who tend to receive lower prices.

It was also not possible to use disaggregated information to calculate income for self-employed family members in the non-agricultural sector. Although there is detailed information on the costs of business activities, there is no question about gross revenues. The only possibility in this case was to use the answer to the single question about net income of the business activity, which we can assume, under-represents the real income.

Despite these caveats, the values reported in this study should represent rural household income values better than the usual values from single questions. In addition to including informa-

---

18. The imputed rental value of owned property where the family lives is also added. Value from leasing property and from interest on savings are not included because of a problem with the related questions in the survey, which mix monthly income from rental of property and interest on savings accounts with one-time income from sale of property and sale of bonds (see questions 11 and 17 in section 8 of survey).

19. See Ferreira et al. (1999).

20. In the cases where the only farm activity is cattle or animal raising, farm income is obtained from the answer to the single question about net farm income available form another section in the survey.

tion on income from jobs other than the main one, whether self-employed or salaried, as well as on benefits and non-labor income, it was also possible to include an estimation of the rental value of housing for those families who own their houses.[21] The value of public services such as health and education, which are likely to represent an important component of the real income of rural households, particularly poor families, cannot be estimated. The reader should be aware of these omissions when analyzing poverty estimates.

The other main household survey covering rural areas in Brazil is the *Pesquisa Nacional por Amostra de Domicilios* (PNAD), which is representative on a national basis and conducted annually since the mid 1970s, covering both urban and rural areas (except in Northern region), with a sample size of approximately 105,000 households. Despite its wide coverage in space and time, the range of questions in the PNAD is more limited than the PPV and, particularly with respect to farmers and the self-employed, the reliability of the data on income is rather poor given the fact that the questions for sources of income, other than wage employment, are dealt with in an aggregated manner.[22] Therefore, in comparison to the PNAD and despite its limited coverage, the strength of the PPV data is that it allows for in-depth analysis of questions involving income and poverty.[23]

As a final point, the reader should be aware that in the PPV (as well as in the PNAD), rural households are classified according to administrative criteria. IBGE defines as rural all population that resides outside the urban limits, while "urban" is defined according to the administrative condition of the place of residence. There are, therefore, no criteria related to population size, or any type of infrastructure and services that can consistently be associated with the definition of rural.[24] Given the political and financial advantages of becoming an "urban space," there has been a tendency in Brazil to create "cities" even in very sparsely populated areas. In addition, rural spaces that continue to have rural characteristics, but that become more dynamic and link-up to metropolitan areas, tend to become "urban," thus removing from the rural sample many of the cases of rural areas with active economic sectors.[25] Another important point to be made is that the basis of analysis in these surveys is the household location, not the place of employment. Therefore, rural inhabitants that have non-farm jobs may or may not be employed in rural areas.[26]

Main Characteristics of Rural Households

Table 1.1. (and 1.A1, 1.A2 in the appendix) provides a summary of the main characteristics of rural households for the Northeast and Southeast regions, by per capita income quintiles defined according to the distribution within each region.[27] The average annual per capita income in 1996 for the NE and SE regions was R$2,123 and R$3,056, respectively, well below the national level GNP per capita for 1996 of 4,945 reais.[28] In order to compare the average income between the two regions, income values should be deflated. According to the price index calculated in Ferreira et al. (1999) for Brazil, the price indexes are 0.95 and 0.89 for the NE and SE, respectively, using

21. The estimations were carried-out in Ferreira et al. (1999) for rural and urban households, based on location and house characteristics. Since most of the observations available on house rental come from urban areas, it is probable that the values are over-estimated for rural areas, particularly for the more remote localities.
22. For instance, questions on in-kind benefits do not ask for their specific money value separately, and income from secondary and other occupations are dealt with in only one question.
23. The work by Lanjouw (2000) is an important attempt to use the wider coverage of the PNAD together with the in-depth questions of the PPV.
24. In Graziano da Silva (1999) the PNAD data was disaggregated according to the new criteria utilized in the 1991 Census which created 5 distinct categories for place of residence, permitting a much better characterization of the rural/urban. Lanjouw (2000) also utilizes these new categories.
25. For in-depth analysis of the implications of these definitions of "rural" see Abramovay (1999).
26. For a more detailed discussion see Graziano da Silva and Del Grossi (1997).
27. The sample is separated into income quintiles using household per capita income adjusted for adult equivalency (using the Rothbar criteria, described in section 5). All values presented are weighted averages since the sample is not self-weighting.
28. National GNP per capita estimated in Ferreira and Paes de Barros (1999).

TABLE 1.1: BRAZIL NORTHEAST AND SOUTHEAST REGIONS (1996/97):
DISTRIBUTION OF MEANS OF RURAL POPULATION—
CHARACTERISTICS ACROSS INCOME GROUPS[1]

| | Southeast | | | Northeast | | |
	All	Poorest 20 percent	Top 20 percent	All	Poorest 20 percent	Top 20 percent
Income						
Household income	9,910	1383	31,897	8,052	1,101	26,786
Per capita income	3,056	339	10,066	2,123	230	7,256
Per capita income adjusted[2]	3,801	455	12,602	2,739	323	9,423
Monthly household expenditure	451	340	673	408	322	717
Monthly per capita expenditure	141	82	238	109	81	192
Income from farming	3,731	233	16,053	4,397	318	15,600
Income from agricultural wages	1,605	175	2,501	314	159	653
Income from non-agriculture sector	2,981	221	10,709	1,658	113	5947
Non-labor income	554	248	801	1,066	143	3178
Sources of Income (as percent of total income[3])						
Farming	23.8	32.8	41.0	49.0	48.7	59.2
Non-agriculture (wages and self-employment)	28.9	27.0	35.0	22.0	16.0	26.6
Agricultural wages	31.6	22.2	17.4	9.6	23.6	3.8
Non-labor income (excluding imputed rental)	15.6	18.0	6.6	19.3	11.4	10.4
Public pension	15.0	16.9	6.3	18.1	8.4	8.2
percentage of households where at least one person receives pension	24.4	15.6	22.6	29.8	8.1	27.8
Demographic Characteristics						
Number of people in household	3.8	4.6	3.4	4.5	5.0	4.3
Number of children of head of household	1.8	2.6	1.4	2.4	2.8	2.1
Age of head of household	45.9	44.4	45.5	47.2	42.6	45.6
Average age of family	32.0	26.9	34.5	30.2	24.9	28.0
Dependency ratio (N° of family members divided by N° of workers)	1.3 1.2	1.8	1.1	1.3	1.6	
percentage of heads of household white	57.5	38.0	78.1	30.9	32.2	25.3
percentage of heads of household black or Mulatto	42.5	62.1	21.9	69.1	67.8	74.7
percentage of heads of household that migrated from different state	12.6	11.0	13.5	8.3	8.6	6.5
Education						
percentage of heads of households illiterate	33.3	39.7	14.7	62.4	75.3	43.8
percentage of illiterates aged 10 and above	24.0	27.2	14.1	50.6	59.3	41.5
Years of education of head of household	2.7	2.2	4.1	1.8	1.1	3.8
percentage of heads of household that h had no formal schooling	29.5	27.1	18.4	56.4	62.4	36.6

(continued)

TABLE 1.1: BRAZIL NORTHEAST AND SOUTHEAST REGIONS (1996/97): DISTRIBUTION OF MEANS OF RURAL POPULATION— CHARACTERISTICS ACROSS INCOME GROUPS[1] (CONTINUED)

| | Southeast | | | Northeast | | |
	All	Poorest 20 percent	Top 20 percent	All	Poorest 20 percent	Top 20 percent
Years of education of male household members over 18	4.0	3.0	5.5	3.7	2.6	5.6
Years of education of female household members over 18	4.2	3.6	5.2	4.2	3.7	5.9
Years of education of household members aged between 6 and 12	1.8	1.7	2.3	1.0	0.7	0.9
Years of education of household members aged between 13 and 17	4.7	4.6	5.7	3.2	2.5	4.1
percentage of household members between 6 and 17 attending school	78.5	81.0	83.7	76.4	71.6	81.0
Education gap of household members aged between 6 and 18	2.5	2.5	1.3	3.7	4.4	3.2
percentage of household members between 6 and 17 in ideal or better grade	24.0	22.8	42.1	10.4	6.8	16.7
Access to Services						
percent of households with access to piped water	68.8	45.1	87.6	24.4	16.2	42.4
percent of households with access to electricity	82.4	63.2	94.5	54.2	42.5	56.9
percent of households with at least one member covered by private health insurance	25.0	4.3	53.4	12.3	2.1	46.6
Total amount credit received last month (only for households that obtained credit)	519.4	219.7	934.1	109.6	14.9	307.7
percent of households that received credit last month	6.1	7.5	5.9	3.9	1.9	6.1
Wage and Gender Aspects						
Hourly wage of women in salaried jobs	1.13	0.30	1.57	1.15	0.69	2.07
Hourly wage of men in salaried jobs	1.31	0.32	2.72	1.15	0.31	3.54
Number of hours per year worked by women in salaried and self-employment	1,344	1,068	1,525	1,265	1,464	1,346
Number of hours per year worked by men in salaried and self-employment	2,324	2,099	2,451	1,902	1,670	2,036
percent of households headed by a woman	12.1	12.7	9.0	15.7	15.5	13.7
Number of households	483	96	96	599	120	120

[1] Money values in Reais 1996 not adjusted for regional price differences; all income values are annual; income quintiles defined according to the per capita distribution within each region.
[2] Per capita income consumption-adjusted for adult equivalency according to the Rothbarth scale.
[3] Relative to total household income not including imputed rental value.

the metropolitan area of São Paulo as the reference. After this adjustment, the average income per capita in the SE region is about 54 percent larger than in the NE.

Income inequality is high in both regions. The per capita income of the highest income level is about 29 and 31 times larger than the lowest quintile for the SE and NE, respectively. The gini coefficient calculated for the two regions together is 0.64, while the gini coefficients for the Northeast and Southeast regions calculated separately are the same and equal to 0.63. These measures, therefore, also indicate that inequality in income distribution in both regions is high and very similar. They are also larger than the gini measures calculated for the whole country in 1996, which, by the estimations of Ferreira et al. (1999), is 0.57 and by Hoffman (sem data) is 0.59. The difference in per capita expenditure is considerably smaller, between 2.5 and 3 times larger in the highest income quintiles.

The importance of different sources of income to total household income also varies across income levels. Tables 1.1, 1.A1, and 1.A2 in the appendix, present these shares in relation to total income exclusive of the imputed house rental value. Income from farming is more important as a source of household income in the Northeast region, where it reaches, on average, almost 50 percent of total income. By contrast, the sum of agricultural wages and income from the non-agricultural sector make up a much more important proportion of income in the SE, about 60 percent. In both regions the agricultural sector, as a whole (self and salaried income), is more important than the non-agricultural sector, both reaching approximately 70 percent and 55 percent of total income in the NE and SE, respectively. As we observe, in the Southeast, the agricultural sector as a whole contributes with only a little over half of total rural income.

In both regions, the share of total income from farming is highest in the top quintile, but also important for the poorest family group, being relatively less important for the mid-income groups. Mid-income families seem to rely more on income from the non-agriculture sector and in the SE only, on agricultural wages also. The poorest families in the Northeast depend mostly on farming for their income. Yet, they also depend on agricultural wages much more than the "less poor" families in the region do, with 24 percent of income coming from that source versus the 4 percent corresponding to the wealthier families.

In the Southeast the mid-income families depend more on agricultural wages, while the poorest depend almost equally on farming and non-agricultural income. This suggests that the higher demand for agricultural labor in this region is responsible for increasing the income of many families, which, otherwise, would fall under the lowest income-level groups. It is noteworthy that wage salaries in the agricultural sector in the Northeast region only account for 9 percent of all income, whereas in the Southeast region, this figure reaches 32 percent of total income. This difference in the structure of the rural population between the two regions is analyzed in more detail in the next section.

The importance of the non-agricultural sector increases with income as observed in other studies.[29] In the SE it is interesting to note that the share of non-agricultural income is slightly higher in the poorest families than in families corresponding to the next two income levels, while, again, only the top two quintiles become more important. This seems to be related to the findings in Chapter 6 on Rural Non-Farm Employment that there is a group of people in the non-agricultural sector that works in low-paying jobs. Thus the poorest rural families may be more involved in low-return employment while the wealthier are involved in high-return jobs.

Non-labor income, which includes unemployment, pension, remittances, life insurance, food, and transport subsidies,[30] is slightly more important in the NE. The average proportion of total income from non-labor sources is 16 percent in the SE and 19 percent in the NE, and the average absolute value of income from that source is twice as large in the Northeast. By far, the main source of non-labor income is pension (it is responsible for about 95 percent of the total non-labor income) and within that, public pension is basically the only source (private pension is almost non-existent). The middle-income quintiles have the highest share of pension in total income, reaching

---

29. For example, see Graziano da Silva. 1999 and the case studies in López and Valdés (forthcoming).
30. Values of non-labor income do not include imputed rental value.

32 percent in the NE and 19 percent in the SE. The proportion of households receiving pension follows the same pattern, with a higher percentage in the mid-quintiles.

Given the fact that pension is such a large share in the income of families that are just beyond the poorest group, it is important to verify what happens to their level of income if we remove the value they receive from pension. When we remove pension from the total household income and re-evaluate each household's position across the same income levels, we observe that in the Northeast 10 percent of all households go down to the bottom income level, most of which coming from the mid-low and mid- income levels. And another 5 percent go down from the mid- to the mid-low income level. The same exercise applied to the Southeast results in 7 percent more households in the bottom income level, coming mainly from the mid-low quintile and another 5 percent go down to the mid-low quintile. The same exercise is carried out in the section on Poverty Estimates to analyze the change in poverty headcount levels.

As expected, the average family size is higher and the average family age is lower in the NE. Family size and number of children decrease, and average age of family and age of head of household increase with income, as expected. The dependency ratio, here defined as the number of family members per worker, decreases with income and is overall very similar for both regions.

Migrants are more common in the SE, where on average 13 percent of all heads of household come from a different state, and the proportion is higher in the wealthier 40 percent of the households than among the poor. In the SE, there is also a more apparent distinction between income levels in terms of the race of the head of household, where higher-income households are headed more frequently by white people. In the NE, there is no large distinction between income levels.

Educational level is quite different in the two regions. In the NE illiteracy is strikingly high, reaching 62 percent of all heads of household and 51 percent of all family members above 10 years of age. In the poorest fifth households, 75 percent heads of households are illiterate, compared to 44 percent in the wealthier quintile. In the SE these figures are 40 percent and 15 percent, respectively. Education is strongly correlated with income, with almost all indicators improving as income rises in both regions.

Younger generations have had better access to education, on average with double the number of completed years of education compared to the heads of household. The inequality in the indicators of educational level between income levels and regions is also larger with respect to the head of household than to the younger family members, particularly in the NE. The average number of completed, or effective, years of education of men and women 18 years of age and older, as well as the percentage of children attending school, are more similar among income levels and between regions than education of the head of households. The average number of years of completed schooling for men over 18 in the SE and NE is very similar at 4 and 3.7, respectively, while heads of household have on average 2.7 and 1.8 completed years of education.

In the poorest families the education of men and women over 18 is about 37 percent less than that of the wealthier families in the Southeast and 43 percent less in the Northeast. When we compare to differences between income levels but with respect to the years of education of the heads of household we get sharper differences of 46 percent and 71 percent for SE and NE, respectively.

Gini measures of inequality in the distribution of education confirm that education is less unequal for the younger generation, but still high. The gini coefficient for completed years of education for heads of household is 0.69 for the two regions together: 0.76 within the Northeast, and 0.53 within the Southeast region, showing that inequality is high in both, but particularly so in the Northeast. The same measure applied to household members aged 18 and above shows a better picture in both regions. The gini coefficient in this case for the Northeast is 0.63, while in the Southeast, it is 0.42, both indicating a less unequal distribution of education.

It is interesting to note that there is a sizeable difference between regions in the number of years of education completed for children between 6 and 17, being fewer in the Northeast. This would seem to indicate the opposite of what was discussed above, that is, that for the younger generations, the gap in education between regions is smaller. However, analyzing the figures for educational gaps (the difference between the grade children attend and that which they should be attending according to their age) and proportion of children in ideal grade, it becomes apparent that children in the Northeast start school later or have a higher rate of grade repetition than those in the Southeast, although they attend school at a similar rate than children in the Southeast. It seems, therefore, that the differences found are related to the fact that children in the NE complete their education at a later age.

Access to services is quite limited in the NE and a little better in the SE. Access to piped water and electricity is about 24 percent and 54 percent, respectively, in the NE, compared to 69 percent and 82 percent in the SE. The situation is much worse for the lowest income quintiles, where only 16 percent of the NE rural households have access to piped water versus 45 percent in the SE. The wealthier quintiles in both regions have about double the rate of access to piped water as opposed to the poorest quintiles.

Private health insurance is very low in the four lowest quintile groups in the NE, averaging about 4 percent of all households in these groups, while the highest income group's coverage is 47 percent. In the Southeast only the poorest fifth of the population has private health coverage as low as the rate in the Northeast. The average coverage in the Southeast is about twice that in the Northeast region as a whole. This indicates the strong tendency to enroll in private health insurance as soon as income levels permit.

Access to credit is very limited also. The information on credit obtained is not very representative since the question in the survey referred only to the month before the survey was applied. It can be noted, however, that the SE region has, in genera, higher levels of credit than the NE. In general, the SE also shows a higher proportion of households receiving credit, though the figures are very low in both regions. Only 6 percent of the households in the SE and 4 percent in the NE had access to any credit during the month before the survey.

Wages in the NE are, in general, lower than in the SE across income levels, except for the highest quintiles. According to these figures, the hourly wage received by men in the wealthier category is about 8 to 10 times higher than the wage in the poorest group in both regions. When wage is averaged for men and women we obtain hourly wages of R$1.15 and R$1.22 for the Northeast and Southeast regions, respectively.[31]

On average women work less than men in terms of hours per year in salaried and self-employment (not including housework), but the gender difference is more apparent in the SE. In the NE the poorest women work more than their counterparts in the SE, but the situation is inverted for the higher income levels where women in SE work more hours, a situation most likely related to the higher opportunities the latter have in the non-agricultural sector.

Comparison among Different Rural Population Groups

Table 1.2 presents characteristics of the rural population according to the division of the sample into different groups and by region. Tables 1.A3 and 1.A4 in the appendix compare the same groups across income levels and describe production technology variables for farmers. Farmers are defined as households where at least one family member operates land for agricultural production (not necessarily owned land). The division within the landless (or non-farmers) is effected according to the proportion of total household income that originates in agricultural activities. Agricultural workers have at least 50 percent of total income coming from agriculture and workers in the non-agriculture sector have less than 50 percent coming from agriculture.[32]

---

31. Paes de Barros et al. (1999) calculates average wages of R$1.6 and R$1.3 for the NE and SE, respectively.

32. Although the criteria utilized to separate the two groups of non-farmers is the source of at least 50 percent of total work income, 93 percent of the 348 households classified as landless in non-agriculture have zero income from agricultural activities. Of these only 2.5 percent have more than 35 percent of total income originating in agriculture.

TABLE 1.2: BRAZIL SOUTHEAST AND NORTHEAST REGION 96/97: COMPARISON OF MEANS OF RURAL POPULATION GROUPS[1]

| | | Southeast | | | Northeast | |
	Farmers	Landless In Agri-culture	Landless Non Agriculture	Farmers	Landless In Agri-culture	Landless Non-Agriculture
Income						
Household income	12996	5329	9655	8804	2117	7421
Per capita income	3647	1713	3377	2284	592	2034
Per capita income adjusted[2]	4516	2146	4215	2979	805	2545
Monthly household expenditure	490	346	487	377	300	498
Monthly per capita expenditure	140	113	164	93	77	152
Income from farming	9025	0	0	6653	0	0
Income from agricultural wages	1232	4030	142	365	1181	34
Income from non-agriculture	1060	134	7688	730	142	4088
Non-labor income	720	195	629	646	303	2180
Sources of Income (as percent of total income[3])						
Farming	55.8	0.0	0.0	70.1	0.0	0.0
Non-agriculture (wages and self-employment)	14.3	2.8	73.5	9.3	5.4	62.1
Agricultural wages	13.6	92.1	2.4	6.6	82.2	1.3
Non-labor income (excluding imputed rental)	16.3	5.1	24.1	13.9	12.4	36.4
Public pension	16.2	4.2	23.1	13.6	12.4	32.2
percentage of households where at least one person receives pension	30.4	11.3	27.2	29.9	16.9	32.0
Demographic Characteristics						
Number of people in household	4.2	3.8	3.4	5.0	4.5	3.5
Number of children of head of household	2.1	1.8	1.6	2.7	2.3	1.5
Age of head of household	48.9	41.0	45.9	48.9	38.1	45.0
Average age of family	32.9	28.5	33.4	30.1	23.7	31.5
Dependency ratio (N° of family members divided by N° of workers)	1.4	1.4	1.2	1.1	2.0	1.7
percentage of heads of household that migrated from different state	9.0	12.3	17.3	9.1	5.7	6.7
Education						
percentage of heads of households illiterate	33.9	37.5	29.3	67.7	81.4	46.5
percentage of illiterates aged 10 and above	23.5	27.9	21.6	53.6	64.5	41.2
Years of education of head of household	2.7	2.3	3.2	1.1	0.6	3.7
percentage of heads of household that had no formal schooling	29.7	32.6	26.7	61.6	63.4	42.9
Years of education—male household members over 18	4.1	3.4	4.4	2.8	1.8	6.5

(continued)

TABLE 1.2: BRAZIL SOUTHEAST AND NORTHEAST REGION 96/97: COMPARISON OF MEANS OF RURAL POPULATION GROUPS[1] (CONTINUED)

	Southeast			Northeast		
	Farmers	Landless In Agri- culture	Landless Non Agriculture	Farmers	Landless In Agri- culture	Landless Non- Agriculture
Years of education—female household members over 18	4.1	3.6	4.7	3.3	3.6	6.1
Years of education of household members aged between 6 and 12	1.7	1.4	2.1	0.8	0.5	1.7
Years of education of household members aged between 13 and 17	4.7	3.9	5.7	2.9	2.7	5.0
percentage of household members between 6 and 17 attending school	77.2	74.1	84.6	76.0	60.7	82.1
Education gap of household members aged 6 to 18	2.5	3.0	2.0	3.9	4.7	2.6
percentage of household members between 6 and 17 in ideal or better grade	23.0	17.4	31.5	5.6	4.6	29.2
Access to Services						
percent of households with access to piped water	60.1	71.8	77.4	13.7	10.2	51.7
percent of households with access to electricity	77.1	82.9	88.6	44.1	33.5	81.2
percent of households with at least one member covered by private health insurance	15.4	37.0	27.6	6.1	0.0	28.9
Total amount credit received last month (only for households that obtained credit)	769.2	828.5	95.1	107.4	—	115.5
percent of households that received credit last month	7.8	2.2	7.1	4.3	0.0	3.6
Wage and Gender Aspects						
Number of hours per year worked by women in salaried and self-employment	1,230	1,512	1,367	1,216	1,114	1,461
Number of hours per year worked by men in salaried and self-employment	2,274	2,603	2,140	1,865	2,203	1,942
percent of households headed by a woman	10.0	5.2	20.1	10.0	8.7	30.2
Number of households	201	127	155	365	41	193

[1] Money values in Reais 1996 not adjusted for regional price differences; all income values relate to annual income.
[2] Per capita income consumption-adjusted for adult equivalency according to the Rothbarth scale.
[3] Relative to total household income not including imputed rental value.

This sample division allows for interesting insights into the structure of rural groups, their main characteristics, and differences in welfare status. In the Southeast region, this division of the rural sample turned out to be relatively balanced among groups, resulting in 201 farmer households, 127 agricultural workers and 155 non-agricultural workers. It is very interesting to note that in the Northeast very few households actually fall in the category of agricultural workers, representing only 7 percent of the sample,[33] while farmers make up the largest group with 365 households, or 61 percent of the sample.[34]

In both regions the group of non-farmers employed in the non-agricultural sector constitutes about 33 percent of the rural families sampled and they have better indicators than the other groups in terms of expenditure, education, and access to services. In terms of per capita income, the data actually shows that farmers and households in the non-agriculture sector have similar income. Here it is important to point out that while it was possible to estimate income from farming with much detail about value of sales and costs of production, the same is not true for self-employment activities in the non-agricultural sector (as discussed in section 2). Therefore, it is very likely that income related to earnings from self-employment[35] are under-reported.

Looking at Tables 1.A3 and 1.A4 in the appendix, we can also observe that non-agricultural workers from poorest to wealthier have higher expenditures than all equivalent income levels in the other groups. However, the third poorest families within this group are not much better as compared to the poorest farm households. Their characteristics in terms of education and income/expenditure are similar to those of poor farmers. This seems, again, to be related to the findings in Chapter 6 that there exists a group of the people dependent mainly on the non-agricultural sector that are employed in low-paying jobs.

Agricultural workers, as a whole, have the lowest measures of welfare of all groups, and the differences are more accentuated in the Northeast region. There, their average per capita income is about three times smaller than that of the other groups, and the average per capita expenditure is 20 percent less than that of farmers with half the per capita expenditure of non-agricultural workers. In the Southeast region they have about half the per capita income of the other households, and per capita expenditure between 25 percent and 45 percent smaller.

These figures focus on the overall means for all groups, but they also apply to the comparison between equivalent income levels among groups. However, we note that at least a third of the agricultural workers, the wealthier group, live in similar conditions to the mid-income level families of farmers and non-agricultural workers, in terms of per capita expenditure and income, many education indicators, and, access to services (the latter applies only in the SE). This is particularly clear in the Southeast region and relates to what was discussed in the previous section, which is that families in the mid-income level in this region are quite dependent on wage employment.

Non-agricultural workers' share of income from public pension is the highest among the rural groups in both regions, reaching 32 percent in the NE and 23 percent in the SE. Agricultural workers receive the lowest proportion of income from public pension; in the Southeast this proportion is 4 percent. In the Northeast 12 percent of agricultural workers' income comes from pension. In absolute terms, the differences are also large, as can be seen in the tables by the average values of non-labor income received per household, which is comprised mostly by public pension. The average amount of pension received by workers in agriculture is about four times less than that received by the other groups in the Southeast, and seven times less than that of workers in the non-agriculture sector in the Northeast. Overall, the importance of public pension is much higher in the Northeast rural areas and for non-agricultural workers.

---

33. Because of its small sample size, the averages for the group of agricultural workers in the NE have to be interpreted more carefully.

34. When we incorporate the weights associated with each household—since the sample is not self-weighting—the importance of farmers in the Northeast is even stronger.

35. When income values are taken from the single question about yearly income, the average income figures are higher for non-farmers in non-agricultural activities.

As expected, family size is highest for farmers and lowest for workers in the non-agriculture sector. For households employed mainly in the agriculture sector, the age of the head of household and the average age of family are lowest and the dependency ratio (number of family members to worker) is highest.

The indicators of the educational level are also lowest for agricultural workers. In the Northeast, the proportion of illiterate heads of household in this group reaches the very high rate of 81 percent, while 65 percent of all adults over 10 years of age are also illiterate. In the Southeast, the incidence of illiteracy is much smaller, although still high, reaching 28 percent of all adults in the group of agricultural workers. With the exception of education of adult women in the NE, all other indicators are the worst for this group also.

By contrast, workers employed in the non-agriculture sector are significantly more educated than all other groups in both regions. However, farmers and non-agricultural workers of the lowest income terciles in the Southeast have very similar education. Only in the highest income levels the difference widens. In general the educational indicators in the Northeast are worse than in the Southeast for all groups.

In terms of access to services farmers and agricultural workers are not very different, but the gap between the two regions is enormous. In the Northeast only 14 percent of all farmers have access to piped water and 44 percent to electricity, while in the Southeast 60 percent and 77 percent have access to these services. Actually, in the Southeast agricultural workers have higher access to water and electricity than farmers, indicating that probably in this region, they tend to live closer to cities, while in the Northeast the opposite holds. The same can be said about coverage by private health insurance. The group with the highest access to services is non-agricultural workers.

Finally, it is very striking that, on average, 30 percent of all non-agricultural households in the Northeast are headed by women; the same figure for the Southeast is also relatively high, reaching 20 percent. The percentages for the other groups are much smaller. These results should be further explored, but they indicate that these families are likely to have remained in the rural areas after the husband migrated or died, and their income is increased by pension payments. Indeed, analyzing only woman-headed households, the proportion of total income from pension increases from 32 percent to 55 percent in the group of non-agricultural workers. Pension in rural areas goes mainly to the elderly poor (WB, 1999) and the analysis here seems to indicate that rural women get a large share of it.

Tables 1.A3 and 1.A4 in the appendix present additional characteristics for farmers only, according to income levels.[36] Land operation is increasing in income and is higher in the SE. The average land size for the lowest income terciles is 5 and 16 hectares in the NE and SE, respectively, while the top terciles operate farms of 37 and 67 hectares on average, respectively. A measure of land inequality, the gini coefficient calculated for land size operated (where the universe is the total number of establishments operated), is 0.85 for the NE and 0.83 for the SE, and the inequality in land distribution is not much different when calculated for the two regions, at 0.85. Thus, the distribution of land is only slightly worse in the NE region, but in both regions it is quite high.

There seems to be a higher proportion of farmers that own their land in the NE region, and the poorest farmers seem to own more of the land they operate. Wealthier farmers in both regions use more technology. In the NE farmers use more animal traction than in the SE in all income levels, while in the SE farmers use more machinery (tractors, etc.), though at very low levels, with the exception of the wealthier farmers where 41 percent have some type of heavy farm equipment.

Technical assistance is used only in 1 percent and 3 percent of the poorest farms in the NE and SE regions respectively. Only in the SE, a more significant proportion of the wealthier farmers

---

36. The rural component of the PPV sample includes only rural residents. As such, there is an under-representation of large farmers who more likely live in urban areas. Here farms smaller than 10 hectares represent 80 percent of the sample, while according to the Agricultural Census 1995/96 this land size category represents 59 percent of all farm establishments in the Northeast and Southeast regions.

(24 percent) uses the services of technical assistance. Government subsidized-financing reaches a very small proportion of farmers in both regions, but it is higher in the NE, with an average of 4 percent, as opposed to approximately 2 percent in the SE.

Poverty Estimates

In this section, the poverty level is compared across rural population groups. These numbers should be seen primarily as indications of the relative ranking of rural population groups and, given the small sample of the PPV, it is important to consider the standard errors associated with each number presented.

Table 1.3 provides estimates of poverty incidence by the headcount index, for the Northeast and Southeast regions, as well as for the three rural population groups. It uses, as welfare measurement, the per capita expenditure figures calculated from the PPV data and adjusted for regional price differences. The expenditure headcount measure indicates that 50 percent and 24.6 percent of the rural population in the NE and SE, respectively, fall under the extreme poverty line (equal to the minimum necessary for basic food requirements), which is equal to R$781 per capita annually.[37] These numbers are very similar to the ones obtained by Lanjouw in Chapter 6 based on a much larger sample for rural NE and SE, using PNAD consumption expenditure calibrated on the PPV. These numbers indicate that rural poverty incidence is higher than the average for the country as a whole. The poverty figure for Brazil is 22.6 percent (presented in Ferreira et al., 1999, using the same poverty line).

If we consider the total poverty line (a poverty line equal to approximately double the extreme poverty line), not less than 82 percent and 65 percent of the rural population in the NE and SE is poor. Ferreira et al. (1999) obtain that 45 percent of the population for Brazil as a whole is poor.

As mentioned earlier, it is important to analyze the significance of pensions in bringing families out of poverty. We can have a preliminary idea of the impact of pension on poverty by looking at if and how many families that do not, at this point, fall under the poverty line, would change position if not receiving pension. One way to verify this is to calculate the headcount index for both regions using the per capita income as welfare indicator and removing from it the value of pension payments. In both regions the extreme poverty figures calculated with income per capita are 45.8 percent (std. error = 4.2 percent) and 32 percent (std. error = 5.2) for the Northeast and Southeast, respectively. If pension is removed, the Northeast poverty figure increases to 51.9 percent and the Southeast to 37.1 percent, an increase that is statistically significant in the Northeast region only.

The regional average figures compared across rural population groups also indicate that the Northeast has higher incidence of poverty in all groups. The head count figures show that workers in agriculture and farmers in the NE have the highest incidence of poverty, with 59 percent and 57 percent falling under extreme poverty, respectively. These measures are very close and the positions may be reverted if we consider the standard errors associated with each measure. Also in the Southeast, a similar proportion of the population of agricultural workers and farmers, about 28 percent, live in extreme poverty. Workers in the non-agricultural sector in the Southeast have the lowest incidence of extreme poverty, 15 percent, which is also below the national poverty index.

Measures of total poverty follow the same pattern, but with much higher numbers, showing that 92 percent of the group of agricultural workers in the Northeast lives in poverty, followed by 86 percent of farmers in the same region, and 76 percent of agricultural workers in the Southeast. Again, workers in the non-agricultural sector form the group that is the least poor.

The next measures presented in Table 1.3 are per capita expenditure values adjusted to account for the different consumption demands of children.[38] These numbers are presented as an

---

37. The indigence line is R$65.07 monthly per capita and total poverty line is R$131.97 monthly per capita in Reais 1996. All values are regionally deflated with reference to Metropolitan São Paulo.

38. The adjustment for adult equivalency uses the Rothbarth scale that assumes that: children between 0–4 consume 15 percent of that of the average adult, children 5–10 consume 20 percent, and children between 11–15 consume 43 percent.

TABLE 1.3: POVERTY INCIDENCE—NE AND SE RURAL GROUPS: HEADCOUNT INDEX
(welfare measure: expenditure per capita)[1]

	Northeast				Southeast			
	Total	Farmers	Agricultural workers	Non-Agricultural workers	Total	Farmers	Agricultural workers	Non-Agricultural workers
Extreme poverty	50.0 (4.7)	57.1 (4.2)	59.1 (10.8)	24.7 (8.1)	24.6 (4.3)	29.2 (7.0)	27.3 (6.0)	15.0 (4.2)
Poverty	82.2 (3.2)	86.5 (2.8)	92.3 (5.3)	64.6 (4.7)	66.6 (6.2)	75.9 (4.3)	75.9 (4.3)	51.4 (6.1)
Extreme poverty adjusted[2]	—	30.03	19.36	8.36	—	11.63	10.99	3.70
Poverty adjusted	—	70.53	75.93	40.99	—	49.48	43.99	29.52
Extreme poverty theta=0.9[3]	—	22.12	15.57	4.08	—	6.00	9.94	2.39
Poverty theta=0.9	—	64.24	68.22	35.63	—	41.95	34.14	25.78

[1] Extreme poverty line=R$781/year per capita and poverty line=R$1562/year per capita, in 1996 prices. All income values have been deflated by regional price indexes. Standard errors in parenthesis for the main poverty measures.

[2] Income values adjusted for adult equivalency according to the Rothbarth scale using same poverty line. These numbers should be used exclusively for comparisons of rankings across groups and should not be seen as alternative head count measures since here the poverty line is not adjusted to take into account the average scaling effect of this adjustment.

[3] Income values adjusted for adult equivalency and economies of scale in consumption, where no economies of scale is theta=1; smaller values of theta indicate assumptions of increased degrees of economies of scale in consumption. These numbers should also be used exclusively for comparisons of rankings across groups and should not be seen as alternative head count measures since here the poverty line is not adjusted to take into account the average scaling effect of this adjustment.

indication of how the ranking of poverty levels across different rural groups can change and should not be seen as alternative headcount measures, since the poverty line here is not adjusted to take into account the average scaling effect of this adjustment. The consumption adjustment shows higher poverty for farmers relative to the group of agricultural workers. This is a consequence of the fact that there are more very young children in the families of agricultural workers and that their consumption is discounted more heavily. The ranking with respect to the other group and the ranking in the Southeast remain the same.

The analysis of adjustments for economies of scale in consumption[39] should also be used only for comparisons of positions among rural groups. These adjustments assume that, as family sizes increase, there are economies of scale in consumption of food, clothing, shelter, and other goods. With these adjustments, there is a change in the relative position between farmers and agricultural workers in the Southeast (again, if we consider the statistical errors involved, the change may not be significant). The stability of the relative measures of poverty for non-agricultural workers in all different methods gives support to the conclusion that this group is the least affected by poverty in both regions. Farmers and agricultural workers in the Northeast are also consistently the poorest, although their relative position may change with different measures.

Summary of Main Findings

According to the analysis based on the PPV data, the average annual per capita income in the rural areas of the Northeast and Southeast regions in 1996 was approximately R$2,100 and R$3,000, representing about 40 percent and 60 percent of the national GNP per capita, respectively. The average income of the poorest 20 percent households was approximately R$230 in the NE and R$340 in the SE, equivalent to about 30 times less than the income of the wealthier 20 percent in both regions, indicating a very unequal income distribution. Indeed, the gini coefficient for rural areas is similar in both regions at around 0.63, a higher inequality than that estimated by other authors for the whole country in the same year, of 0.57 (Ferreira et al., 1999) and 0.59 (Hoffman, not dated). If poverty is defined according to a poverty line of R$781 yearly per capita, equivalent to the minimum food requirements, approximately 50 percent and 25 percent of the rural population is poor in the Northeast and Southeast regions, respectively.

The analysis of the sources of income shows that the rural population in the Northeast is much more dependent on own-farming income than in the Southeast. In the Northeast 50 percent of total income comes from farming compared to 24 percent in the Southeast. The poorest families in the Northeast depend mostly on own-farming revenues, but they also depend on agricultural wages for 24 percent of their income, compared to only 4 percent among the wealthier families.

By contrast, agricultural wages and income from the non-agricultural sector are together a much more important share of income in the Southeast, reaching on average of 60 percent of total income. Mid-income families are the most dependent on agricultural wages, while the poorest depend almost equally on farming and non-agricultural income. This suggests that the higher demand for agricultural labor in this region is responsible for increasing the income of many families, which, otherwise, would fall in the lowest income level groups.

Families whose main economic activity is in the non-agricultural sector have more income, better education, and access to services than farmers and landless workers whose main source of income is agricultural wages. About 33 percent of the rural families have their main income from the non-agricultural sector, in both regions. However, when we analyze the characteristics of non-agricultural workers by income level we observe that the third poorest families, within this group, are not much better compared to the third poorest farm households. Their characteristics in terms of education and income/expenditure are similar to those of poor farmers. This seems to support

---

39. The values for Theta relate to economies of scale in consumption of a household, which increases as family size increases. Theta=1 means no economies of scale, and as theta decreases, economies of scale become more important.

the findings by Lanjouw in Chapter 6 that part of the people dependent mainly on the non-agricultural sector are employed in low-paying jobs.

Among rural families, landless agricultural workers have the worst welfare indicators: they are significantly less educated, earn between half and one-third of the average income of the other rural families and those in the Northeast, they also have the worst indicators of access to services. In the Northeast, only a small proportion of the rural population, 7 percent, fall in this category, while 60 percent are farmers; in the Southeast the distribution is more homogeneous with 26 percent and 42 percent being landless agricultural workers and farmers, respectively. Therefore, although poverty seems to be more widespread within the group of agricultural workers, the absolute numbers are less important than that of farmers, especially in the Northeast.

As expected, when we analyze the incidence of poverty separately for each group of rural households, we find that among non-agricultural workers, the incidence of poverty is the lowest, while farmers and agricultural workers have higher and similar proportions of poor families. However, since farmers make up a larger share of the population, particularly in the NE, the absolute number of poor people is higher among farmers. Using the level of expenditure per capita as the welfare measure, we find that the headcount index in the Northeast is about 57 percent for both farmers and agricultural workers, whereas in the Southeast, this figure is about 28 percent. The headcount index among non-agricultural workers is 24 percent and 15 percent in the NE and SE, respectively.

Public pension seems to be an important source of income to poor households, but more so to mid-income households. In the Northeast 44 percent of the households in the mid-income level receive pension, averaging over 30 percent of their total income. The poorest 20 percent in the SE and NE receive about 17 percent and 8 percent of their income from pension, respectively. When the sample is separated according to the main economic activity of the household, we observe that it is the rural group of workers in the non-agricultural sector that receive the highest pension share, reaching over 30 percent in the Northeast and over 20 percent in the Southeast. Among these, woman-headed households are prominent.

Given the importance of pensions for a large share of the rural population, it is important to analyze its weight in bringing families out of poverty. As mentioned above, we can have a preliminary idea of pension's impact on poverty by looking at if and how many families, which now do not fall under the poverty line, would change position if not receiving pension. This exercise shows that without pension the mean poverty figure would increase in both regions by about 5 percent, but this change is statistically significant only the Northeast region.

The educational level in rural areas is very low, particularly in the Northeast, and is also quite correlated with income. Illiteracy is very high for the poorest 20 percent of the rural population, reaching 75 percent of the heads of household in the Northeast and 40 percent in the Southeast. Younger generations show improved education, but still far from acceptable levels. About 51 percent of all people over 10 years of age are illiterate in the Northeast and 24 percent in the Southeast. The average number of completed years of education for men and women over 18 years of age is about 4 in both regions. The distribution of education is also quite unequal, though better for younger generations. The average number of completed years of education of the poorest families is about half the average educational level of the wealthier families. The gini coefficient calculated for years of completed education of adults is 0.63 in the NE and 0.42 in the SE. Given the increasing importance of non-agricultural economic activities in rural areas and the higher educational demands of higher-paying jobs in this sector, providing better education to the rural poor would considerably improve their chances of benefiting from the growth of this sector.

The inequality of land distribution is very high in both regions, even considering the fact that the largest farms are not included in the PPV sample. The average land size of the poorest third of farmers in the NE is 5 hectares compared to 37 hectares in the wealthier third of the households, while in the SE, these are 16 and 67 hectares. The gini coefficient calculated for land area is about 0.85 in both regions. The use of farm machinery is very low in all groups with the exception of the top third in the SE, where 41 percent of farmers possess some farm machinery. Technical assistance also reaches a very small percentage of farmers, being only significant, again, for the wealthier farmers in the SE. Access to subsidized credit is low across income levels, on average being used by 4 percent and 2 percent of farmers in the NE and SE, respectively. These numbers suggest that lack of access to capital, technical assistance, and credit is a severe constraint among small, poor farmers.

The gap between the Northeast and Southeast regions with respect to access to services is large, as is the difference across income levels within regions. For instance, on average, only 24 percent of the rural population in the Northeast has access to piped water compared to 69 percent in the Southeast. Only 16 percent of the poorest Northeast families use piped water versus 43 percent of the wealthier. About 82 percent rural households have access to electricity in the Southeast and 54 percent in the Northeast. Thus, lack of access to basic infrastructure is quite correlated to poverty in rural areas.

References

Abramovay, R 1999. "Do Setor ao Território: Funções e Medidas da Ruralidade no Desenvolvimento Contemporáneo." Primeiro relatório-Projeto BRA/97/013. IPEA, Rio de Janeiro.

Ferreira, F., and R. Paes de Barros. 1999. "The Slippery Slope: Explaining the Increase in Extreme Poverty in Urban Brazil, 1976–1996." Draft paper presented at LACEA 1998 conference, Buenos Aires

Ferreira, F., P. Lanjouw, and M. Neri. 1999. "The Urban Poor in Brazil in 1996: A New Poverty Profile Using PPV, PNAD and Census Data." Background Paper for the World Bank's Urban Poverty Strategy Report, 1998.

Graziano da Silva, J. 1999. *O Novo Rural Brasileiro*. Universidade de Campinas, Instituto de Economia, Campinas, SP.

Graziano da Silva, J., and M. Del Grossi. 1997. "A Evolução do Emprego Não-Agrícola no Meio Rural Brasileiro, 1992–1995." Working Paper, Instituto de Economia, UNICAMP, Campinas.

Hoffman, R. (forthcoming). "Desigualdade e pobreza no Brasil no período 1979–97 e a influência da inflação." Working Paper, Instituto de Economia, UNICAMP, Campinas.

López, R. and A. Valdés. (forthcoming) *Rural Povery inh Latin America: Analytics, new empirical evidence and policy*. St Martin's Prss, N.Y. and McMillan, London.

Paes de Barros, R., C. H. Corseuil, and R. Mendonça. December. 1999. "Uma análise da estrutura salarial brasileira baseada na PPV." Texto para discussão #689. IPEA, RJ.

World Bank. 1999. "Brazil: Critical Issues in Social Security." Volume 1: Summary Report # 19641-BR. Confidential Draft, World Bank, Washington, D.C.

Appendix

TABLE 1.A1: BRAZIL NORTHEAST REGION: DISTRIBUTION OF MEANS OF RURAL POPULATION CHARACTERISTICS ACROSS INCOME GROUPS[1]

	All	Low	Mid-low	Mid	Mid-high	High
Income						
Household annual income	8052	1101	2969	4269	7496	26786
Per capita annual income	2123	230	631	1160	1980	7256
Per capita income adjusted[2]	2739	323	851	1486	2444	9423
Monthly household expenditure	408	322	306	326	404	717
Monthly per capita expenditure	109	81	70	92	119	192
Income from farming	4397	318	1341	1802	4347	15600
Income from agricultural wages	314	159	287	284	227	653
Income from non-agriculture sector	1658	113	504	840	1418	5947
Non-labor income	1066	143	439	925	914	3178
Sources of Income (as percent of total income[3])						
Farming	49.0	48.7	47.0	38.1	53.0	59.2
Non-agriculture (wages and self-employment)	22.0	16.0	22.6	22.4	21.9	26.6
Agricultural wages	9.6	23.6	11.7	6.7	4.2	3.8
Non-labor income (excluding imputed rental)	19.3	11.4	18.8	32.7	20.9	10.4
Public pension	18.1	8.4	18.2	32.3	20.3	8.2
percentage of households where at least one person receives pension	29.8	8.1	25.9	44.1	45.2	27.8
Demographic Characteristics						
Number of people in household	4.5	5.0	5.1	4.1	4.1	4.3
Number of children of head of household	2.4	2.8	2.9	2.0	2.0	2.1
Age of head of household	47.2	42.6	45.2	52.9	50.1	45.6
Average age of family	30.2	24.9	26.6	37.4	34.0	28.0
Dependency ratio (N° of family members divided by N° of workers)	1.3	1.6	1.3	1.3	1.2	1.2
percentage of heads of household white	30.9	32.2	30.1	31.7	34.7	25.3
percentage of heads of household black or mulatto	69.1	67.8	69.9	68.3	65.3	74.7
percentage of heads of household that migrated from different states	8.3	8.6	8.6	6.0	11.6	6.5
Education						
percentage of heads of households illiterate	62.4	75.3	61.8	67.7	60.4	43.8
percentage of illiterates aged 10 and above	50.6	59.3	45.0	58.7	46.7	41.5
Years of education of head of household	1.8	1.1	1.3	1.1	1.9	3.8
percentage of heads of household that had no formal schooling	56.4	62.4	60.1	65.2	55.0	36.6

(continued)

TABLE 1.A1: BRAZIL NORTHEAST REGION: DISTRIBUTION OF MEANS OF RURAL POPULATION CHARACTERISTICS ACROSS INCOME GROUPS[1] (CONTINUED)

			Income Levels			
	All	**Low**	**Mid-low**	**Mid**	**Mid-high**	**High**
Years of education of male household members over 18	3.7	2.6	3.2	3.0	3.8	5.6
Years of education of female household members over 18	4.2	3.7	3.8	3.2	4.2	5.9
Years of education of household members aged between 6 and 12	1.0	0.7	1.1	1.0	1.4	0.9
Years of education of household members aged between 13 and 17	3.2	2.5	3.0	3.1	4.0	4.1
percentage of household members between 6 and 17 attending school	76.4	71.6	75.8	70.3	85.0	81.0
Education gap of household members aged between 6 and 18	3.7	4.4	3.8	3.6	3.1	3.2
percentage of household members between 6 and 17 in ideal or better grade	10.4	6.8	8.8	5.6	15.1	16.7
Access to Services						
percent of households with access to piped water	24.4	16.2	17.9	19.1	28.8	42.4
percent of households with access to electricity	54.2	42.5	52.9	54.5	65.7	56.9
percent of households with at least one member covered by health insurance	12.3	2.1	0.3	12.0	4.0	46.6
Total amount credit received last month (only for households that obtained credit)	109.6	14.9	18.7	33.8	35.5	307.7
percent of households that received credit last month	3.9	1.9	2.6	5.0	3.9	6.1
Wage and Gender Aspects						
Hourly wage of women in salaried jobs	1.15	0.69	0.42	1.05	1.32	2.07
Hourly wage of men in salaried jobs	1.15	0.31	0.51	0.69	1.25	3.54
Number of hours per year worked by women in salaried and self-employment	1,265	1,464	1,090	1,193	1,201	1,346
Number of hours per year worked by men in salaried and self-employment	1902	1670	1752	2003	2105	2036
percent of households headed by a woman	15.7	15.5	10.3	15.6	23.7	13.7
Number of households	599	120.0	120	119	120	120

[1] Money values in Reais 1996.
[2] Per capita income consumption-adjusted for adult equivalency according to the Rothbarth scale.
[3] Relative to total household income not including imputed rental value.

TABLE 1.A2: BRAZIL SOUTHEAST REGION: DISTRIBUTION OF MEANS OF RURAL POPULATION—CHARACTERISTICS ACROSS INCOME GROUPS[1]

	All	Low	Mid-low	Mid	Mid-high	High
Income						
Household annual income	9,910	1,383	3,449	5,230	7,922	31,897
Per capita annual income	3,056	339	898	1,604	2,482	10,066
Per capita income adjusted[2]	3,801	455	1,139	1,968	2,972	12,602
Monthly household expenditure	451	340	380	416	451	673
Monthly per capita expenditure	141	82	106	131	149	238
Income from farming	3,731	233	611	814	1,063	16,053
Income from agricultural wages	1,605	175	1,164	1,720	2,523	2,501
Income from non-agriculture sector	2,981	221	530	1,179	2,388	10,709
Non-labor income	554	248	453	653	620	801
Sources of Income (as percent of total income[3])						
Farming	23.8	32.8	20.3	15.6	11.2	41.0
Non-agriculture (wages and self-employment)	28.9	27.0	23.7	23.9	35.0	35.0
Agricultural wages	31.6	22.2	37.9	40.2	38.3	17.4
Non-labor income (excluding imputed rental)	15.6	18.0	18.0	20.3	15.5	6.6
Public Pension	15.0	16.9	17.4	19.3	15.4	6.3
percentage of households where at least one person receives pension	24.4	15.6	24.9	33.4	25.4	22.6
Demographic Characteristics						
Number of people in household	3.8	4.6	4.1	3.5	3.4	3.4
Number of children of head of household	1.8	2.6	2.1	1.6	1.5	1.4
Age of head of household	45.9	44.4	45.4	47.1	47.1	45.5
Average age of family	32.0	26.9	29.4	33.9	35.3	34.5
Dependency ratio (N° of family members divided by N° of workers)	1.3	1.8	1.5	1.2	1.1	1.1
percentage of heads of household white	57.5	38.0	45.2	59.6	67.5	78.1
percentage of heads of household black or mulatto	42.5	62.1	54.8	40.5	32.6	21.9
percentage of heads of household that migrated from different state	12.6	11.0	10.5	12.1	15.8	13.5
Education						
percentage of heads of households illiterate	33.3	39.7	44.7	39.3	27.7	14.7
percentage of illiterates aged 10 and above	24.0	27.2	28.8	28.4	21.3	14.1
Years of education of head of household	2.7	2.2	2.3	2.5	2.7	4.1
percentage of heads of household that had no formal schooling	29.5	27.1	38.9	35.9	26.8	18.4
Years of education of male household members over 18	4.0	3.0	3.6	3.7	4.0	5.5

(continued)

TABLE 1.A2: BRAZIL SOUTHEAST REGION: DISTRIBUTION OF MEANS OF RURAL POPULATION—CHARACTERISTICS ACROSS INCOME GROUPS[1] (CONTINUED)

			Income Levels			
	All	**Low**	**Mid-low**	**Mid**	**Mid-high**	**High**
Years of education of female household members over	4.2	3.6	3.7	4.1	4.3	5.2
Years of education of household members aged between 6 and 12	1.8	1.7	1.9	1.1	2.0	2.3
Years of education of household members aged between 13 and 17	4.7	4.6	3.9	4.9	5.1	5.7
percentage of household members between 6 and 17 attending school	78.5	81.0	75.0	70.5	81.0	83.7
Education gap of household members aged between 6 and 18	2.5	2.5	3.2	3.0	2.2	1.3
percentage of household members between 6 and 17 in ideal or better grade	24.0	22.8	16.2	21.3	20.1	42.1
Access to Services						
percent of households with access to piped water	68.8	45.1	58.8	70.8	82.6	87.6
percent of households with access to electricity	82.4	63.2	76.8	89.1	88.9	94.5
percent of households with at least one member covered by health insurance	25.0	4.3	10.4	19.5	38.6	53.4
Total amount credit received last month (only for households that obtained credit)	519.4	219.7	1212.7	121.0	100.3	934.1
percent of households that received credit last month	6.1	7.5	6.1	4.9	6.2	5.9
Wage and Gender Aspects						
Hourly wage of women in salaried jobs	1.13	0.30	0.72	1.16	1.46	1.57
Hourly wage of men in salaried jobs	1.31	0.32	0.74	1.09	1.50	2.72
Number of hours per year worked by women in salaried and self-employment	1,344	1,068	1,167	1,308	1,662	1,525
Number of hours per year worked by men in salaried and self-employment	2,324	2,099	2,249	2,395	2,431	2,451
percent of households headed by a woman	12.1	12.7	15.4	13.1	10.0	9.0
Number of households	483	96	97	99	95	96

[1] Money values in Reais 1996.
[2] Per capita income consumption-adjusted for adult equivalency according to the Rothbarth scale.
[3] Relative to total household income not including imputed rental value.

TABLE I.A3: BRAZIL NORTHEAST REGION: COMPARISON ACROSS RURAL GROUPS AND INCOME LEVELS[1]

	Farmers			Agricultural Workers			Non-agricultural Workers		
	Low	Mid	High	Low	Mid	High	Low	Mid	High
Income									
Household annual income	2,231	5,205	19,480	973	2,281	3,654	1,150	3,567	20,489
Per capita annual income	417	1,257	5,322	228	515	1213	314	1,256	5,258
Per capita expenditure	68	87	127	64	68	108	94	119	268
percentage farming in total income	68.2	63.0	78.9	0.0	0.0	0.0	0.0	0.0	0.0
percentage non-agriculture in total income	10.3	10.1	7.5	3.9	2.9	10.3	60.1	55.5	71.7
percentage agricultural wages in total income	10.2	5.3	4.1	96.1	71.2	72.6	3.1	0.6	1.2
percentage public pension in total income	11.3	20.8	9.1	0.0	25.8	17.1	25.7	42.8	22.5
percentage of households where at least one person receives public pension	17.4	38.1	36.0	0.0	32.7	25.9	13.8	50.1	32.0
Number of people in household	5.7	4.5	4.6	4.9	4.9	3.3	3.7	3.2	3.6
Average age of family	26.4	33.8	30.6	19.0	22.9	31.7	25.6	39.3	29.1
Dependency ratio (N° of family members divided by N° of workers)	1.2	1.2	1.1	2.2	2.8	1.0	1.7	1.8	1.6
percentage heads of household illiterate	68.7	71.0	63.5	81.9	83.9	78.0	65.1	54.1	12.8
percentage of illiterates aged 10 and above	51.8	55.8	53.5	71.5	59.2	59.5	54.8	49.3	13.2
Years of education of head of household	0.9	0.9	1.5	0.4	0.5	0.9	2.1	2.4	7.4
Years of education of men over 18	2.5	2.6	3.2	1.7	2.4	1.4	3.9	5.7	8.9
Years of education of women over 18	3.3	3.1	3.5	3.5	3.0	4.4	4.5	4.4	8.7
percentage of households with access to piped water	11.4	11.7	18.1	9.1	5.9	16.4	28.6	44.8	90.5
percentage of households with access to electricity	38.0	46.1	49.0	32.4	34.2	34.3	70.5	77.3	100.0
percentage of households with at least one member covered by health insurance	2.0	10.0	7.0	0.0	0.0	0.0	0.3	6.0	95.2
percentage of households headed by a woman	6.8	13.8	10.0	6.5	15.7	4.8	28.4	33.6	28.0
Farmers' Production Characteristics									
Total land size operated (ha)	5.1	7.9	37.2						
percentage of land operated that is owned	64.8	57.8	52.1						
percentage of households that received technical assistance	1.1	2.2	5.2						

(continued)

TABLE 1.A3: BRAZIL NORTHEAST REGION: COMPARISON ACROSS RURAL GROUPS AND INCOME LEVELS[1] (CONTINUED)

	Farmers			Agricultural Workers			Non-agricultural Workers		
	Low	Mid	High	Low	Mid	High	Low	Mid	High
percentage of households that own a truck	1.9	0.0	4.7						
percentage of households that own farm machinery	11.4	8.6	17.7						
percentage of households that use animal traction	12.0	21.0	30.2						
percentage of farms with irrigation system	0.0	0.0	1.9						
percentage of households that received subsidized credit	0.8	2.7	5.4						

[1]Money values in Reais 1996.

TABLE 1.A4: SOUTHEAST REGION: COMPARISON ACROSS RURAL GROUPS AND INCOME LEVELS[1]

	Farmers			Agricultural Workers			Non-agricultural Workers		
	Low	Mid	High	Low	Mid	High	Low	Mid	High
Income									
Household annual income	2,063	6,120	31,324	2,734	4,560	8,441	1,648	4,947	22,329
Per capita annual income	485	1,664	8,944	694	1,421	2,927	445	1,706	7,968
Per capita monthly expenditure	82	121	220	70	108	158	96	180	216
percentage farming in total income	59.8	43.1	64.2	0.0	0.0	0.0	0.0	0.0	0.0
percentage non-agriculture in total income	14.6	14.3	13.9	2.6	3.5	2.5	70.8	64.5	84.1
percentage agricultural wages in total income	7.4	23.1	10.4	91.8	88.2	95.9	2.7	2.6	2.2
percentage public pension in total income	18.2	19.4	11.0	5.1	6.1	1.7	24.8	31.7	13.7
percentage of households where at least one person receives public pension	23.6	41.8	26.3	10.5	16.4	7.5	17.7	36.9	27.2
Number of people in household	4.7	4.0	3.7	4.4	3.6	3.4	4.1	3.1	3.0
Average age of family	27.8	36.1	35.3	26.6	27.5	31.3	27.9	37.3	35.3
Dependency ratio (N° family members divided by N° workers)	1.7	1.0	1.4	1.6	1.6	0.9	1.8	0.8	0.9
percentage heads of household illiterate	39.2	44.3	18.0	58.0	34.4	21.2	37.1	33.3	17.7
percentage of illiterates aged 10 and above	27.8	28.3	14.2	37.8	26.5	19.9	22.3	27.1	15.6

(continued)

TABLE 1.A4: SOUTHEAST REGION: COMPARISON ACROSS RURAL GROUPS AND INCOME LEVELS[1] (CONTINUED)

	Farmers			Agricultural Workers			Non-agricultural Workers		
	Low	Mid	High	Low	Mid	High	Low	Mid	High
Years of education of head of household	2.4	2.0	3.7	1.7	2.6	2.6	2.7	2.6	4.2
Years of education of men older than 18	3.5	3.7	4.9	2.7	3.4	3.9	3.3	4.1	5.5
Years of education of women older than 18	3.6	3.9	4.9	2.8	3.4	4.6	4.5	4.2	5.3
percentage of households with access to piped water	36.4	66.3	79.2	56.3	73.6	84.4	58.7	80.5	93.1
percentage of households with access to electricity	60.0	79.5	92.8	67.2	92.3	89.0	77.9	91.6	96.4
percentage of households with at least one member covered by health insurance	1.5	23.5	22.1	8.5	2.5	95.1	4.6	38.4	40.3
percentage of households headed by a woman	10.8	15.9	3.5	6.6	7.2	2.2	20.6	20.1	19.5
Farmers' Production Characteristics									
Total land size operated (ha)	16.3	12.5	67.4						
percentage of land operated that is owned	50.7	49.9	58.2						
percentage of households that received technical assistance	3.4	1.7	24.2						
percentage of households that own a truck	3.6	3.6	13.8						
percentage of households that own farm machinery	6.1	14.4	41.6						
percentage of households that use animal traction	9.2	12.3	24.6						
percentage of farms with irrigation system	0.0	0.0	3.1						
percentage of households that received subsidized credit	1.6	0.0	3.3						

[1] Money values in Reais 1996.

CHAPTER 2

DYNAMICS OF THE BRAZILIAN SMALL FARM SECTOR

Introduction[40]

The present chapter intends to address the main structural transformations undergone in Brazilian agriculture over the past 20 years. The central objective is to extract the implications that the changes in Brazilian agriculture have had on small family farms. The chapter is divided into two sections. The first describes the main structural changes the sector has undergone in the country, extracting the implications of these transformations on small family farming. The second discusses the most appropriate policies for small production in the context of the macroeconomic scenario examined in the first part of the chapter.

The history of Brazilian agriculture has always been marked by concentration. Since the beginning of agricultural exploration, the concentration of land possession was the most evident characteristic. This characteristic, in turn, ended up reinforcing the income concentration in the sector. This is nothing new. However, throughout the past 20 years, a new type of concentration has been marking agricultural production in the country, namely, one induced technologically. In recent years, a relatively small group of farmers began to follow a course of increasing productive efficiency, rationalization in the use of modern inputs, and the incorporation of those technologies developed in centers of public research and by private enterprises. This movement generated a significant rise in productivity, making it possible for this group of farmers to continue expanding production even in an unfavorable macroeconomic environment.

This new form of concentration substantially alters the manner of dealing with income distribution in the sector. In a certain sense, land possession loses relative importance in the face of technological concentration when explaining income distribution. The division that comes to be relatively more applicable is not between the groups that possess land and those that do not, but

40. This paper was prepare by Guilherme Leite da Silva Dias, Professor of the School of Economics and Business of USP; and Alexandre Lahóz Mendonça de Barros, Visiting Professor of the Department of Economics, Business, and Sociology of ESALQ/USP. Both the authors would like to thank Leila Campos Vieira and Cicely Moitinho Amaral for their collaboration.

rather, between those that rely on modern technology of production and those that do not. It is true that the concentration of capital remains important: modern technology requires a significant amount of capital (machines, fertilizers, agrochemicals, facilities, irrigation, etc.). Nevertheless, land possession per se does not guarantee the survival of the dynamism of the firm, as it once did.

The objective of the present chapter is to clarify this process of transition through an analysis on the past 20 years of Brazilian agriculture. The aim is to develop a line of reasoning that shows that the process of a group of farmers' increasing productive efficiency was the form of survival found in an environment of high macroeconomic instability where the instruments of public policies were being dismantled. In particular, we intend to elucidate the implications of this transformation on small-farm owners. The combination of the increased competitiveness of a group of farmers, an unfavorable macroeconomic environment, together with greater market liberalization, associated with the central government's incapacity to prepare an agricultural policy of income sustenance was especially harmful to small-farm owners.

The Structural Changes of Brazilian Agriculture and their Implications on Family Agriculture

The relationship of the public sector with agriculture in Brazil has always been profound. It is difficult to understand the evolution of the sector in the country without taking into consideration the central government's policies of intervention. It seems unnecessary for the purposes of the present chapter to go over all the aspects of Brazilian agricultural policies. There is vast literature that addresses its evolution. It is important, however, to emphasize that in the past 20 years, the degree of interventionism has been substantially reduced. Throughout this period, the pillars of agricultural policy constructed in the1960s and 1970s have been so corroded that the resulting model at the end of the 1990s holds little correlation with the old one.

The central objective of the model developed in the 1960s and 1970s was to guarantee the stability of the internal food supply, allowing the process of urbanization of the Brazilian economy to follow its course without major leaps in the inflation rates. For this purpose, a set of policies was created in order to stimulate the adoption of modern production inputs. The system was based on subsidized credit policies and income stabilization mechanisms like minimum prices and regulating stocks. Associated with these mechanisms of stimulus toward modernization were innumerable mechanisms of taxation on certain products, import and export quotas, tariff barriers on inputs and agricultural products.

The disarray of interventions of the federal government (including minimum prices, subsidized credit, taxes, tariff barriers, import and export quotas) made it difficult to identify the resulting vector of the Brazilian agricultural policy. The conjunction of policies of stimulus toward production with those of food price control, as well as export product taxation, generated an environment in which the effect of the public policies on agricultural production was unknown.

The work of Brandão and Carvalho (1990) and an earlier one by Oliveira (1976) constitute a referential milestone in understanding the distortions generated by the governmental interventions in Brazilian agriculture, as well as the compensating role played by subsidized rural credit. The first authors make use of a model of partial equilibrium seeking to investigate the direction of the market forces reflected in the movements of relative prices. The results of the study make clear the discrimination agriculture suffered as a result of the direct and indirect interventions in the prices of agricultural products. Excluding the policy of rural credit, the authors estimate that approximately 8.9 percent of the agricultural GDP (on average for the period of 1975 to 1983) was shifted from the agricultural sector to the other sectors of the economy.

The distortions in product prices ended up reducing the amount of food that would be produced in perfect market conditions. According to Brandão and Carvalho (1990), actual production was below that which would be expected in a situation of free trade for all the products analyzed (cotton, soybean, corn, rice, and wheat). Corn production, for example, was between 4 and 39 percent below what it could have been. Furthermore, the food-producing sector was favored during the period. The exporting sector faced prices that were an average 10 percent to 30 percent lower than they would have been in market conditions without any intervention whatsoever. These distortions reduced the total supply of exportable products by nearly 10 percent.

Though interventions in the markets generated a draining of resources from the sector, signaling a "bias against agriculture," the policy of subsidized rural credit would compensate this movement. According to Brandão and Carvalho (1990), when the subsidized rural credits were introduced in the analysis, it was noted that, on average, the agricultural sector received the equivalent to eight percent of the agricultural GDP in the period from 1975 to 1983. This inversion in of the surplus received by the sector gives an indication of the magnitude of the rural credit conceded between the mid-1970s and the mid-1980s.[41]

Indeed, the pattern of accumulation generated by the rural credit policy was significant. The volumes of resources involved in the program, as well as the negative real interest rates originating from inflationary acceleration, had a non-neutral effect on the relative prices of inputs and products. There were mechanisms of rationing that clearly favored the adoption of modern inputs, especially machines and equipment.

The growth of agriculture in that period took on an extensive pattern, in which the functioning of the rural credit policy stimulated an increase of those cultivated areas associated with the use of machines and fertilizers. Though there was a significant rise in the use of modern factors of production and in the occupied areas throughout the 1970s, the productive efficiency gains were relatively low (Barros and Graham, 1978; Barros and Dias, 1983; Barros, Graham and Gautier, 1987; and Goldin and Rezende, 1993). At any rate, the amount of capital injected into the sector was of such magnitude that the growth rates of production were remarkable, reaching annual increases to the order of 4 percent to 6 percent.

The macroeconomic imbalance that began to characterize the Brazilian economy at the beginning of the 1980s would make it unfeasible for Brazilian agriculture to maintain this level of growth. The conjunction of the second oil shock and the external financing crisis of 1982 exhausted the capacity of the central government to transfer resources to the private sector. The recessive adjustment with public spending cuts combined with a restrictive monetary policy heavily affected the agricultural sector, reducing the amplitude of both the policy of minimum prices and the rural credit system. The guaranteed prices were progressively lowered, approaching actual market prices.

The magnitude of the reduction in the volumes of conceded rural credit can be better visualized with the help of Figure 2.1. It presents the ratio between the amounts conceded by the formal system of rural credit and the agricultural GDP. It is possible to note clearly the break in the trend of the series as of the mid-1980s. In truth, already in 1984 there was a reduction in the amounts conceded; the Cruzado Plan in 1986 would, for the last time, restitute the previous patterns of resource liberation, but lasted only one year. We can see that, while the volume of government induced credit was close to the agricultural GDP in the 1970s, at the end of the 1990s this ratio fell to levels that fluctuated between 8 percent and 10 percent.

The Figure further allows us to measure the amount of capital received by Brazilian agriculture between the mid-1970s and 1980s. As Goldin and Rezende (1993) attest, considering the negative real interest rates that fluctuated between −1.5 percent and −37.7 percent in the period from 1970 to 1987, we can perceive that the transfer of income to the rural sector was very significant for the period in question, as already shown in the work of Brandão and Carvalho. The aggregated numbers masked, however, the magnitude of concentration in the rural credit distribution. According to a study by the World Bank (1989), it is estimated that in the 1970s only 20 percent to 25 percent of the farmers received credit conceded by the official system; of these, less than five percent of the farmers received more than half of the total conceded credit.

---

41. It should be remembered, however, that part of the subsidy was absorbed by the inputs industries. As shown in the work of Oliveira (??), the protection conceded to the modern inputs industry in the 1970s, particularly fertilizers and farm machinery, caused the subsidies in the interest rate to be partially appropriated by these firms.

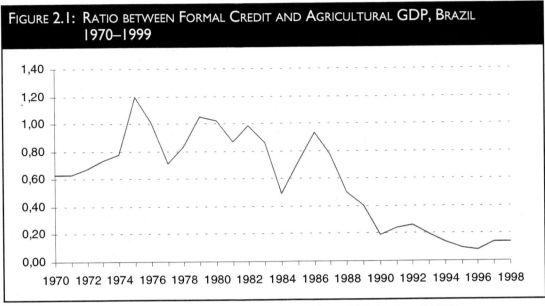

FIGURE 2.1: RATIO BETWEEN FORMAL CREDIT AND AGRICULTURAL GDP, BRAZIL 1970–1999

Source: The credit data was taken from Almeida (1996). The agricultural GDP data from BACEN.

One would expect such a drastic reduction in the volume of capital transferred to agriculture to alter its growth pattern. The rhythm of capital accumulation would have to slow down. This fact is clearly perceivable when inspecting the evolution of cultivated areas in the country, as well as in the behavior of the tractor stock during the 1980s.

As can be observed in Figure 2.2, the area with permanent and temporary cultivation remained practically constant in the period following 1980. It is possible to note that since the 1960s, the cultivated areas had been increasing consistently in the country. The inflection of the series is quite visible at the beginning of the 1980s.

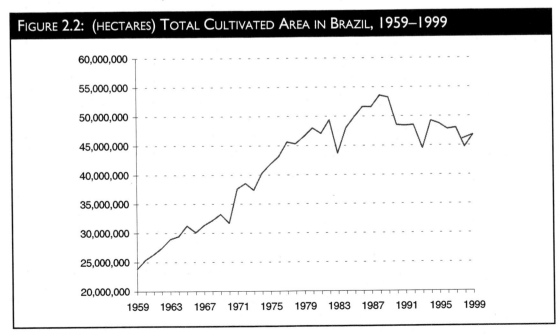

FIGURE 2.2: (HECTARES) TOTAL CULTIVATED AREA IN BRAZIL, 1959–1999

Source: FIBGE.

Another way to evaluate the reduction in agricultural investments is by means of an analysis on the evolution of the machinery stock used in agriculture. While working with the sales series of wheel tractors, Barros (1999) created alternative means to measure the stock of tractors in Brazil. The author made use of price series of second-hand tractors in order to estimate the economic depreciation of the tractor stock. The function of depreciation assumed a declining geometric format with depreciation rates fluctuating between six percent and seven percent a year, depending on the model of the tractor considered. With the annual sales of wheel tractors according to class of engine power, the data contained in the Agricultural Censuses, and the estimated rate of depreciation, Barros constructed, year by year, the stock of wheel tractors expressed in engine power (hp), in the number of tractors (units), and in value (1995 R$), considering the depreciation rates of 6 percent and 7 percent).

The results can be seen in Figure 2.3. The aspect to be highlighted is the aging process of the tractor stock in Brazil. The value of the fleet reached its peak at the end of the 1980s, when its value was four times greater than in 1970. However, from that point on, the trend changed clearly, having reduced its valued by more than 20 percent. It is perceivable, therefore, that the alterations in the economic conditions in the 1980s heavily affected investments. Note that the amount of capital invested in tractors in 1995 was equivalent to the amount in 1979.

Further inspection of Figure 2.3 allows a better visualization of the relative movements of the series. The growth rate of the stock value was greater (from the beginning of the 1970s until the mid-1980s) than that of the number of tractors. This movement is typical of economies in expansion. Starting with a small stock, high annual increases raised the value of the stock more than it did in proportion to the number of tractors. We see, however, that this trend was reverted and, as of the 1980s, the rate of decline in the value became much more accentuated than that of the number of tractors, indicating the aging of the fleet. It is worthwhile noting that the stock of tractors increased almost five times in number between 1970 and 1990. What is most remarkable, however, is the evolution of the accumulated engine power. Between 1970 and 1994 the stock of tractors measured in engine power increased more than six times, suggesting an elevation of the average engine power of the tractors. Even so, one can perceive that all the series indicate a trend of reduction of the stock as of 1994, which, in fact, could be anticipating an environment of uncertainty in a not-too-distant future.

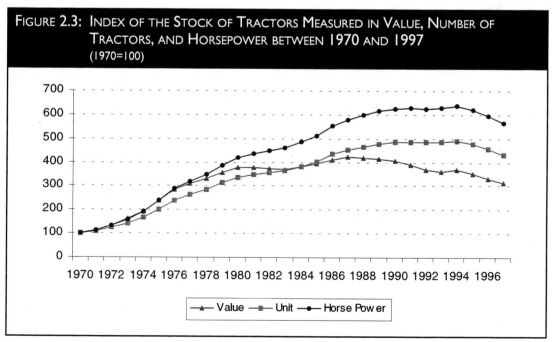

FIGURE 2.3: INDEX OF THE STOCK OF TRACTORS MEASURED IN VALUE, NUMBER OF TRACTORS, AND HORSEPOWER BETWEEN 1970 AND 1997 (1970=100)

Source: Barros (1999).

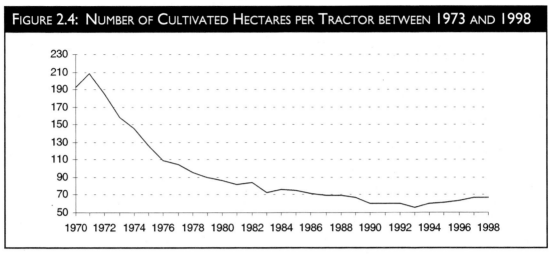

FIGURE 2.4: NUMBER OF CULTIVATED HECTARES PER TRACTOR BETWEEN 1973 AND 1998

Source: Barros (1999).

The process of capital accumulation in agriculture in the 1970s and mid-1980s was, in fact, significant. The increase in the number of tractors in the country caused the number of hectares per tractor to drop notably. While 165 ha per tractor were cultivated in 1973, in 1995 this number was 64 (Figure 2.4).

Table 2.1 gives us a better notion of the process of capital accumulation in Brazilian agriculture from 1973 to 1995. It is observed that the capital/labor ratio increased considerably in the period. While there was one tractor for every 63 people employed in agriculture in 1973, in 1995 this number corresponded to 18. However, when considering the value of capital per person, we see an increase until the beginning of the 1990s at which point it began to decline (there was a ten percent drop in the value of the stock of capital per employed person between 1990 and 1995). Finally, we can see that there was indeed an elevation in the average engine power in the period studied, reaching an average of 81 hp per tractor in the 1990s.

Cultivated area and wheel tractors are used here as indicators of a pattern of extensive growth. The expansion of these two elements, combined with the level of public investments in roads and an agrarian policy anticipating property rights on frontier lands—reproducing the elevated concentration of land possession of the older areas of occupation—ended up inducing large capital gains for a group of farmers.

One would also expect that, with the abrupt cut in inter-sectoral transfers of income, agricultural production would be heavily hit. What occurred in the 1980s and, particularly, throughout the 1990s, surprised a good part of agricultural economists. Despite the unstable macroeconomic environment and the contraction in the level of activity of the industrial sector, agriculture continued to expand its aggregated supply. Figure 2.5 illustrates the evolution of agricultural production in the period from 1969 to 1998. Note that between 1980 and 1998, there was an increase of more than 70 percent in the total product.

The central question to be extracted from the considerations woven thus far refers to how it was possible for the sector to grow in such an unfavorable environment. As will be seen later on, in addition to the aforementioned transformations in the agricultural policy, Brazilian agriculture was the sector that first exposed itself to international competition, facing a scenario of exchange rate valorization from the mid-1980s and, particularly, after the Real Plan.

Some elements can be examined in order to try to understand this peculiar dynamic of agriculture.[42] A first set of arguments relates to microeconomic efficiency gains associated with significant

42. The articles of Dias (1988, 1989, and 1990) summarize the arguments presented here.

TABLE 2.1: NUMBER OF HECTARES PER TRACTOR, PEOPLE PER TRACTOR, HORSEPOWER PER PERSON, AND CAPITAL VALUE PER PERSON IN BRAZILIAN AGRICULTURE, FROM 1973 TO 1995

Year	Hectares per Tractor	People per Tractor	Horse Power per Tractor	Capital (R$) per person
1973	165	64	70	239
1974	151	53	72	292
1975	131	44	74	363
1976	113	36	75	441
1977	108	35	75	458
1978	99	31	76	506
1979	93	28	77	548
1980	89	23	77	662
1981	85	23	78	629
1982	87	24	78	586
1983	75	22	79	621
1984	79	24	79	563
1985	78	23	79	573
1986	75	20	79	639
1987	71	19	79	662
1988	72	18	80	655
1989	70	18	80	658
1990	63	18	80	636
1991	63	16	80	689
1992	63	19	80	549
1993	58	18	80	547
1994	63	17	81	579
1995	64	18	81	540

Source: Barros (1999). The data relative to people employed in agriculture were taken from PNAD.

FIGURE 2.5: INDEX OF THE EVOLUTION OF AGRICULTURAL PRODUCTION, 1962–1998

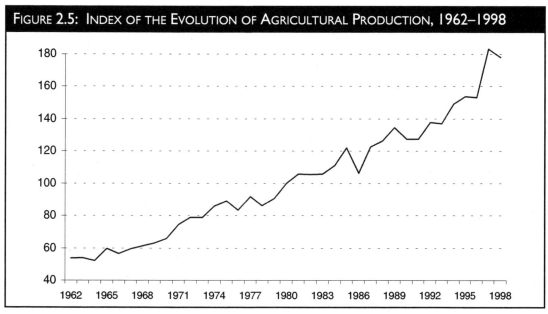

Source: FIBGE

Year	Crops	Animal Products	Sub-Sectors
1987	100.0	100.0	100.0
1988	96.1	101.9	98.0
1989	100.5	103.8	101.6
1990	94.9	105.8	98.5
1991	97.1	107.9	100.7
1992	103.6	110.0	105.7
1993	110.8	112.1	111.3
1994	111.3	114.3	112.3
1995	112.5	116.6	113.8
1996	114.2	118.9	115.8
1997	116.4	121.3	118.0
1998	122.4	123.6	122.8
1999	128.7	129.1	128.8

TABLE 2.2: EVOLUTION OF THE PRODUCTIVITY INDICES, 1987/1999 (1987=100). Sub-Sectors.

Source: IBGE, elaboration by MBAssociados.

changes in the relative prices of the factors of production. The main point to be noted is that the simultaneous movements of trade liberalization and restriction of subsidized resources ended up forcing an increase in the productive efficiency of the most capitalized firms. This pressure for increased efficiency and the concomitant favorable evolution in the exchange ratio (product/input) reinforced the movement of increased productivity. Small farms with traditional technology, the semi-subsisting type of organizations, would have been left out of this adjustment process.

Several works address the productivity gains of Brazilian agriculture in the 1980s and, mainly, in the 1990s: Bonelli and Fonseca, 1998; Dias and Bacha, 1999, Gasques and Conceição, 1998; Ávila and Evenson, 1995. Barros (1999) estimated that the gains in the total factor productivity (TFP) as of 1987 were to the order of 1.8 percent a year. Labor productivity increased to more elevated rates: 27 percent a year between 1986 and 1996. As can be seen in Table 2.2, land yield also increased from 1987 to 1998. The index constructed separated the crop component from husbandry. In each of these indices, the various components were weighed by the participation of the value of each crop (or animal product) in the total value of the production in the base year. The growth rate of land yield (measured by the crop component) was to the order of 1.85 percent a year in the period in question. Taking the average of the triennium 1996–1998, the crop yield suffered a 22 percent increase.

The husbandry yield indicator was constructed from data contained in the Agricultural Censuses of 1985 and 1995–96. This procedure was adopted because no indicator existed to convert food kilos into meat kilos, nor was there any annual data on the size of the herd of poultry, pork, and beef. The solution was to carry out a linear interpolation between the Censuses, thus obtaining an estimate of the average growth in the period in question. The result was very similar to that obtained for crops: an annual growth rate of productivity to the order of 1.94 percent a year. The yield in the triennium 1996–1998 was 23.6 percent greater than in 1987. Taking the aggregate (weighted sum of the value of crops and husbandry), an annual yield increase of 1.88 percent was reached.

However, the increase in land yield was not homogeneous among the main crops that make up Brazilian production. As can be seen in Table 2.3, the crops presenting the highest gains of land productivity, were corn, beans, and soybean. These cultures are the most important in the consumption of the working class and the poorer population. Cotton showed a notable rise in yield in the period, reaching a gain of over 52 percent.

The products traditionally geared to the external market (cacao and coffee) did not show the same pattern of increased productive efficiency as the other crops. This can be explained somewhat by the low international prices faced for several years running. It is interesting to note that the bean crop, which is the most traditional and typical of the internal market, was the one that showed the highest increase in yield, reaching a gain of 58 percent.

TABLE 2.3: PRODUCTIVITY INDEX OF THE MOST IMPORTANT CROPS, 1986/99
(86/88=100)

Year	Productivity					
	Cotton	Soybean	Coffee	Cacao	Corn	Beans
86/88	100.0	100.0	100.0	100.0	100.0	100.0
87/89	106.3	100.0	75.0	104.7	99.7	113.7
88/90	110.3	98.0	63.7	103.7	97.7	121.3
89/91	116.3	95.0	68.0	101.0	96.7	122.7
90/92	121.3	96.0	68.7	91.7	100.3	131.0
91/93	126.3	103.7	71.3	89.7	111.3	144.7
92/94	127.3	115.0	74.7	89.3	120.3	154.3
93/95	136.0	118.0	73.7	86.3	125.7	158.3
94/96	139.7	119.0	78.3	82.7	123.7	152.7
95/97	148.7	121.3	76.0	78.3	127.0	153.3
96/98	152.2	124.3	87.0	77.0	130.7	158.3
97/99	189.5	127.4	93.2	70.6	136.1	170.3

Source: IBGE.

This asymmetric pattern of performance among the various crops left little doubt as to the superior performance of the domestic market crops in comparison with export products. These observations suggest that Brazilian agriculture became more oriented toward meeting the needs of the domestic market than the external one. There is an important side effect: modern technology and new varieties were introduced into the production systems oriented toward the domestic market, small farms organized in a cooperative framework had access and took advantage of this opportunity, but small semi-subsisting farmers had to face competition in the traditional channels of commercialization. For illustration, old bean varieties became inferior products, much less valued, with respect to modern varieties that upheld taste and fast cooking qualities for a longer period.

The critical role played by cooperatives in the diffusion of technological innovations between small farmers should not be underestimated. The economy of scale aspect of technical assistance is better known in the sense of organizing demonstration plots on the properties of small-farm owners, but continued effort, quality of service, and trustworthiness are not as common to public service as it is with the cooperative system. Performance of new varieties is sometimes site specific, requiring local observation and selection that goes beyond the activities performed by research institutions. Large-farm owners can do it with their own employees and only cooperatives can do it for small-farm owners. The same thing goes for seed reproduction, disease detection and appropriate control, and many other factors required in advanced technological production systems.

Part of the productivity gains presented above can be explained by a correlation with the investments in public research and extension. During the 1970s various institutions of agricultural research were created around the country (see Alves and Contini, 1992). The results obtained in these centers began to be disseminated in the growing schools of agronomy, forestry, and veterinary medicine. In 1969, these courses were given in 49 units that added up to 1008 academic places. In 1986, this number rose to 7203 places in 96 institutions (Alves and Contini, 1992). In 1994, there were 12,142 places available in 177 different institutions (Araújo et al., 1996). A growing number of technicians linked to the sector were utilized a good deal by the extension centers created by the Brazilian state in order to disclose the research and modern farming techniques. The increased investments in research and development and in the endowment of human capital linked to agriculture were part of the structural requisites to the growth of the sector (Barros, 1979).

As is well known, the returns on investment in research, mainly in agriculture, are quite slow. As one would expect, there is lag between the creation of the research centers and their results in terms of technological innovations. The same occurs with the process of diffusing new techniques. It takes time before agents have a perfect knowledge of how new technology works. The productivity increases coming from the use of new techniques ("learning-by-doing") only appear with time. Thus, it was unsurprising that the productivity increases would not occur vigorously during the 1970s. The returns on investments would only have an effect in the following decade. In other words, that period would have served as a basis for the growth that would follow. Even with the recession of the Brazilian economy in the 1980s, some foundations for growth had already been constructed.

Another important aspect in understanding the efficiency gains of the sector relates to the weak performance of investments in the country's transportation infrastructure since the mid-1980s. The worsening in the transportation conditions ended up forcing the intensification of the land factor, utilizing traditional areas closer to urban centers and new areas of the Center-west.

The pressure for intensification of the cultivated area was not caused solely by the lower efficiency in the transportation system. The relative prices of the factors contributed to accentuating that trend. The liberalization process of the Brazilian economy in mid-1980s, accentuated in the Collor administration in 1990, served to reduce substantially the prices of imported inputs.

The growing dependence on importation of fertilizers and agrochemicals pressured the liberalization of imports. The rise in imports began in the early 1990s, when the central government prepared a schedule of import tariff reductions. Table 2.4 presents the evolution of the import tariffs between 1991 and 1993. It is possible to see that the tariffs on fertilizers were practically nonexistent as of 1993. The agrochemical tariffs were around 10 percent. Only the sector of machinery and equipment maintained protectionist barriers of the order of 30 percent. In other words, with the exception of the machinery sector, it can be said that the prices of inputs consumed by Brazilian agriculture were adjusted to the international market.

TABLE 2.4: AGENDA OF TARIFF REDUCTION OF AGRICULTURAL PRODUCTS AND INPUTS (1991/1993)

Items	Jul-90	Aug-90	Feb-91	Jan-92	Oct-92	Jul-93
Inputs						
Fertilizers	25	0–10	0–10	0–10	0–10	0–10
Tractors	65	40	40	40	30	20
Equipment	40	25	25	25	20	20
Chemicals	40	20	20	20	20	20
Ag.Products						
Average	30.6	30.6	24.5	19.9	15.5	12.6
Maximum	79.6	79.6	70.0	60.4	37.5	23.5
Minimum	6.3	6.3	4.5	1.8	0.0	0.0

Source: Kume, H.—Chapter 8 in "Comércio Internacional e Comercialização Agrícola," Viçosa, UFV, 1995.

Apart from the tax reform, which also effected the importation of agricultural products in general,[43] a set of complementary reforms was implemented with the purpose of improving the system of statistical information on foreign trade and simplifying the customs control mechanisms. An agile electronic system was developed permitting that the control of the importation process be

---

43. See Dias and Amaral (2000) for greater details.

carried out in a centralized and efficient manner. These mechanisms served to reduce the transaction cost of imported products.

The liberalization of the inputs market guaranteed a significant improvement in the terms of trade in favor of agriculture. Between 1987 and 1998, agriculture obtained a rise of 30 percent in its terms of trade. These gains would be much more remarkable if not for the husbandry sector. While the sub-sector crops saw an increase of 46 percent in the prices received/prices paid ratio, husbandry suffered a reduction of 3 percent in this same ratio. Table 2.5 below presents the terms of trade of the crops and husbandry sub-sectors, and those of agriculture in the period from 1987 to 1998.

From among the 20 products analyzed from the crops sector, almost all experienced improvement in the ratio between prices received and prices paid. It was noted, as shown in Table 2.6, that the gains were 25 percent for corn, 60 percent for beans, 68 percent for rice, 46 percent in the case of coffee, and only 10 percent for soybean. These significant gains allowed the sector to continue expanding the supply throughout the decade. An important point to stress, however, relates to the form of calculating the index of prices paid. In the composition of the index are expenditures on labor, fertilizers, agrochemicals, machines, and fuel.

TABLE 2.5: EVOLUTION OF THE TERMS OF TRADE— PRICES RECEIVED/PRICES PAID, 1987/99 (1987=100)

Year	Crops	Animal Products	Agriculture
1987	100.0	100.0	100.0
1988	118.1	92.1	109.5
1989	93.4	96.9	94.6
1990	122.0	119.6	121.2
1991	120.1	108.9	116.4
1992	121.2	102.8	115.2
1993	133.2	120.4	129.0
1994	149.4	127.5	142.2
1995	128.8	100.1	119.3
1996	122.5	90.2	111.8
1997	139.9	98.5	126.2
1998	145.7	97.7	129.9
1999	118.1	84.8	107.1

Source: IBGE, elaboration by MBAssociados.

TABLE 2.6: TERMS OF TRADE OF SELECT CROPS, 1987/1999 (1987=100)

Year	Rice	Beans	Corn	Soybean	Coffee
1987	100.0	100.0	100.0	100.0	100.0
1988	121.4	99.4	128.1	140.3	118.1
1989	95.1	110.8	98.2	84.8	93.4
1990	150.3	126.0	145.7	83.4	122.0
1991	173.3	111.7	143.9	102.5	120.1
1992	139.7	106.7	134.7	109.6	121.2
1993	157.3	141.9	158.0	121.3	133.2
1994	156.9	155.3	137.8	106.7	149.4
1995	132.0	101.9	127.2	99.6	128.8
1996	125.3	106.3	123.2	100.8	122.5
1997	146.9	108.2	112.5	122.9	139.9
1998	167.7	159.6	125.0	108.4	145.7
1999	140.3	104.1	117.7	92.3	159.5

Source: CONAB, elaboration by MBAssociados.

The indicator reproduces, therefore, a technological standard that encompasses the group that adopts technologies that are more advanced. Thus, though it is impossible to quantify or even identify precisely what the benefits of this improvement are in relation to exchanges, certainly those farmers that do not make use of modern inputs would not be able to appropriate such favorable relative prices: It could indeed be worse if the prices received by agricultural products fell with respect to the consumption package of the small farmer household.

In a recent study, Ferreira Filho (1997) showed that the decrease in the prices of factors of production made possible a significant reduction in the average costs of several crops. From a series of production costs gathered by the Institute of Agricultural Economics of the State of São Paulo (IEA) from 1980 to 1994, the author studied the behavior of said costs for corn, rice, beans, cotton, manioc, soybean, and wheat. The decrease in the unit costs is very clear in the period. From an index of 100 in 1981, in 1994 it reaches a value of 44 for cotton, 43 for rice, 22 for beans, 37 for corn, 59 for manioc, and 57 for soybean. In other words, in the majority of products, there was a drop of more than 50 percent in production costs.

The main cause pinpointed for the reduction of production costs was the drop in the prices of factors. As Homem de Melo (1992) states that in the 1980s there was a drop in the prices of fertilizers, agrochemicals, and fuel. Only the prices of agricultural machinery showed a rising trend. However, parallel to the reduction in the price of the factors, there was a drop in the prices of almost every agricultural product. It would be worthwhile knowing, therefore, whether the drop in prices of the products would be enough to more than compensate the reductions in average costs.

Table 2.7, extracted from Ferreira Filho (1997, page 11), calculates the ratio between the prices received and the indices of unit cost. We can observe that despite the downward variations in some years, there is a rising trend of the prices received/unit cost ratio, indicating improvement in the economic situation of farmers. The series clearly shows that the margin, at the level of farm properties, increased systematically in the period. The only exception is the manioc crop, which presented a systematic reduction in its margins.

The relative cheapening of fertilizers radically altered the path of growth of Brazilian agriculture. As will be seen in the next chapter, throughout the successive heterodox plans for economic stabilization, land prices fluctuated quite a bit, but, in general, were relatively high. As various

TABLE 2.7: INDEX OF THE RATIO PRODUCT PRICE/UNIT COST OF PRODUCTION
(1981=100)

Year	Cotton	Rice	Beans	Corn	Manioc	Soybean
1980	137	177	123	130	147	179
1981	100	100	100	100	100	100
1982	102	135	59	98	58	94
1983	94	147	86	136	72	110
1984	108	127	108	121	99	119
1985	119	186	37	141	101	110
1986	110	121	73	172	40	147
1987	86	71	122	64	22	111
1988	96	80	81	99	101	78
1989	47	59	122	81	56	59
1990	57	84	86	82	21	49
1991	61	122	144	114	19	78
1992	82	107	138	142	47	94
1993	148	172	252	204	75	125
1994	108	112	216	114	46	86

Source: Ferreira Filho (1997).

studies developed over the past few years attest, land came to serve as a value reserve against the successive shocks the Brazilian economy suffered. This fact ended up inflating the value of land, favoring its intensification.

One form of evaluating the degree of production intensification, as well as the level of productive efficiency, is to establish a ratio between the total nutrients extracted each year by agricultural production, comparing it with the volume of chemical fertilizers expended on that crop. With the purpose of determining the rhythm of exportation of nutrients by Brazilian agriculture, a study was carried out using response-to-fertilization curves. For a given genetic pattern of the different cultures, there is a strong correlation between production per hectare and the volume of nitrogen, phosphorus, and potassium extracted from the soil. Thus, taking as a basis the nutrient extraction curve, the average productivity, and total productivity of each crop produced, it was possible to determine the total extraction of nutrients per culture and per state in the past 30 years.

The response-to-fertilization curves were gathered in several fertilization trials as well as on high-technology properties that constituted the frontier of the response to fertilization. Once the pattern of response to fertilization was determined, equations of fertilization were estimated for the cultures of cotton, rice, banana, potato, cacao, coffee, sugarcane, beans, tobacco, orange, corn, soybean, tomato, wheat, and grapes. These crops together respond to about 90 percent of the total consumption of chemical fertilizers in Brazil.

With the fertilization curves in hand, it was possible to calculate the volume of nutrients extracted from each crop during the past few years in Brazilian agriculture. The procedure adopted consisted in obtaining, year to year, the average productivity of each crop in each state of the country based on data from IBGE and, from there, calculating total consumption of fertilizers based on total production in each state. This is how the results presented in the Figure were reached.

Figure 2.6 helps to identify the different cycles of agricultural expansion over the past years. As can be noted, rural credit played a central role in the sales of fertilizers throughout the 1970s and early 1980s. Note that the total of fertilizers sold was higher than the total amount of nutrients extracted from the main crops produced in the country. The distance between the two curves in the period gives some dimension as to the degree of low technical efficiency associated with distorted relative prices, as mentioned previously.

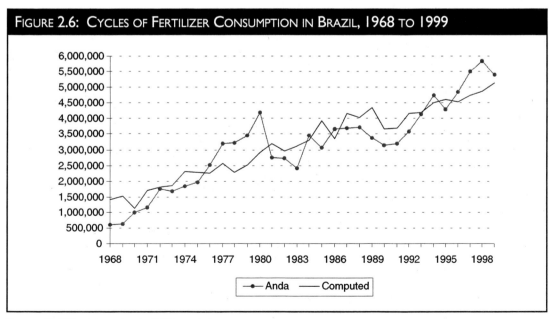

FIGURE 2.6: CYCLES OF FERTILIZER CONSUMPTION IN BRAZIL, 1968 TO 1999

Source: ANDA, elaboration by MBAssociados.

With the economic crisis that characterized the 1980s and with the change that occurred in agricultural policy, we can perceive that the volume of nutrients extracted from the system was higher than the total replaced with fertilization. This fact explains the process of decapitalization of part of Brazilian agriculture. Nevertheless, as we move into the 1990s, it becomes visible that the process of increased productivity, mentioned in the previous chapter, was accompanied by a significant rise in fertilizer sales, indicating a re-composition of the nutrients extracted throughout the 1980s. It is curious to observe that Brazilian agriculture assumed, as of the mid-1980s, a path of growth of the biological type, according to the classic categorization of Hayami and Ruttan.

The "biological route" of Brazilian agriculture can be appreciated through the inspection of Figure 2.7. The graph shows the quantity of fertilizers (NPK) consumed per hectare in Brazil from 1970 to 1999. The intensification in the use of chemical fertilizers becomes clear: in 1999, it reached a level of 120 kilos per hectare. According to the data from FAO (FAOSTAT), this amount is similar to the American, indicating that, in a certain way, the cycle of growth by intensification may be reaching the end.[44]

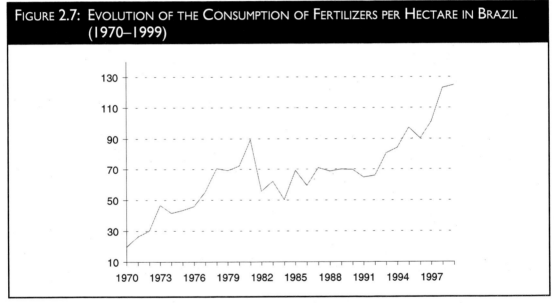

FIGURE 2.7: EVOLUTION OF THE CONSUMPTION OF FERTILIZERS PER HECTARE IN BRAZIL (1970–1999)

Source: ANDA and FIBGE.

From what is exposed above, it is now possible to prepare an explanation for the good aggregate performance of the sector even under such adverse macroeconomic conditions. The joint increase of productivity and terms of trade of the sector guaranteed a notable rise in the purchasing power of agriculture. Figures 2.8 and 2.9 illustrate this argument well. An indicator of the profitability of the activity (purchasing power) was constructed. It is composed of the combination of the productivity gains and the evolution of the terms of trade. Elevations in the terms of trade and/or in the productivity of the firms guarantee an increase in profitability. Figure 2.8 permits us to evaluate that, despite the slight decline in the terms of trade of husbandry in the period, the productivity gains achieved by the sector allowed an increase of about 21 percent in its purchasing power between 1987 and 1998.

---

44. Another additional indication of a possible alteration in the pattern of growth over the past years is raised by Ferreira Filho (1999). Utilizing a similar argument to that presented here, the author attributes the alteration in relative prices of land and fertilizers after the devaluation of 1998 with a potential change in the route of agriculture. Land prices, according to the author, should be relatively cheaper than the modern inputs prior to the devaluation.

FIGURE 2.8: EVOLUTION OF THE PURCHASING POWER OF THE ANIMAL PRODUCTS
SECTOR, 1987–1999
(1987=100)

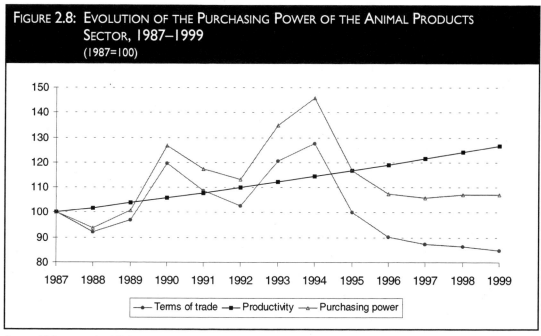

Source: Elaboration by MBAssociados.

The sector of crops showed a much more vigorous performance in the period considered. As seen in Figure 2.9, the ratio between prices paid and prices received increased by 46 percent in the 11 years of the series. This evolution, combined to a rise of 22 percent in productivity, guaranteed an increase in the sector's purchasing power equivalent to 78 percent.

This advantage, measured in terms of productivity and improvement in exchange ratios, is what allows the high-technology farmer to find substitute financing for the traditional system of

FIGURE 2.9: EVOLUTION OF THE PURCHASING POWER OF THE CROPS SECTOR, 1987–1999
(1987=100)

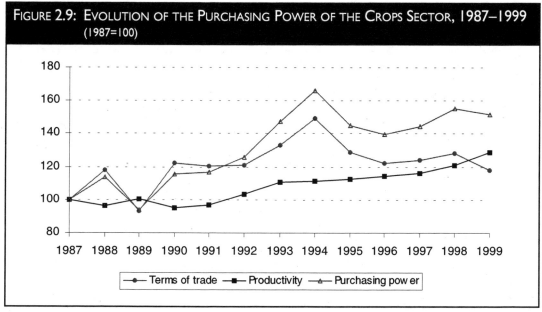

Source: Elaboration by MBAssociados.

rural credit. The means producers found to finance the production, compensating the financial restriction imposed by the reduction in the fiscal capacity of the state, generated a rather dynamic autonomous system. It is certain that the returns on agricultural activity do not allow a very high growth rate. However, the pattern of increase in the internal supply was enough to meet the expansion of internal demand at falling prices. It is important to observe that, in this new system, all the producers with below average productivity were undoubtedly undergoing a process of decapitalization and gradually being expelled from the activity.

Self-financing does not completely explain how it was possible to finance the growth of agriculture throughout its process of structural change. The transformations in the structures of food commercialization should additionally be taken into consideration. The financial restriction of the public sector, as previously discussed, forced a progressive reduction in the minimum price and regulating stock mechanisms. The entry of the private sector was making up for the withdrawal of the state from financing and commercialization of production. The food processing industries, the traders, and the supermarkets began to develop a sophisticated informal system of production financing. The logic behind this movement has to do with the ability of these segments to gather capital in a macroeconomic environment marked by instability and high interest rates. Part of the food industry and all of the exporters began to gather resources abroad, transferring these resources to producers integrated into their productive chain. In the case of the food industry, not only the funds to finance production, but also all the genetic material, and production technology began to be furnished to the producers. This link, built up over the period, constituted an additional explanation as to the referred productivity gains of Brazilian agriculture, in particular, of small animal husbandry.

The supermarkets, on their part, guaranteed significant gains in the period of high inflation rates, resulting from cash sales and post-dated sales. This capitalization made possible a rapid expansion and concentration of the retail sector, altering the relationships with food suppliers, especially vegetable and fruit producers. Again, this process of transformation in the structure of production financing reinforced the discrimination in favor of those more technologically advanced producers, because the standards of quality imposed by the private sector required technologies that were more sophisticated. In other words, the alteration in the commercialization system ended up favoring the gains in scale and the standardization of production.

The reduction in food prices did not occur merely because of the increased internal efficiency of some producers. The process of market liberalization started in the mid-1980s, intensified as of 1990, and imposed a new pattern of internal food prices. In particular, the integration of MERCOSUR altered the ratio between the prices received by the farmers and the prices paid by the urban wage earner. To elucidate this last argument, an indicator of the margin of commercialization was constructed. The indicator was prepared from the index of prices received by farmers divided by the food prices paid by the urban consumers. As can be seen in Figure 2.10, as of the years 1989–1990 there was an abrupt drop in the margin of food commercialization. In the previous period, the inflationary peaks of 1982, 1985, 1987, and 1989 seem to have pressured the agricultural sector. However, after every shock there was a recomposition of the margin of commercialization. The same cannot be said of the 1990s. It seems clear that there was a structural change in food commercialization consolidating a new margin of commercialization level.

The reduction in the margin of commercialization of the sector was compensated, somewhat, by the elevation in the internal demand for food. This fact constituted an additional explanation as to the performance of agriculture in the period in analysis. The expansion in the purchasing power of the real salary provided by the reduction in the relative price of food, guaranteed a growing demand throughout the period. To give shape to the real salary gains of laborers, Dias and Amaral (1999) calculated the ratio between the nominal salary in civil construction and food prices (taking the food and clothing component of the Consumer Price Index, FIPE). The salary in civil construction was utilized because it is the most flexible in the economy, in addition to reflecting the least skilled group of laborers. The result can be seen in Figure 2.11. We perceive that, mainly, since the economic opening of the 1990s, the gains in real salary of the laborers were quite substantial.

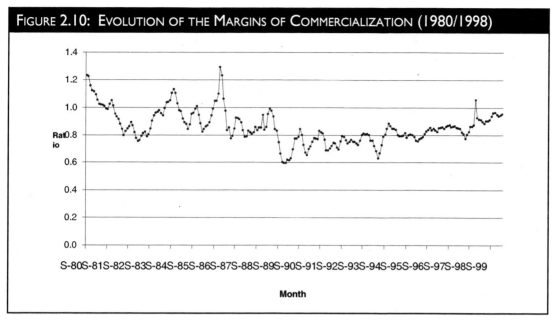

FIGURE 2.10: EVOLUTION OF THE MARGINS OF COMMERCIALIZATION (1980/1998)

Source: FGV—index *f* prices received by farmers divided by FIBGE—Consumer price index-Food items only.

The perception that the internal market was vital to the growth of agriculture in the period, or, in other words, that agriculture grew geared toward the internal economy, can be perceived by means of a measurement of the degree of liberalization to the external market. For this, an index of liberalization was constructed taking, as a basis, the main crops and products of animal origin produced in the country. Based on the exportation data, the amount of product absorbed in the domestic market was calculated. The result is presented in Figure 2.12. Note that throughout

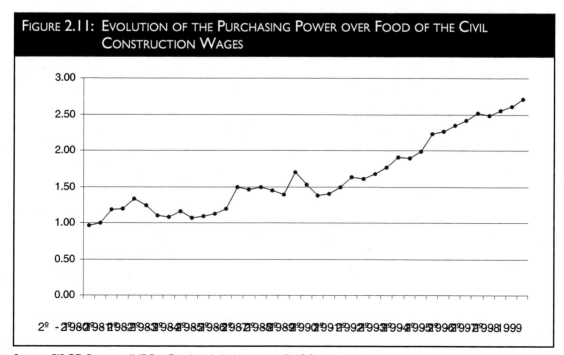

FIGURE 2.11: EVOLUTION OF THE PURCHASING POWER OVER FOOD OF THE CIVIL CONSTRUCTION WAGES

Source: FIBGE. Ration = INPC—Food and clothing items/INCC—average wage construction industry.

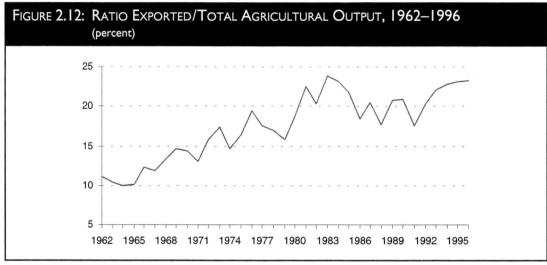

FIGURE 2.12: RATIO EXPORTED/TOTAL AGRICULTURAL OUTPUT, 1962–1996
(percent)

Source: Barros (1999).

the 1970s and 1980s the exported portion of national production was on the rise. However, as of the 1990s, the exported percentage stabilized and, some years, even decreased. This trend characterized the previously discussed exchange valorization, associated with the elevated level of competition in the external market, together with the strong increase in domestic demand for cheaper food.

Implications on Family Farming

The main implication of the macro scenario and the productivity gains was the drop in labor absorption. The adjustment of the sector via productivity growth at the level of agricultural firms propitiated the sustained growth of agriculture in the period, but brought with it an expansion of rural unemployment and alteration in the structures of agricultural firms.

An important point to be observed is that only one group of farmers can appropriate the gains in the terms of trade. In reality, inasmuch as part of the prices paid refer to modern inputs (especially fertilizers, agrochemicals, machinery), only those producers that adopt a technological standard of high intensity of capital could take advantage of the improvement in the relative prices.

Moreover, inasmuch as the prices received fell throughout most of the period, the farmer that continued using an older technological standard and, therefore, did not manage to present significant productivity gains, saw the profitability of his business drop heavily. The loss of margin threw several establishments into a very low income-level, to the point of generating an average gain per laborer of R$ 40/month in the North and only R$ 30 in the Northeast, as Alves, Lopes, and Contini (1999) attest. The authors, working with data from the Agricultural Census of 1995–1996, register the difference between the average income of the properties and the expenses, including land rent (4 percent of the value), by class of area. Table 2.8 synthesizes the results. The net revenue, thus obtained, was divided by occupied family labor, resulting in an average gain per laborer for each size group of establishments. Note that in all regions considered, the income per employed family member on properties with less than 50 hectares is less than one minimum salary. It should be stressed that in Brazil, properties with less than 50 hectares correspond to 81 percent of the total: those with less than 100 hectares make up 89 percent of the total. Of a national total of 4.86 million establishments, only 541,000 contain an area greater than 100 hectares.

In the case of the Northeast, it is possible to perceive that only the class of areas, greater than or equal to 200 hectares, presents remuneration equivalent to one minimum salary. Of the 2,309,074 establishments that exist in the region (47.5 percent of the national total), 94.2 percent constitute an area under 100 hectares.

TABLE 2.8: MONTHLY PAY OF FAMILY LABOR BY CLASS OF AREA AND BY REGION
(R$ per employed family members)

Classes (ha)	North	Northeast	Center-west	Southeast	South
Under 10	36.67	15.43	50.76	69.89	57.34
10–20	44.44	27.97	52.02	98.87	79.71
20–50	37.74	34.81	71.27	114.53	119.63
50–100	38.14	48.42	78.24	210.97	223.93
100–200	39.83	64.26	137.33	360.07	426.40
200–500	56.89	177.82	303.93	591.36	850.72
500–1000	99.80	380.80	663.37	1,662.18	1.993.99
1000–10000	142.51	1,017.43	1,453.77	2,527.05	3.259.62
10.000 and over	−2,083.00	1,157.98	−2,890.90	−9,369.00	−2.076.70
Region	40.08	29.99	201.97	175.75	135.64

Source: Alves, Lopes and Contini (1999).

With remuneration of this nature, one could only expect that labor absorption would diminish over the past 10 years. In reality, in the period comprehended between the Agricultural Censuses of 1985 and 1995, there was a reduction of approximately 23 percent in the personnel employed in the sector (Dias and Amaral, 1999). This result may be somewhat misleading, as a study of the Institute of Agricultural Economics within the State of São Paulo, points out. According to the authors, methodological alterations between the censuses of 1985 and 1995 may have caused a downward bias in this result. The period of information gathering, in particularly, was changed to a period between harvests, which is a moment notorious for lower labor absorption. At any rate, the result is strong enough to sustain the structural employment change within the sector.

There is, however, a way to conciliate the results. Because of the low remuneration in most of the establishments, there has been a process of "urbanization" of agricultural labor over the past 20 years. Working with data from PNAD, Graziano da Silva et al. (1999) find that there was an increase in the number of resident laborers in the agricultural sector, but with primary employment in the urban zone. As can be observed in Table 2.9, of the 13.3 million people residing in the rural zone in 1981, 2.6 million worked in the urban zone, whereas in 1997, this number jumped to 3.3 million. On this issue, see Chapters 3 and 6 by Carneiro and Lanjouw respectively for a more extensive treatment.

This is a generalized phenomenon in the country, but it gains clearer contours in the more developed regions, signaling that urban development favors this change in employment composition. Taking, for example, the case of the State of São Paulo, we can perceive that almost half the people, residing in the rural zone, develop economic activity in the non-agricultural sector (Table 2.10). Even in the Northeast, about 24.6 percent of the residents in the rural zone make their living in activities in the non-agricultural sector.

One of the most relevant aspects regarding the withdrawal of government from financing and commercialization of the harvest relates to the compensation of regional

TABLE 2.9: POPULATION WITH RURAL RESIDENCE BY SECTOR OF ECONOMIC ACTIVITY, BRAZIL, 1981, 1992, AND 1997

Year	Agricultural	Non-agricultural	Total
1981	10.736	2.564	13.300
1992	11.193	3.669	14.861
1997	10.056	3.373	13.429

Source: Adapted from Graziano da Silva et al. (1999). Original data from PNAD—IBGE.

TABLE 2.10: POPULATION WITH RURAL RESIDENCE BY SECTOR OF ECONOMIC ACTIVITY, BRAZIL AND REGIONS, 1997

Regions	Agricultural	Non-agricultural	Total
Northeast	5,308	1,735	7,042
São Paulo	454	526	979
Southeast (less Sao Paulo)	1,543	742	2,285
South	2,066	764	2,830
Center-west	686	320	1,006
Brazil	**10,056**	**4,086**	**14,142**

Source: Adapted from Graziano da Silva et al. (1999). Original data from PNAD—IBGE.

imbalances. While there was a structure of reigning minimum prices for the entire country and the abundant rural credit was being distributed all over the nation, there was, to a certain point, a generalized stimulus toward production. Federal agricultural policy ended up, then, concealing the comparative advantages of the different regions of the country. Inasmuch as these instruments were exhausted and the public sector replaced by the private sector, the investments began to shift slowly to the regions with greater competitive advantages.

This movement was especially intense in the southern region of the country. The exchange rate appreciation and commercial liberalization of MERCOSUR, along with the migration of production to the Center-west region, put double pressure on southern agriculture. On one hand, there was a flight of physical and human capital from the region to the Center-west; on the other, the proximity with the large-scale agriculture of Argentina imposed a very heavy level of competition. This can be inferred from the evolution of cultivated areas. As can be seen in Figure 2.13, the cultivated area in Rio Grande do Sul increased significantly throughout the 1970s, accompanying the expansion of official rural credit. In 1970, 6.5 million hectares were cultivated, whereas in 1979, this figure reached 9 million hectares. We see, however, that during the 1980s, the cultivated area regressed to a level of 7.5 million hectares. As of the 1990s, when the process of market liberalization intensified, there was an additional reduction of 1 million hectares.

FIGURE 2.13: TOTAL CULTIVATED AREA IN RIO GRANDE DO SUL, 1973–1999
(hectares)

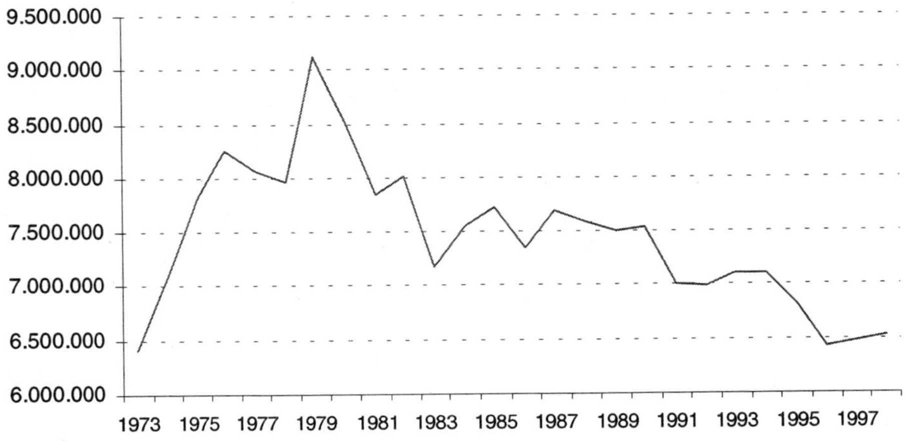

Source: IBGE.

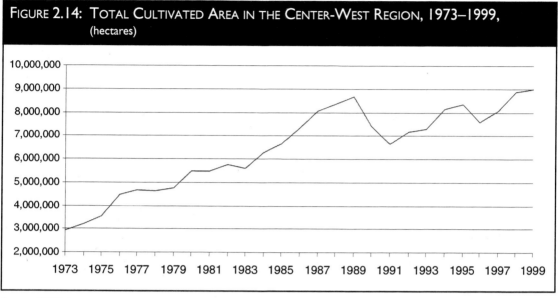

FIGURE 2.14: TOTAL CULTIVATED AREA IN THE CENTER-WEST REGION, 1973–1999, (hectares)

Source: IBGE.

An opposing movement occurred in the Center-west. Though the effects of the reduction of rural credit conceded are perceivable since the mid-1980s when there was a reduction in cultivated areas, as we enter the 1990s, the trend of expansion in the area is seen to recover (Figure 2.14). Behind this recovery is private capital expanding its horizons within a region in which gains in scale are possible thanks to favorable climactic and topographical conditions. However, the characteristics of fertility of the Cerrado soils force, from the implementation of agriculture, an occupation based on high fertilizer consumption. This pattern of occupation demanded a high technological level ever since day one. The public research in the region of the Cerrado would facilitate the development of agriculture in the Center-west, but the private sector would guarantee part of the capital necessary for occupation as well as the state-of-the-art technology developed in other regions (or countries). This is the case of poultry and pig breeding: the firms that were set up in the south of the country began to develop concentrated plants in the Center-west in pursuit of abundant raw materials (especially corn) existent in the region. Indeed, this movement takes away the capacity of producers integrated into agro industry in the south to survive. In conclusion, it can be said that a profound regional alteration occurred in the country.

The combination of all these elements, discussed in the present section, generated a rather accentuated concentration of production: a small group of establishments generated most of the value of production. In recent work, Abramovay (1999) performed some special tabulations of the Agricultural Census 1995–1996, seeking to measure the level of concentration of agricultural production in the country. Separating the farmers into employer segment and family segment, the author finds that, indeed, a small group of farmers produced the majority of the value of agricultural production. Table 2.11, extracted from Abramovay (1999), shows just how concentrated land possession in the country was: the employer segment with above average income, together with the family segment with above average income, hold 34.6 percent of total area, though they make up 17.6 percent of the total producers.

However, the concentration of the value of production is even more accentuated. It is possible to perceive that the conjunction of the employer segment with above average income and the family segment with above average income produced almost the totality of the value of agricultural production in 1995 (see Tables 2.12 and 2.13). The level of concentration speaks for itself.

TABLE 2.11: EMPLOYER AND FAMILY FARM SEGMENTS—NUMBER AND AREA

		Establishments			Area		
		1000 units	percent Total	percent Segment	1000 Hectares	percent Total	percent Segment
Total		**4,860**	**100.0**		**353,611**	**100.0**	
P	**Employer Segment**	**785**	*16.1*	**100.0**	**224,042**	*63.4*	**100.0**
P$_a$	Above average income	88	*1.8*	11.2	76,708	*21.7*	34.2
P$_b$	Between average and median	189	*3.9*	24.1	43,800	*12.4*	19.5
P$_c$	Income below median	266	*5.5*	33.8	31,191	*8.8*	13.9
P$_-$	Negative income	242	*5.0*	30.8	72,344	*20.5*	32.3
F	**Family Segment**	**4,075**	*83.9*	**100.0**	**129,569**	*36.6*	**100.0**
F$_a$	Above average income	769	*15.8*	18.9	45,649	*12.9*	35.2
F$_b$	Between average and median	922	*19.0*	22.6	23,909	*6.8*	18.5
F$_c$	Income below median	1,634	*33.6*	40.1	30,034	*8.5*	23.2
F$_-$	Negative income	750	*15.4*	18.4	29,977	*8.5*	23.1

Source: Primary Data IBGE—Agricultural Census 1995–1996—Special tabulations—ABRAMOVAY, Ricardo, VEIGA, José Eli e NUNES, Rubens (1999)—"O bimodalismo da agricultura brasileira—Instantâneo 1996"–FAPESP, projeto temático, relatório final.

TABLE 2.12: EMPLOYER AND FAMILY FARM SEGMENTS—NET MONETARY INCOME

			Net Monetary Income	
		R$ million	percent Total	percent Segment
Total		**16,745**	**100.0**	
P	**Employer Segment**	**8,768**	*53.6*	**100.0**
P$_a$	Above average income	10,422	62.2	116.1
P$_b$	Between average and median	1,893	*11.3*	21.1
P$_c$	Income below the median	472	2.8	5.3
P$_-$	Negative income	−3,810	−22.8	−42.4
F	**Family Segment**	**7,768**	46.4	**100.0**
F$_a$	Above average income	6,534	39.0	84.1
F$_b$	Between average and median	11,408	8.4	18.1
F$_c$	Income below median	641	3.8	8.2
F$_-$	Negative income	−814	−4.9	−10.5

Net Monetary Income = Revenues—Expenses.
Source: Primary Data IBGE—Agricultural Census 1995–1996—Special tabulations—ABRAMOVAY, Ricardo, VEIGA, José Eli e NUNES, Rubens (1999)—"O bimodalismo da agricultura brasileira—Instantâneo 1996"—FAPESP, projeto temático, relatório final.

Main Implications on Public Policies

Main Determinants

The principal idea to be extracted from what has so far been exposed is that the macroeconomic conditions have been, and will continue to be, very unfavorable both for agricultural production and for the labor market in the case of rural workers that do not achieve a technologically advanced standard. In other words, conditions for income maintenance for traditional farmers in the short and medium terms will not come from the agricultural world and from the labor market. The

TABLE 2.13: EMPLOYER AND FAMILY FARM SEGMENTS—INCOME AND CREDIT

	Receipts /ha. R$ha	Expenditure /ha. R$ha	Net Income /ha. R$ha.	Inve stim. /ha. R$ha.	Total Credit /ha. R$ha.	Credit		
						Short Run R$ha.	Long Run R$ha.	Commercialization R$ha.
Total	**123.4**	**76.0**	**47.4**	**21.8**	**10.5**	**7.3**	**2.6**	**0.5**
P Employer Segment	**128.8**	**88.8**	**40.1**	**24.1**	**12.8**	**9.2**	**2.9**	**0.7**
P_a Above average income	236.5	100.6	135.9	30.2	15.4	12.3	2.5	0.7
P_b Between average and median	108.3	65.1	43.2	19.0	9.1	6.8	2.1	0.2
P_c Income below the median	6.7	51.6	15.1	14.4	5.3	3.7	1.5	0.1
P_- Negative income	53.9	106.6	−52.7	24.9	15.5	9.8	4.4	1.4
F Family Segment	**113.9**	**53.9**	**60.0**	**18.0**	**6.4**	**4.1**	**2.2**	**0.2**
F_a Above average income	213.1	70.0	143.1	24.5	9.0	6.4	2.3	0.2
F_b Between average and median	106.4	47.6	58.9	15.1	5.4	3.5	1.8	0.1
F_c Income below median	52.0	30.7	21.3	10.6	3.4	1.8	1.6	0.1
F_- Negative income	30.7	57.9	−27.2	17.7	6.4	3.2	1.6	0.1

Source: Primary Data IBGE—Agricultural Census 1995–1996—Special tabulations—ABRAMOVAY, Ricardo, VEIGA, José Eli e NUNES, Rubens (1999)—"O bimodalismo da agricultura brasileira—Instantâneo 1996"–FAPESP, projeto temático, relatório final.

relevant question to be extracted from the framework constructed in the previous section is how to sustain the income of small family properties.

Every question consists of how to ensure survival of the different regional systems of family production. There are two lines of action encompassing, respectively, the most dynamic part of small production and the group that will not be in a position to enter the world of new technology.

It is important to remember some aspects brought up in the previous sections. The terms of trade were especially favorable to those farmers with a more advanced technological standard. Access to this technology depended on the combination of the organization of farmers, the financing of the investments required, and the training of the rural man within higher levels of formal education. These factors in themselves would only serve to accentuate the dualism of Brazilian agriculture. Furthermore, the most dynamic region of Brazilian agriculture, especially throughout the 1990s, was intimately associated with the land policy of the 1970s, which radically favored the access to land by large-farm owners.

Improving the terms of trade was fundamental to the good performance of a group of Brazilian agriculturers because there was a significant reduction in the volumes of official credit available for the financing of crop. The greatest group of production financing began to occur with the heightening of the purchasing power of the most advanced farmers, that is, through self-financing.

Main Alternative Policy Actions

It is of ultimate importance that the government seek political support to sustain a division line between a group that can survive in a competitive agriculture market and those that will be sustained in a rural environment that is close to the poverty line. For the first group, two actions should be stressed: a) organization at a local level through a diversified form of associations, supported by local community and local government (in most instances this means supplying to the local market or local industry); b) strong support for a capillary system of agricultural credit, at the initial stage, based on government funding with risk sharing arrangements that will induce an increasing participation of private funds.

A potential form of approach to satisfy the more dynamic group of Brazilian agriculture could be transfer via official rural credit. The Brazilian historic experience has shown that this mechanism would not be very recommendable given its natural propensity to concentration. However, it is possible to imagine a set of public policies that would facilitate the process of production financing and that would expand the horizon of survival of the more dynamic small farms. It seems important to increase the capillary structure of the financing system. Given the low volumes of capital required in each transaction, as well as the regional dispersion of the farmers, the banking system will have little stimulus to involve itself in production financing. It is fundamental, then, that the public sector deepen the financing in the PRONAF line, stimulating the different forms of micro-credit.

An interesting possibility would be the stimulus toward the development of local credit agencies, that is, organizations that form and manage a credit portfolio whose financing is sought within the financial system itself and also government credit agencies. These local agencies would not necessarily be financial middlemen in the sense of assuming the risk of resource gathering.

There is evidence of the emergence of this type of organization in the south of the country (Bittencourt, 1999). In a certain sense, PRONAF has already been stimulating these forms of structuring by seeking to satisfy the demand for credit at the community level of small-farm owners.

A more formal structure that has been assuming significant proportions is the credit coop. These organizations present the great advantage of having a light and autonomous administrative structure. Additionally, farmers that know each other join and, in this sense, there is a natural selection among the agents themselves. It is fundamental that none of the cooperatives grow too much. Throughout the past few years, a very interesting system has developed in this direction (Cresol Coops, Parana State). There are examples of associations that restrict the growth of the coop: when it passes a certain size, it is divided into two.

Another important line to be followed by the public authorities is that of production organization. Maintaining a production structure of high technological standard requires the presence of a superstructure that organizes the actions of small farmers, purchase of inputs, sale of products, technical assistance, and, even more importantly, the formulation of commercialization strategies that guarantee access to the more dynamic markets. There are concrete examples of organizations that are heading in the direction proposed above, from more informal associations of farmers to production coops, and in the systems of agro industrial integration, where industry rules the process.

As stated in the previous sections, the recent transformations in retail have gone in a direction opposite to that of farmers with less capacity to guarantee volume and quality of production. There is room, therefore, for the development of channels of commercialization to be organized at a community level in order to guarantee access, of the small farm production, to the local market. It would be important to revitalize the structure of rural extension, seeking to gather farmers in associations or cooperatives of production sales, ensuring that purchasers receive stable supply and quality.

In general terms, it is fundamental that small production find itself integrated into the supply of its own regions with the purpose of ensuring the participation of the small-farm owners in the political organization of the community. This would allow them to demand, with greater legitimacy, a greater supply of services from the local public authorities. Thailand, South Korea, and China are symbolic examples in this direction.

These policies could be combined with the expansion of access to non-agricultural rural employment. This could be achieved by means of a flexibilization in the labor laws, allowing for different forms of temporary labor. These transformations would be especially relevant in the states in which the non-agricultural rural job already assumes respectable proportions, as is the case of the southeast of the country.

For the second group, those that fail to achieve market competitiveness, a minimum income policy should be ensured through government transfer, as was the case with the pensions program in the early 1990s. Further universalized and associated to a variable transfer to compensate the loss of income caused by severe drought, mostly in the Northeast. Other actions should be associated with improved access to education by younger age groups and labor qualification for non-agricultural activities.

In terms of the less dynamic group of small production, a universal social policy seems more important than a traditional farm policy. First, Brazilian experience has shown that those that most benefit from the farm policy are not this target group. Moreover, transfers, via prices, generate significant distortions in the product market. These distortions end up affecting the processing agro industry, altering its decisions regarding location. Changes in the decisions of processing, in turn, directly affect employment perspectives in the non-agricultural sector.

It would be interesting to consider the association of a minimum income program (such as the pension system) with an income insurance program. Due to the droughts in the Northeast and South, the conjunction of these two policies would confer selectivity, precisely in the sense of reaching the target group, thus lowering the risk of the minimum income system spreading to groups that do not need the policy. In this manner, the waste, typical of generalized programs, may be avoided. Any program must have as its basic presupposition, the identification of the government's political capacity to guarantee a line of division separating the target group from the rest. This would surely be difficult in a program of minimum income insurance. There would be, however, some alternative indicators that would serve as control variables. Some examples are climactic catastrophes, objective characterization of drought, level of market prices that compromise farmer income, etc.

Another potential line to be followed would be a further extension of the pension program. As discussed in other chapters, in many regions, the municipality's greatest source of income is the old-age pension fund. Under certain edapho-climactic conditions, one would expect this characteristic to be maintained for a long period of time.

It should further be stressed that the universal policies of income maintenance will be relevant even in some regions of land reform. The competitive pressure imposed by the modern sector of agriculture will continue forcing the margins downward, which makes the survival of farmers entering production, difficult. Furthermore, given the low intensity of capital that is typical of the establishments resulting from agrarian reform, some line of financing that confers minimum conditions of production on these farmers becomes necessary.

In general terms, it is fundamental to guarantee the maintenance of income by means of a broad spectrum of specific and regionalized policies. The central idea is to guarantee time for the second generation to expand its possibilities of employment within the non-agricultural sector. The maintenance of income, for as long as possible, becomes vital in order to keep the family environment from disintegrating. Throughout this period, it is fundamental also that the second generation acquire skills, hence, expanding its possibilities of employment. Scholarships would serve well in this direction. The greater survival in the rural area will guarantee the reduction of social costs in the urban area.

References

Abramovay, Ricardo, José Eli Veiga, and Rubens Nunes. 1999. "O bimodalismo da agricultura brasileira—Instantâneo 1996."—FAPESP, projeto temático, relatório final.

Alves, E., and E. Contini. 1992. "A modernização da agricultura brasileira." In : Brandao, A. S. P. (Ed). *Os principais problemas da agricultura brasileira.* 2.ed. Rio de Janeiro: IPEA/INPES,. p.49–98.

Alves, E., M. Lopes, and E. Contini. 1999. "O empobrecimento da agricultura brasileira." "*Revista de Política Agrícola*," Ministério da Agricultura, CONAB. Brasília, 8 (3), p. 5–19.

Araújo, P. F. C. et al. 1996. Descrição do Ensino na Área de Ciências Agrária. Brasília: Ministério da Educação e do Desporto, Secretaria de Educação Superior, Comissão de Especialistas de Ciências Agrárias, mimeo.

Ávila, A. F. D., and R. E. Evenson. 1995. "Total factor productivity growth in the brazilian agriculture and the role of agricultural research." In: Congresso Brasileiro de Economia e Sociología Rural, 33., Curitiba, 1995. Anais. Brasília: SOBER, p.631–657.

World Bank. "The Management of Agriculture, Rural Development"

Barros, A. L. M. 1999. "Capital, Produtividade e Crescimento da Agricultura: o Brasil de 1970 a 1995." Piracicaba, p.149 Doctoral Thesis—Escola Superior de Agricultura Luiz de Queiroz, Universidade de São Paulo.

Barros, J. R. M. 1979. "Política e desenvolvimento agrícola no Brasil." In : Veiga, A. (Coord.) *Ensaios sobre política agrícola brasileira.* São Paulo: Secretaria da Agricultura, p.9–36.

Barros, J. R. M. 1983. "Transição e descontinuidade no crescimento agrícola." In : Dias, G. L. S.; Barros, J. R. M. *Fundamentos para uma nova política agrícola.* Brasília: Companhia de Financiamento da Produção, p.23–39. (Coleção Análise e Pesquisa, n.26).

Barros, J. R. M., and D. H. Graham. 1978. A agricultura brasileira e o problema da produção de alimentos. *Pesquisa e Planejamento Econômico,* v.8, n.3,.

Barros, J. R. M., D. H. Graham and H. Gautier 1987. Thirty years of agricultural growth in Brazil: crop performance, regional profile and recent policy review. *Economic Development and Cultural Change,* v.35.

Bittencourt, Wilson. 1999. Sistema CRESOL: Sistema de Cooperativas de Crédito Rural com Interação Solidária—Projeto CUT?CONTAG de formação sindical—Série Experiências, No. 9—São Paulo.

Bonelli, R. and R. Fonseca. 1998, "Ganhos de produtividade e de eficiência: novos resultados para a economia brasileira." Brasília: IPEA, (Texto para Discussão n.557).

Brandão, A. S. and J. L. Carvalho. 1990. "Economia Politica de las Intervenciones de Precios em Brasil". In Krueger, A. O., M. Schiff and A. Valdes, *Economia Politica de las Intervenciones de Precios em America Latina.* BIRD/BIRD.

Dias, G. L. S. and C. M. Amaral 2000. "Mudanças Estruturais na Agricultura Brasileira, 1980–1998." In Baumann, R, (Org) *Brasil: Uma Década em Transição.* Rio de Janeiro: Editora Campus,. p 223–253.

Dias, G. L. S. 1990. "Avanços e perspectivas do agribusiness brasileiro." In: *Congress Brasileiro e Sociología Rural,* 28., Florianópolis, 1990. Anais. Brasília: SOBER.

Dias, G. L. S. 1988. "O Papel da agricultura no processo de ajustamento estrutural do Brasil." In: ROCCA, C.A. (Org.). *Brasil 1980*. São Paulo: FIPE/USP, p.259–272.

Dias, G. L. S. 1989. "O papel da agricultura no processo de ajustamento estrutural do Brasil: nota adicional." In: *Congresso Brasileiro de Economia e Sociología Rural*, 27., Piracicaba,. Anais. Brasília, SOBER.

Dias, G. L. S. and J. R. M. Barros. 1983. "Fundamentos para uma nova política agrícola." *Brasília: Companhia de Financiamento da Produção*, (Coleção Análise e Pesquisa, v.26).

Dias, R. S., and C. J. C. Bacha. 1998. "Produtividade e progresso tecnológico na agricultura brasileira: 1970–1985." In: *Congresso Brasiliero De Economia e sociologia Rural*, 36., Poços de Caldas, 1998. Anais. Brasília: SOBER, p.211–221.

Ferreira Filho, J. B. S. 1997. "Ajustamento estrutural e crescimento agrícola na década de oitenta: notas adicionais." Piracicaba: DESR/ESALQ/USP. (Mimeo).

Ferreira Filho, J. B. S. 1999. "Os Desafios da Estabilização Econômica para a Agricultura Brasileira." In: Gomes, M. S. M. and F. A. COSTA, (Des) *Equilíbrio Econômico e Agronegócio*. Viçosa. Universidade Federal de Viçosa. p 41–50.

Gasques, J. G., and J. C. P. R. Conceição. 1998. *Crescimento e produtividade da agricultura brasileira*. Brasília: IPEA, (Texto para discussão, n° 502).

Goldin, I., and G. C. Resende. 1993. *Agricultura brasileira na década de 80: crescimento numa economia em crise*. Rio de Janeiro: IPEA,

Graziano Da Silva, J. et al. 1999. *The Evolution of Rural non-Agricultural Activities and Inter-sectorial Linkages in Brazil*. Campinas. IE/UNICAMP, (Texto para discussão, n° 75).

Hayami, Y., and V. W. Ruttan. 1988. *Desenvolvimento agrícola: teoria e experiências internacionais*. Brasília: EMBRAPA,.

Homem de Melo, F. B. 1988. *Padrões de crescimento da oferta agrícola*. In: Rocca, C.A. (Org.). *Brasil 1980*. São Paulo: FIPE/USP, p.245–258.

Homem de Melo, F. B. 1992. "Tendência de queda nos preços reais de insumos agrícolas" *Revista de Economia Política*, v.12, n.1, p.141–146, jan/mar.

World Bank. "The Management of Agriculture, Rural Development"

CHAPTER 3

AN ASSESSMENT OF RURAL LABOR MARKETS BRAZIL

Abstract

The paper assess the role of labor legislation and of economic development in affecting rural labor markets. For that purpose, the paper presents an assessment of rural labor markets in Brazil throughout the 1990s, discussing how labor is organized and what are the costs of formal employment. Then, major trends in agricultural employment are examined followed by an assessment of rural poverty indicators. Finally, the paper presents some policy recommendations aimed at improving rural labor markets in Brazil.

Introduction

It is an established pattern that, in the process of economic growth, the percentage of the labor force employed in agriculture falls consistently as a result of rural-urban migration and/or development of non-farm employment in rural areas. During the 1970s, Latin American rural agricultural employment fell by 0.8 percent per year while rural non-agricultural employment grew by 3.4 percent per year, a rate higher than the average growth of the total economically active population for all of the Latin American countries (Klein, 1992). The same trends can be observed in Brazil. During the 1960s and 1970s, a significant contingency of rural workers moved from the countryside to the outskirts of large cities provoking the urbanization of a large part of the agricultural labor force that had previously lived in farms.

More recently (1980s and 1990s), however, this trend has been replaced with the urbanization of the countryside through the growth of non-agricultural employment in rural areas (see Graziano da Silva, 1996 and Del Grossi and Graziano da Silva 1999). In 1990, for example, only two out every five rural residents in the state of São Paulo were engaged in agricultural activities. The remaining three were employed in non-agricultural activities, particularly in manufacturing industries (agro industries), personal services, building, commerce, and social services. It is argued that, in Brazil, one of the reasons for the growth of non-agricultural activities in the rural sector is the high cost of relocating in the cities. These high costs are materialized in the distance from basic inputs, the existence of a highly unionized and organized labor force in the cities, difficulties with transportation, and a more effective pollution control policy.

At the same time, however, several economists are suggesting that the labor laws in Brazil are a very important factor affecting rural employment. Recent analysis suggests that the labor laws could represent a substantial indirect cost on employment in farming, not only due to the law itself, but also due to the way the local labor courts enforce the legislation (Paulillo, 1996). In the current system, workers can go to court and claim anything, including land ownership, and the employer has to respond to this claim with lawyers. The high costs associated with the hiring and firing of workers in the rural sector could be encouraging the substitution of labor-intensive agriculture with capital-intensive farming.

This overall view was confirmed by a World Bank report, which concluded that the July 1991 legislative change on the financing of social security in rural areas had substantially increased the payroll taxes for farm firms (from 2.5 percent to 2.8 percent, of which 20 percent went to social security) and the employee who had to pay nothing, now had to pay a tax of 8–10 percent. The self-employed now have to pay 10–20 percent on their earnings. Such changes increased the burden of labor-intensive agriculture relative to capital-intensive farming. For instance, taxes paid by coffee producers in 1992 rose by 1140 percent and for sugar producers by 830 percent, while taxes fell by 60 percent for mechanized corn producers. It was shown that shifting from production to payroll taxes raised real labor costs for the employer by 25 percent and created incentives to use temporary workers and adopt non-monetary payments for workers. The report concluded that the new tax laws induced tax evasion, increased labor market informality, and reduced formal employment by 17 percent (World Bank, 1994).

Labor adjustment lies at the core of the adjustment process. Rural labor markets are an important element in an overall strategy for rural development and poverty alleviation. Thus, the analysis of the present situation regarding the role of labor legislation and of economic development in affecting rural labor markets could provide valuable insights for the analysis of rural poverty. Till now, Brazilian labor economists have not addressed these issues. Indeed some observers actually submit that the role of labor regulation in the agricultural sector is largely overestimated. For instance, one plausible scenario is that the non-agricultural sectors that cannot avoid labor legislation via informalities are in part responsible for the lower labor absorption out of agricultural. Clearly, the ongoing rural labor debate has generated some very interesting and policy-relevant questions. However, thus far, this—currently largely subjective—debate still awaits the input of empirically generated evidence. This paper aims, in part, to contribute towards filling that gap.

In what follows, we present an assessment of rural labor markets in Brazil throughout the 1990s. Since labor market flexibility largely depends on labor contract legislation, the analysis of the main trends in Brazilian rural labor markets is preceded by an examination of Brazil's labor legislation. The paper discusses how labor is organized in Brazil and what the costs of formal employment in the labor market are. It analyzes major trends in agricultural employment and the evolution of earnings and poverty indicators in the rural sector. Finally, it concludes with policy recommendations aimed at improving the workings of rural labor markets.

Labor Organization in Brazil

Effective and efficient labor adjustment requires a degree of labor market flexibility that in turn facilitates labor reallocation across regions, skills and types of employment. In this respect, labor contract legislation is critical because it largely determines the degree of market flexibility. In this section, we focus on the functions and on the characteristics of labor legislation in Brazilian labor markets. In particular, we investigate whether labor legislation has been responsible for increasing labor market rigidity in the rural sector. Also, we present evidence on the recent appearance of workers' cooperatives in the rural sector, which has been seen as a way of escaping excessive legislation and the high costs of hiring temporary rural labor.

The basic legislation governing rural and urban labor was unified under the 1988 Constitution. Before that, urban labor was regulated by the *Consolidação das Leis do Trabalho* (CLT) of 1943, while rural labor was governed by the *Estatuto do Trabalhador Rural* (ETR). The labor code has a very paternalistic character and was created under the general view that the State held sole responsibility for the protection of workers' individual rights. Furthermore, the collective bargaining framework prevailing in Brazil is believed to be conducive to bad macroeconomic performance in terms of employment generation and inflation control (Carneiro, 1999). Thus, it is important to understand the changes that have taken place in rural labor markets.

Labor contracts in Brazil are of two types: individual contracts and collective wage bargaining by rural workers' unions. Individual contracts, which are either fixed-term or open-ended and must be registered in the labor card, guarantee all workers' rights as established by the prevailing labor laws. Each worker is free to join a trade union. Trade unions for rural workers are organized on a territorial basis centered on each municipality. Once a year, unions conduct collective wage negotiations on behalf of their members in the so-called base-dates (*datas-bases*). Non-unionized workers are afforded the same rights and benefits as union labor workers. It is estimated that in the Northeast alone, rural labor unions have more than 1,400 local-level affiliates representing more than five and a half million members in the nine states of the Northeast (Amadeo and Camargo, 1993).

Local trade unions are organized into state-level federations with departments responsible for legal rights, agricultural policy, land reform, education, and women's organization. These federations in turn have a coordinating body at a national level, the *Confederação Nacional dos Trabalhadores na Agricultura* (CONTAG). This structure resembles that of urban workers and their central labor unions, such as the *Central Única dos Trabalhadores* (CUT) and the *Central General dos Trabalhadores* (CGT). Overall, the normal unit of collective bargaining in Brazil is that of federations, which represent the demands of an entire professional category in a given state. The effects of this sort of intermediate level of collective bargaining have been found to be negative in terms of economic performance (c.f., Calmfors and Driffill, 1988), whereas a more decentralized framework seems to yield better results (World Bank, 2000).

Furthermore, the existence of a single piece of legislation concerning wages and terms of employment, as the one prevailing in Brazil in the form of the CLT, have been found to distort productivity (Heckman, 1997). Economy-wide bargaining regulations in labor negotiations suppress the creation and use of situation-specific knowledge because the parties involved are not free to act on what they know as good in any specific context, as do government regulations of the employment contract. Rent seeking and not wealth creation is what emerges out of sectoral and national bargaining policies that favor some groups over others and draw government into wage and employment determination. On the other hand, there seems to be convincing evidence that decentralized bargaining with flexible labor markets are conducive to wealth creation and declining unemployment (World Bank, 2000).

The conditions of employment for farm workers are, in principle, the same as those for urban workers. The normal workweek is forty-four hours and the normal workday is eight hours. In addition, workers employed full time under individual or collective labor contracts are entitled to thirty days paid vacation a year (plus a special wage increase of 30 percent of the wage during the vacation month). All other benefits granted to urban workers are extended to rural workers, such as maternity and paternity leave, family wage, education salary, Christmas bonus, annual bonus, etc. However, only a minority of the labor force actually enjoys the various benefits to which workers are entitled. This excludes casual labor and all other workers without formal contracts (those without signed labor cards). For instance, sharecroppers and workers who are paid by the day lack basic wage protection or access to the most basic social benefits. Furthermore, there are still significant disparities in employment conditions between rural and urban areas.

BOX 3.1: THE CURRENT COMPOSITION OF THE COST OF LABOR IN THE FORMAL SECTOR

Taxes and Wage Deductions (percent)

A—Social Contributions	
Social Security	20.0
Severance Payment (FGTS)	8.0
Education Salary	2.5
Accident Insurance (Average)	2.0
Sesi	1.5
Senai	1.0
Sebrae	0.6
Incra	0.2
Sub-Total A	*35.8*
B.—Time Not worked—1	
Weekly Rest	18.9
Vacations	9.5
Vacation Bonus	3.6
Short Notice	1.3
Injury Benefit	0.6
Sub-Total B	*38.2*
C.—Time Not Worked—2	
13th Salary	10.9
Dismissal Costs	2.6
Sub-Total C	*13.5*
D.—Cumulative Effects	
Groups A and B	13.7
FGTS over 13th Salary	0.9
Sub-Total D	*14.6*
Total	**102**

Source: Pastore (1994), based on the Constitution and the CLT.

The total cost of hiring a formal employee in Brazil is estimated at 102 percent of the basic salary, as illustrated in Box 3.1. Taxes and wage deductions corresponding to workers' benefits comprise social contributions and the cost of time not worked.[45] There is a social security tax composed of an employer contribution of 20 percent of the worker's total wage, and an 8 to 10 percent employee contribution (depending on the wage level). Unemployment insurance is funded out of a contribution paid by the employee (PIS/PASEP). Brazil's severance pay scheme (FGTS) is funded with an earmarked monthly wage deduction of 8 percent. Upon dismissal without just cause, the employer must pay a fine equivalent to 40 percent of the total balance of the FGTS account that accumulates the deposits (of 8 percent of the worker's salary) made during the time of employment. This provision is believed to be a reverse incentive for workers to seek dismissal and the government is currently examining how to modify unemployment insurance and severance rules in Brazil.[46]

The Appearance of Cooperatives

Some commentators have claimed that the high labor costs and the increasing tax burden on employers have favored increased mechanization and the reduction of permanent employment in agriculture (Anderson, 1990, Mueller and Martine,1997). In addition, another recent trend in the sector is the appearance of workers cooperatives. They have acted as contractors mediating the hiring of labor between farmers and farm workers. The appearance of cooperatives was encouraged by a change in article 442 of the CLT in December 1994 (Law No. 8,409), which established that there are no formal labor links between farmers and cooperative workers. In the state of São Paulo alone there were more than 50,000 workers affiliated to cooperatives in 1998. The same trend seems to be taking place in the Northeast (Graziano da Silva, 1999).

In practice, cooperative workers receive a wage that is, in average, 30 percent higher, while farmers hire cheaper labor and are freed of any eventual judicial claims in the future by farm workers. Actually, the cooperatives are the ones responsible for the employees, and the farmers see

---

45. Some commentators criticize the inclusion of paid holidays, weekly rest, injury benefits and other items in the calculation of the cost of labor on the grounds that these are not taxes on labor but well established benefits in any civilized society. Thus, if one decides to reconsider the calculations and exclude the benefits listed above, the cost of labor could be estimated at some 80 percent of the basic salary, which is still high.

46. This view is supported by evidence that labor turnover rates have increased after the 1988 Constitutional revision that allowed for an increase in the fine for dismissals without just cause from 10 percent to 40 percent of the balance of FGTS accounts—see Pastore (1994) and Camargo (1996).

themselves exempt from any burden involved in the hiring of labor. Workers hired under this scheme give up benefits like paid vacations, 13th salary, weekly rest, and severance pay (FGTS). The reported savings under this scheme varies from 15 percent to 45 percent for farmers, but the most attractive feature of cooperatives is that farmers cannot be taken to court by labor. In the past, when farmers hired temporary labor through contractors and a labor claim arose, both contractors and farmers were taken to court. With the change in the CLT, cooperatives are the ones responding to labor while farmers are free of any judicial burden.

The cooperatives have proliferated mainly in labor-intensive cultures that have the longest harvest periods, such as coffee, sugarcane, and orange. In labor-intensive cultures like cotton, which have shorter harvests and where workers are less organized (usually family workers who become wage earners only during harvest time), very few farmers register their labor and the only attractiveness in doing so through cooperatives is to avoid any judicial claims in the future. In most cases, the agro-industries themselves take the initiative of firing their workers setting up cooperatives for them and hiring the same workers back again through the cooperatives, breaking therefore any formal ties with labor and avoiding the taxes and deductions listed in Box 3.1 above.

The rapid growth of cooperatives highlights how heavy the labor burden is for formal employment in Brazil and how important the search for flexibilization in rural labor markets is. In an opinion poll with rural industrials, Paulillo (1996) concluded that the main results obtained with the practice of sub-contracting workers though cooperatives presented a reduction in the number of employees, a reduction in taxes and labor costs paid by farmers, avoidance of union activism, and reduction in the number of unionized workers. The overall picture, therefore, seems to be favorable for the development of informal and precarious labor relations with the gradual reduction of permanent salaried employment.

Government Reaction to Cooperatives

The Federal Government is reacting to the widespread appearance of cooperatives in the rural sector. Recognizing the precarious situation of cooperative workers who have to give up a number of labor rights when joining a cooperative to work in temporary crops, the government is now encouraging a new form of hiring temporary labor in agriculture. Following earlier attempts by the Federation of Agriculture of the State of São Paulo (FAESP) and some isolated initiatives in the state of Paraná, the Ministry of Labor has allowed rural farmers to form a pool of employers, the so-called "Condomínio de Empegadores," to hire temporary rural workers.

While cooperatives are associations of workers offering temporary labor at a lower cost (and at the expense of legal rights), *condomínios* are associations of employers hiring rural labor for temporary work for different farmers. Under this modality of employment, a *condomínio* is responsible for all legal obligations in terms of labor rights. This means that each worker hired by a *condomínio* will have a signed labor card and access to all of the benefits extended to workers in the formal sector. Farmers alternate the use of labor in their temporary crops and the workers are paid for the number of days of work used by the *condomínio,* maintaining their legal labor rights, which will be shared by all employers affiliated to the *condomínio.* The costs of hiring a formal worker in this way are, therefore, divided by as many employers there are in the *condomínio* and this is expected to encourage formality in agriculture.

Rules and recommendations as to how to set up a *condomínio* are available in a manual published by the Ministry of Labor (Ministry of Labor, 2000). There are several positive points regarding the creation of a *condomínio:*

- ▨ **Avoiding Intermediaries:** Employers will no longer have to hire temporary labor through intermediary agents (or the so-called "gatos")—a widespread practice in crops such as sugarcane, coffee, orange etc. The hiring of temporary labor through "gatos" is always confusing and farmers are constantly subject to labor claims.
- ▨ **Eliminating Risk of Future Labor Claims:** *Condomínios* should honor all legal obligations when hiring temporary labor and, in doing so, they practically eliminate future labor

claims. *Condomínios* are also preferable to cooperatives, since both employers and employees are covered by legislation.

▪ **Reduces Hiring Costs:** There should be a considerable reduction in hiring costs since all bureaucracy is to be taken care of by the *condomínio* and all expenses shared by all affiliated farmers.

▪ **Advantages to Employees and Society:** From the point of view of employees, the most favorable result is the guarantee that all legal rights will be respected, including health insurance, which tends to be neglected in other modalities of temporary employment. From the point of view of society as a whole, the main benefit is the reduction in informality and the improvement in labor relations and conditions of work in rural areas with consequent positive outcomes in terms of poverty alleviation.

Cooperatives or Condomínios?

As affirmed earlier, the appearance of cooperatives of agricultural workers and of *condomínios* of employers represent attempts to reduce the growing uncertainty regarding the risk of future labor claims involved in the process of hiring temporary labor in Brazil. Cooperatives have proliferated because of a change in the labor code that has been interpreted as if there were no labor links between farmers and cooperatives. *Condomínios* represent a new scheme that is being proposed by the Labor Ministry to keep all temporary workers within the boundaries of formality.

In practical terms, workers hired under cooperatives give up a number of social benefits and receive a wage that is, in average 30 percent higher, while farmers perceive savings that vary from 15 percent to 45 percent of the cost of labor because of the benefits forgone by the workers. In the case of *condomínios,* all legal obligations in terms of labor rights are fully met by the employers who are members of a particular *condomínio.* The government encourages the association of employers in *condomínios* and recognizes the precarious situation of labor relations in the case of cooperatives.

In both cases, the main concern of employers is the high labor costs and the complexity of the legislation involving the hiring of temporary workers. As we have seen, the cost of hiring a formal worker is 102 percent of the basic salary. As for the legislation regarding the process of hiring a temporary worker, there are so many taxes and contributions to be met by farmers that it is usually necessary to hire an accountant and/or a lawyer to make sure that all formalities have been fulfilled. Furthermore, it takes at least 15 days to register a temporary contract in the labor card of the worker, a period which many times exceeds the demand of farmers in some crops. The whole process of hiring a temporary worker, therefore, is conducive to informality and carries a constant risk, giving rise to onerous labor claims.

The interest of the government in promoting the organization of *condomínios* reflects the fact that cooperatives are not exempt from risks in terms of labor claims. Actually, the number of claims connected to cooperatives has increased substantially recently. This is because labor courts are revising their interpretation of article 442 of the labor code, which had served as a benchmark for the intermediation of cooperatives in the hiring of temporary workers, and ruling that cooperatives are not legally allowed to act as subcontractors.[47] On the other hand, despite the fact that *condomínios* fulfill all legal obligations concerning labor rights, the wages paid to workers hired by them would be lower than the earnings of cooperative workers. Thus, for workers with a high inter-temporal discount rate, it would always be preferable to be hired through a cooperative.

---

47. According to many lawyers, although cooperatives break the formal tie between farmers and labor, workers can still go to court and make claims with a great probability of success. An existing alternative to cooperatives is the so-called *sindicatos de avulso* or professional unions. However, they can only hire temporary labor in the case of harbor workers. This is the only exception in the law, as stated by Laws No. 8630/93 and 9719/98, which extend to harbor unions the possibility of acting as intermediary agents in the hiring of temporary labor. Many lawyers also see this practice as illegal, as Article 8 of the Federal Constitution determines that labor unions should defend the individual and collective rights of their professional categories and not being responsible for hiring their members.

In view of the above, what would be the best way of hiring temporary labor? How could the uncertainty regarding the risks of future labor claims be eliminated? How could labor be benefited in this process and remain within the formal sector? The answer to these questions may lie between what happens in the cases of cooperatives and *condomínios*. That is, in the case of cooperatives, earnings are higher and the cost of labor is lower, whereas in the case of *condomínios*, wages are lower and the cost of labor remains high. As in the latter case, the workers remain worse off, whereas in the former case, there still remains a risk of labor court action against farmers in the future; neither is strictly preferable over the other. The solution then demands further changes in the legislation to allow for a reduction in the number and the value of taxes and social contributions in order to reduce the incentives that induce workers and employers to resort to illegal practices.

Ideally, to be able to assess the likely gain that reductions in labor taxes could represent to workers, one would need to provide an elasticity of earnings with respect to changes in labor costs. Up to this moment, however, there are no studies by Brazilian economists that present such elasticity for the rural sector. In an attempt to illustrate the likely effects of changes in social security contributions in the rural sector, a World Bank report has argued that wage elasticities of employment in the Brazilian rural sector could range from 0.5 to 2.0 (World Bank, 1994, p. 153). Under this wide scenario, the report concluded that the 28 percent increase in the payroll tax introduced in 1991 to finance the new social security scheme for rural workers could represent an average reduction of employment of 17.5 percent in agriculture.

Carneiro and Henley (2000), on the other hand, have estimated a wage equation for the urban sector of Brazil where the cost of labor enters as an explanatory variable. Using time series data to estimate a wage equation in the context of a bargaining model of the labor market, they derived an elasticity of earnings with respect to changes in labor costs that ranged from 0.66 to 0.76. By assuming that labor costs are the same in both rural and urban sectors, these estimates can be used as a rough indicator of what the expected effects of reductions are in labor costs in the rural sector. Thus, considering a reduction in the cost of labor of about 30 percent, for example (the average savings that farmers face when hiring temporary labor through cooperatives), the rural wage bill is expected to rise by 21 percent, in average.

These numbers highlight the potential damage and benefits of changes in labor legislation. On the one hand, the Bank estimates illustrated the employment effects of a rise in payroll taxes. On the other hand, the estimates by Carneiro and Henley (2000) suggest that there are important employment and wage gains if labor costs are reduced. In a sense, a reduction in the cost of labor is already one of the concerns of the government. What has to be stressed further is the need to facilitate the process of hiring temporary employment in a way that will eliminate completely the risks of future labor claims.

The Evolution of Agricultural Employment

Overall, the previous section highlights the fact that labor legislation in Brazil has imposed a substantial indirect cost on employment in farming. It seems appropriate now to investigate recent trends in rural labor markets in this context. Thus, this section describes and identifies the salient features of rural labor markets in Brazil focusing on major migration trends and on the composition of rural labor. The section starts with a picture of migration flows over the last five decades, presents recent estimates on urbanization rates and the profile of migrants. Additionally, the section addresses the composition and structure of agricultural employment in Brazil. Specifically, it seems appropriate to assess whether or not there has been a clear trend toward informality in rural labor markets in the recent period.

Driving Forces of Migration

In Latin America, the proportion of the total population living in urban areas grew from about 40 to 70 percent between 1950 and 1990. Rural-urban migration occurred because living standards, employment opportunities, and general economic growth improved steadily in the cities relative to the countryside. Urban-biased policies were also gradually implemented to pull or push rural inhabitants to the cities to supply labor to the growing industrial sector. Latin American governments embarked on numerous public projects in the cities, including the construction and furnishing of schools and health facilities and the provision of electricity, water, and other utilities. Furthermore, roads and other means of transportation were improved or constructed to facilitate rural emigration to the cities (Williamson, 1988).

Intersectoral income differences are also seen as an important determinant of migration. As institutional factors help to explain differences in the economic environment and in economic dynamics, it is important to look at institutional features that might create differences in sectoral incomes. Loayza (1994) investigated the role of labor legislation in fostering the appearance of a significant urban informal sector in Latin America. He argued that Latin American economic policies for most of the period between the 1950s and 1980s were extremely populist and characterized by strong state intervention. One of the most prominent forms of intervention was through labor regulations. In the entire region, rather extensive labor codes were enacted to purportedly further workers' welfare. These regulations, by effectively raising labor compensation above its market levels, diminished incentives for the industrial sector to provide work to the growing number of city inhabitants. On this respect, Cardoso and Helwege (1991) observed that the mandated benefits introduced via labor codes promoted the welfare of relatively small groups at the expense of larger groups.[48] As a result of the state-induced excess labor supply in the cities, a significant informal sector emerged in urban labor markets in the region fed mostly by rural migrants.

Larson and Mundlak (1995) studied the factors that induced intersectoral migration of agricultural labor in a large number of countries. They argued that since the decision to migrate is based on the expected lifetime income of an individual, the age and level of education of rural workers are important factors. Other things being equal, the younger the person is, the longer is the period over which s/he will benefit from the higher income in the new occupation. Also, as changing sectors is costly, the cost of migration should be lower for younger workers than for the old. The level of education is also expected to reduce the cost of migration as it should be easier for a better-educated person to find a job in the urban sector.

In studies of migration, a recurrent conclusion is that migration takes place in spite of existing unemployment in non-agriculture. In this context, the migrant may find himself unemployed. Furthermore, the first job a migrant takes after migration is likely to be low paying and therefore kept for a relatively short duration. Todaro (1969) suggested that the decision to migrate is based on the expected rather than the actual wage rate. Therefore, when the wage differential is high, it maybe rational to migrate even when the probability of getting a job is less than one.[49] As more people leave agriculture, the economic base of non-agriculture increases and that has a positive effect on migration rates. Also, as labor leaves agriculture, labor productivity in agriculture increases, the income differential decreases and the migration rate declines. As such, off-farm migration simultaneously leads to an increase of income in the rural sector and to the development of non-agriculture.

Rural-Urban Migration Trends in Brazil

The agricultural labor force in Brazil has remained quite stable as compared to the rapid growth in the urban labor force. Agricultural labor grew from 12.3 million in 1961 to peak at 15 million in 1991 and then gradually declined to 14.5 million in 1997. The rural population has followed the same path as the agricultural labor force peaking at 42.4 million in the early 1970s and drop-

---

48. This is also the one of the conclusions of Ferranti et al. (2000) who have shown that benefits such as severance payment and unemployment insurance in Brazil cover mostly high income groups and are, therefore, wrongly targeted.

49. Ramos and Araújo (1999) argue that high unemployment rates are observed in areas of high per capita income in Brazil and as such help to explain migration flows to urban centers.

ping to 29 million in 1998. This is in stark contrast with the growth path of the urban population that has more than tripled, from 34.4 million in 1961 to 136 million in 1998. The reduction in the share of the rural population is due to migratory trends observed in Brazil in the last five decades.

In the 1970s, roughly 40 percent of the rural population migrated to the urban sector while in 1980 one third of the total rural population migrated to urban areas. Overall, the number of rural migrants in the 1980s reached 13 million people. Between 1990 and 1995, the number of rural migrants exceeded 5.5 million people. If this trend persisted during the 1990s, some 28 percent of the rural population would have migrated to the cities by the year 2000. Nevertheless, the 1990s have witnessed the stabilization of migratory movements in all regions of the country but the Northeast. In what follows, we present the most salient features of migratory flows in Brazil over the last five decades. The information we present is based on previous work that has made use of the demographic censuses and appear in Tables 3.1 and 3.2.

The 1950s: Some 11 million people migrated from the rural to the urban sector during the 1950s. Out of this total, 46.5 percent were from the Northeast. The contribution of the other regions was as follows: 19 percent from the South, 19 percent from the Center-West and 30 percent from the Southeast. Despite the significance of these migration rates, the rural population remained stable during the 1950s due to growing fertility and declining mortality rates.

The 1960s: During this decade, rural-urban migration in the country totaled 11 million people and the main migratory flows were observed in the Southeast region. Some 46 percent (or roughly 6 million people) of this total were from the Southeast. The main reasons for this significant rural exodus in the region were attributed to the substitution of coffee plantations by cattle farms and the effects of the labor legislation at the time. With the introduction of the Rural Labor Code (*Estatuto do Trabalhador Rural*—ETR), the legislation created the possibility of future judicial claims of land ownership for those workers who previously lived and worked in farms. As a result, employers decided not to keep workers living in their properties any longer and this is believed to have fueled rural-urban migration, especially in the Southeast (Alves 1995; Camarano and Abramovay, 1999; Couto Filho and Schmitz, 2000).

In the 1960s, rural-urban migration in the Northeast totaled 3 million people (or 20 percent of the total rural population in the region) and represented 27 percent of the total rural-urban migratory flows in the country. Reduced work opportunities in the Southeast with the end of coffee plantations and with the slow down in economic activity added to improvements in climate conditions in the region and a delay in the effects of the change in the rural legislation help to explain the lower rural-urban migration rates in the Northeast during the 1960s.

The 1970s: The number of people who migrated to the cities in the 1970s reached 14 million, of which 5 million were from the Northeast and 4.5 million from the Southeast. During this period, rural-urban migration occurred because living standards, employment opportunities, and general economic conditions improved steadily in the cities relative to the countryside. Additionally, some authors attribute to increased mechanization, the growth of cattle farming, and again to the effects rural of labor legislation on labor relations in agriculture the significant migration flows in the 1970s (Alves, 1995; Camarano and Abramovay 1999).

The South region contributed with 29 percent of all of the rural

TABLE 3.1: NET GROWTH RATE OF RURAL-URBAN MIGRATION IN BRAZIL—1950/95

| Period | Balance | | | Net Growth Rate (percent) |
	Male	Female	Total	
1950/60	−4839	−5984	−10824	−33.0
1960/70	−6318	−5146	−11464	−29.9
1970/80	−6959	−7453	−14413	−34.1
1980/90	−5621	−6814	−12135	−31.4
1990/95	−2696	−2959	−5654	−29.3

Source: Censuses data as tabulated by Camarano and Abramovay (1999).

TABLE 3.2: REGIONAL MIGRATION RATES—1950–95					
	1950/60	**1960/70**	**1970/80**	**1980/90**	**1990/95**
North	−18.5	−22.6	6.3	9.6	21.5
Northeast	−30.8	−14.9	−20.1	−22.4	31.1
Southeast	−30.6	−46.5	−40.6	−35.2	25.9
South	−18.9	−22.0	−45.5	−37.7	−30.2
Center-West	−11.6	−17.0	−35.2	−48.8	−38.5
Brazil	−25.4	−26.5	−31.6	−28.4	−29.3

Source: Censuses data as tabulated by Camarano and Abramovay (1999). (*) Ten-year rates.

migratory flows in the 1970s, when nearly half of the rural population (45.5 percent) from that region left the countryside. Some commentators believe that the reason for the significant rural exodus from the South in this period was the distortion in relative prices of production factors that implied in the closure of a large number of family units in agriculture (Binswanger and Von Braun 1993).

The 1980s: The development of capital intensive cultures in the Center-West and the increase in cattle farming were responsible for rural migration flows in the 1980s. The total of people who moved from the rural sector to the cities in the period reached 12 million, of which 5.4 million were from the Northeast. In the Center-West, 49 percent of the rural population migrated to the cities in the 1980s. There is evidence, however, that during the 1980s, migratory flows were mainly intra-regional, with a large amount of rural migrants moving to small and medium-sized cities of their own regions (Andrade, Santos and Serra, 2000).

The 1990s: For the 1990s, there are estimates on rural-urban migration only up to 1995. In the first half of the decade, 54.6 percent of all rural migrants of the country were from the Northeast. As a result of the rural exodus in the region, the rural population in the Northeast declined by 1.2 million people during these five years. However, a significant change in migratory patterns can be observed in this period. There was a homogeneous decline in migration rates for all regions, and most importantly, an almost halt in rural-urban migrations in the Southeast and South regions. This new pattern has been termed as the urbanization of the countryside by Graziano da Silva (1996), who argues that rural-rural migrations have now become more important than rural-urban migration in the most developed regions of the country.

Using household survey data from the PNADs, Graziano da Silva et al. (1999) observed that in 1990, out of every five rural residents in the state of São Paulo, only two were engaged in agricultural activities.[50] The remaining three were employed in non-agricultural activities. As Graziano da Silva et al. (1999, p. 13) argue, the occupational migration of the rural population towards non-rural sources of employment demonstrates, on the one hand, the low demand for agricultural labor, and on the other, the search for paid work and higher-paying jobs. The main occupations taken on by this rural non-agricultural population are linked to personal services, the transformation industry, commerce and building.

---

50. As noted by Graziano da Silva et al. (1999), the definition of the economically active population in rural areas has changed in the PNADs of the 1990s, making it difficult to carry on direct comparisons between the data published in the new surveys of 1992 to 1997 and the earlier surveys. To avoid this problem, the data quoted in this paper are based on the micro-data of the PNADs and remove from the agricultural EAP those who have worked only in subsistence agriculture and consider only those non-paid workers who have worked 15 hours a week or more. In this way, the series from 1992 on were reconstructed by Graziano da Silva et al. (1999), using the same criteria as of 1981.

TABLE 3.3: PROJECTED URBANIZATION RATES FOR BRAZIL IN THE PERIOD 2000–2015
(in percentage)

Years	Brazil	North	Northeast	Center-West	Southeast	South
2000	79.9	64.8	67.6	87.6	91.8	79.9
2005	83.3	67.9	71.3	90.6	93.4	83.3
2010	86.3	70.8	74.7	93.0	94.8	86.2
2015	88.8	73.5	77.8	94.8	95.9	88.8

Source: Alves et al. (1999).

TABLE 3.4: SPEED OF URBANIZATION FOR BRAZIL AND REGIONS

Years	North	Northeast	Center-West	Southeast	South	Brazil
1940	0.5447	0.6184	0.0106	0.0118	0.0092	0.0091
1950	0.5869	0.6703	0.0116	0.0123	0.0095	0.0097
1960	0.6368	0.7731	0.0141	0.0121	0.0107	0.0105
1970	0.6735	0.8393	0.0156	0.0098	0.0113	0.0104
1980	0.6793	0.8624	0.0137	0.0070	0.0108	0.0092
1991	0.6635	0.8237	0.0096	0.0052	0.0088	0.0078
1996	0.6382	0.7828	0.0083	0.0047	0.0081	0.0071

Source: Alves et al. (1999)—calculated using the following formula: $dy(t)/dt=y(t)(1-y(t))(-b)$ where $y(t)$ is the ratio of the urban population to the total population in time t and b is the growth rate of urbanization estimated by a linear trend model.

Projected Urbanization Rates. Alves et al. (1999) estimated urbanization rates for the period 1991/2015. The results are reported in Tables 3 to 5. The authors claim that by 2015 all regions of the country will have urbanization rates in excess of 70 percent (Table 3.3). The speed of urbanization was also calculated and appears in Table 3.4. The results show stabilization of urbanization rates for the South, Southeast and Center West, but indicate that the North and Northeast still hold a significant stock of migrants. Table 3.5 reports the number of migrants per region and decade until the year 2000, as calculated by Alves et al. (1999). The data for the period 1991/2000 are based on the assumption that the rates observed for the period 1991/96 remain unchanged. The results in Table 3.5 point to a significant decline in the rate of growth of the total population in Brazil, from 1.92 percent per year in the period 1980/91 to 1.35 percent per year in the period 1991/96. They also show that all regions lost rural workers through migration, with the exception of the North in the period 1991/96, which observed an increase in its rural population.

Age and Gender: In the 1950s, most of the rural migrants in Brazil were male workers. This situation has now changed and young and female workers form the largest part of rural migrants. According to the evidence presented by Abramovay (1999), in 1996 the number of male rural workers in the age range of 15 to 24 years was 14 percent higher than that of female rural workers for the total of Brazil. This pattern is also observed at the regional level and the region with the largest male/female ratio in the rural sector is the Northeast. This overall trend is consistent with the growth of new job opportunities in the services sector, which tend to attract more women. Also, as schooling levels among women are higher than for men in the rural sector (while 55 percent of the rural male workers have less than 4 years of schooling, the share of rural female workers in the same situation is of 42 percent), women tend to find it easier to get a job out of the rural sector.

TABLE 3.5: NUMBER OF RURAL MIGRANTS PER REGION AND RATE OF RURAL-URBAN MIGRATION

Region	Period	Rate of Growth Rural	Rate of Growth Brazil	No. Of Migrants (1,000)	Migration percent of Base Year
North	40/50	1.79	2.31	59.99	5.7
	50/60	2.38	2.99	86.89	6.9
	60/70	2.09	2.85	134.56	8.4
	70/80	3.63	2.45	−281.64	−14.0
	80/91	3.82	1.92	−738.15	−26.0
	91/00	0.68	1.35	285.96	6.96
Northeast	40/50	1.80	2.31	619.53	5.6
	50/60	1.04	2.99	2,717.14	20.5
	60/70	1.08	2.85	2,739.63	18.7
	70/80	0.53	2.45	3,229.92	19.7
	80/91	−0.28	1.92	4,106.71	23.8
	91/00	−1.43	1.35	4,326.70	25.9
Southeast	40/50	0.62	2.31	1,933.41	17.4
	50/60	1.07	2.99	2,395.56	20.3
	60/70	−1.90	2.85	5,694.12	43.2
	70/80	−2.00	2.45	4,410.55	40.5
	80/91	−1.50	1.92	3,107.18	34.9
	91/00	−0.92	1.35	1,628.50	21.7
South	40/50	2.88	2.31	−274.21	−6.6
	50/60	2.91	2.99	55.70	1.0
	60/70	2.18	2.85	550.06	7.4
	70/80	−2.50	2.45	4,032.08	43.9
	80/91	−2.00	1.92	2,780.35	38.9
	91/00	−1.33	1.35	1,438.60	25.12
Center West	40/50	2.85	2.31	−61.77	−6.3
	50/60	3.88	2.99	−142.01	−11.0
	60/70	3.09	2.85	−54.71	−2.8
	70/80	−0.81	2.45	826.07	31.3
	80/91	−2.80	1.92	1,087.17	44.7
	91/00	−1.52	1.35	469.09	26.6
Brazil	40/50	1.60	2.31	2,280.98	8.0
	50/60	1.56	2.99	5,137.40	15.5
	60/70	0.57	2.85	9,068.54	23.4
	70/80	−0.63	2.45	12,240.18	29.8
	80/91	−0.62	1.92	10,382.53	26.9
	91/00	−1.06	1.35	8,185.40	22.8

Source: Alves et al. (1999). For the period 1991/00 the authors assumed the same growth rates as for 1991/96.

The Structure of Employment in the Agricultural Sector

Despite the fact that urbanization rates are stabilizing in the major and more dynamic cities of the country, there are some important changes in the structure of employment in the agriculture sector taking place. Data from the Agricultural Census appear in Table 3.6 below. This census classifies rural labor by type of access to land. As one can see, the rate of ownership has increased considerably since 1970, from 68.8 percent to 78 percent in 1996. This category accounts for the largest

TABLE 3.6: COMPOSITION (PERCENT) OF ACTIVE LABOR FORCE BY TYPE OF ACCESS TO LAND, 1970–96

Types of Access to Land	1970	1980	1985	1996
Proprietor	68.9	72.2	70.2	78.6
Renter	10.9	9.5	8.4	5.3
Share-Cropper	6.5	4.9	6.2	4.6
Occupant	13.7	13.4	14.2	11.4

Source: IBGE, Agricultural Census.

share of rural labor. The share of renters and other non-owners has declined substantially over the same period. The share of occupants, which had been growing since 1970, has dropped from 14 percent in 1985 to 11 percent in 1996. The total of all categories of non-owners amounted to 3.3 million workers (at the age of 14 and above). These are the workers who compose the bulk of the informal sector and that have very limited access to formal, commercial rural credit, except when special programs are in place.

The Growth of Temporary Employment

Mueller and Martine (1997) have analyzed the evolution of agricultural employment in Brazil in face of the increased modernization process observed in the agricultural sector during the 1980s. They have documented significant increases in the number of tractors followed by equally significant reductions in permanent agricultural employment and increases in temporary work. This trend was accompanied by greater concentration of land use and access to credit and deterioration in income distribution. The process of mechanization, however, provoked reductions in agricultural employment only in the most modern agricultural regions of the country (Tables 3.7 and 3.8). While in the most modern agricultural regions, the number of agricultural workers declined followed by an increase in the number of tractors between 1980 and 1985, in the less dynamic regions the reverse trend was observed.

TABLE 3.7: AGRICULTURAL EMPLOYMENT AND NUMBER OF TRACTORS IN MODERN REGIONS* OF SELECTED STATES, 1980 AND 1985

	Number of Occupied (1000)		Average Annual Growth	Number of Tractors (1000)		Average Annual Growth
	1980	1985		1980	1985	
Modern Rio Grande do Sul	515.5	506.8	−0.34	33.71	38.95	2.89
"Colonial" RS, SC, PR	1,361.6	1,395.1	0.48	63.24	74.96	3.39
Modern Paraná	799.1	783.4	−0.39	50.58	63.20	4.46
Modern São Paulo	876.2	849.0	−0.63	101.27	115.24	2.62
Small and Diversified SC	156.4	162.5	0.76	12.82	17.51	6.24
Modern Cattle Area of SP, PR	395.2	395.1	−0.02	20.44	24.92	3.96
Total	4,104.0	4,091.9	−0.06	281.86	334.78	3.44
Modern Cerrados	886.8	1,006.1	2.52	53.82	75.31	6.72
Frontier Cerrados	906.2	1,017.5	2.32	12.95	19.05	7.72
Total	1,793.0	2,023.6	2.42	66.77	94.36	6.92

Source: Agricultural Census, 1980 and 1985; Mueller and Martine (1997).
(*) See Mueller and Martine (1997, pp. 88–91) for the delimitation of the modern agricultural regions.

Table 3.8: Agricultural Employment and Number of Tractors in Less Dynamic Regions of Selected States, 1980 and 1985

	Number of Occupied (1000)		Number of Tractors (1000)	
	1980	1985	1980	1985
São Paulo	331.9	336.8	23.61	27.99
Paraná	563.2	621.0	18.43	22.13
Santa Catarina	318.3	347.2	12.39	17.60
Rio Grande do Sul	450.8	450.2	37.33	43.55
Sul				
Total	1,664.2	1,755.2	91.76	111.27

Source: Agricultural Census, 1980 and 1985; Mueller and Martine (1997).
(*) See Mueller and Martine (1997, pp 88–91) for the delimitation of the modern agricultural regions

Table 3.9: Distribution of the Population per Household Status, Occupation, and Activity Sector, 1981/97

	Number of People (1,000)					
	1981	1992	1993	1995	1996	1997
Total Population Aged 10 or more	88,903	113,295	115,658	120,600	123,378	125,074
Total Economic Active Population	47,489	65,983	66,954	70,063	69,593	71,638
Occupied	45,465	61,236	62,400	65,394	64,309	65,586
Agricultural	13,300	14,861	14,481	14,405	13,349	13,430
Non-Agricultural	32,166	46,375	47,918	50,989	50,960	52,156
Not Occupied–Seeking work	2,023	4,747	4,554	4,669	5,284	6,058
Non-Economically Active	41,414	47,312	48,704	50,537	53,785	53,436
Retired, On Pension, Other Income	7,338	10,277	11,240	11,779	12,726	13,121
Other Non-Economically Active	34,076	37,035	37,464	38,758	41,059	40,315
Urban Population Aged 10 or more	64,669	89,511	91,898	96,571	99,167	100,756
Total Urban EAP	33,553	50,982	51,956	55,128	55,284	57,066
Occupied	31,669	46,547	47,697	50,781	50,404	51,443
Agricultural	2,564	3,669	3,656	3,676	3,399	3,374
Non-Agricultural	29,105	42,878	44,041	47,106	47,005	48,069
Not Occupied–Seeking work	1,884	4,435	4,259	4,346	4,880	5,628
Non-Economically Active	31,117	38,529	39,943	41,443	43,883	43,690
Retired, On Pension, Other Income	6,098	8,760	9,541	9,889	10,681	11,048
Other Non-Economically Active	25,018	29,769	30,402	31,554	33,202	32,642
Rural Population Aged 10 or more	24,234	23,785	23,760	24,029	24,211	24,318
Total Rural EAP	13,936	15,001	14,998	14,935	14,309	14,572
Occupied	13,797	14,689	14,702	14,613	13,905	14,144
Agricultural	10,736	11,193	10,826	10,730	9,950	10,056
Non-Agricultural	3,061	3,497	3,877	3,883	3,955	4,087
Not Occupied–Seeking work	139	312	295	322	404	430
Non-Economically Active	10,298	8,783	8,762	9,094	9,902	9,746
Retired, Pension, Other Income	1,240	1,517	1,699	1,890	2,045	2,073
Other Non-Economically Active	9,058	7,266	7,063	7,204	7,857	7,673

Source: Special tabulations of PNAD for Project Rurbano, IEA-Unicamp.

Anderson (1990) documented this same pattern for the rural workers of the Northeast for the period 1960–80. She argued that rural labor legislation introduced in the early 1960s, which required employers to pay indemnities for firing workers without "just cause," induced fundamental changes in the scope and structure of relationships between permanent employees and employers. These changes increased the relative costs and reduced the relative benefits of hiring workers under permanent contracts, and induced farmers to substitute away from permanent labor. Mueller and Martine (1997) have also argued that despite the increase in temporary work observed in the 1980s as a result of mechanization in agriculture, the share of temporary work in agriculture declined fast in the 1990s. This is because employers have found it more attractive to invest in machinery than to have to deal with increasingly organized temporary workers.

Table 9 shows the evolution of the economically active population in agricultural and non-agricultural activities in rural and urban areas. The economic active population in agriculture represented roughly 20 percent of the total labor force in 1997, and roughly 75 percent of this total resided in rural areas. Thus, the amount of people in urban areas represented 80 percent of the country's labor force in 1997, as opposed to approximately 70 percent in 1981. The growth rate of the urban population over the period 1981–97 was of 2.9 percent implying that some 36 million people have become urban residents throughout this period.

Non-Agricultural Employment

The intensification of this urbanization process was due to the dynamics of the urban population since the rural population showed positive growth rates during the 1990s. Although the rural population has shown non-negative growth rates in the 1990s, the number of people engaged in agricultural occupations has dropped. Thus, a significant structural change in the composition of the rural labor force is the growth of non-agricultural employment in rural areas.[51]

The increase in the share of inactive workers in the rural sector, and the rapid growth of the number of people seeking work in rural areas were other important characteristics of the 1990s. The declining demand for agricultural workers in the rural sector was analyzed by Balsadi (1995), who showed that nearly a million workers were dismissed from the 30 main crops in the country, as a whole, between 1988 and 1995. According to the author, this declining demand was mainly the result of improvements in productivity and only marginally due to reductions in the cultivated areas (stet. Graziano da Silva, Balsadi and Del Grossi 1997).

The pattern of urbanization and the relative stability of the rural labor force can also be observed for the different regions in Brazil. In all of the regions but the South, the growth rate of the rural population was higher than the national average in the period 1992–97. In the South, the rural labor force actually declined over this period at a rate of 1 percent a year. In the Northeast, the growth of the urban labor force was faster than in the other regions, but the rural labor force also increased.[52] At the same time, within the rural labor force, the number of workers engaged in agricultural activities declined in all regions. Such decline has been faster in the South and in São Paulo, where the process of mechanization and the correspondent increase in productivity have taken place earlier relative to the other regions. This points to the growth of non-agricultural employment opportunities in the rural sector in all regions of Brazil (see Figure 3.1).

The labor force engaged in non-agricultural activities is concentrated in 5 occupations. With Table 3.10, one can see that jobs in manufacturing, personal services, commerce, construction, and social services concentrated more than 85 percent of the workers in the rural sector in the period

---

51. Another likely explanation for this trend could be attributed to changes in participation rates in rural areas.

52. The increase in the total population engaged in agricultural activities for the country, as a whole, in the period 1981–92 was mainly due to the Northeast. This region concentrated roughly 40% of the population linked to agriculture in 1981, 46 % in 1992 and 49% in 1997 (see Laurenti and Del Grossi, 1999).

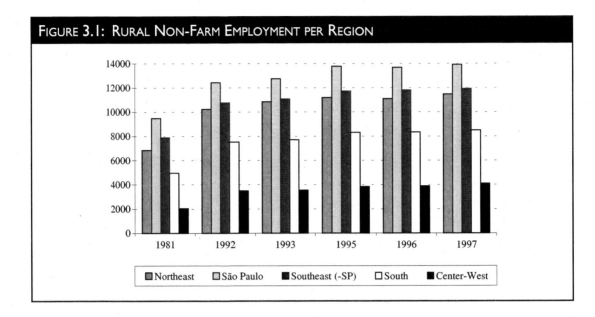

FIGURE 3.1: RURAL NON-FARM EMPLOYMENT PER REGION

Legend: ■ Northeast   □ São Paulo   ■ Southeast (-SP)   □ South   ■ Center-West

1981–97. Altogether, this represented 35 million people in the rural sector with non-agricultural employment. It is worthwhile stressing that the public sector plays an important role in the creation of non-agricultural employment through public administration or by way of social services. The total number of workers in social services in Brazil was of 718,000 people in 1997. It is also important to note that the highest rates of growth of non-agricultural employment were found in the sectors of commerce, personal services, transport and communication, and public administration over the period 1981–97.

TABLE 3.10: RURAL EAP BY OCCUPATIONAL STATUS AND ACTIVITY SECTOR, 1981–97

Activity Sector	Number of People (1,000)					
	1981	1992	1993	1995	1996	1997
Total Rural EAP	13,936	15,001	14,998	14,935	14,309	14,572
Occupied	13,797	14,689	14,702	14,613	13,905	14,144
Agriculture	10,736	11,193	10,826	10,730	9,950	10,056
Non-Farm	3,061	3,497	3,877	3,883	3,955	4,087
Services	618	975	970	1,106	1,105	1,207
Manufacturing Industry	646	773	814	791	741	780
Commerce	313	452	449	517	543	532
Social Services	309	469	507	507	538	506
Construction	735	312	558	396	434	446
Public Administration	96	162	231	199	205	212
Transport and Commun.	117	146	130	147	171	173
Other Industrial Activities	126	115	126	119	103	111
Auxiliary Services	55	55	54	64	71	75
Other Activities	45	38	39	37	44	47
Job Seekers	139	312	295	322	404	430
People with + 10 Years of Age	24,234	23,785	23,760	24,029	24,211	24,318

Source: Special tabulations of PNAD for the Project Rurbano, NEA-IE/Unicamp.

Table 3.11 presents the distribution of the rural labor force engaged in non-agricultural occupations. Nearly 50 percent of the rural non-agricultural employees is engaged in domestic services, construction, self-employment, sales, drivers, tailors and other such occupations that do not demand high skill levels. The larger number of workers in non-agricultural activities in the rural sector is found in domestic services, which employed 13 percent of the rural labor force in 1997 in the country as a whole, and roughly 20 percent in the state of São Paulo. According to Graziano da Silva (1997), this reflects: (i) women's increasing difficulty in finding a place within the agricultural labor market, where attributes linked to physical resistance are considered important for the unskilled labor force; (ii) the growth in wealthy residences in rural areas, mostly for leisure purposes; and (iii) the growth of a low-income population that works in the cities but lives in rural areas due to lower costs and less restricted housing regulations.

Less Formal Jobs in Agriculture

The composition of the rural labor force in terms of occupational status is presented in Table 3.12. Overall, there is a remarkable stability in all categories, in percentage terms. Except for the category of employees in both agricultural and non-agricultural activities, whose share in total employment declined in 1981, from 31 percent and 74 percent, respectively, to 28 percent and 70 percent in 1997, the shares of the self-employed, employers, and unpaid workers have remained roughly at the same levels throughout the 1980s and 1990s (see Figures 3.1 and 3.2). An overall reduction in formal employment is also apparent from the data collected by the Ministry of Labor. Figure 3.4 reports the

TABLE 3.11: MAIN OCCUPATIONS OF THE RURAL NON-AGRICULTURAL EAP

Occupations	1997 (1000)	(percent)
Domestic worker	537	13.1
Bricklayer	245	6.0
Autonomous service provider	207	5.1
Sales clerks	174	4.3
Primary schoolteacher	162	4.0
Driver	158	3.9
Janitor	137	3.3
Bricklayer's assistant	129	3.2
Assistants diverse trades	120	2.9
Others	105	2.6
Seamstress & tailor	89	2.2
Brickmaker	83	2.0
Handyman	69	1.7
Sub-Total	2,215	54.2
TOTAL	4,086	100.0

Source: Special tabulations of PNAD for Project Rurbano.

TABLE 3.12: BRAZIL, POVERTY INDICATORS— 1979–97

Period	S	H	P	FGT
1979	1.65	0.208	0.130	0.0619
1980	1.90	0.219	0.128	0.0567
1981	1.83	0.213	0.135	0.0647
1982	1.82	0.217	0.136	0.0649
1983	2.15	0.263	0.168	0.0810
1984	1.92	0.259	0.163	0.0773
1985	1.53	0.226	0.140	0.0660
1986	1.54	0.152	0.098	0.0474
Period	S	H	P	FGT
1987	1.77	0.222	0.142	0.0685
1988	1.79	0.233	0.148	0.0708
1989	1.90	0.214	0.138	0.0669
1990	2.25	0.265	0.173	0.0853
1992	3.02	0.251	0.151	0.0694
1993	2.93	0.243	0.146	0.0669
1995	3.23	0.175	0.109	0.0529
1996	3.74	0.170	0.111	0.0557
1997	3.65	0.190	0.119	0.0582

Notes: S = percentage of families without income in the total of families which have reported income; H—Proportion of poor families; P—Sen's poverty index; and FGT—Index of poverty of Foster, Greer and Thorbecke. Poverty line defined as the real value of the minimum wage of August 1980 (deflated by INPC).
Source: Hoffman (1999)—Primary data from PNADs.

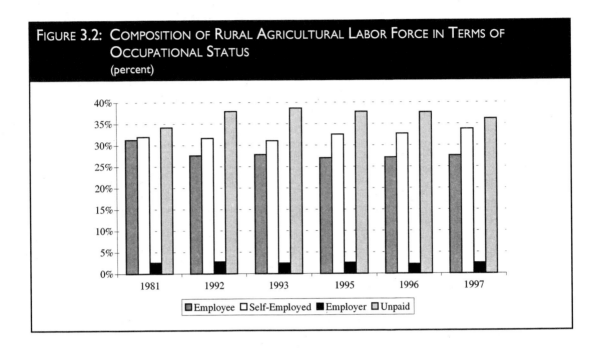

FIGURE 3.2: COMPOSITION OF RURAL AGRICULTURAL LABOR FORCE IN TERMS OF OCCUPATIONAL STATUS
(percent)

evolution of formal employment in agriculture as compared to all other occupations. In both cases, a declining trend is noticeable. In agriculture, however, that trend is visibly more pronounced.

The number of salaried workers in agricultural activities dropped from 3,359 in 1981 to 2,776 in 1997, following the fall in the economic activity population in agriculture from 10.7 million to 10 million over the same period. On the other hand, in the non-agricultural sector, the number of salaried workers increased from 2,257 in 1981 to 2,857 in 1997, whereas the total labor force in this sector increased by 1 million people over the same period.

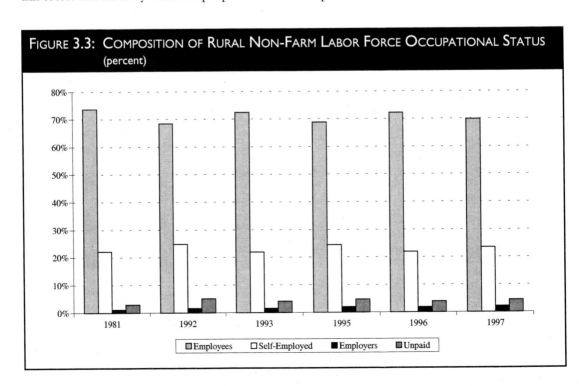

FIGURE 3.3: COMPOSITION OF RURAL NON-FARM LABOR FORCE OCCUPATIONAL STATUS
(percent)

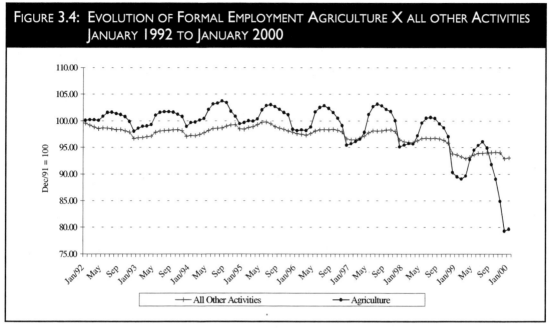

FIGURE 3.4: EVOLUTION OF FORMAL EMPLOYMENT AGRICULTURE X ALL OTHER ACTIVITIES JANUARY 1992 TO JANUARY 2000

Source: Caged—Law N°4,923/65—MTE

In relative terms, the self-employed and the unpaid workers are the two most important categories in agriculture, employing roughly 65 percent of the agricultural labor force in the rural sector. In non-agricultural activities, the most important category is that of salaried workers, employing around 70 percent of the non-agricultural labor force; the self-employed, and the unpaid workers employed in average 25 percent of the non-agricultural labor force between 1981 and 1997. The total number of employers averaged 2 percent for the two sectors in the whole period.

Regional Differences in Rural Labor Markets

Laurenti and Del Grossi (1999) have investigated whether the different regions followed the pattern observed for the whole the country. They have found different outcomes for the different regions. In the Northeast, for example, while there was an increase in the agricultural labor force, the number of salaried workers declined causing a shrink in the share of employees in the labor force, which dropped from 41 percent in 1981 to 32 percent in 1997. The number of unpaid workers, however, increased significantly and its share in the agricultural labor force increased from 22 percent to 30 percent over the same period. The very same pattern was observed in the non-agricultural rural sector of the Northeast. This suggests that the rural-urban migration in the Northeast is still significant and that the region remains as an important source of informal work.

In stark contrast to what has happened in the Northeast, the state of São Paulo has shown a substantial increase in the share of salaried workers in the labor force of both the agricultural and non-agricultural sectors while the share of unpaid workers has dropped by half since 1981. In the South, the share of employees in agriculture increased from 26 percent in 1981 to 32 percent in 1997, while the share of unpaid workers in the agricultural labor force declined from 43 percent to 36 percent in the same period.

A slight distinct pattern can be observed for the Center-West (including the state of Tocantins). There, the number of employees has grown substantially and the share of salaried workers in both agriculture and non-agricultural activities has risen since 1981. On the other hand, the number of self-employed and unpaid workers both in agriculture and in non-agricultural activities has remained relatively stable.

Overall, formal job opportunities have risen in the rural sector of frontier regions, as suggested by the increase in the share of salaried workers in the Center-West. In the poorest regions, however, there has been a decline in the number of salaried workers while typically informal occupations have risen, as in the case of the Northeast. In the wealthiest regions, typically informal occupations have declined while the share of salaried workers has either increased or remained stable. The regional pattern, therefore, is different from that observed for the country as whole and highlights the significant regional disparities still present in Brazil.

Policy Recommendations

In an effort to highlight some possible policy strategies towards the reduction of rural poverty in Brazil, we present below a set of alternatives to guide policy discussions. As the information gathered previously cover mostly workers in the formal sector, the measures proposed should have only marginal impacts for those in semi-subsistence in the rural sector. However, improvements in areas such as infrastructure, education, and legislation are likely to raise welfare overall and as such contribute towards reductions in poverty levels. Among the possible strategies to be followed we list:

(a) *Measures aimed at reducing intersectoral income differentials via improvements in infrastructure and in the provision of education.* This strategy should be more effective in the Northeast since that is the region that remains as the main provider of rural migrants. Measures to reduce intersectoral income differentials necessarily involve the development of better infrastructure and improvements in the provision of education in rural areas. Better infrastructure raises the welfare condition of rural residents and better education is expected to increase expected income (by increasing both actual wage rates and the probability of finding a job), reducing thus poverty prospects.

(b) *A selective revision of the labor code.* Although labor legislation covers only some 30 percent of the agricultural labor force, measures aimed at reducing the cost of labor as those outlined in previous sections should increase the prospects of formal employment either in the rural or the urban sector. This should have a positive impact on welfare, as formal sector workers enjoy better pay and social benefits not directly available in the informal sector. In less developed regions, it should also accelerate the path of rural-urban migration if decisions to migrate are based on expected income (the product of the current wage rate and the probability of finding a job). In either case, incentives to formalization of labor relations should contribute to reduce poverty levels in the rural sector.

(c) *Incentives to activities directly linked to rural non-farm employment.* This may involve microenterprise promotion programmes designed to stimulate this sector. Measures with such orientation should also contribute to reduce the intersectoral income differential and contribute to the development of the so-called "new rural sector." They should also help to provide paid work and higher paid jobs to the young and the women (the group identified as the main rural migrants in the most recent period). However, care should be taken with the possibility that the income generated by such activities be even more unequally distributed in favor of the wealthy.

Earnings and Poverty in the Rural Sector

The last section highlighted relevant trends in rural labor markets that point to the decline of permanent employment and the rise of temporary and informal employment in agriculture. In this section, we investigate the behavior of earnings and poverty trends in agriculture. The growth of informality itself points to the appearance of more precarious employment opportunities and this process can be associated to poverty. It is appropriate to investigate now whether this trend toward informality was accompanied by falling real wages and growing rural poverty.

There are differences regarding the way rural workers are paid in Brazil. Permanent workers receive a fixed wage in the same fashion as urban workers, but for casual or temporary labor typical of rural areas, wages and forms of payment vary by region and type of crop. During the sugarcane harvest or orange picking, for example, each worker receives a fixed amount per ton of the product that is cut/picked and loaded. Overall, workers earn much less than the minimum wage between harvests and see their income peak at harvest time.

Figures 5 to 7 below present the evolution of wage indices for farm administrators, permanent workers, and temporary workers in agriculture. Nominal wages in these categories of employment are adjusted twice a year, in June and December. Real wages were calculated using the General Price Index (IGP-DI) of the Getúlio Vargas Foundation as deflator. The time series chosen reflect four distinct periods of the country's economic history. The first period (1977–80) marks the end of the so-called "Brazilian miracle" of the 1970s, when annual GDP growth exceeded 10 percent a year, and coincides with the period of the second *Plano Nacional de Desenvolvimento Econômico*, when the government promoted an import substitution program. The second period (1981–83) is that of severe macroeconomic adjustment and economic recession in the immediate aftermath of the 1980 debt crisis. The third period (1984–94) shows the impact of failure to control hyperinflation, while the final period (1994–99) presents the results of macroeconomic adjustment and inflation control.

Overall, real wages of agricultural workers for all categories of employment has declined by 30 percent since 1977. It is interesting to see, however, that during the 1980–83 recession, wages fell less than during the inflationary period. In the mid-1980s, with the Cruzado Plan, real wages of both skilled and unskilled rural workers recovered their peak levels following the widespread growth in the demand for agricultural products and the significant increase in employment in the urban sector, which is believed to have contributed to increasing the earnings of rural workers (Hoffman, 1991). This positive result, however, was rapidly reversed with the return of high inflation rates in 1987. In 1994 with the "Real Plan" the government regained control over inflation and real wages stabilized.[53] Although that trend ran across all wage categories, the wages of temporary workers fell more than did those of permanent workers and farm administrators. The same pattern can be observed at the state level, even for the state of São Paulo where workers are more organized.

The behavior of land prices was quite similar to that of the agricultural real wages. Figure 8 below shows the evolution of land prices deflated by the IGP-DI/FGV from 1977 to 1999. In the period 1977–80, land prices remained stable in real terms to decline during the economic recession of 1981–83. In the next two years, there was a slight growth, but in 1986, land prices reached their highest level in 20 years with the Cruzado Plan. This significant growth of land prices in 1986 resulted from widespread speculation in the land market, following the end of the formal indexation mechanism. In the following months, land prices returned to their normal level as speculation eased and have remained remarkably stable since 1994.

Poverty

Following the effects of rising wages during the Cruzado Plan, income distribution showed a temporary improvement in agriculture in 1986. As per Table 3.13, inequality increased between 1981 and 1985, but declined in 1986 reducing the number of poor in the rural sector allowing them to be better off. This situation is consistent with the increase in the demand for agricultural products and the appearance of more job opportunities in the rural sector with the consequent real increase in rural wages in 1986 reported above. However, this was just a temporary improvement as the levels of income inequality and poverty deteriorated again after 1987, returning to the levels observed in the early 1980s.

The evidence on the profile of the rural poor is scattered and scarce. Most of the rural poor are temporary workers and self-employed farmers with small farms with no access to mechanization

---

53. Paes de Barros (2000) has found a 4 percent real increase for rural earnings in Brazil between 1992 and 1999, using data from the PNADs. This real growth is mostly due to a lower basis observed in the beginning of the 1990s, as real wages virtually stagnated between 1994 and 1999 (see Figures 5 to 7).

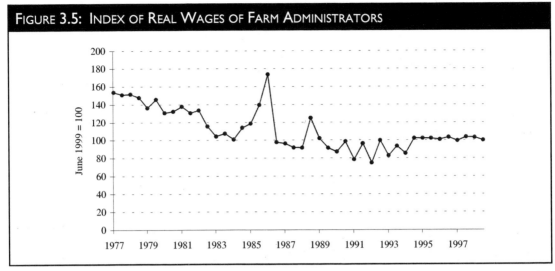

FIGURE 3.5: INDEX OF REAL WAGES OF FARM ADMINISTRATORS

Source: FGV—Estatísticas Agrícolas

FIGURE 3.6: INDEX OF REAL WAGES OF PERMANENT WORKERS IN AGRICULTURE

Source: FGV—Estatísticas Agrícolas.

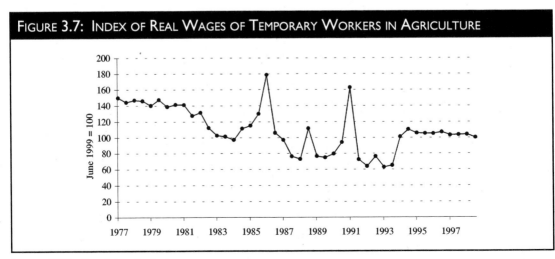

FIGURE 3.7: INDEX OF REAL WAGES OF TEMPORARY WORKERS IN AGRICULTURE

Source: FGV—Estatísticas Agrícolas.

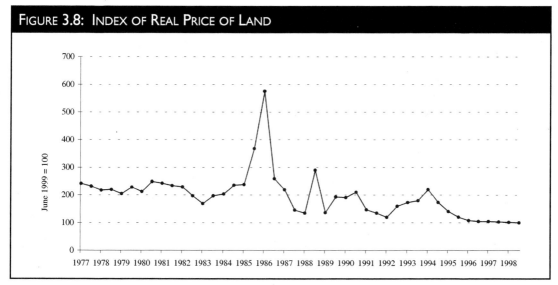

FIGURE 3.8: INDEX OF REAL PRICE OF LAND

Source: FGV—Estatísticas Agrícolas.

TABLE 3.13: BRAZIL—RURAL LABOR FORCE BY OCCUPATIONAL STATUS, 1981–97

	1981	1992	1993	1995	1996	1997
Agricultural Activities	10,736	11,193	10,826	10,730	9,950	10,056
Employees	3,359	3,093	3,015	2,907	2,703	2,776
Self-Employed	3,434	3,546	3,363	3,491	3,255	3,395
Employers	274	312	265	275	219	247
Unpaid Workers	3,669	4,241	4,183	4,058	3,748	3,638
	Share of Total Employment					
Employees	31 percent	28 percent	28 percent	27 percent	27 percent	28 percent
Self-Employed	32 percent	32 percent	31 percent	33 percent	33 percent	34 percent
Employers	3 percent	3 percent	2 percent	3 percent	2 percent	2 percent
Unpaid Workers	34 percent	38 percent	39 percent	38 percent	38 percent	36 percent
Non-Agric Activities	3,061	3,497	3,877	3,883	3,955	4,087
Employees	2,257	2,393	2,807	2,673	2,855	2,857
Self-Employed	677	868	849	948	866	959
Employers	36	57	61	79	76	89
Unpaid Workers	90	179	160	184	157	183
	Share of Total Employment					
Employees	74 percent	68 percent	72 percent	69 percent	72 percent	70 percent
Self-Employed	22 percent	25 percent	22 percent	24 percent	22 percent	23 percent
Employers	1 percent	2 percent	2 percent	2 percent	2 percent	2 percent
Unpaid Workers	3 percent	5 percent	4 percent	5 percent	4 percent	4 percent

Source: PNADs.

		Number of People (1,000)					
Regions	Population	1981	1992	1993	1995	1996	1997
Northeast	**Total**	**25,060**	**32,093**	**32,759**	**33,905**	**34,716**	**35,295**
	Urban	13,758	20,083	20,821	21,863	22,542	22,936
	Rural	11,302	12,010	11,938	12,042	12,173	12,359
São Paulo	**Total**	**20,211**	**25,854**	**26,419**	**27,784**	**28,395**	**28,853**
	Urban	18,474	24,145	24,594	25,910	26,577	26,991
	Rural	1,737	1,709	1,825	1,874	1,818	1,862
Southeast (-SP)	**Total**	**20,921**	**25,208**	**25,620**	**26,567**	**27,038**	**27,263**
	Urban	16,679	21,238	21,609	22,426	22,880	23,118
	Rural	4,243	3,970	4,011	4,141	4,158	4,145
South	**Total**	**14,743**	**17,799**	**18,075**	**18,727**	**19,131**	**19,243**
	Urban	9,247	13,367	13,778	14,497	14,883	15,067
	Rural	5,496	4,433	4,297	4,230	4,248	4,176
Center-West (+TO)	**Total**	**5,704**	**8,193**	**8,475**	**8,958**	**9,230**	**9,429**
	Urban	4,247	6,530	6,786	7,215	7,416	7,653
	Rural	1,456	1,663	1,688	1,743	1,814	1,776

TABLE 3.14: REGIONAL DISTRIBUTION OF THE POPULATION WITH + 10 YEARS OF AGE, 1981/1997

Source: Special tabulations of PNAD for the Project Rurbano, NEA-IE/Unicamp.

living in the Northeast. The special supplement of the 1990 National Household Survey (PNAD) shows that 27.7 percent of the informal workers of the country were in the agricultural sector– a proportion that is much larger in the Northeast, where the average household income of one minimum wage is the lowest in the country (Graziano da Silva, 1998).

The growth in informality and self-employment has contributed to increasing the number of poor in the rural areas of the poorest states. Despite a significant improvement in 1995, probably following the real increase in the value of the minimum wage, rural poverty levels continued growing in the Northeast. In the other regions, rural poverty remained relatively stable between 1995 and 1996 [see Figure 9]. The reason for that stabilization has been attributed to the leveling of rural social security pensions relative to the pensions paid in the urban sector [see next section]. In aggregate terms, however, overall poverty indicators have continued to increase after 1995, as illustrated by Figure 10 and Table 15.

As the poverty line is often defined as a proportion of minimum wages, and most of the workers in agriculture receive only a minimum wage as remuneration, it is important to investigate how changes in the minimum wage impact poverty levels and income distribution. Several previous studies have found strong and robust evidence that changes in the real value of the minimum wage affect negatively income inequality. This result holds true under different methodologies, for different periods and different activity sectors in Brazil. Hoffman (1973) and Hoffman (1999), for example, have shown a negative impact of changes in the real value of the minimum wage over income distribution using household income data for the period 1966–97. Reis (1989) found a positive impact of changes in the minimum wage over average wages of formal workers (with signed labor cards). Neri (1997) used monthly data for six metropolitan regions in the period 1980–97 to conclude in a similar fashion that there is a negative impact of the minimum wage over income inequality (as measured by the ratio of the income of the wealthiest 20 percent and the poorest 50 percent). He also pointed out that the elasticity of the proportion of the poor in relation to the minimum wage is negative and inversely related to the poverty line, which is suggestive that the minimum wage has the greatest impact in the lower tail of the distribution of per capita household income. Carneiro and Faria (1997) also found that changes in the minimum wage lead to changes in the same direction in other wages. In the same line, Gill and Montenegro (2000)

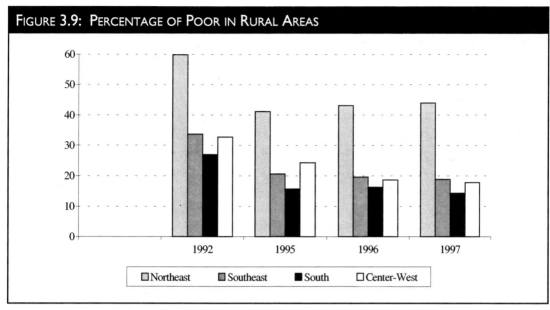

FIGURE 3.9: PERCENTAGE OF POOR IN RURAL AREAS

Source: David et al. (1999).

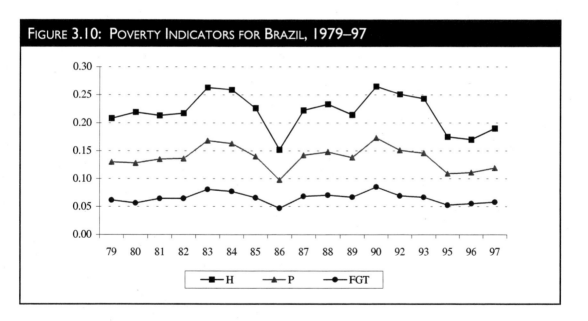

FIGURE 3.10: POVERTY INDICATORS FOR BRAZIL, 1979–97

collected evidence that a large number of workers in Brazil are paid exactly the legal minimum wage even in the "unregulated" sector, and that adjustments in this wage are matched by salary adjustments. Finally, Correa and Hoffman (1997) presented evidence that the minimum wage is an important determinant of income inequality in the rural sector.

Conclusions

This paper has identified some relevant trends in rural employment in Brazil. Overall, agriculture employed a declining share of the population over the 1990s, despite the fact that the economically active population in the rural sector increased from 13.9 million in 1981 to 14.6 million in 1997. There was a decline in the number of salaried workers in agriculture that was followed by an

Regions	REAP Activity Sector	Number of People (1,000)					
		1981	1992	1993	1995	1996	1997
Northeast	**Total**	**12,231**	**17,055**	**17,372**	**18,088**	**17,296**	**18,049**
	Agricultural	5,367	6,824	6,518	6,898	6,191	6,574
	Non-Agricultural	6,864	10,231	10,854	11,191	11,105	11,475
São Paulo	**Total**	**10,641**	**13,694**	**14,041**	**14,875**	**14,801**	**14,848**
	Agricultural	1,166	1,261	1,279	1,102	1,115	924
	Non-Agricultural	9,475	12,433	12,762	13,773	13,686	13,924
Southeast (-SP)	**Total**	**10,243**	**13,111**	**13,421**	**13,978**	**13,961**	**14,031**
	Agricultural	2,351	2,337	2,343	2,249	2,154	2,113
	Non-Agricultural	7,892	10,774	11,079	11,729	11,807	11,918
South	**Total**	**8427**	**10633**	**10689**	**11148**	**11035**	**11057**
	Agricultural	3474	3106	2972	2837	2688	2555
	Non-Agricultural	4952	7527	7717	8311	8347	8502
Center-West (+TO)	**Total**	**2893**	**4634**	**4701**	**4946**	**4886**	**5135**
	Agricultural	837	1123	1153	1107	1000	1032
	Non-Agricultural	2055	3511	3548	3839	3887	4104

TABLE 3.15: REGIONAL DISTRIBUTION OF RURAL ECONOMIC ACTIVITY POPULATION PER ACTIVITY SECTOR: 1981/1997

Source: Special tabulations of PNAD for the Project Rurbano, NEA-IE/Unicamp.

increase in informality in rural labor markets. In regional terms, however, there were significant differences in the trend in salaried versus self-employed workers in agriculture. In the poorest regions, such as the Northeast, where typically informal employment has risen, salaried work declined in contrast with increases in São Paulo and in the Center-West region. We have also noticed a slight increase in rural non-farm employment in Brazil.

As for the observed trends in real wages, we have noticed that the earnings of skilled and unskilled agricultural workers declined by 30 percent between 1977 and 1997, with more important reductions in the earnings of temporary workers. Real wages recovered in periods of low inflation and economic growth, such as the mid-1980s. We have also noticed that the combined effect of declining real wages and growing informality contributed to increasing rural poverty, particularly in the poorest regions.

Overall, the Brazilian history of high income-inequality and the prolonged period of corporatist policies in the country have led to labor laws with a clear pro-labor bias. Labor courts have acquired a similar bias in their verdicts on disputes. The result of increased ambiguity in labor laws, combined with this pro-labor bias of conflict resolution, has resulted the ability of former workers (dismissed from either formal or informal employment) to extract generous severance payments from their formal employers. This general state of affairs has led to higher and more uncertain labor costs in both regulated and unregulated employment. Some of the evidence presented in this paper seems to support this general view.

As we have argued, there seems to be a consensus on the fact that the growth of informality and self-employment in Brazil results from the design of labor legislation and the way in which it is enforced by labor courts (Amadeo and Camargo, 1997) and (Gill and Montenegro 2000). This applies to both urban and rural labor markets, as both of them are subject to the same labor code. The excess of legislation is also responsible for high hiring costs, which, in Brazil, reach 102 percent of the basic salary. Therefore, informality is bound to remain high as long as labor legislation remains ambiguous and enforced with a clear pro-labor bias. Thus, poverty alleviation strategies must seek an improvement in labor market flexibility so that labor contracts can accommodate firm and labor characteristics and discourage informality.

Our analysis suggests that there is room for a labor reform aimed at improving the labor market. In general terms, there should be emphasis on measures directed towards increasing labor market flexibility in order to facilitate labor reallocation across regions, skills and types of employment. Some of these measures, identified as critical in the present paper, include: a) reductions in the number and value of taxes that employers have to pay as social contributions when hiring temporary labor; b) reductions in FGTS deposits and exemption of the 40 percent fine upon termination of contract, in the case of temporary employment; c) changes in the labor code aimed at easing the rules for hiring temporary workers, either through cooperatives or *condomínios*, as long as uncertainty regarding future labor claims is definitely eliminated; d) reduction in the pro-labor bias in conflict resolution by ending the legal power of the Labor Courts while retaining their standing to engage in voluntary arbitration in collective economic conflicts, at the request of the parties.

References

Abramovay, Ricardo. 1999. *Funções e Medidas da Ruralidade no Desenvolvimento Contemporâneo*, Texto para Discussão No. 702, IPEA, Brasília.

Alves, Eliseu. 1995. "Migração Rural-Urbana," *Revista de Política Agrícola*, 4, 15–29.

Alves, Eliseu, Mauro Lopes, and Elísio Contini 1999. "Novas Evidências sobre Migração Rural," Embrapa, Brasília, mimeo.

Amadeo, E. J., and J. M. Camargo. 1993. "Labor Legislation and Institutional Aspects of the Brazlilian Labor Code," *LABOUR*, 7, 157–180.

Amadeo, E. J., and J. M. Camargo. 1997. "Brazil: Regulation and Flexibility in the Labor Market," in: S. Edwards and N. Lustig (org.) *Labor Markets in Latin America: Combining Social Protection with Market Flexibility*, Brookings Institution Press, Washington, DC.

Anderson, J. 1990. *Legislation, development and legislation development in Brazilian rural labor markets: The sugar cane cutters of Pernambuco*, McNamara Fellowships Program, EDI, The World Bank, mimeo.

Andrade, Thompson A., Angela M. S. P. Santos, and Rodrigo V. Serra. 2000. "Fluxos Migratórios nas Cidades Médias e Regiões Metropolitanas Brasileiras: A Experiência do Período 1980/96," Texto para Discussão No. 747, IPEA, Brasília.

Balsadi, O. V. 1996 "Força de Trabalho na Agricultura Brasileira no Período 1988–95," Proceedings of the XXXIV Brazilian Congress of Rural Economics and Sociology (SOBER), Aracajú, 1, 786–815.

Binswanger, H. P. and J. von Braun 1993. "Technological Change and Commercialization in Agriculture: Impact on the Poor," in Lipton, M. and J. Van Der Gaag, *Including the Poor–Proceedings of a Symposium* Organized by the World Bank and the International Food Policy Research Institute, World Bank Regional and Sectoral Studies, pp. 169–189.

Calmfors, L. and J. Driffill 1988. "Bargaining Structure, Corporatism and Macroeconomic Performance," *Economic Policy*, 6, 13–61.

Calmfors, L., and J. Driffill 1988. "Bargaining Structure, Corporatism and Macroeconomic Performance," *Economic Policy*, 6, 13–61.

Camarano, Ana Amélia, and Ricardo Abramovay. 1999. *Êxodo Rural, Envelhecimento e Maculinização no Brasil: Panorama dos Últimos 50 Anos*, Texto para Discussão No. 621, IPEA, Brasília.

Camargo, J. M. 1996. "Flexibilidade e Produtividade do Mercado de Trabalho Brasileiro," in Camargo, J. M. (ed.), *Flexibilidade do Mercado de Trabalho no Brasil*, Editora FGV, Brazil.

Cardoso, Eliana, and A. Helwege. 1991. "Populism, Profligacy, and Redistribution," in *The Macroeconomics of Populism in Latin America*, edited by R. Dornbush and S. Edwards, NBER, The University of Chicago Press.

Carneiro, F. G. 1999. "Insider Power in Wage Determination: Evidence from Brazilian Data," *Review of Development Economics*, 3, 155–169.

Carneiro, F. G., and J. R. Faria. 1997. "Causality between the Minimum Wage and Other Wages," *Applied Economics Letters,* 4, 507–510.

Carneiro, F. G., and A. Henley. 2000. "Real Wages and the Lucas Critique: Can the Government Tax Policy Influence Wage Growth in Brazil?," *Revista de Econometria,* forthcoming.

Corrêa, A. M. C. J., and Hoffmann, R. 1997. "Fatores condicionantes da desigualdade de rendimentos na agricultura paulista: 1981–90," *Revista Brasileira de Economia 51,* 471–487.

Couto Filho, Vitor A., and Arno P. Schmitz. 2000. *Fatores Determinantes da Ocupação da Mão de Obra Agrícola,* Paper presented at the X World Congress of Rural Sociology, Rio de Janeiro.

David, M. D. 1999. "Previdência Rural no Brasil: Uma Análise de Seu Impacto e Eficácia como Instrumento de Combate à Pobreza Rural," Paper Presented at the FAO/CEPAL/RIMISP Seminar on Successful Experiences Against Rural Poverty in Latin America, Brazil, mimeo.

De Ferranti, D., G. E. Perry, I. S. Gill and L. Servén. 2000. *Securing our Future in a Global Economy,* World Bank and Caribbean Studies, Washington.

Delgado, G. C., and J. C. Cardoso Jr. 1999. *A Previdência Social Rural e a Economia Familiar no Brasil: Mudanças Recentes nos Anos 90,* IPEA, Brasília, mimeo.

FAO. 1998. *The State of Food and Agriculture,* NY.

Gill, I., and C. Montenegro. 2000. *Stabilization, Adjustment and Beyond: Quantitative Assessments of Labor Policy Challenges in Latin America,* The World Bank, forthcoming.

Graziano da Silva, F. J. 1997. "O novo rural brasileiro" (*The new rural sector in Brazil*), *Nova Economia 7,* 43–81.

Graziano da Silva, F. J., O. V. Balsadi and M. E. Del Grossi. 1997. "O Emprego Rural e a Mercantilização do Espaço Agrário," *São Paulo em Perspectiva,* Fundação SEADE, 11, 50–64.

Graziano da Silva, F. J. and M. E. Del Grossi. 1997. "A evolução do emprego não-agrícola no meio rural brasileiro–92/95" (*The evolution of rural non-farm employment in Brazil—92/95*), *Proceedings of the XXV Annual ANPEC Meeting,* Vol. 2, pp. 940–54.

Graziano da Silva, J. 1999. *Agroindústria e Globalização: O Caso da Laranja do Estado de São Paulo,* mimeo.

Graziano da Silva, F. J., M. E. Del Grossi, and A. C. Laurenti. 1999. "The evolution of rural non-agricultural activities and intersectoral linkages in Brazil." Paper presented at the 6th International Conference of the Latin American and Caribbean Association of Agricultural Economists, Trinidad and Tobago, July.

Graziano da Silva, J. 1998. *A Nova Dinâmica da Agricultura Brasileira,* Ed. Unicamp, 2nd edition.

Heckman, J. 1997. *Diversity and Uniformity: Labor Market Reform in Argentina,* University of Chicago Discussion Paper.

Hoffmann, R. 1973. "Considerações sobre a evolução recente da distribuição da renda no Brasil." *Revista de Administração de Empresas 13,* 7–17.

Hoffman, R. 1991. "Distribuição de Renda na Agricultura," in Camargo, J. M. and F. Giambiagi, org., *Distribuição de Renda no Brasil,* São Paulo, Paz e Terra.

Hoffman, R. 1999. "Desigualdade e Pobreza no Brasil no Período 1979–97 e a Influência da Inflação e do Salário Mínimo," mimeo.

Klein, E. 1992. *El empleo no agricola en America Latina.* Documento de Trabajo No. 364, PREALC/OIT, Santiago, Chile.

Lanjouw, J. O., and P. Lanjouw 1995. "Rural non-farm employment: A survey," The World Bank, mimeo.

Larson, Donald, and Yair Mundlak. 1995. *On the Intersectoral Migration of Agricultural Labor,* Policy Research Working Paper No. 1425, The World Bank, Washington.

Laurenti, A. C., and M. E. Del Grossi. 1999. *"A Evolução das Pessoas Ocupadas nas Atividades Agrícolas e Não-Agrícolas nas Áreas Rurais do Brasil,"* mimeo.

Loayza, Norman V. 1994. *Labor Regulations and the Informal Economy,* Policy Research Working Paper No. 1335, The World Bank, Washington.

Ministry of Labor. 2000. *Condomínio de Empregadores: Um Novo Modelo de Contratação no Meio Rural,* Ministério do Trabalho e Emprego, SIT, Brasília.

Mueller, C. C., and G. Martine 1997. "Modernização da Agropecuária, Emprego Agrícola e Êxodo Rural no Brasil—A Dédada de 1980," *Revista de Economia Política*, 17, 85–104.

Neri, M. 1997. *O reajuste do salário mínimo de maio de 1995. XIX Encontro Brasileiro de Econometria*, SBE, Anais, vol. 2, p. 645–666.

Paes de Barros, R. 2000. "Pobreza e Trabalho Rural no Brasil: 1992–1999." Paper presented at the Seminar Desafios da Pobreza Rural no Brasil, Rio de Janeiro, 30/08 to 01/09/2000, Brazil, mimeo.

Pastore, J. 1994. *Encargos Trabalhistas no Brasil e no Mundo*, Rio de Janeiro, Sebrae.

Paulillo, L. 1996. "*O Avanço do Setor Serviços nos Complexos Agroindustriais: A Terceirização Agroindustrial e as Cooperativas de Mão-de-Obra Rural na Citricultura*," *Informações Econômicas*, 26, 37–53.

Ramos, Carlos A., and Herton Araújo. 1999. *Fluxos Migratórios, Desemprego e Diferenciais de Renda*, Texto para Discussão No. 657, IPEA, Brasília.

Reis, J. G. Almeida dos. 1989. "*Salário mínimo e distribuição da renda. In: IPEA*," *Perspectivas da Economia Brasileira—1989*, p. 371–391.

Todaro, M. P. 1969. "A Model of Labor Migration and Urban Unemployment in Less Developed Countries," *American Economic Review*, 59, 138–148.

World Bank. 1994. *Brazil: The management of agriculture, rural development and natural resources*. Report No.: 11783-BR.

World Bank. 2000. *Argentina: Labor Market in the New Millennium*, Report No.: 19996-AR.

Williamson, J. G. 1990. "Migration and Urbanization," in *Handbook of Development Economics*, Vol. 1, edited by H. Chenery and T. N. Srinivasan, Amsterdam.

CHAPTER 4

LAND MARKETS AND RURAL POVERTY ALLEVIATION

Executive Summary[54]

This paper reviews recent policies, institutional changes, and price trends in the land market in Brazil and their implications on rural poverty alleviation. It starts by showing the decreasing importance of land as a factor of production in Brazil, which has a declining share in the value and in the cost of production. Moreover, the declining value of land also diminishes its *asset value,* reducing its attractiveness as collateral for lending operations by financial institutions.

The decline in land prices and land rents that has been observed in Brazil after 1994 could be seen as a positive factor in that it reduces barriers to entry into the agricultural sector with favorable implications for the land tenure structure over the long run. The sustainability of this trend depends on the continuation of macroeconomic stability, a very likely event.

Nevertheless, there are still distortions that restrain the operation of the land market (sales and rentals), such as: the extremely high degree of ownership concentration; a deficient system of titling and registration and the lack of a cadastre; deficient value assessment for tax purposes; and restrictive labor and land legislation with a bias against rentals and sharecropping.

The government uses the mechanism of land expropriation and redistribution as the principal instrument to overcome restrictions on land market operation and the solution to the rural-urban migration. Granting that these programs will effectively achieve the stated goals, they are not cost effective. Existing estimates on the potential beneficiaries of land reform vary significantly across studies. Considering a figure of 3.5 million families, an average of 27 ha/family and expropriation cost of R$ 680/ha, the total budget estimated to settle all potential beneficiaries would be equivalent to R$ 64 billions. Meanwhile, there is evidence that socio-economic conditions of the settled families are improving marginally but poverty levels are still very high.

A market-based approach is being implemented in Brazil since 1997, starting out as a pilot project by the World Bank called Land Cooperative Program (Programa Cédula da Terra, PCT).

54. This paper was prepared by Antonio Salazar P. Brandão, Professor of Universidade Santa Ursula (USU) and Universida de do Estado do Rio de Janeiro (UERJ); Guilherme Soria Bastos Filho, Fundação Getulio Vargas, (FGV); and Alexandre P. Brandão, Fundação Instituto Brasileiro de Geografia e Estatística (IBGE).

It differs from the traditional approach in that the beneficiaries receive a collective loan to purchase land, a lump sum as start-up money, and a loan from the official credit program for purchase of inputs (Procera/Pronaf). Up to date, there is no ex-post evaluation of the PCT, although expropriation prices per hectare obtained in the INCRA program are on average 222 percent higher than PCT prices. Nevertheless, the early-perceived success of the program encouraged the government to launch "Banco da Terra," which is a fund for acquisition of land.

The Rural Village Program in the State of Paraná and the Sharecropper and Rural Leasing Exchange in the State of Minas Gerais offer two promising alternatives for rural poverty alleviation. The former is a settlement localized near urban centers with significant investments in education, health, and urban infrastructure. The purpose is to offer conditions for rural families to combine agricultural production with working opportunities in the urban labor market, allowing a better diversification of income sources and better opportunities for investment in human capital of the family members. The latter is an attempt to overcome the restrictions imposed on the lease market by the distortions in the land and labor legislation. This is done through the creation of an institution that will guarantee the contracts. This program has benefited farmers with idle land and has not had any significant impacts on poverty. Nevertheless, the concept is an important one and could be used to increase access to land by the rural poor, even in a context of unfriendly legislation and in an environment of imperfect and incomplete markets.

The main policy recommendations presented in this paper are the following:

- To revise the labor and land legislation and remove the provisions that hamper the operation of the rental and sharecropper markets
- To reform the land administration system, improving the titling situation and creating a national cadastre and registration system
- To revise the land assessment criteria for tax purposes based on the new created cadastre
- To promote alternatives that require less capital mobilization by the rural poor, such as small rural villages or land rentals.

These policies will have only limited impacts on poverty if not accompanied by other measures. The increasing capitalization of agriculture makes entry even into sharecropping more difficult for the poor. Thus, access to alternative sources of credit (such as micro-credit and collective credit is of fundamental importance), education, and training will improve the likelihood of the new entrants in the land market to move up on the agricultural ladder.

The sequence of the proposed reforms is also important. Social movements and large state owners may resist major changes in the legal structure. To pursue this goal, the government must give credible signs to the society, beginning with the reform of the land administration system. In the meantime, the removal of the anti rentals and sharecropping bias in the legislation will foster the development of land markets, provide a mechanism for a more rational use of land, and increase employment in the agricultural sector. In the short run, alternatives to land redistribution, such as the PCT, promotion of rentals by groups of landless or nonviable small farmers, and urbanization of rural areas may be able to reduce the emphasis on expropriations and consequently break the link between its land reform policy and rural conflicts.

Introduction

Land has been a source of political power throughout most of the world's history. Landowners have been able to obtain large rents based on this power, either by passing appropriate legislation or by using brute force or other means.

However, the role of land as a source of power has declined over time. On the one hand, land values comprise only a small part of the value of production since a modern and competitive agriculture requires large amounts of renewable capital and technology. On the other, with the development of financial markets and financial innovations, land has become much less important as a store of wealth in most societies.

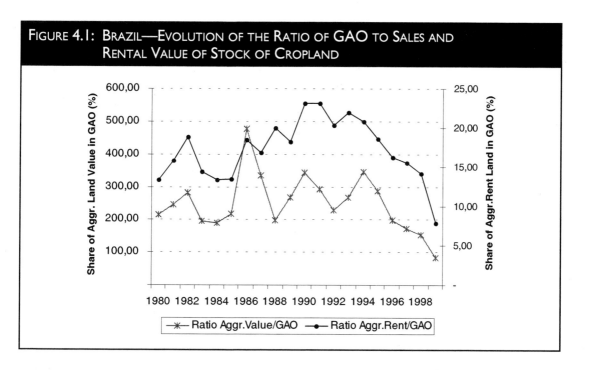

FIGURE 4.1: BRAZIL—EVOLUTION OF THE RATIO OF GAO TO SALES AND RENTAL VALUE OF STOCK OF CROPLAND

Figure 4.1 shows the evolution, for Brazil, of the ratio between the value of agricultural output and the sale and rental values of the corresponding land stock. The dramatic reduction observed in these two ratios since the beginning of the 1990s gives an indication that land is taking a smaller value of agricultural production in Brazil. It is important to stress the fact that the reduction in the ratio has been quite dramatic: it passed from more than 300 percent in 1990 to about 83 percent in 1999. A similar decline is observed for the ratio of the rental value and the value of agricultural production; from over 20 percent to less than 10 percent over the same period.

This fact has important implications on access to credit. Land is a preferred form of collateral by the banking system and most lending operations in Brazil are carried out with guarantees that are larger than 130 percent of the value of the loan. The fact that the stock of land is worth less than the value of agricultural production indicates that land is losing importance in this respect too.

In this paper, we characterize recent policy and institutional changes and price trends in the land market in Brazil. Where are we now? What are the recent land-price trends? What has changed in the ownership structure and average farm size? What has changed in titling and registration situation of lands in Brazil? What has changed in the government's traditional land reform program?

In the second section, we explore some on-going experiences in Brazil on alternatives to traditional view of promoting land ownership through land distribution or land sale markets.

The third section addresses the impact of the recent policy and institutional changes in land markets in Brazil and the listed alternatives on rural poverty alleviation. How sustained is land price decline? What is the impact on the poor population's access to land?

Finally, the last section contains conclusions and policy recommendations.

Recent Changes in Land Markets and Land Policies in Brazil

Recent Evolution of Brazilian Agriculture[55]: Production and harvested area stabilized in the 1990s, after reaching a peak in the middle of the 1980s. But productivity increases were significant in several crops (Figure 4.2). Trade liberalization led to a decline of input prices which affected the

---

55. A detailed description of the recent evolution of Brazilian agriculture is in the chapter by Dias and De Barros.

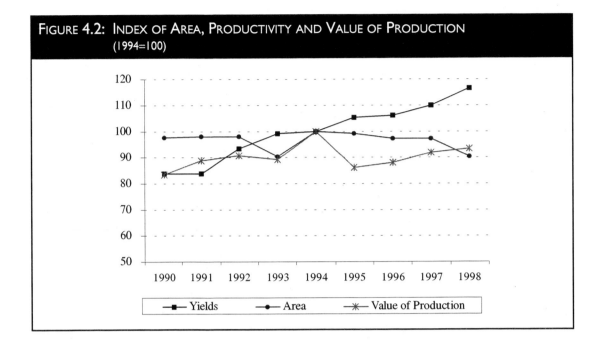

FIGURE 4.2: INDEX OF AREA, PRODUCTIVITY AND VALUE OF PRODUCTION
(1994=100)

domestic terms of trade of agriculture. Figure 4.3, which presents the evolution of the ratio of the producer price index and an index of fertilizer and pesticide prices, shows a significant improvement in this ratio. After the implementation of *Plano Real* in July 1994, agriculture was severely affected by high interest rates and the overvaluation of the currency. In 1999, with the adoption of a floating exchange rate and the devaluation of the domestic currency, output and input prices

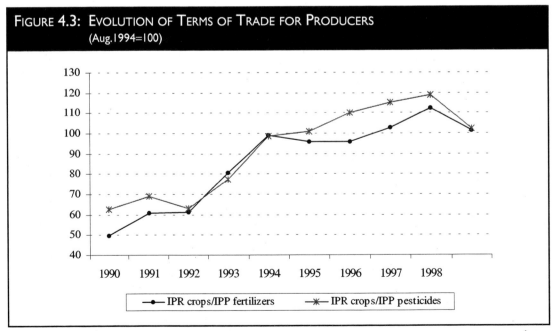

FIGURE 4.3: EVOLUTION OF TERMS OF TRADE FOR PRODUCERS
(Aug.1994=100)

Note: IPR crops—*Índice de Preços Recebidos pelos Produtores—Lavouras* (Producer Price Index for crops); IPP—*Índice de Preços Pagos pelos Produtores* (Prices Paid by Producers Index).
Source: FGV.

were affected. Figure 4.3 shows that the impact on important input prices was larger than the impact on the average basket of production represented by the index of producer prices. The impact on the terms of trade of agriculture is, however, likely to be negative because world prices of commodities exported by Brazil were declining at the time of the devaluation.

Trends in Land Prices: Brazilian land real prices have been falling since 1986 (Figure 4.4). This fall was preceded by a long period of steadily increasing prices that were induced by a number of factors analyzed in the literature (Brandão, 1992; Brandão and Rezende, 1992). The behavior of the economy, of the agricultural terms of trade, credit subsidies, and increasing inflation largely explain this behavior during the 1970s and the 1980s. The rate of decline in land prices increased after 1994, due to the low rates of inflation that prevailed thereafter.

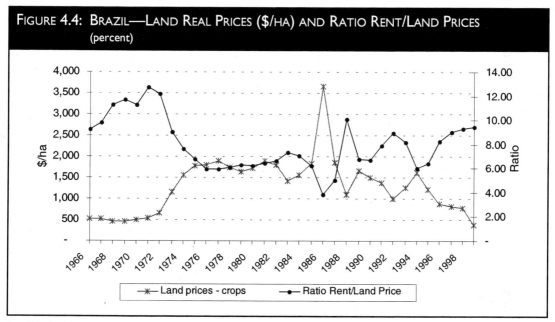

FIGURE 4.4: BRAZIL—LAND REAL PRICES ($/HA) AND RATIO RENT/LAND PRICES (percent)

June/99: $1.00 = R$ 1,75
Source: FGV—Ibre/CEA.

Using the same source of data, Reydon and Plata (n/d) analyzed cropland price trends at the regional level. Except for the North, the study revealed a similar pattern in almost all regions. Cropland prices in the Northeast, North, and Center-west after 1970 were always below the Brazilian average; in the Southeast and South, always above (Appendix Figure 4.1 and Appendix Table 4.1). The similar pattern among different regions indicates that the analysis can proceed using the national average cropland price data.

A closer look at data suggests the following additional observations:

- From 1971 to 1975, the increase in land prices was largely due to the commodity boom observed in that period which led to a significant increase in the terms of trade of agriculture, and to concessionary interest rates in agricultural credit. Furthermore, this was a period of strong economic growth;
- From 1975 to 1983, land real prices were relatively stable. There were a number of relatively opposite forces operating in the economy during that time. On the one hand, the policy of concessionary interest rates persisted (and the subsidy has indeed increased) and inflation rates started to go up. On the other hand, however, the overvaluation of the economy and the reduced rate of growth had an opposite effect.

■ Between 1983 and 1994, land prices oscillated drastically. This was a period characterized by high and unstable inflation and by several pseudo macroeconomic stabilization plans, which have affected deeply the returns of financial assets in the economy, and this has spilled over to land prices.[56] As noted before, the decline in prices was quite significant after 1994: between June 1994 and June 1995, they fell by 42 percent and from June 1995 to December 1998, they fell even more (44 percent). Because of the devaluation of the Brazilian currency and because of expectation of increase in inflation, an increase of about 3.5 percent was observed in the first semester of 1999.

The decline observed during the land rental prices of the 1970's and 1980's was associated with a simultaneous increase in the volume of credit to agriculture and decrease in the rate of interest charged on agricultural credit (Brandão and Rezende, 1992). From 1972 to 1986, credit subsidy as a percentage of value of agricultural production ranged from 0 to 31 percent. During this period, deflated monetary correction of credit varied from 0 to -28 percent.

The decline in land prices observed after 1994 poses a new dimension for the analysis of the role of land markets and rural poverty. In what follows, we review the most significant hypotheses that have been brought up in recent Brazilian literature.

Reydon and Plata (n/d) argue that the effect of high interest rates and low inflation rates have contributed to the downward trend in land prices.[57] The high interest rates, coupled with an environment of price stability, took away from land its attractiveness as an asset since it became easier to find assets with higher liquidity and lower risk-levels.

One additional point is whether there is room for further declines in prices. A simple comparison with neighboring countries lead the authors to find that land prices in Brazil are 3 to 4 times higher than they are in Uruguay (Reydon and Plata, n/d).

Equilibrium land prices in Brazil could be lower than what they actually are, but there are several obstacles to overcome before the land market in Brazil may function adequately to support such a decline: high ownership concentration; difficulties associated with value assessment and enforcement for tax purposes (despite the fact that that land tax legislation has improved in recent years); the need for improvement of titling and land registration; inadequate legislation regarding the rental and sharecropping contracts.

Further on in this paper is a brief update on issues that may affect land prices and, consequently, land access, in Brazil.

The Ownership Structure: Concentration

Brazil's agrarian structure has remained unchanged for the last 25 years (Table 4.1). Large states (some unproductive, others hiring labor and capital intensive) co-exist with a small farm sector, comprised mostly of poor families. Although the number of farms with less than 10 ha decreased by 22 percent, as opposed to the previous agricultural census, it still accounts for nearly 50 percent of the agricultural establishments in Brazil, a proportion that has been kept the same since the 1970s.

Comparing the two last censuses, with the exception of few states (Roraima, Ceará, Espírito Santo, and Mato Grosso), all regions present a reduction in the number of agricultural establishments. The greatest reductions occurred in the Northeast and Southeast (Appendix Table 4.2).

During the 10-year gap between the last two agricultural censuses, a process of ownership concentration took place (Table 4.2). Almost 700,000 small farms were incorporated by larger farms or by other activities (the total area of agricultural farms in Brazil decreased 5.6 percent). Overall, the average size of farms had increased in all regions from 1985 to 1995, except in the states of Ceará, Bahia, Minas Gerais, Espírito Santo, Acre, Amazonas and Amapá (Table 4.2).

---

56. For a greater detailed analysis of the evolution of land prices and the impact of macroeconomic stabilization plans, see Reydon and Plata (n/d).

57. Brandão and Rezende (1986 and 1993) econometric analysis indicated that both the interest rate and the rate of inflation have large effects on the real price of land.

TABLE 4.1: BRAZIL—SHARE OF AGRICULTURAL ESTABLISHMENTS BY GROUPS OF
FARM SIZE: 1970–1995

Farm Size (ha)	Share (percent)				
	1970	1975	1980	1985	1995
0–10	51.2	52.1	50.4	52.8	49.4
10–100	39.3	38.0	39.1	37.2	39.4
100–1000	8.4	8.9	9.5	8.9	9.7
>1000	0.7	0.8	0.9	0.9	1.0
Undeclared	0.4	0.2	0.2	0.2	0.4
Total (`000 farms)	4,924	4,997	5,160	5,802	4,860

Source: IBGE Agricultural censuses 1970, 1975, 1980, 1985, 1995/96.

TABLE 4.2: BRAZIL—EVOLUTION OF AVERAGE SIZE OF FARM BY GROUPS OF
FARM SIZE: 1970–1995

Farm Size (ha)	Average size (ha/farm)				
	1970	1975	1980	1985	1995
0–10	3.6	3.5	3.5	3.3	3.3
10–100	31.1	31.7	32.0	32.2	32.7
100–1000	262.2	259.8	259.6	254.0	262.9
>1000	3,152.6	3,347.6	3,435.6	3,252.1	3,231.4
Average size	59.7	64.8	70.7	64.6	72.8
Total Area (`000 ha)	294,144	323,896	364,655	374,925	353,611

Source: IBGE Agricultural censuses 1970, 1975, 1980, 1985, 1995/96

Gasques and da Conceição (2000) estimated land concentration indexes based on data from IBGE agricultural censuses. The results indicated that the concentration process was halted in 1980, but since then, the concentration index did not change from the 0.856–0.857 levels. An analysis by region reveals interesting differences. The North region is where the strongest concentration process occurred during the past 10 years. In the Northeast, states of Ceará and Alagoas have been under a land concentration process during the past 15 years. The Center-west is the region with greater reduction in concentration of land, a process that has been taking place since 1975 (Appendix Table 4.A3.).

In summary, the Brazilian farm structure seems to be moving towards the American archetype. According to Tables 4.1. and 4.3., a fraction of farms (10.7 percent of agricultural establishments

TABLE 4.3: BRAZIL—SHARE OF VALUE OF PRODUCTION (VOP) BY GROUPS OF
FARM SIZE: 1970–1995

Farm Size (ha)	Share (percent)				
	1970	1975	1980	1985	1995
0–10	17.8	14.8	13.0	11.8	12.2
10–100	40.0	38.5	37.7	36.4	34.4
100–1000	29.3	32.9	33.2	34.9	32.3
>1000	12.6	13.6	16.0	16.8	21.0

Source: IBGE Agricultural censuses 1970, 1975, 1980, 1985, 1995/96.

over 100 ha) produce the bulk of production (53 percent of the value of production registered in the 95/96 census).

The process of ownership concentration between the two agricultural censuses took place simultaneously with several changes in the Brazilian economy and in Brazilian agricultural policies. Interest rate subsidies were severely reduced, tariffs for agricultural products and inputs were reduced, and the volume of credit drastically reduced (see Chapter 2 on the Dynamics of the Brazilian Small Farm Sector). But, during most of the time that has elapsed between these two censuses, Brazil has struggled with high and unstable inflation rates and this has always been an important force pushing real land prices up (Brandão and Rezende, 1992) and accelerating ownership concentration.

Tax Assessment

In theory, land taxes were to be an economic instrument to constrain the process of land concentration and promote the dynamics of land markets. However, until 1990, this instrument was almost ineffective, representing only a small fraction of federal revenue with tax collection. After April 1990, law N° 8.022 changed the agency responsible for collection of land taxes from INCRA (the National Institute for Colonization and Agrarian Reform) to the Ministry of Finance. Because of this change, in 1992, the Federal revenue generated from this tax collection jumped from 0.2 percent of the GDP to 0.5 percent. In 1999, the situation did not change much from the previous period with INCRA, when U$ 273 million was collected, approximately 0.2 percent of the Brazilian GDP.

Taxes are progressive, and establishments with less than two fiscal modules (*módulos fiscais*) are exempt from paying land taxes.[58] Farms with an area greater than 100 fiscal modules pay 3.5 percent of the total land value of unexplored land. Still, this payment can be reduced by almost 90 percent, according to the intensity of exploration of land and productivity levels attained. In fact, these exemptions eliminate the progressive feature of the land tax, reducing its effectiveness.

Experiences in many developing countries suggest that collecting a uniform land tax may be a more realistic goal than using a progressive system, Deininger and Feder (1998). A flat tax could be applied based on the location and size of the farm (Guanziroli et al., 1995). The possibility of transferring the tax collection responsibility to local agencies may also improve its efficiency.

Titling and Registration

In Brazil, land is either public or private. Public land becomes private through its transfer from the Union or States to settlers pertaining to land reform programs (Land Statute, 1964), through the application of "usucapião" laws (Civil code, Land Statute and the 1981 Special Law for "usucapião"— through which squatters have their property rights recognized), and transfer to the private sector through sale (auction or bidding).

Private ownership is the rule (Table 4.4) and accounts for almost 75 percent of farm establishments.[59] There are some regional disparities, mainly in the Northeast, where only 64 percent

---

58. The fiscal module is obtained by dividing the total area utilized by the *município* fiscal module. The *município* fiscal module is calculated as total area (-) legal reserve (-) area of permanent conservation (-) areas of ecological interest (-) forested area with native species (-) not arable area (-) area occupied by constructions (-) mining area.

59. Different situation observed in other countries. According to Lopez and Valdes (1999), in most Latin American countries relatively few small and medium-sized farmers have legal title to their land; less than 55 percent of the farmers in Honduras, Paraguay and Colombia. On the other hand, part-time farming and rentals are the most common sources of land tenure in developed countries.

TABLE 4.4: BRAZIL—SHARE OF NUMBER OF FARMS BY LAND TENURE
(percent)

	1970	1975	1980	1985	1995
Owners	66.76	64.06	65.72	64.60	74.16
Renters	13.76	11.41	11.36	9.91	5.51
Sharecroppers	1.98	5.98	6.18	7.65	5.70
Squatters	17.49	18.55	16.76	17.84	14.61
# Farms (`000)	4,636	4,997	5,160	5,802	4,860

Source: IBGE Agricultural censuses 1970, 1975, 1980, 1985, 1995/96.

of the farmers are landowners. Maranhão, Piauí and Ceará are the only states in Brazil with less than 50 percent of landowners (Table 4.A4). Farms with squatters are relatively numerous in the Northeast and North, 21.6 percent and 18.2 percent; a situation that changed significantly from the 1985 Agricultural census for the North (34.1 percent), but not significantly for the Northeast (22.7 percent).

The inconsistency of institutions prepared to handle the technical and legal aspects of land registration, the registries or "*cartórios,*" lead to multiple titles for the same parcel and improper specification of boundaries (called *grilagem*).[60]

In fact, land market transactions in Brazil take place based in widely accepted titles of property, not so much affected by its reliability. Nonetheless, deficiencies in the land information system compromise the well functioning of the markets due to higher transaction costs.

When there are market and institutional failures inhibiting or contributing to the mal-functioning of land markets (both sales and rental), "individual titling programs that represent the ultimate in making private ownership complete may be neither necessary nor sufficient to achieve efficiency in land use" (De Janvry et al., 1999). Under incomplete specification of property rights or market failures, there are other alternatives where land access can improve for example, through developing land rental markets. The relative low and declining participation of renters and sharecroppers in the Brazilian agriculture suggests that there are still obstacles against access to land markets.[61]

Recent Changes in Legislation and Impact on Land Rental Markets

Three legal documents regulate the temporary use of land and other agrarian contracts[62]:

- The Land Statute, law N° 4,504, of November 30th, 1964 (particularly sections I, II and III of Chapter IV, from Title III)
- Law N° 4,947, of April 6, 1966, which set Agrarian Rights;
- Decree N° 59,566, of November 14, 1966, which regulates the above.

---

60. Entries in the registries are not the same as the "rural property cadaster" maintained by INCRA. The INCRA cadaster is based on landholder's self-declaration, and it was used for fiscal purposes, but still being used for expropriation purposes.

61. For the last agricultural census, some methodological changes occurred. These changes were on the definition of agricultural establishments to avoid double counting of agricultural production from sharecropping areas and larger farms that contained the sharecropping areas. Thus, the drastic decline on other forms of land tenure, but private land ownership, may be partially explained by this methodological change.

62. See appendix Table 4.5. for a chronological list of laws and decrees associated to land markets.

It is important to observe that those instruments were created to give support to Land Reform objectives to regulate labor relations in the rural areas, rather than regulate land access for renters and sharecroppers (Romeiro and Reydon, 1994).

In general, these laws require a very detailed description of agrarian contracts (Article 12 from Decree N° 59,566), and are effective even under verbal agreements. The provisions of the Land Statute set fixed and ceiling prices for rentals (Articles 17 and 95, from Land Statute), and conditions and percentages for sharecropping (Article n. 96, from Land Statute).

Notwithstanding, the provision in the Land Statute "provides nearly permanent rights to tenants after a few years . . . In addition, the Land Statute contains other provisions that relate the incidence of renting and sharecropping to the possibility of expropriation of farms" (World Bank, 1993). Under the widespread condition of informal sharecropping contracts, landlords run the risk of having the sharecroppers claim rights granted by the labor legislation which are often recognized by the labor courts as evidence of "occupation" provided by the sharecroppers (or lack of counter-evidence provided by the landlords).

Another source of land insecurity is in the Land Statute, which says that land can be expropriated if it does not fulfill its social function. However, the criterion to classify whether land is made productive is not very clearly specified. According to Alston et al. (1998), this is a major cause for rural conflicts and invasions.

The most recent changes are described in Dias (2000) and summarized below:

- Complimentary laws, N° 76/93 and 88/96, defined the Summary Rite ("Rito Sumário"), which expedites the process of acquiring ownership from expropriated land through the previous deposit of TDA's (Agrarian Debt Titles) relative to the price of land, and the deposit in cash relative to the buildings and other constructions on the property.
- A provisory measure giving INCRA authorization to visit an establishment without previous authorization of the landowner, and also delegated States to cadastre land and evaluate properties.
- Complimentary law N° 93/8, decrees 2614/98 and 2680/98, provisory measure 1901–2899 creating a fund to finance land acquisition by rural landless or household farmers without enough land to generate sufficient income for subsistence. The fund is called *Banco da Terra*. These laws also authorize INCRA to buy and sell land for agrarian reform purposes where there is a high local demand for land or social pressures.

A second reading of these changes suggests that not much has been done to diminish land insecurity. Thus, the development of formal sharecropping/tenancy arrangements is deterred. Informal/verbal agreements may occur, but cannot be long lasting otherwise sharecroppers/tenants could invoke land-right claims granted via land and labor legislation.

Situation of land reform in Brazil. The government has two tracks on land reform, the older INCRA program and the most recent *Banco da Terra,* a market-assisted land reform. The *Banco da Terra* was created after the experience of *Cédula da Terra* program (See box 4.1 for a description of *Cédula da Terra* program—PCT and comparison with *Banco da Terra*).

However, land expropriation and official settlements are still the main instruments for agrarian reform in Brazil. Only in 1998, more than 100,000 families were settlers, representing almost 22 percent of the total families settled since 1985 (Table 4.5).

The traditional model of land distribution adopted in Brazil can be seen as an instrument of force used to distribute land from large farmers (*latifundiarios*) to landless workers (Teofilo

BOX 4.1: THE LAND COOPERATIVE PROGRAM AND *BANCO DA TERRA*

The Land Cooperative Program (*Programa Cédula da Terra* - PCT), negotiated with the World Bank and implemented at the end of 1997, consists of forming groups/associations of workers or small farmers to buy a tract of land, which they are interested in. After the identification of the area, the group prepares a legal brief for its acquisition, and presents it to the state-level technical entity. If the proposal is approved, the group will receive financing for the purchase, with a repayment period of 20 years. For this purpose, INCRA signs agreements with the Bank of Brazil (BB) and with regional banks like the Bank of the Northeast (BN), which will initially administer the program.

Project implementation, originally planned to benefit 15,000 families over three years, is running well ahead of schedule. At the end of January 1999, 7,619 families had received land and titles to 204,395 ha, or about 27 ha per family (see Appendix Table 8.26. in Amsberg's Chapter (9) on Public Policies to Reduce Rural Poverty). The remaining 7,000 families have negotiated land purchases and will receive loans shortly. Demand is running far ahead of the Project, with another 28,000 families currently in line for approval of purchase proposals totaling about 808,000 ha.

A prior evaluation of the program shows that prices for one hectare negotiated under the PCT were much lower than the expropriation costs of INCRA or the land reference value calculated by Getulio Vargas Foundation (see table). On average, prices were 62 percent lower in Maranhão, 66 percent in Ceará, 14 percent in Pernambuco, 43 percent in Bahia, and 49 percent in Minas Gerais.

The success of PCT encouraged the government to expand its ideas through the Land Bank Program (*Banco da Terra* - created on February 4, 1998 but regulated only on April 13, 1999 by the Decree N° 3.027), which offers subsidized credit to rural workers, small producers, or organizations of workers and producers, to buy land and invest on infrastructure. The loans can be repaid in 20 years and include a 3-year grace period.

TABLE: CROPLAND PRICES (FGV), COST PER HECTARE IN CÉDULA DA TERRA, AND EXPROPRIATION COST BY INCRA, IN R$ (REAIS)

Region	FGV[a]	Cost per hectare Cédula da Terra[b]	Expropriation cost INCRA[c]
Northeast	396.0	167.3	539.4
Maranhão	189.2	93.6	244.6
Ceará	171.2	132.2	385.6
Pernambuco	659.7	593.2	687.8
Bahia	572.1	191.9	333.9
M. Gerais	978.7	306.5	604.6

[a]Land real price—FGV—IBRE/CEA (prices at June/1998).
[b]Average cost per hectare, Informe Cédula da Terra, September 1998, Núcleo de estudos Agrários e Desenvolvimento—NEAD
[c]Average price of expropriated land by INCRA per hectare 1996–1998, Department of Finance—INCRA. In Gasques, J. e Conceição Da, J. Demanda de terra para a reforma agrária no Brasil Box 5, p 38, Brasília Nov. 1998.

Programs like *Banco da Terra* exist in other countries (Guatemala—Penny Foundation, El Salvador, Costa Rica, Equador—*Fondo Popularum Progression*, and Chile—*Fondo de Tierras Indigenas*), but there are major problems related to availability of enough funding and repayment capacity (Raydon and Plata, n/d)

et al, 1998). The heavy government participation in the entire process of expropriation and land distribution results in expropriated prices that are usually more than three times the average land prices. The World Bank (1997) estimated that there is approximately 33 percent of cost savings per family using the market-assisted-land-reform approach instead of the traditional approach (Appendix Table 4.6).

TABLE 4.5: SETTLED FAMILIES AND PROJECTS 1985/1998		
Year	Number of families	Number of Projects
1985–1989	83,732	506
1990–1992	45,137	229
1993–1994	36,481	111
1995	42,827	314
1996	61,674	433
1997	81,944	644
1998	101,094	965
Total	452,889	3,202

Source: 1985–1994, Guanziroli (1999) and 1995–1998, INCRA.

Notwithstanding, estimates of potential beneficiaries are high (but vary substantially across studies), ranging from 1.8 million to 4.5 million (David et al., 1999; Russo, 1998; Gasques and Conceição, 2000).[63, 64, 65]

Given the cross-regional variability in land prices, the estimated number of beneficiaries, and per-beneficiary cost estimate, based only on land price (not taking into account working capital and investment subsidies), if there were 3.5 million families who could be benefited, with an average of 27 ha/family and an average expropriated cost of land of R$ 680/ha (see Table 4A.7), then the total project cost would be R$64 billions. This is a lower bound estimate and is more than forty times larger than the national land-reform budget for 1999.[66] Clearly, the cost of reaching such a vast number of beneficiaries would require a considerable increase in the Brazilian fiscal budget. Due to fiscal constraints, land expropriation, or the program that gives incentives to buy land, will not be a viable solution to solve the problems of rural poverty in Brazil.

Another important point to consider is the generation of land conflicts in Brazil caused by the current expropriation policies (Alston et al., 1998). The large time gap between the identification of areas for expropriation and the actual settlement indirectly stimulates occupation and other rural conflicts. In addition, political pressures from social movements preclude the possibility of substituting the INCRA land reform program and give support to the traditional form of agrarian reform (Navarro, 1999).

"Therefore it (the government) has been forced to seek new land reform policies while still persisting with the old land reform model. As these new policies and others start to take effect, the government may be able to reduce the emphasis on expropriations and consequently break the link between its land reform policy and rural conflicts. Doing so will require that the government be in a position to provide credible commitments, and not respond to invasions by expropriating the land and settling the group that invaded. Until now, however, it has not been able to do so, since expropriation is often the path of least resistance to solve any given conflict" (Alston et al., 1998).

---

63. David et al. (1999) estimated that only for the North Region, there is a potential demand of 1,6 million people for agrarian reform, 80 percent of the total rural poor in the North Region with less than a quarter of the minimum wage per month.

64. Based on INCRA data, Russo estimated the potential demand for Agrarian Reform. Taking into account the area landowners declared as being arable (*explorável*) and the average size of *municípios* fiscal modules (North: 65 hectares; Northeast: 45 hectares; Southeast: 24 hectares; South: 18 hectares; Center-west: 52 hectares), there is a potential to settle 2,6 million of families of rural workers country-wide, using the instrument of land expropriation. If the area declared by landowners as being arable is not taken into account and non-arable land is maximized according to the law (area of permanent preservation, legal reserve, and not usable) in 70 percent for the North, 40 percent in the Northeast and Center-west (except Mato-Grosso, 60 percent) and 30 percent in the South and Southeast, there is a potential demand of 1,8 million families of rural workers to be settled in Brazil.

65. Gasques and da Conceição based their estimates on the last agricultural census data. They considered the following categories as potential beneficiaries, sharecroppers, squatters, renters, landowners with size of farm less than the family property, and landless rural workers. The total number of families under the categories listed added to 4.52 million.

66. In 1999, Congress approved R$ 1.4 billion to agrarian reform conducted by INCRA, R$ 30 million to PCT, and R$ 122 million to the Fund of land and agrarian reform ("*Fundo de Terrras e Reforma Agrária*").

These difficulties indicate the need for reform, both in the legislation and in the land administration system, in order to eliminate the existing barriers that allow improvement of this market. The discussion of these reforms lies beyond the scope of this paper. Needless to say, a careful cost benefit analysis of the reform of the land administration system vis a vis the traditional land settlement programs is badly needed. The authors suspect that cost benefit ratios for the land administration reform are much lower than for traditional land reform programs.

Alternatives to the Traditional Land Reform Program

In our view, under current Brazilian conditions, the land sale market is not the main road to rural poverty alleviation. Under an environment of capital scarcity and credit limitation, alternatives that require less capital mobilization should be preferred, such as sharecropping or renting. There are some on-going experiences in different regions of Brazil that promote access to land without altering the land-ownership structure. Two interesting experiences are worth describing, the Small Rural Villages and the Sharecropper and Rural Leasing Exchange. The latter will be commented in detail.

■ Small Rural Villages (vilas rurais)

The government of the state of Paraná, in partnership with the municipalities, is also innovating. It is buying land around the medium-sized cities and transforming them into urban lots to be distributed to the so-called "bóias-frias"—temporary rural workers, who migrate following the harvest-cycle.

The rural villages are plots of ½ hectare. They are associated with a school, health-center and complete urban infrastructure: potable water, basic sanitation and public lighting. With better living conditions, the migrant worker tends to stay on the plot and has an incentive to produce vegetables, both for his own consumption and for sale in the local market.

Such policies to urbanize rural zones have had good results and have had an immediate positive impact on the quality of life of these people. At the same time, they inhibit migrations to the large-urban-center slums. However, this alternative is not applicable everywhere in Brazil.

■ Sharecropper and Rural Leasing Exchange.

In the Triângulo Mineiro region, an experience proved that even without expropriating land or altering the land-ownership structure, it is possible to form partnerships that improve the economic situation of the landless farmers. In 1985, Uberaba, in Minas Gerais, had the same problem that affects most of Brazil's agricultural sector: a low level of land utilization and a great potential to attract capable professional farmers. There were 200,000 idle hectares in the region.

The Bank of Brazil's Agricultural Credit Department (*Carteira de Crédito Agrícola*), in conjunction with the municipal government and the rural landowners, proposed a simple, viable and innovative solution to resolve the problem: to create the Sharecropper and Rural Leasing Exchange in Brazil (*Bolsa de Parceria e Arrendamento Rural do Brasil*). In the following harvest (1986/87), through the rental exchange, 72 leasing contracts were signed to cultivate more than 21,000 hectares. There was no government bureaucracy in this process.

The contracts had a term of five years and were renewable. The leaseholder's payment varied from 5 percent of his annual income as of the second harvest, to 15 percent for the last two harvest years. Access to the land was granted with the knowledge of the municipality and was financed with normal bank credit. Professional farmers from Minas Gerais, São Paulo, Goiás and even Japan, along with farmers from Rio Grande do Sul and Santa Catarina—who has German and Italian traditions—formed the pioneer group of lessees.

The experience has also expanded to Uberlândia, with twenty-five tenants producing on 21,000 hectares, an average of 850 hectares per tenant. As far as we can observe, this initiative has worked very well—in both regions—for a very selective category of producers (those with ability to cultivate large areas, not necessarily landless, and most likely well educated, with some managerial skill).

Romeiro et al carried out a survey on the profile of the landowners and renters, in Uberaba, Uberlândia (Minas Gerais) and Nova Andradina (São Paulo).

In Minas, the survey detected two types of landowners. In most of the sample (60 percent) the landowners were cattle raisers who rented from 5 percent to 75 percent of their pastures, with the main objective of having renovated fields for pastures at the end of the contract. Another group of landowners, also cattle raisers, decided to rent land because they were unable to explore it, either due to aging or for not having descendants working in agriculture. In São Paulo, the main justification for renting land was lack of conditions to run their own business.

In general, the Rural Leasing Exchange experience is not oriented to social goals, but to increase agricultural output. Most of the renters came from the South region of Brazil (with the exception of Uberaba). At least 50 percent of the renters are landowners in their place of origin. Labor in rented areas is usually from the household or hired. The rented area is usually greater than 100 ha. Therefore, in general, these are medium to large size areas, and the renter is an agent with some entrepreneurial capacity, not an uneducated rural landless or temporary rural worker (*bóia-fria*).

Notwithstanding, we believe that the Rental Exchange idea contains elements that might work as a good strategy for rural poverty alleviation. The literature has given full support to the development of rental markets as an instrument to address the problem of rural poverty and land access under incomplete and imperfect market environment.

The Impacts on Rural Poverty Alleviation

Lower land prices. As noted above, the decline in land prices is likely to be sustained as long as macroeconomic conditions improve. However due to legal, economic, and physical obstacles it may not represent significant improvement in land access.

Lower land prices are necessary but not sufficient conditions for rural poor to gain access to land. Other factors may constitute a barrier for the entry of rural poor into the land market. The lack of formal education, limited access to information, and other characteristics in addition to limited availability of long-term credit reduce the demand for land by low-income households and, thus, should be considered in the overall analysis.

Traditional land reform and market-based assisted land reform. Poor rural families are constrained by credit availability, lack of efficient commercialization channels, and production of low aggregated value products. Thus, settler or farmer under land programs with the objective to promote private ownership of land may not generate enough income to remain beyond the poverty line. Consequently, the propensity to sell the plot of land and migrate to urban centers would be high.

A study from the National Confederation of Agriculture and Getulio Vargas Foundation, (CNA, 1999) found that the willingness to migrate is mainly influenced by the search for better educational opportunities for siblings, insufficient agricultural income to support family standard of living, and desire to change activity. Analyzing siblings separated from the entire family, the propensity to migrate considerably increases in all samples (South, Southeast, Center-west, Pernambuco and Ceará).

Lopez and Valdes (1999) showed that land redistribution from large to small farmers might contribute to increase farm output but have a limited impact on household income.[67] To have a sizeable impact on rural poverty, massive land redistribution would be necessary. They give the

---

67. The contribution of land to per capita income was small, as measured by the elasticity of income with respect to land which in most cases was not higher than 0.15. On the other hand, the elasticity of farm output to land fluctuated between 0.36 and 0.46.

example of Colombia, where raising per-capita income of the poorest 40 percent of farm house-holds up to the poverty line would require almost quadrupling their current land area.

In Chapter 5, Lopez and Romano found that the marginal effect of having more land is practically negligible for small farmers (revenue elasticity of 0.008), while it is large and highly significant for large farmers (revenue elasticity of 2.04).

▓ Land Cooperative Program.

Until the completion of this report, there was not any official report with an ex-post evaluation of the program.

There is an on-going passionate debate on the relative success of the PCT. While the World Bank and Brazilian government finds the program a great success, the program has been attacked by the leaders of the main Brazilian social movements related to land reform.

The claims refer to unattained objectives, concern that beneficiaries will be unable to repay debts entered into under the Project (the Project is leading to increased prices of agricultural land available to rural workers). In general, the major social movements are concerned that the Project be transformed into an alternative/substitute model instead of a complement to Brazil's Constitutionally mandated land reform program. To evaluate the PCT lies beyond the scope of this study. A complete assessment of the impacts of an expansion of the PCT countrywide must be carried out once a series of evaluation reports are completed by the Bank (see appendix Table 4.8.).

Navarro (1999) claims that the innovative idea of giving credit to associative forms of workers and/or producers may not be sustainable unless a program to support the organization or association is created.

The national forum for Agrarian Reform and Rural Justice (*Fórum Nacional pela Reforma Agrária e Justiça no Campo*) pointed out many cases in which the price per hectare under the PCT program was much higher than the average published by Getulio Vargas Foundation. To overcome this problem, Navarro (1999) suggested the creation of a State Commission of the PCT, a neutral and "public space" that would evaluate the final decisions in the negotiations for the acquisition of properties, instead of government doing so. This would prevent PCT from becoming a land-price speculation program.

Another important issue to address is the farmer's payments capacity under PCT or *Banco da Terra*. In the literature there is evidence demonstrating that indebted farmers deviate money received to invest in production for consumption.[68]

According to Rezende (1999), there are strong reasons behind deviation and default of Procera loans. In the past, during high inflation periods, Procera loans were corrected by half of the inflation of the month.[69] Unclear operations and successive debt forgiveness invited default, while new loans were being offered.[70] Lack of Incra monitoring allows indebted settled farmers to transfer rights to a new settler, who in turn has access to new credit lines from Procera. The risk of financial institutions lending Procera money is absorbed by the National Treasury, thus project viability is neither important, nor is technical assistance or monitoring.

---

68. According to Buainain and Souza Filho (1998[0]), money from loans is spent on consumer goods (TV's, fridges, etc) instead of investment in production. Bruno and Medeiros (1998[0]) found that the effect of highly subsidized interest rates in PROCERA had contrary effects. Instead of increasing the probability of success of the settled, it was increasing evasion—so the debt was not paid, and the new owner of the plot of land did not carry past debts.

69. After the "Real" Plan, with lower inflation rates, the real value of the debt is not lowered unless the debt was paid. If payments are not due, the farmer can be eligible for a 50 percent rebate on interest rates.

70. One important feature of the Procera system is that resources come mainly from constitutional funds, which are not under fiscal or budget pressures. They are considered "lost funds." Therefore, even if there are high default rates, the system does not halt, as there is permanent injection of new resources from the constitutional funds.

The capacity of payment also relates to the inherent conditions of family farming activities in Brazil: low rates of return and very high discount rates on consumption. In theory, the settled could graduate only if sufficient income was generated to meet household demands and necessary savings to allow investments in productive activities. However, this is not the case. Family farm production usually faces adverse conditions for commercialization, thus resulting in lower prices when selling the products and lower agricultural income. According to Dias and de Barros (Chapter 2 on "Dynamics of the Brazilian Small Farm Sector"), the rapid concentration of the retail sector favored gains in scale and standardization of production, reinforcing the discrimination in favor of the more technologically advanced producers.

Bittencourt (1999) carried out some payment capacity simulations for farmers who borrowed from *Banco da Terra* to acquire land. The simulations showed that family farms were not able to pay the debt after 20 years. The equivalence-product should be considered as an alternative. Again, the problem is related to the high interest rates and low rates of returns on crops produced by family farming.

According to the Bank, the overall project Internal Economic Rate of Return (IERR) estimated is 32 percent. Even with total failure of 33 percent of subprojects (abandonment of farm after all investments and sale at the purchase prices), the IERR reduces to 25 percent (World Bank, 1997). This is still higher than the cost of a medium-term Government financing estimated at 16 percent (based on the market discount rate of Government land reform bonds with 5–10 year maturity).

Alternatives to land distribution program. The two alternatives presented should not be considered as a substitute but as a complement to the on-going land reform program.

In the case of the Rural Leasing Exchange, it is clear that the experience is not oriented toward social goals but toward increasing agricultural output. Renters are not poor, nor uneducated or low-skilled agricultural landless workers, but the idea contains elements that might work as a good strategy for rural poverty alleviation. The literature gives support to the development of rental markets as instruments that address the problem of rural poverty and land access under incomplete and imperfect market environment.

According to Sadoulet, Murgai and de Janvry (2000), the most important reason why the rental market is superior to the sales market is that the entry subsidy needed for poor households to purchase land is high.[71]

Gasques and da Conceição (2000) estimated from the last agricultural census that renters earned the highest annual gross income, R$28,782, when compared to other categories, such as landowners (R$17,437), sharecroppers (R$12,564) and squatters (R$5,905). This is a rough indication of the potential use of land-rental markets for poverty alleviation in Brazil.

The Small Rural Villages are another interesting alternative to the traditional land reform program conducted by INCRA. Lanjouw's chapter on "Poverty and Non-farm Employment in Rural Brazil" shows relatively low poverty figures based on headcount for rural locations considered as urban extensions, for the Northeast and Southeast regions (Tables 6.3A. and 6.3B.).

Conclusion and Policy Recommendation

a) The declining trend in land prices is likely to continue as long as macroeconomic conditions keep improving. However, it may occur at a lower pace since there are still existing obstacles for land market improvement.

b) Lower land prices can facilitate the access to land on the part of the poor but may not be sufficient to alleviate poverty. Credit, training/education, and conditions for commercialization are also badly needed.

---

71. There are four components to this subsidy: the mortgage payment, the value of side benefits of land ownership (store of wealth, collateral value, insurance value, speculative value, value for tax breaks and access to subsidized credit lines, and political and social capital value), the current costs of capital net of labor earnings, and the transaction costs on land sales market.

c) Legal constraints deter the development of land rental contracts, which in the past were viewed as sources of exploitation of landless workers.

Excessive security regarding continued access to land is given to tenants; and tenants are entitled to ownership based on investments they have made. Insecure property rights for landlords can also deter this market as they see tenants as a threat to regaining control over land.

This view has changed significantly with the understanding that contracts of this type involve trade of several inputs, particularly agent specific non-tradable inputs, such as labor supervision and managerial skills. However, the problem is that the legislation has not changed yet.

d) The government model of land reform through land distribution is a vicious cycle: land is redistributed where there is a social conflict, and social conflicts put pressure on the government land redistribution program.

e) Alternatives to land redistribution co-exist with the traditional model but are not accepted by the social movements.

f) As new alternatives start to take effect, the government may be able to reduce the emphasis on expropriations and consequently break the link between its land reform policy and rural conflicts.

g) Under an environment of capital scarcity and credit limitation, alternatives that require less capital mobilization should be investigated, such as sharecropping or renting.

h) Ideas from the land market-assisted land reform could be applied to land rental contracts such as decentralized and participatory targeting and training of beneficiaries, collective bargaining of contracts and community endorsement.

i) Of course, increasing capitalization of agriculture also makes entry into sharecropping more difficult for the poor. Thus, access to wealth, independent sources of credit (informal credit), and training in management (through extension services) can play a significant role giving potential tenants a better chance to participate in land markets.

References

Alston, Lee J., Gary D. Libecap, and Bernado Mueller. 1998. "A model of rural conflict: violence and land reform policy in Brazil". Unpublished paper.

Binswanger, H. P., K. Deininger and G. Feder, 1995. "Power, Distortions, Revolt and Reform in Agricultural Land Relations", in J. Behrman and T. N. Srinivasan, eds., *Handbook of Development Economics*. Vol. III, Amsterdam: North Holland Publishers.

Bittencourt, Gilson Alceu. Banco da Terra: Análise Econômica e Exemplos de Financiamentos. DESER, 25/06/99 (http://www.dataterra.org.br/Documentos/deser.htm)

Brandão, Antonio Salazar P. 1992. "O Mercado de Terra e Estrutura Fundiária," in Antônio Salazar P. Brandão ed., *Os Principais Problemas da Agricultura Brasileira:* Análise e Sugestões, Serie PNPE, Rio de Janeiro, pp. 139–180.

Brandão, Antonio Salazar P., and Gervasio de Castro Rezende. 1992. *Credit, Subsidies, Inflation and the Land Market in Brazil: A Theoretical and Empirical Analysis.* World Bank, Agricultural Policies Division, Washington, D.C.

Buainain, Antonio Marcio, José Maria da Silveira e Edson Teófilo. 1999. *Reforma agrária, desenvolvimento e participação: uma discussão das transformações necessárias e possíveis.* NEAD documents.

Confederação Nacional da Agricultura/Fundação Getulio Vargas. 1999. *Um perfil do agricultor brasileiro.* Brasília: CNA.

David, Maria Beatriz de Albuquerque, Enali Maria de Biaggi, Mônica dos Santos Rodrigues, Antonio Cesar Schewenk, Antônio Carlos de Albuquerque David, and Rosane Girão Peres. 1996. *II Relatório de Andamento do Projeto Mão-de-Obra, Emprego e Demanda por Reforma Agrária.* PNAD.

Deininger, Klaus and Gershon Feder. 1998. "Land institutions and land markets." Washington: The World Bank. *Policy Research Working Paper,* n. 2014.

Dias, Guilherme. 2000. *Avaliação da legislação e da organização institucional.* unpublished manuscript.

de Janvry, Alain Gustavo Gordillo, Jean-Philippe Platteau, and Elisabeth Sadoulet. 1999. "Access to land, rural poverty, and public action." (Author's preliminary copy, April 1999).

Gasques, J. and J. Conceição Da, 2000. "A Demanda da terra para a reforma agrária no Brasil". In: *Reforma Agrária e Desenvolvimento Sustentável,* Pedro Sisnando Leite et alii (orgs.). Brasília: Ministério do Desenvolvimento Agrário.

Guanzirolli, Carlos E. 1999. "*Reforma Agrária e a Globalização da Economia—o caso do Brasil.*'" Projeto de Cooperação Técnica INCRA/FAO, Brasília, DF.

IBGE, Censo Agropecuário, 1970.

IBGE, Censo Agropecuário, 1975.

IBGE, Censo Agropecuário, 1980.

IBGE, Censo Agropecuário, 1985.

IBGE, Censo Agropecuário, 1995–96.

Lopez, Ramon, and Alberto Valdes. 1999. "Fighting Rural Poverty in Latin America: New Evidence on the Effects of Education, Demographics, and Access to Land". Unpublished.

Navarro, Zander. 1999. O projeto-piloto "Cédula da Terra"—comentário complementar. Report to the World Bank office at Brasilia.

Reydon, Bastiaan P., and Ludwig Agurto Plata. N/d. *Evolução recente do preço da terra rural no Brasil e os impactos do Programa da Cédula da Terra.* (http://www.dataterra.org.br/Documentos/Bastiaan.htm)

Romeiro, Ademar, and Bastiaan Philip Reydon. 1994. "Análise Geral do Mercado de Aluguel de Terras, Aspectos legais e Institucionais," in A. Romeiro and B. Reydon ed., *O Mercado de Terras.* Estudos de Política Agrícola—n. 13, Relatórios de Pesquisa, Março.

Russo, Osvaldo. 1999. Reforma agrária e capacidade de assentamento Brasil, Grandes Regiões e Estados. August 20, (http://www.dataterra.org.br/Documentos/russo2.htm)

Sadoulet, Elisabeth, Rinku Murgai, and Alain de Janvry. 2000. "Access to land via land rental markets". Unpublished.

Teofilo E. et al. 1998. *Diretrizes para a política de desenvolvimento agrário.* Brasília: NEAD.

World Bank. 1993. *Brazil—The Management of agriculture, rural development and natural resources—vol II, background papers.* Environment and Agriculture Division. Latin American and the Caribbean Region. May 27, 1993.

World Bank. 1997. Project appraisal Document on a Proposed Loan in the Amount of US$ 90.0 million equivalent to the Federative Republic of Brazil for a Land Reform and Poverty Alleviation Pilot Project. The World Bank: Natural Resources, Environment and Rural Poverty Division, Country Department I, Latin America and the Caribbean Region. April 3, 1997 (report n. 16342-BR).

Appendix

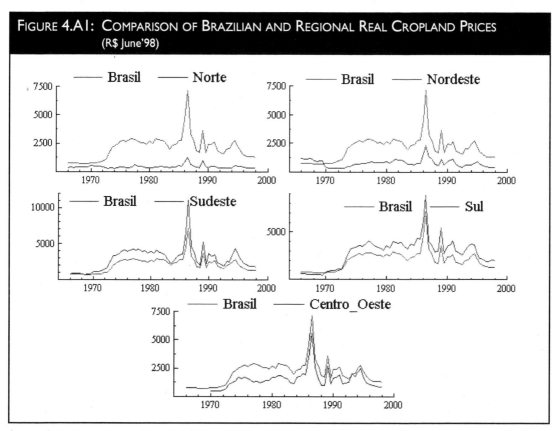

FIGURE 4.A1: COMPARISON OF BRAZILIAN AND REGIONAL REAL CROPLAND PRICES (R$ June'98)

Source: Reydon and Plata (n/d) from FGV-IBRE/CEA

APPENDIX TABLE 4.A1: AVERAGE REAL CROPLAND PRICE FOR BRAZIL AND REGIONS (R$ june '98)

	Brazil	North	Northeast	Southeast	South	Center west
June/1966–dec/1972	788	467	379	1.154	880	545
June/1975–dec/1985	2.607	429	821	3.663	3.680	1.549
Dec/86	7.148	1.267	2.341	11.114	8.801	5.545
June/1988–dec/1994	2.897	489	936	4.095	4.038	1.808
June/1995–dec/1997	1.568	412	571	2.402	2.156	1.089
June/98	1.286	339	396	1.785	2.013	845

Source: Reydon and Plata (n/d) from FGV-IBRE/CEA

TABLE 4.A2: NUMBER OF FARMS, AREA, AVERAGE AREA, BY STATE/REGION

Region/State	Year	# farms	Area (ha)	Avg. size by farm
Brazil	**1985**	**5,804,679**	**374,767,985**	**65**
	1995	**4,859,865**	**353,611,246**	**73**
North Region	**1985**	**543,583**	**62,570,453**	**115**
	1995	**446,175**	**58,358,880**	**131**
Rondônia	1985	80,615	6,032,639	75
	1995	76,956	8,890,440	116
Acre	1985	35,049	5,238,568	149
	1995	23,788	3,183,065	134
Amazonas	1985	116,242	5,859,506	50
	1995	83,289	3,322,566	40
Roraima	1985	6,389	2,149,534	336
	1995	7,476	2,976,817	398
Pará	1985	253,222	24,727,791	98
	1995	206,404	22,520,229	109
Amapá	1985	4,816	1,208,018	251
	1995	3,349	700,047	209
Tocantins	1985	47,250	17,354,397	367
	1995	44,913	16,765,716	373
Northeast Region	**1985**	**2,799,239**	**92,054,621**	**33**
	1995	**2,326,413**	**78,296,096**	**34**
Maranhão	1985	532,413	15,548,463	29
	1995	368,191	12,560,692	34
Piauí	1985	270,443	11,828,019	44
	1995	208,111	9,659,972	46
Ceará	1985	324,278	11,009,154	34
	1995	339,602	8,963,842	26
Rio Grande do Norte	1985	115,736	4,383,313	38
	1995	91,376	3,733,521	41
Paraíba	1985	203,277	4,872,090	24
	1995	146,539	4,109,347	28
Pernambuco	1985	356,041	6,699,918	19
	1995	258,630	5,580,734	22

(continued)

TABLE 4.A2: NUMBER OF FARMS, AREA, AVERAGE AREA, BY STATE/REGION (CONTINUED)

Alagoas	1985	142,774	2,363,766	17
	1995	115,064	2,142,460	19
Sergipe	1985	115,271	1,918,503	17
	1995	99,774	1,702,628	17
Bahia	1985	739,006	33,431,395	45
	1995	699,126	29,842,900	43
Southeast Region	**1985**	**993,975**	**73,244,330**	**74**
	1995	**841,661**	**64,085,893**	**76**
Minas Gerais	1985	551,488	45,836,646	83
	1995	496,677	40,811,660	82
Espírito Santo	1985	69,140	3,895,320	56
	1995	73,288	3,488,725	48
Rio de Janeiro	1985	91,280	3,267,143	36
	1995	53,680	2,416,305	45
São Paulo	1985	282,067	20,245,221	72
	1995	218,016	17,369,204	80
South Region	**1985**	**1,200,545**	**47,794,215**	**40**
	1995	**1,003,180**	**44,360,364**	**44**
Paraná	1985	466,397	16,624,990	36
	1995	369,875	15,946,632	43
Santa Catarina	1985	234,976	7,419,535	32
	1995	203,347	6,612,846	33
Rio Grande do Sul	1985	499,172	23,749,690	48
	1995	429,958	21,800,887	51
Center-west Region	**1985**	**267,337**	**99,104,366**	**371**
	1995	**242,436**	**108,510,012**	**448**
Mato Grosso do Sul	1985	54,631	31,108,806	569
	1995	49,423	30,942,772	626
Mato Grosso	1985	77,921	37,817,644	485
	1995	78,763	49,849,663	633
Goiás	1985	131,365	29,864,098	227
	1995	111,791	27,472,648	246
Distrito Federal	1985	3,420	313,818	92
	1995	2,459	244,930	100

Source: Agricultural Census (1995–1996) from IBGE.

Appendix Table 4.A3: Concentration Index, by Region/State

	1970	1975	1980	1985	1995
BRAZIL	**0.843**	**0.854**	**0.857**	**0.857**	**0.856**
North Region	**0.831**	**0.863**	**0.841**	**0.812**	**0.820**
Acre	0.607	0.623	0.691	0.619	0.717
Amazonas	0.734	0.921	0.870	0.819	0.808
Amapá	0.870	0.853	0.850	0.864	0.835
Pará	0.881	0.867	0.842	0.827	0.814
Rondonia	0.678	0.620	0.647	0.655	0.765
Roraima	0.617	0.887	0.787	0.751	0.813
Tocantins	0.692	0.705	0.739	0.714	0.726
Northeast Region	**0.854**	**0.862**	**0.861**	**0.869**	**0.859**
Alagoas	0.835	0.845	0.846	0.858	0.863
Bahia	0.800	0.811	0.825	0.840	0.834
Ceará	0.790	0.783	0.779	0.815	0.845
Maranhão	0.924	0.926	0.925	0.923	0.903
Paraiba	0.822	0.844	0.828	0.842	0.834
Pernambuco	0.837	0.828	0.824	0.829	0.821
Piauí	0.891	0.898	0.898	0.896	0.873
Rio Grande do Norte	0.853	0.861	0.850	0.853	0.852
Sergipe	0.853	0.853	0.847	0.858	0.846
Southeast Region	**0.760**	**0.761**	**0.769**	**0.772**	**0.767**
Espírito Santo	0.602	0.626	0.655	0.671	0.689
Minas Gerais	0.749	0.755	0.766	0.770	0.772
Rio de Janeiro	0.789	0.789	0.804	0.815	0.790
São Paulo	0.777	0.774	0.773	0.770	0.758
South Region	**0.725**	**0.733**	**0.743**	**0.747**	**0.742**
Paraná	0.699	0.725	0.740	0.749	0.741
Rio Grande do Sul	0.754	0.753	0.761	0.763	0.762
Santa Catarina	0.644	0.656	0.677	0.682	0.671
Center-west Region	**0.876**	**0.876**	**0.861**	**0.857**	**0.831**
Distrito Federal	0.794	0.780	0.753	0.767	0.801
Goiás	0.751	0.760	0.753	0.766	0.740
Mato Grosso do Sul	0.918	0.909	0.871	0.860	0.822
Mato Grosso	0.941	0.943	0.921	0.909	0.870

Source: Gasques and da Conceição (2000) from IBGE Ag. Censuses.

TABLE 4.A4: SHARE OF NUMBER OF FARMS BY LAND TENURE AND BY STATE/REGION
(in percent)

Region/State	Year	Landowners	Renters	Sharecroppers	Squatters
Brazil	**1985**	**64.6**	**9.9**	**7.7**	**17.8**
	1995	**74.2**	**5.5**	**5.7**	**14.6**
North Region	**1985**	**57.7**	**5.1**	**3.1**	**34.1**
	1995	**79.9**	**0.7**	**1.3**	**18.2**
Rondônia	1985	58.3	2.1	11.5	28.1
	1995	85.7	1.2	5.4	7.8
Acre	1985	36.9	15.2	2.9	44.9
	1995	69.4	0.4	0.2	30.1
Amazonas	1985	49.0	11.4	0.4	39.2
	1995	65.7	0.8	0.2	33.4
Roraima	1985	57.4	0.0	0.0	42.6
	1995	88.9	0.2	0.3	10.7
Pará	1985	61.4	2.4	2.2	34.0
	1995	83.0	0.5	0.6	15.9
Amapá	1985	24.5	0.1	0.1	75.3
	1995	76.6	0.1	0.0	23.3
Tocantins	1985	77.3	2.9	1.1	18.7
	1995	86.0	1.0	0.5	12.6
Northeast Region	**1985**	**56.4**	**13.2**	**7.8**	**22.7**
	1995	**64.3**	**6.6**	**7.6**	**21.6**
Maranhão	1985	19.5	38.0	4.4	38.1
	1995	31.8	20.0	6.4	41.8
Piauí	1985	33.9	13.8	22.7	29.5
	1995	45.2	9.2	15.2	30.4
Ceará	1985	53.1	8.0	21.8	17.1
	1995	49.6	5.7	21.9	22.8
Rio Grande do Norte	1985	59.0	9.3	8.4	23.4
	1995	65.1	4.8	10.0	20.1
Paraíba	1985	59.2	12.5	7.5	20.8
	1995	66.2	5.2	5.7	22.9
Pernambuco	1985	61.9	9.5	5.1	23.4
	1995	72.0	3.7	4.3	20.0
Alagoas	1985	60.5	11.7	5.5	22.4
	1995	64.4	9.0	5.9	20.7
Sergipe	1985	76.7	8.0	1.8	13.5
	1995	79.8	4.4	1.0	14.9
Bahia	1985	84.7	1.0	1.2	13.1
	1995	88.7	0.7	1.4	9.3
Southeast Region	**1985**	**79.8**	**5.7**	**6.7**	**7.7**
	1995	**86.6**	**4.4**	**4.3**	**4.7**
Minas Gerais	1985	85.7	3.9	3.0	7.4
	1995	88.5	3.2	3.2	5.2
Espírito Sant	1985	89.5	0.8	1.9	7.8
	1995	93.1	1.1	3.8	2.0

(continued)

TABLE 4.A4: SHARE OF NUMBER OF FARMS BY LAND TENURE AND BY STATE/REGION (CONTINUED)
(in percent)

Rio de Janeiro	1985	68.8	4.6	13.1	13.4
	1995	78.7	4.2	12.3	4.8
São Paulo	1985	69.4	10.8	13.2	6.6
	1995	82.1	8.6	4.9	4.4
South Region	**1985**	**72.8**	**7.8**	**10.6**	**8.8**
	1995	**80.8**	**6.5**	**5.7**	**6.9**
Paraná	1985	65.0	10.4	14.8	9.8
	1995	76.3	7.3	7.6	8.8
Santa Catarina	1985	77.8	6.6	6.9	8.8
	1995	84.3	6.0	3.0	6.7
Rio Grande do Sul	1985	77.6	6.0	8.5	7.9
	1995	83.1	6.2	5.3	5.4
Center-west Region	**1985**	**71.9**	**10.5**	**5.9**	**11.8**
	1995	**87.5**	**3.9**	**1.0**	**7.6**
Mato Grosso do Sul	1985	70.4	11.9	5.0	12.6
	1995	83.8	5.8	0.9	9.5
Mato Grosso	1985	62.7	13.3	6.4	17.7
	1995	86.6	2.1	1.2	10.1
Goiás	1985	78.9	7.4	6.0	7.6
	1995	90.5	3.5	0.9	5.1
Distrito Federal	1985	33.8	40.4	0.9	24.9
	1995	55.3	36.6	2.4	5.7

Source: IBGE - Agricultural Censuses.

of FEDERAL LAWS RELATED TO

	ions of concessions and land alienations made for *elece prazo para as ratificações de concessões e s na faixa de fronteira, e dá outras providências)*
	bagamento em TDA)
	ributions to INCRA (*Reduz alíquotas de con-*
	cking accounts to the program of agrarian reform *ão recadastradas ao programa de reforma agrária)*
	oposition III of art. 82 of Law N° 5.869, 11 of *(Dá nova redação ao inciso III do art. 82 da Lei n° igo de Processo Civil)*
9 9 8.	Tax (*Aplicação da Taxa de Juros de Longo Prazo)* õe sobre o Imposto sobre a Propriedade Territorial
8.	s related to the agrarian reform (*Regulamentação reforma agrária)*
8. 7.	15 of September of 1965, and revokes the and 7.511, of 7 of July of 1986 (*Altera a redação 965, e revoga as Leis n°s 6.535, de 15 de junho)*
7.4	its (*Requisitos para lavratura de escrituras*
6.9	ecial)
6.7	solo urbano)
6.6	
6.4	ônia (*Expansão municipal na Amazônia Legal)*
5.9	erties administratively discriminated or *para o registro de bens imóveis discriminados ião)*
5.95	settlement nucleus (*Doação de imóveis*
5.86	ltural Credit (*Regulamenta o Sistema Nacional*
5.70	oreigners (*Aquisição de imóveis por Estrangeiro)*
4.947—06/04/1966:	Establishes Norms of Agrarian law (*Estabelece Normas de Direito Agrário)*
4.829—05/11/1965:	Institution of the Agricultural Credit (*Instituição do Crédito Rural)*
4.771—15/09/1965:	Institutes the New Forest Code (*Institui o Novo Código Florestal)*
4.755—18/08/1965:	It legilsates on the form of fixing the Union Tax due for the rural establishments (*Dispõe sobre a forma de fixação do Imposto Sindical devido pelos estabelecimentos rurais)*
4.504—30/11/1964:	Land Statute (*Estatuto da Terra)*
601—18/09/1850:	Legislates on vacant lands of the Empire (*dispõe sobre as terras devolutas do Império)*

APPENDIX TABLE 4.A6: PER FAMILY COST OF MARKET-BASED V. TRADITIONAL LAND REFORM (R$)

Northeast	Admin.	Land (Including Improvements)	Start-up Money	Infrastructure	Total
NPV Costs					
Traditional	1,930	6,578*	2,331	2,407	13,246
Market-based	441	3,521	1,300	3,258	8,519
Savings	77 percent	46 percent	44 percent	−35 percent	36 percent
Initial Costs					
Traditional	2,941	8,229*	2,980	3,193	17,343
Market-based	478	4,847	1,300	3,758	10,383
Savings	84 percent	41 percent	56 percent	−18 percent	40 percent

*Excluding costs related to frequent judicial action.
Source: World Bank, 1997. Project appraisal Document.

APPENDIX TABLE 4.A7: AVERAGE PRICE PER HECTARE OF EXPROPRIATED LAND BY INCRA, BETWEEN 1996 AND 1998, IN CURRENT VALUES (R$)

BR	680.73								
North	346.58	**Southeast**	690.21	**C.West**	492.27	**Northeast**	539.42	**South**	1,335.19
AM	357.63	SP	861.10	MT	263.07	MA	244.60	PR	1,261.48
RO	709.63	MG	604.59	MS	745.99	CE	85.65	SC	1,421.30
PA	283.53	RJ	297.72	GO	467.74	AL	630.16	RS	1,322.79
AC	132.24	ES	997.42			PE	846.19		
TO	249.89					BA	333.97		
						PB	687.86		
						SE	728.70		
						RN	463.97		
						PI	533.69		

Source: Gasques and da Conceição (2000) from INCRA - *Departamento de Finanças.*

APPENDIX TABLE 4.A8: LIST OF STUDIES UNDERTAKEN FOR PROJECT *CÉDULA DA TERRA*

Study	Status	Objectives
Case Studies on Implementation and Impact of Land Reform Pilot in Ceara and *Cedula da Terra(CdaT)Project*	Completed 9/98 and 2/99	Detect implementation problems or particular successes in *CdaT* in order to adjust it during implementation and improve the design of any proposed follow-up project. Validate economic and financial parameters used for the economic analysis of the Project
Farm Models and Financial Analysis	Completed 1/97	Evaluate the economic benefits, the financial viability and the family income effect of market-assisted land reform in different regions of the country
Impact of Market-Based Land Reform Pilot in Ceará	Ongoing	Analyze the implementation and the impact of market based land reform for the 43 subprojects included in the first phase pilot in Ceara.
Social Sustainability	Completed 8/98	Provide orientation for the positioning of market-based land reform within the political conflict surrounding land reform in Brazil.
Financial Options Study	Completed 11/98	Analyze and propose alternatives to current financial arrangements in respect to: Commercial risk associated with land loans (see how bad disincentive for collection) Participation of private Banks in the administration of land loans Participation of private capital in land loans or agriculture credit Link with PROCERA and agriculture credit
Cost of Traditional Land Reform Programs	Completed 12/98	An update of the cost of traditional land reform in different regions and agro-zones of the country
Long-term Financing for Land Reform	Draft completed 12/98	Identify sources of financing for market-assisted land reform and policies to mobilize these resources
Impact of Large-Scale Market-Assisted Land Reform (*Banco da Terra*) on Land Markets	Draft completed 12/98	Analyze the impact of large-scale market-based land reform on land prices in different regions of the country Assess the quantity of land available for sale in different regions at different prices
Social Demand for Land Reform	Draft completed 11/98	Determine the number and social situation of potential program beneficiaries Estimate the number of likely beneficiaries of land reform in Brazil by region, current occupation and income Determine expected impact of program on rural poverty and relative size of per-family benefits compared to other social programs.
Small Farm Viability	Ongoing	Evaluate the economic benefits and the financial viability of different scales of agriculture production in different regions for different products
Impact of Large-Scale Market-Assisted Land Reform on Product Markets	Ongoing	Analyze the impact of large-scale market based land reform on product markets in different regions of the country Identify likely constraints in product markets
Institutional Support, Technical Assistance and Environmental Sustainability	Ongoing	Assess institutional and other aspects of Market-Based Land Reform in the Southern part of Brazil

Source: World Bank, 1997. Project appraisal Document.

CHAPTER 5

DETERMINANTS OF FARM REVENUES AND FACTOR RETURNS FOR POOR FARMERS IN BRAZIL

Introduction[72]

There is a high degree of correspondence between income level and farm size among farmers. The vast majority of small farmers are poor, while farmers owning large land areas are generally not poor. Table 6.1 shows the household income of farmers classified into four categories[73] by land size. Farmers in the category minifundia operate land areas of up to 2 hectares; small farmers operate land of between 2.1 and 10 hectares. Each of these smaller groups constitutes about 40 percent of the sampled farm households. Farmers with medium-sized farms operate areas of 10.1 to 50 hectares, while those with large farms range between 50.1 and 2,000 hectares and make-up for approximately 5 percent of the sample.[74]

The average household income of the minifundia is about 5,800 reais, while that of the medium-sized and large farms is about 18,000 and 45,000, respectively. Given this high correlation between income and farm size among farmers, the analysis will focus on characteristics of minifundia vis-à-vis large farms. We thus assume that policies that benefit small farmers will benefit poor farmers, while policies that benefit large farmers are generally doing so for non-poor farmers.

Table 5.2 shows the farm production characteristics of farmers by land size. Comparing minifundia and large farms, we see that the average farm gross revenue among the poorest group

---

72. This paper was prepared by Ramón López and Claudia B. Romano of the University of Maryland at College Park

73. All data analysis in this paper is based on the "*Pesquisa sobre Padrões de Vida*" (PPV), implemented by the Brazilian Statistical Agency (IBGE) in 1996/1997. The sample covers the Northeast and Southeast regions of Brazil, with approximately 1,100 rural households of which around 520 are farmers. For more details about the PPV sample design and characteristics see Romano (2000).

74. The PPV sample was designed to be representative of the resident population. Therefore, the rural component includes only rural residents. As such, there is an under-representation of farmers with large farms that more likely live in urban areas. Here farms smaller than 10 hectares represent 80 percent of the sample, while according to the Agricultural Census 1995/96 this land size category represents 59 percent of all farm establishments in the Northeast and Southeast regions.

TABLE 5.1: INCOME AND DEMOGRAPHIC CHARACTERISTICS BY FARM SIZE CATEGORY[1]				
	Minifundia (up to 2ha)	Small (2.1–10ha)	Medium (10.1–50 ha)	Large (50.1–2000ha)
Household size	4.7	5.0	4.7	4.5
Household income	5,807	9,382	17,511	43,769
percent of farm (self-employment) income in total income	58.5	75.7	72.4	69.5
percent wage income in total income	15.7	5.5	2.5	10.0
percent non-agricultural labor and capital income in total income	9.5	7.1	12.4	13.2

[1]Money values in Reais 1996. Tabulation based on PPV sample.

is approximately one fifth that of farmers with medium-sized farms and twelve times less than that of large farmers. There are also quite important differences in the structure of production of small and large farms, as shown in the share of the various outputs in total farm revenue. We have classified farm outputs into three categories to facilitate the evaluation of the impact of trade and exchange rate policies: (i) import substitutes; (ii) exportable commodities; and (iii) non-trade commodities. Among group (iii) we have commodities that are not traded internationally, including many of subsistence commodities such as tubers, manioc, vegetables, and most fruits. Import substitutes include cereals, cotton, and bean, while exportables include coffee, sugar, orange, and cocoa.[75, 76]

As can be seen in Table 5.2, the share of non-trade commodities in total farm revenues is higher in minifundia than in large farms, 43 percent and 24 percent, respectively. The opposite occurs with exportable commodities that are much less important, as a source of revenues, for minifundia than for large farmers, with 7 percent and 29 percent, respectively. In fact, the share of exportables in total farm revenues for large farmers four times that for minifundia farmers. The share of import substitutes is more similar between minifundia and large farms, at around 50 percent, but higher in the two-intermediate-sized farm groups, reaching 56 percent for small farmers.

One likely implication of these differences in productive structures is that increased trade liberalization that raises the prices of exportables and real exchange rate devaluation that reduces the real price of non-tradables are more likely to be beneficial for large farmers than for those with small (poor farmers) farms. Increasing prices of exportables improves revenues of large farmers to a larger extent than it does for small farmers. Furthermore, lower prices for non-tradables affect small farmers more negatively than it does those with large farms.

With respect to the structure of inputs used, a much greater proportion of large farmers owns capital and livestock and uses more purchased inputs than small farmers. Since a large portion of purchased (variable) inputs are import substitute goods; trade liberalization that reduces their prices is more beneficial for large farmers than it is for those with small farms. Additionally, small farms practically do not receive technical assistance or credit while a significant proportion of large farms does.

Farm Revenues and Prices

The purpose of this section is to provide quantitative insights into the impact of trade policy reform and real exchange rate devaluation on minifundia and large farmers. In Table 5.2, we pre-

---

75. See also Helfland and Rezende (2000), who evaluate the impact of policy reforms on exportables, importables, and non-tradables in the 1990s in Brazil.

76. Soybean is not produced by any of the sampled farms in the Northeast and Southeast region; animal products are not included in this data analysis due to lack of appropriate data in the PPV survey.

TABLE 5.2: FARM PRODUCTION CHARACTERISTICS BY FARM SIZE[1]

	Minifundia (up to 2 ha)	Small (2.1–10ha)	Medium (10.1–50ha)	Large (50.1–2000ha)
Total land operated per household (hectares)	1.0	4.9	21.7	242.2
Share of land operated that is owned	0.40	0.57	0.75	0.79
Farm revenues per household (including imputed values of own-produced goods)	3,170	7,244	15,169	40,181
Share of importables in total revenue	0.51	0.56	0.55	0.48
Share of exportables	0.07	0.11	0.15	0.29
Share of non-tradables	0.43	0.33	0.30	0.24
Share of purchased inputs in total revenue	0.01	0.01	0.03	0.04
percent receiving technical assistance	2	2	8	31
percent owning machinery, equipment or vehicles	7	13	34	53
percent that uses animal traction	5	23	34	44
percent that received government subsidized credit	1	3	0	19

[1]Money values in Reais 1996. Tabulation based on PPV sample.

sent the shares of importables, exportables, and non-tradables on total farm revenue for different land size categories. We observe that the main difference between farmers with smaller and larger farms is that the former is more dependent on non-tradables and less dependent on exportables than the latter.

It is shown below that, under certain conditions, the elasticities of farm revenue with respect to output prices are equal to their respective shares. That is, the elasticity of farm revenue with respect to the price of exportables, for example, is equal to the share of exportables in the total revenues. Consider a farm revenue function:

$$R = R(P_x, P_M, P_N; H) \equiv \max_{Q_x, Q_M, Q_N} \{p_x, Q_x + p_M Q_M + p_N Q_N : F(Q_x, Q_M, Q_N; H) = 0\},$$

where R is equal to farm revenues; P_x, P_M, and P_N are prices of exportables, importables, and non-tradables, respectively; H is a vector of factor endowments and household characteristics including, among others, land, capital and education. Q_x, Q_M and Q_N are outputs produced from exportables, importables, and non-tradables, respectively; and $F(\cdot)$ is a production possibility function. The impact of price changes on revenues in elasticity form is,

$$\frac{\partial R}{\partial P_x} \frac{P_x}{R}, \quad \frac{\partial R}{\partial P_M} \frac{P_M}{R}, \quad \text{and } \frac{\partial R}{\partial P_N} \frac{P_N}{R} \tag{1}$$

If farmers maximize expected revenues, that is, if they allocate their resources (H) to the production of the three outputs so that the sum of their revenues $P_x Q_x + P_M Q_M + P_N Q_N$ is maximized, then Hotelling's lemma applies,

$$\frac{\partial R}{\partial P_x} = Q_x, \quad \frac{\partial R}{\partial P_M} = Q_M; \quad \frac{\partial R}{\partial P_N} = Q_N. \tag{2}$$

In this case, using (2) in (1) we obtain,

$$\text{(i)} \quad \frac{\partial R}{\partial P_x} \frac{P_x}{R} = \frac{Q_x P_x}{R} \equiv S_x,$$

$$\text{(ii)} \quad \frac{\partial R}{\partial P_M} \frac{P_M}{R} = \frac{Q_M P_M}{R} \equiv S_M, \qquad (3)$$

$$\text{(iii)} \quad \frac{\partial R}{\partial P_N} \frac{P_N}{R} = \frac{Q_N P_N}{R} \equiv S_N,$$

where S_i $(i = x, M, N)$ are the shares of each output group. We note that nominal revenue is homogenous of degree one, in all prices (for example, if all prices increase by 10 percent, nominal revenues should also increase by 1 percent). That is, the price elasticities add up to one, or, $S_x + S_M + S_N = 1$.

Policies and Real Farm Revenues

Under this assumption, one can analyze the effects of trade liberalization and devaluation on the farm revenues of small and large farms separately. Before this, however, it is necessary to define *real* revenue as

$$\tilde{R} = \frac{R}{\text{CPI}}, \qquad (4)$$

where CPI is the aggregate price index that includes prices of agricultural and non-agricultural goods consumed by farmers. We are, thus, interested in determining the likely impact of exchange rate and trade policies on $\tilde{R}$. We note on starting out that both $R(\cdot)$ and CPI are allowed to be different for farmers with small and large farms. The revenue, R, and the CPI index corresponding to farmers with smaller and larger farms are affected by price changes in a different way depending on differences in revenue elasticities and differences in the price weights of the CPI index.

Nominal Devaluation: Nominal devaluation has a direct and an indirect effect on prices. The direct effect is its impact on the price of tradables that increases in proportion to devaluation. If the nominal exchange rate increases by x percent, the direct effect is to increase prices of tradables by x percent (assuming a small open economy case). The indirect effect is the spillover of these price increases on the non-tradable sectors of the economy and on the CPI.

Using (4), it is clear that farmers' real revenue is affected by nominal devaluation as

$$\%\Delta\tilde{R} = \%\Delta R - \%\Delta\text{CPI} \qquad (5)$$

Let us define the aggregate price index,

$$\text{CPI} = p_T^{\alpha_1} p_N^{\alpha_2} q_T^{\alpha_3} q_N^{1-\alpha_1-\alpha_2-\alpha_3}, \qquad (6)$$

where p_T is the price index of agricultural tradables, p_N is the price index of agricultural non-tradables, q_T is the price index of non-agricultural tradable commodities, and q_N is the price of non-agricultural non-tradable commodities. The coefficients α_i $(i = 1, 2, 3) < 1$ are the weights in the CPI basket of agricultural tradables, agricultural non-tradables, and non-agricultural tradables. It is reasonable to assume that the CPI index is linearly homogenous with respect to the prices.

However, the weights α_i are assumed to be different for farmers in different land size categories, according to their respective expenditure shares of the four goods. Since the effect of nominal devaluation is to increase p_T and q_T proportionally we obtain,

$$\Delta\%p_T = \Delta\%q_T = x, \tag{7}$$

where x is the rate of nominal devaluation.

Next, let us consider the "spillover" effects of devaluation on the nominal price of non-tradables. In general non-tradable nominal prices will also rise but at a lower rate than that of devaluation. Assuming that devaluation causes prices of non-tradables to increase by a proportion $0 < \beta < 1$ of the devaluation,

$$\Delta\%p_N = \Delta\%q_N = \beta x, \tag{8}$$

where we have assumed that the impact of nominal devaluation on the prices of agricultural and non-agricultural non-tradables is the same. Using (6), (7) and (8) we obtain,

$$\begin{aligned} \Delta percentCPI &= \left[\alpha_1 + \alpha_3 + \beta(1 - \alpha_1 - \alpha_3)\right]x \\ &= \left[(1 - \beta)(\alpha_1 + \alpha_3) + \beta\right]x. \end{aligned} \tag{9}$$

Obviously, the term $(1 - \beta)(\alpha_1 + \alpha_3) + \beta \equiv \gamma$ is less than one since $\beta < 1$ and $\alpha_1 + \alpha_3 < 1$. Thus, γx is the impact of nominal devaluation on CPI and $(1 - \gamma)x$ is a frequently used definition of the *real devaluation*.

Using (3) and (8), the effect of devaluation on nominal farm revenue, R, is

$$\%\Delta R = \left(S_x + S_M + \beta S_N\right)x \tag{10}$$

Also, using the fact that $S_x + S_M + S_N = 1$, we obtain

$$\%\Delta R = \left[(1 - \beta)(S_x + S_M) + \beta\right]x \tag{11}$$

where the price of agricultural tradables increases by x percent and the price of agricultural non-tradables increases by βx percent.

Using (5), (9) and (10) we obtain the effect of devaluation on real farm revenues,

$$\%\Delta\tilde{R} = \left[S_x + S_M - (\alpha_1 + \alpha_3)\right](1 - \beta)x. \tag{12}$$

Since $S_x + S_M < 1$, $0 < \alpha_1 + \alpha_3 < 1$, the term in brackets on the right-hand-side is necessarily less than one. Also, $(1 - \beta)x$ can be interpreted as nominal devaluation minus the increase of the price of non-tradables induced by devaluation. That is, $(1 - \beta)x$ is the increase in the *relative* price of tradables vis-à-vis that of non-tradables, which is the most commonly used definition of real devaluation. That is, real revenue increases less than real devaluation. Thus, the effect of nominal devaluation on farmers' real revenues will be positive if the sum of the *production shares* of traded agricultural goods is greater than the sum of the *consumption shares* of the traded consumption goods (including agricultural and non-agricultural goods) in the consumption basket of farmers. If, however, the traded output production shares are less than the consumption shares of traded goods, then, devaluation will have a negative effect on farmers' real revenue. Additionally, the

TABLE 5.3: CONSUMPTION EXPENDITURE SHARES: PERCENT OF TOTAL EXPENDITURES BY FARM SIZE CATEGORY[1]

	Minifundia	Small	Medium	Large
Food traded	38	39	36	25
Food non-traded	21	24	25	17
Manufactured (non-agricultural traded goods)	11	11	11	10
Others (services, housing, etc.)	29	26	29	48

[1]Tabulation based on PPV sample.

TABLE 5.4: EFFECTS OF A 40 PERCENT NOMINAL DEVALUATION FOR FARM REVENUES BY FARM SIZE CATEGORY AND UNDER VARIOUS VALUES OF β

percent Δ of Real Revenues for	Values of β Assumed		
	0.20	0.30	0.50
Minifundia Farmers	2.6 percent	2.2 percent	1.6 percent
Farmers with Small Farms	5.4 percent	4.8 percent	3.4 percent
Farmers with Medium-sized Farms	7.4 percent	6.4 percent	4.6 percent
Farmers with Large Farms	13.4 percent	11.8 percent	8.4 percent

absolute impact of nominal devaluation on real farmers' revenues (whether positive or negative) will be reduced by a greater spillover of devaluation on the prices of non-tradables (β). Of course, if $\beta = 1$ there is no real devaluation, and the impact on real revenues is zero.

We know S_x and S_M for the different farmer groups (Table 5.2). The consumption shares α_1, α_2, α_3 are also likely to vary among groups. Poorer farmers (with smaller farms) represent greater consumption shares of food and smaller shares for manufacturing and non-agricultural services (Table 5.3). Using expenditure shares for the different farm size categories obtained from the expenditure component of the survey, we can estimate (1) under alternative assumptions regarding the price transmission coefficient, β, for which we do not have information. Table 5.4 simulates the impact of a 40 percent nominal devaluation under various assumed values for β.

As can be seen from Table 5.4, devaluation increases real farm revenues for all farmers. Large farmers are able to increase their real revenues by more than 13 percent as a consequence of a 32 percent real devaluation ($\beta = 0.20$) compared to a 2.6 percent increase for farmers in the minifundia category. Across the farm size categories, the pattern is clear where farmers with larger farms gain more with devaluation than those with smaller farms do. Farmers with small farms and poor farmers are able to increase their real revenues only by a modest proportion. The rather limited benefits of devaluation for the farmers with the smallest farms is due to the fact that their revenues are highly dependent on non-tradables and that their consumption basket includes a relative large component of traded goods. By contrast, large farmers tend to focus their production much more on traded agricultural commodities, and their consumption expenditures include a larger proportion of non-traded non-agricultural goods, including services, housing, education, and transportation.

Thus, devaluation is not likely to play an important role in increasing the incomes of the poorest farmers. But it does have an important effect the revenues of large farmers. This could indirectly benefit the rural poor, especially the landless. Landless rural workers could benefit if large farms substantially increase their labor demand as a consequence of devaluation. We provide some quantitative evidence of this later.

The fact that devaluation also affects prices of intermediate inputs in production could further reduce the benefits for farmers. However, for most small farmers, the share of purchased inputs (fertilizers, pesticides, seeds, etc.) in farm revenue is rather small. If we repeat the exercise above using net revenues instead of gross revenues, the results do not change much even if we assume that all purchased inputs are tradables. In this case the real benefits of devaluation assuming $\beta = 0.20$ in Table 5.4. are reduced by 0.2 percent for farmers in the minifundia groups and 0.1 percent for large farmers.

Trade Liberalization: Reducing Nominal Protection to Agricultural and Non-agricultural Goods

Reducing nominal protection implies a fall in the price of agricultural import substitutes and of non-agricultural importables. Also, since importable goods are important, both in production and consumption, a fall in their prices means that demand for non-tradables decreases as consumers substitute non-tradable goods for cheaper goods (but the increased real income goes in the opposite direction). At the same time, producers change the composition of their output reducing supply of importables and increasing supply of both exportables and non-tradables. Thus, reducing import protection causes: (i) a fall of the price of import substitutes goods, both agricultural and non-agricultural; (ii) a likely decrease in the price of non-tradables, both agricultural and non-agricultural. Here we assume a *uniform* reduction of import protection that applies to all importables including agricultural and non-agricultural goods.

Thus, to evaluate the effect of lowering import protection on the real revenue of farmers, $\tilde{R}$ in equation (5), we need to estimate how R and CPI are affected by the direct and indirect impacts of a uniform decrease of import protection. The nominal farm revenue changes as follows,

$$\%\Delta R = S_M \hat{p}_M + S_N \hat{p}_N, \tag{12}$$

where a ^ means rate of change. If the uniform change of import protection is $y(\hat{p}_M = y)$ then,

$$\%\Delta R = S_M y + S_N \hat{p}_N (y), \tag{12'}$$

where $\hat{p}_N$ is an increasing function of y. If we assume that $\hat{p}_N = \beta_N y \, (0 < \beta_N < 1)$, we obtain

$$\%\Delta R = (S_M + S_N \beta_N) y. \tag{13}$$

In the case of reducing import protection, y is negative and, therefore, the effect on nominal farm revenues is negative because the prices of both importables and non-tradables fall.

The cost of living (CPI), however, also falls. If η is the expenditure share of all importables (including both agricultural and non-agricultural goods) and if η is the expenditure share of all non-tradables in the consumption basket of farmers, then

$$\%\Delta CPI = (\eta + \epsilon\beta_N) y. \tag{14}$$

Thus, the cost of living is, of course, reduced if y is negative because all importable good (both agriculture and non-agricultural) prices fall by y percent and all prices of non-tradables (both agricultural and non-agricultural) also fall. Thus, the effect of reducing protection on the real farm revenues is

$$\%\Delta \tilde{R} = [(S_M + S_N \beta_N) - (\eta + \epsilon\beta_N)] y. \tag{15}$$

TABLE 5.5: EFFECTS OF A 20 PERCENT UNIFORM DECREASE IN IMPORT PROTECTION UNDER VARIOUS PRICE TRANSMISSION COEFFICIENTS BY LAND SIZE CATEGORY			
	Values of β_N assumed		
percent Δ of Real Revenues	0.10	0.20	0.30
Minifundia Farmers	−2.85	−2.70	−2.56
Farmers with Small Farms	−3.25	−2.91	−2.58
Farmers with Medium-sized Farms	−2.13	−1.65	−1.16
Farmers with Large farms	−0.83	0	0.82

We know the value of S_M and S_N for farmers with small and large farms. From expenditure surveys, we see that the consumption expenditure share of importables (η) is estimated at 36 percent for minifundia farmers and 40 percent for large farmers. The expenditure share in non-tradables (ε) is estimated at 50 percent for small farmers and 65 percent for large farmers. Table 5.5 presents an evaluation of the impact of a 20 percent uniform reduction of protection to all importables[77] under various assumptions for the unobserved coefficient β_N. As can be seen from the table, the farm revenue effect of reducing protection is not very large and the actual value is not very sensitive to the unknown parameter β_N. Farmers with smaller farms are more negatively affected by import liberalization than are those with larger farms. Actually, the effect on farmers in the large category is either a very small decrease in real revenue or even a positive effect, depending on the β_N assumed. Minifundia and small farmers reduce their real farm revenues by about 3 percent while the effect on large farmers ranges between a loss of 0.83 percent and a gain of 0.82 percent.

Determinants of Farm Revenue
Here we present the estimates of a farm revenue function using a flexible functional form specification. The function R is

$$R = R\left(p_x, p_M, p_N; Z, T, E, L; K, TA, A; N, D\right), \tag{16}$$

where R is defined as farm revenue per capita, Z are purchased inputs used per capita, T is land per capita, E is education of the household head, L is labor per capita, K is a dummy variable equals one if the farmer uses trucks or mechanized equipment, TA is a dummy for technical assistance, A is a dummy if a farmer uses animal traction; N is family size, and D represents other variables reflecting geographical location of the farm,[78] age of the farmer, etc.

Since $R(\cdot)$ is linearly homogenous with respect to the three prices, p_x, p_M and p_N, we can normalize by any of the prices to obtain a normalized revenue function. We choose p_N as the numeraire price. Thus R/p_N is now a function of the relative prices p_x/p_N and p_M/p_N.

We specify a generalized quadratic function for the R/p_N. Apart from being a flexible form, this functional specification has the advantage of allowing the effects of the explanatory variables on R/p_N to vary across the sample as land, inputs used, capital, technical assistance, etc. change. That is, since the elasticities are functions of these variables rather than fixed values as in, for example, a

---

77. Kume (1996) reports that nominal protection rates in Brazil decreased from about 39 percent in 1988 to 14 percent in 1995, while estimates of the real protection rates were 50 percent in 1988 and 20 percent in 1993.

78. The only variable reflecting geographical location included in the regression is a dummy for the Northeast region. Due to the high number of other dummy variables (by themselves and in interactive variables) and the relatively small sample, it was not possible to use geographical indicators at a more disaggregated level.

Cobb-Douglas specification, the possible biases that could result from the inclusion in the same sample of farmers with large and small farms, poor and rich, etc., are not likely to be large. We obtain elasticities that vary according to the specific characteristics of each farm group. The normalized quadratic revenue function is thus

$$R/p_N = \sum_{i=1}^{2} \sum_{j=1}^{2} b_{ij}(p_i/p_N p_j/P_N) + \sum_{i=1}^{2} a_{zi}(p_i/p_N)(Z/N)$$

$$+ \sum_{i}^{2} a_{Ti}(p_i/p_N)(T) + \sum_{i}^{2} a_{Ei}(p_i/p_N)E \qquad (17)$$

$$+ \sum_{i}^{2} a_{Li}(p_i/p_N)(L/N) + \sum_{i}^{2} a_{Ki}(p_i/p_N)K(D)$$

$$+ \sum_{i}^{2} a_{TA,i}(p_i/p_N)TA(D) + \sum_{i}^{2} a_{Ai}(p_i/p_N)A(D)$$

$$\sum_{i} \sum_{j} c_{ij} x_i x_j,$$

where $b_{ij}, a_{zi}, a_{Ti}, a_{Ei}, a_{Li}, a_{Ki}, a_{TA, i}, a_{Ai}, c_{ij}$ are coefficients to be estimated, x_i and x_j are vectors $[Z, T, E, L, K(D), TA(D), A(D)]$ and the D indicates which are the dummy variables.

Table 5.6 presents the estimated coefficients of (17). The goodness-of-fit of the estimated revenue function is very high with a large number of statistically significant variables including many interactive variables. The regression is able to explain more than 65 percent of the variance of farm revenues across households $\tilde{R}^2 = 0.656$). The high degree of significance of the interactive and quadratic variables indicates that the (marginal) returns on assets is highly dependent on the levels of other assets, and demographic characteristics of the household. This suggests that various characteristics of farmers such as their asset wealth, age, education, strongly affect the rates of return of the various factors of production. Additionally, the fact that many interactive terms involving prices and assets are significant suggests that the returns on assets are quite dependent on relative prices.

Table 5.7 presents an evaluation of the effects of various assets and demographic factors on per capita farm revenues based on the coefficients estimated for the per capita farm revenue function. The flexibility of the specification for the revenue function allows us to obtain elasticities specific to each farmers' groups. In Table 5.7, we provide estimates for all land size categories.

Land Elasticities: The effect of per capita land on per capita farm revenues varies dramatically between large farmers and those with the smallest farms. The marginal effect of having more land is practically negligible for the latter while it is large and highly significant for the farmers with large farms with a revenue elasticity of about 12.

This result goes against conventional wisdom that suggests an inverted U-shaped relationship where land productivity is low for small farms, high for medium-sized farms, and low again for large-sized farms. One interpretation is that without certain other complementary assets and demographic characteristics the value of land by itself is very small. Remember that these are partial elasticities, as such, they measure the marginal contribution of land to farm revenues *given* all other assets and demographic characteristics. For land to have a large impact, it is necessary that farmers have fewer restrictions on liquidity to acquire purchased inputs, more education (which, as we will see later, has a larger positive effect only if farm size is large) and more capital. More land in itself will have little impact, but without a minimum land area the returns on other factors of production and to desirable demographic characteristics also tend to be small (as we show below). There is a synergy between land and other assets where their productivity is mutually reinforced. This has often been neglected in previous analyses.

Liquid Capital (purchased inputs): The elasticity of purchased inputs is quite large for small farmers. The fact that these elasticities are much larger than the observed input shares (which are

TABLE 5.6: LEAST SQUARES ESTIMATES OF THE PRODUCTION FUNCTION[1]

	Parameter Estimates (std. errors)		
Intercept	−33.082	***	(9.383)
Dummy for Northeast Region	−1.576		(1.979)
Average price of exportable crops	44.051	***	(15.369)
Average price of exportable crops squared	−9.216	*	(5.726)
Average price of importable crops	28.030	***	(6.510)
Average price of importable crops squared	−3.743	***	(1.564)
Cross of prices of exportables and importables	−23.464	***	(5.318)
Land size per capita	3.157	***	(0.567)
Land size per capita squared	0.132		(0.079)
Cross of price exportables and land size	−0.415	*	(0.238)
Cross of price importables and land size	−3.052	***	(0.449)
Family workers per capita	−2.237	*	(1.332)
Workers per capita squared	0.239		(0.421)
Cross of workers per capita and prices of exportables	1.025	*	(0.576)
Cross of workers per capita and prices of importables	0.734		(0.678)
Cross of workers per capita and land size	0.105		(0.096)
Family size	−0.224		(0.143)
Age of the head of household	−0.557	**	(0.247)
Education of the head of household	−0.329		(0.423)
Education of the head squared	0.061		(0.065)
Cross of education and price of exportables	0.020		(0.220)
Cross of education and price of importables	0.225		(0.267)
Cross of education and land size	0.131		(0.142)
Total expenses with intermediate inputs	−0.768	**	(0.315)
Expenses with inputs squared	−0.259	***	(0.042)
Cross of inputs and price of exportables	0.202		(0.129)
Cross of inputs and price of importables	0.927	***	(0.221)
Cross of inputs and land	0.229	**	(0.098)
Dummy = 1 if received technical assistance	1.029		(3.546)
Dummy = 1 if has truck or heavy farm machinery	−0.831		(1.415)
Dummy = 1 if uses animal traction	1.097		(1.504)
Cross of technical assistance and price of exportables	−3.641	*	(2.049)
Cross of technical assistance and price of importables	2.929	*	(1.801)
Cross of machinery and price of exportables	−0.640		(0.951)
Cross of machinery and price of importables	1.626	**	(0.776)
Cross of animal traction and price of exportables	−0.806		(0.761)
Cross of animal traction and price of importables	−0.403		(1.094)
Cross of technical assistance and education	−0.925	***	(0.315)
Cross of machinery and education	0.065		(0.148)
Cross of animal traction and education	0.321	**	(0.157)
Cross of technical assistance and inputs	0.363	***	(0.064)
Cross of machinery and inputs	0.002		(0.092)
Cross of animal traction and inputs	−0.003	**	(0.001)
Cross of technical assistance and land	−0.429	***	(0.154)
Cross of machinery and land	−0.094		(0.179)
Cross of animal traction and land	1.110	***	(0.173)

[1]Dependent variable: farm revenue from crops per capita
*indicates p < 10 percent; **p < 5 percent; ***p < 1 percent

TABLE 5.7: EFFECTS OF ASSETS AND DEMOGRAPHIC CHARACTERISTICS ON PER CAPITA FARM REVENUES BY FARM SIZE GROUPS
(Elasticities of revenues with respect to the indicated variables)[79]

Elasticity of Revenue per capita with respect to:	Minifundia	Small	Medium	Large
Land	0.008	0.018	0.541	12.223
Liquid capital	0.151	0.107	−0.539	−0.019
Labor	0.042	0.012	0.064	0.239
Education of operator	0.003	0.113	0.182	0.973
Access to technical assistance	0.071	0.036	0.106	0.068
Physical capital	0.021	0.030	0.057	−0.046
Use of animal traction	0.021	0.115	0.279	1.369
Age Operator	−1.397	−0.709	−0.347	−0.126

about 0.014) suggests that small farmers are indeed liquidity constrained.[80] That is, the marginal revenue of purchased inputs is much higher than their marginal cost.[81] Comparing this with the land effect, it appears that facilitating the access of small farmers to credit in order to relieve their apparent liquidity constraints could be a much more effective way to increase their revenues than that of simply giving them more land.

It is strange and does not seem plausible that the elasticity for farmers with medium-sized and large farms is not positive. However, evidence by Dias (2000) based on the Agricultural Census 1995/96, suggests that there is a significant group of farmers with average land sizes of about 40 hectares who are above average in their use of intermediate inputs per hectare, while their revenue per hectare is the lowest of all farm groups. This situation may be indicating that a large proportion of farms in this size category are in a transition period where investments have not started to pay-off; otherwise these farms will not be feasible in the medium-run.

Labor: Not surprisingly, the marginal impact of (unskilled) labor on the farm revenue of small farmers is almost negligible. There probably exists an excess supply of labor among the small farmers. What is more interesting is the fact that the labor revenue elasticity is so much greater among the large farmers. In fact while the labor elasticity is lower than the estimated labor shares in the case of small farmers, it is higher for large farmers. This may suggest labor market restrictions affecting the ability of large farmers to hire small farmers.

Education: The effect of education on farm revenues is practically negligible for small farmers. By contrast, the education elasticity is many times larger, about 0.97, for large farmers. The value of education is probably higher when farmers have larger, and possibly more complex operations.[82] In such a context, it is natural that education contributes little to increase farm revenues. Another factor that should be taken into consideration is the large difference in the level of farmers' education, which is

---

79. See appendix for factor marginal return equations.

80. de Janvry et al. (1991) show that market failures, including lack of access to the credit market, affect the elasticity of the responses of small farmers to various factors.

81. If farmers were not constrained then there would be an optimal allocation of purchased inputs z. That is, $\partial R/\partial Z = p_z$. This implies that $\partial R/\partial Z \, Z/R = pZ^2/R$, the revenue elasticity $\partial R/\partial Z \, Z/R$ is equal to the factor share $p_z Z/R$. The fact that in reality the elasticity is 10 times larger than the share in the case of small farmers suggests, therefore, that there is a big gap between $\partial R/\partial Z$ and p_z. In other words, since $\partial R/\partial Z > p_z$, small farmers could greatly benefits if they could increase Z.

82. In López and Valdés (2000) it is shown that education does not seem to play any role in increasing the farm revenue with the exception of Chile, where the agricultural sector requires more skilled labor.

much higher in the group of farmers with larger farms. One more year of education at the elementary level is likely to have a smaller impact on revenues than one more year of education at a higher level.

Technical Assistance: The effect of technical assistance is quite similar for groups of farmers with small and large farms. Farmers that have access to technical assistance have about 7 percent more revenues, ceteris paribus, than those that do not. So the potential for increasing farm revenues through increased technical assistance is quite significant and can be approximately equally beneficial to poor and non-poor. The group of farmers in the medium size category is even more positively affected, with an elasticity of 0.11.

Use of animal traction: Only large farmers obtain large returns on the use of equipment that use animal traction. The difference is also strong in the proportion of farms that use animal traction, 5 percent and 44 percent for minifundia and farmers with large farms, respectively.

Farm Operator Age: Farm operators are relatively old and, thus, the effect of increasing age is negative for all farm groups. But the negative effects of aging on farm revenues are dramatically different across the groups. For farmers in the minifundia groups, it is devastating, with an elasticity of -1.4, while for large farmers, the negative effect is much more modest with an age elasticity of -0.13. That is, the loss of farm revenues of a 60-year-old compared to a 50-year-old farmer is about 28 percent among the farmers with the smallest farms compared to only 3 percent among those with large farms. Farmers with large farms presumably can compensate their physical decline by increasing hiring and/or by acquiring more machinery.

The Role of Prices on Factor Returns

Table 5.8. shows how prices and other variables affect factor returns. Higher relative export prices tend to reduce the value of technical assistance and increase the value of purchased inputs and labor. This suggests that exportable commodities are intensive in purchased inputs and labor. Also, it is possible that technical assistance is biased, emphasizing more production of import substituting crops, thus explaining the negative effect of export prices and positive effects of importable prices on the returns to technical assistance. The negative effect on land is small.

The positive effect of the relative price of export prices is quite large and is by far the most important factor affecting labor returns. In fact, a 10 percent increase in p_x rises the marginal value of labor by about an equal percentage. This suggests that policies, such as exchange rate devaluation and trade liberalization (that increase the relative price p_x/p_N), are likely to have an important positive impact in the agricultural labor market by inducing higher real wages.

By contrast, import protection leading to higher domestic relative prices of importables tends to increase the value of inputs but does not seem to affect labor returns.

The effect of increased prices of importables on land rent is negative and quite strong. As shown in Table 5.8., the price of importables exerts a negative effect on land rents. The elasticity of land rents with respect to p_M/p_N is about -3, meaning that a 10 percent increase in p_M/p_N decreases the returns to land by about 30 percent.

TABLE 5.8: EFFECTS OF PRICES, AND OTHER VARIABLES ON THE RETURNS TO FACTORS

| | RETURNS ON | | | | | |
	Land	Tech. Assist.	Education	Inputs	Labor	Capital
Price+ of export	−	−	0	+	+	0
Price of importables	−	+	0	+	0	+
Price of non-tradables	+	−	0	−	−	−
Land	+	−	0	+	0	0
Education	0	−	0	n.a.	n.a.	0
Technical assistance	−	n.a.	−	+	n.a.	n.a.

Technical assistance tends to reduce land rents but to increase the value of purchased inputs. This suggests that technical assistance promotes the demand for purchased inputs, which is not always satisfied, especially in the case of small farmers. The returns on purchased inputs is positively affected by higher prices of exportables and importables but is reduced by higher prices of non-tradables. Thus, real exchange rate devaluation is likely to substantially increase the demand for purchased inputs. The shift in the structure of production towards exportables and importables, and against non-tradables is responsible for this to the extent that production of agricultural tradables is more intensive in purchased inputs than production of non-tradables. Thus, the substantial real devaluation that Brazil has experienced is likely to make lack of credit and liquidity much more costly than before. Or, equivalently, the benefits of increasing credit to farmers are probably going to be much larger now than before devaluation.

Conclusion

There is a high degree of correspondence between the size of land operated by a farmer and his level of income. Generally, farmers with small farms are poor and those with large farms are not. Therefore, policies that benefit those with small farms will likely benefit those that are poor. Farmers with small and large farms differ, not only in revenue levels, but also in the structure of farm production. Large farmers tend to produce more tradable crops while small farmers produce more non-tradable crops. Moreover, the use of intermediate inputs, farm machinery, credit, and technical assistance is much higher in the case of large farms.

Because of these differences in production structure, the impact of trade liberalization and exchange rate devaluation on farmers' revenues is different. Moreover, farm households also differ in the composition of their consumption basket, which also affects the impact on real revenue. We find that devaluation benefits large farmers considerably more than it does those with small farms. A real devaluation of 32 percent would increase real revenues of large farmers by more than 13 percent, while small farmers would increase their revenue by less than 3 percent. However, the rural poor could benefit from these effects if farmers with large farms increase their labor demand as a consequence of devaluation. Indeed, we observe that higher prices of exportable commodities increase labor returns significantly; basically a given percentage increase in exportable prices would cause an equal percentage increase in the marginal returns to labor.

Trade liberalization impacts farm revenues negatively across farm sizes, but the effect is small. Still, farmers with small farms are the most negatively affected. A 20 percent cut in nominal import protection may decrease real revenues of small farmers by 3 percent while the effect on those with large farms is almost zero. On the other hand, we also observe that a decrease in the price of non-tradables, a result of decreased import protection, would have a positive effect on the marginal value of labor (the impact of decreased price of importables does not seem to have an impact of returns to labor). Thus, again, trade liberalization could help farmers with smaller farms by favoring higher wages.

Returns on factors of production also differ significantly depending on the size of the farm and other assets. Characteristics such as education and age of the farm operator also affect factor returns. The impact of most factors on farm revenue is highly dependent on the level of other assets, thus, there seems to be a strong synergy among farm household assets, including human capital.

The quantitative effect of various factors of production on farm revenues was analyzed across different land size groups. Farm revenue responds positively and strongly to land size for farmers who operate large land sizes (average of 240 hectares). For farmers with smaller farms, the impact is practically negligible. This may be indicating that without other complementary assets, the value of land in itself is very small. Therefore, it would be necessary that small farmers have fewer restrictions on liquidity to acquire inputs, more education, and capital so that more land could have a significant impact on their farm revenues. Indeed, the results indicate that small farmers are liquidity constrained. Comparatively, it seems that relieving liquidity constraints of small farmers would be a more effective way to increase their revenues than by simply giving them more land.

One factor that seems to benefit farmers more or less equally across land sizes is technical assistance, which has a relatively large impact on revenues; having access to it increases farm revenues by between 7 percent and 11 percent. Policies that increased access to technical assistance would benefit poor and non-poor farmers alike.

References

Brandão, A. S., Soria Bastos Filho, G. and A. Brandão. 2000. "Land Markets and Rural Poverty Alleviation," in *Rural Poverty in Brazil: Towards an Alleviation Strategy*, World Bank, Brasília.

de Janvry, A, M. Fafchamps, and E. Sadoulet. 1991. "Peasant Behavior with Missing Markets: Some Paradoxes Explained," *The Economic Journal*, (101), pp. 1400–1417.

Dias, G. L. S. "Dynamics of the Brazilian Small Sarm Sector," in *Rural Poverty in Brazil: Towards an Alleviation Strategy*, World Bank, Brasília.

Helfland, S. M., and G. C. de Rezende. 1999. "Brazilian Agriculture in the 1990s: Impact of the Policy Reforms." Paper presented at the Latin American Studies Meeting, March 16–18, Miami.

Kume, H. 1996. "A política de importação no Plano Real e a estrutura de proteção efetiva." Rio de Janeiro, IPEA, maio 1996 (Texto para discussão, 423).

López, R. and A. Valdés. 2000. *Rural poverty in Latin America: analytics, new empirical evidence and policy*. St. Martin's Press, N.Y. and MacMillan, London

Romano, C. B. 1996/97 "Poverty Profile in Brazil. A Comparative Analysis Based on the PPV", in *Rural Poverty in Brazil: Towards an Alleviation Strategy*. World Bank, Brasília.

Appendix

Marginal returns of various assets

(1) $\dfrac{\partial R}{\partial Z} = -0.77^* - 0.50^* Z + 0.23^* T + 0.2^* p_x$
$+ 0.93^* p_M + 0.36^* TA + 0.002K - 0.0026^* A$

(2) $\dfrac{\partial R}{\partial Z} = -0.32 + 0.12E + 0.13T + 0.02p_x$
$+ 0.22p_M + 0.92^* TA + 0.06K - 0.32^* A$

(3) $\dfrac{\partial R}{\partial L} = -2.23^* + 0.46L + 1.02^* p_x + 0.73p_M + 0.10T$

(4) $\dfrac{\partial R}{\partial K} = -0.833 - 0.64p_x + 1.63^* p_M - 0.09T + 0.002Z + 0.065E - 0.09TA$

(5) $\dfrac{\partial R}{\partial T} = 3.15^* + 0.26T + 0.23^* Z - 0.43^* (TA)$
$- 0.09K + 1.1^* A - 0.41p_x - 3.05^* p_M + 0.13E + 0.11L$

(6) $\dfrac{\partial R}{\partial TA} = 1.03 - 3.6^* p_x + 2.93^* p_M - 0.92^* E + 0.36^* Z - 0.43^* T$

CHAPTER 6

POVERTY AND NON-FARM EMPLOYMENT IN RURAL BRAZIL

Introduction[83]

Rural poverty in Brazil is a subject of widespread interest. This is true within Brazil itself, but also in the broader Latin American context. The country looms so large on the geographic, social and economic landscape of the continent that distributional outcomes in Brazil directly influence any assessment of aggregate welfare in the region. For example, at least one study estimates that in 1980, the rural poor in Brazil accounted for roughly 40 percent of rural poverty, and as much as 25 percent of *total* poverty in Latin America as a whole (Morley, 1994).

Brazil's unequal distribution of land, the debate about policies of land redistribution, and the high-profile activities of its large and influential land reform movement provide perhaps the most immediate entry points into discussions of rural living standards and the prospects for poverty alleviation in the country. Recent years have also seen a growing interest in understanding better how livelihoods of the rural poor are influenced by the presence of a non-agricultural sector in rural areas, and whether there exist policy levers which can help to support that sector's contribution to rural poverty alleviation.

The relationship between poverty and the rural non-farm economy in Latin America has received attention by academic researchers and policymakers for some time.[84] Building on earlier work by Klein (1992), Reardon, Berdegue, and Escobar (2000) indicate that non-farm employment growth in rural Latin America has been positive and generally very rapid during the last three decades—certainly more rapid than farm employment growth. Lanjouw and Lanjouw (2000) draw

83. This Chapter was prepared by Peter Lanjouw (World Bank and Free University, Amsterdam), as a background chapter for a World Bank study on Rural Poverty in Brazil, directed by Alberto Valdés. The author is grateful to Johan Mistiaen, Alberto Valdés, and participants at the Workshop on Rural Poverty, held in Rio de Janeiro, May 30–32, 2000, for comments and suggestions.

84. Recent examples include de Janvry and Sadoulet, 1993; Elbers and Lanjouw, 2000; Lanjouw 1999a, 1999b; Lopez and Valdés, 1998; Reardon, Berdegue and Escobar, 2000. For a broader survey see Lanjouw and Lanjouw, 2000.

attention to the sector's great heterogeneity within as well as across countries, effectively spanning a full spectrum of manufacturing and service-sector activities, and argue that this heterogeneity makes it particularly difficult to devise general policies to promote the sector.

Mellor (1976) highlighted the potential interrelationship between the non-farm sector and the agricultural sector, pointing to the myriad linkages that bind these two sectors together. He pointed to potential forward linkages from agriculture to the non-agricultural sector, as well as backward linkages, supporting production as well as consumption growth. The argument stemming from these observations is that the farm and the non-farm sectors can mutually support each other in a "virtuous" cycle of development in which both sectors strengthen simultaneously. While examples of such linkages can be readily identified in Latin America, it is also thought that the particularly skewed distribution of land in the region may act as a constraint (de Janvry and Sadoulet, 1993). In addition, consistent with the observation of the sector's great heterogeneity, it is clear that at least some rural non-farm activities (relating for example to the tourism sector and urban-led manufacturing activities in rural areas) are only tenuously linked to the agricultural economy (Reardon, et al, 2000).

An important emerging "stylized fact" about the non-farm sector has been the large share of non-farm employment in total remunerated employment of women in Latin America. Reardon et al (2000) document that in 9 out of 11 Latin American countries for which they had data, rural women's share of rural non-farm employment during the 1990s was much higher than that of rural men: accounting for between 65 percent and 93 percent of overall labor market participation of women.[85] Lanjouw (1999a and 1999b) observes similar patterns for Ecuador and Mexico respectively, but indicates that women's earnings tend to be much lower than that of men's in the non-farm sector, controlling for education and other individual and household characteristics.[86]

A second stylized fact that has proven quite general in most developing countries is that returns to formal education in the non-farm sector are high, especially in comparison with returns to education in agriculture. This has been documented extensively in Latin America (summarized in Reardon et al, 2000) as well as in Africa and Asia.[87] Reardon et al (2000) emphasize, in addition, the importance of transport infrastructure, mainly roads, in stimulating non-farm employment growth in Latin America.

The relationship between poverty and the non-farm sector is often rather subtle. The most direct impact on poverty can be discerned when the sector offers employment opportunities to the poor with remuneration levels that are sufficiently high to lift them out of poverty. However, Lanjouw and Lanjouw (2000) describe how non-agricultural activities can in general be divided into two groups of occupations: high labor productivity/high income activities, and low labor productivity activities which serve only as a residual source of employment—a "last-resort" source of income. These latter activities can be quite common among the very poor, particularly among women. Even if "last resort" non-farm incomes are very low and, therefore, offer no realistic prospect of lifting individuals out of poverty, such income sources may nevertheless be very important from a social welfare perspective. For example, off-farm employment income may serve to reduce aggregate income inequality; or where seasonal or longer-term unemployment in agriculture exists, households may benefit even from low non-agricultural earnings during the off-season. In addition, for certain subgroups of the population who are without land and who are also unable to participate in the agricultural-wage labor market (due perhaps to ill-health, discrimination and/or cultural restrictions), these non-agricultural incomes may offer the only means to some economic security (a safety net). It is important to recognize, therefore, that even low-productivity activities can play an important role in poverty alleviation—helping to keep many of the poor from falling into further deprivation.

---

85. Although overall labor market participation of women may well be much lower than that of men.

86. Although it is unclear whether this is due to lower returns, shorter employment spells, or some combination of both.

87. Jolliffe, 1998, provides some recent evidence on Africa, for Ghana; Lanjouw, Quizon, and Sparrow—2000, for Tanzania; and Fafchamps and Shilpi (2000) provide some recent evidence for Nepal. Van de Walle (2000), and Lanjouw, and Shariff (2000) do the same for Vietnam and India, respectively.

The purpose of this paper is to bring together some basic empirical material with which to consider the role of the non-farm sector in rural Brazil. The analysis draws on two household surveys fielded in 1996, (the *Pesquisa Sobre Padroes de Vida,* PPV, and the *Pesquisa Nacional por Amostra de Domicilios,* PNAD) and the focus is on the northeast and southeast of Brazil. We apply a recently developed methodology to combine these two data sources so as to present a tentative breakdown of rural poverty by state and urban/rural areas. Against this background we scrutinize occupational patterns and income shares, so as to obtain a sense of the sector's contribution to rural poverty reduction.

The plan of the paper is as follows. We present an initial snapshot of poverty in the northeastern and southeastern regions of Brazil. We describe the method utilized to combine these two data sets so as to be able to present a breakdown of poverty exploiting the large coverage of the PNAD survey and employing the PPV definition of wellbeing based on consumption expenditures. Then we provide a broad breakdown of employment patterns distinguishing between the northeast and southeast of the country, between urban and rural areas, and paying attention to gender and locational characteristics. We summarize the various correlates of non-farm employment on the basis of probit model estimates. Then we turn to a brief discussion of employment trends in the non-farm sector, drawing on analysis by Del Grossi (1999) comparing across various PNAD surveys. Then we consider income shares from non-farm activities and relates these to different segments of the per capita consumption distribution and the distribution of land ownership classes. We report results from econometric estimates of the determinants of labor earnings in rural areas.

Rural Poverty in Brazil[88]

Poverty in Brazil is often described as a largely urban phenomenon. This common impression is based, partly, on three features of the Brazilian setting: (a) only 21 percent of the total population is rural, (b) urban slums are widespread, and (c) so far, both the data collection process and the analysis of poverty has been largely urban oriented. However, recent studies suggest that we may have underestimated the importance of rural poverty in Brazil, and that the traditional rural-urban dichotomy might be a rather misleading notion. In particular, recent work by Ferreira, Lanjouw, and Neri (2000) concludes that the incidence of poverty is not only higher in rural vis-à-vis urban areas, but it is also typically higher in small urban areas compared to larger cities and metropolitan areas.[89] These findings are significant in the context of rural poverty for at least two reasons. Firstly, the urban versus rural dichotomy is inevitably somewhat subjective (depending on, usually, some population-related cut-off) and secondly, it is quite likely that the economies of smaller towns are linked more closely to the rural economy than they are to the economies of larger urban areas. These recent findings are sufficiently compelling to warrant a reconsideration of the conventional focus on poverty in Brazil. In this section we take a step in that direction by presenting a preliminary spatially disaggregated poverty profile for the Northeast (NE) and Southeast (SE) of Brazil.

As described in Section 1, our preliminary poverty profile is based on two data sets: the 1996 *Pesquisa Nacional por Amostra de Domicilios* (PNAD) data and the 1996 *Pesquisa sobre Padrões de Vida* (PPV) survey implemented by the *Instituto Brasileiro de Geografia e Estatística* (IBGE), based on the World Bank's LSMS survey design. Both data sets suffer from strengths and weaknesses.[90] On the one hand, the PPV reports quite detailed consumption expenditure data and permits the construction of price indices to account for spatial price variation (the data suggest that this is substantial across a large country such as Brazil). However, the PPV sample size is not large enough to be representative at levels of spatial disaggregation much below the regional and large metropolitan area level. The PNAD sample is many times larger than the PPV and is representative at the state level.

---

88. This section is based on joint work with Fransisco Ferreira and Johan A. Mistiaen.

89. These areas were defined according to population size criteria: small urban areas (population < 20,000), larger cities (20,000 ≤ population < 100,000), and metropolitan areas (population > 100,000).

90. For a detailed discussion regarding the relative merits of these data sets, see Ferreira, Lanjouw, and Neri, 2000a

However, the PNAD does not report expenditure data and the income measures are somewhat unreliable (particularly in rural areas).[91] By employing a recently developed small-to-large survey imputation technique—see Elbers, Lanjouw, and Lanjouw (2000); and Hentschel, Lanjouw, Lanjouw, and Poggi (2000)—we are able to capitalize on the individual strengths of both data sets while eschewing their respective weaknesses. These econometric techniques essentially enable us to impute the expenditure data sampled via PPV into the larger PNAD sample.

Based on the approach outlined in Elbers, Lanjouw, and Lanjouw (2000), we use data from the PPV survey to estimate 10 models of per-capita *consumption expenditure* (corresponding, in turn, to each representative stratum in the PPV data set). We divide the PNAD data set into the same strata, and then use the PPV parameter estimates to weight PNAD-based characteristics of the population (selected on the basis of their identical definition to the characteristics in the PPV) in each respective stratum. We then calculate each household's expected welfare level. Elbers *et al* (2000) show that this merging of data sources yields an estimator which can be clearly interpreted, extended in a consistent way to any aggregated welfare measure (poverty rate, measure of inequality, etc.), and which can be assessed for statistical reliability.[92]

Preliminary Regional Poverty Estimates for the NE/SE of Brazil

Our preliminary regionally disaggregated headcount poverty estimates, P (0), are presented in Table 6.1. The first column contains the headcount poverty measures, $P_I(0)$, based on the conventionally used PNAD per capita *income* data (employed also by Ferreira, Lanjouw, and Neri (2000)).[93] We note that according to this welfare criterion, the rural Northeast has the highest proportion of poor at 68.5 percent, and that, with exception of the rural Southeast, the northeastern regions are poorer compared to the southeastern regions. These income-based numbers represent a useful upper bound benchmark against which to evaluate our subsequent consumption expenditure-based estimates. This is because, as FLN (2000) argue, the income figures available from the PNAD are likely to understate self-employment earnings. Particularly, in rural areas, where a large fraction of households are self-employed farmers, measured poverty is likely to be overstated. The next column presents the headcount poverty estimates, $P_{ppv}(0)$, and standard errors based on the PPV data only, and based on per capita consumption expenditure as the welfare criterion.[94] Comparing these columns, we notice that, with the exception of Sao Paulo, the PPV expenditure-based measures of poverty are indeed lower. Interestingly, while an expenditure-based incidence of poverty in Rio de Janeiro is almost half as high as the income-based incidence, measured poverty in Sao Paulo increases across data sources and welfare criterion.[95]

Next we present our estimates for the PNAD imputed expenditure-based measures calibrated on the PPV estimates. The $P_i(0)$ estimates are based on the most basic version of the model. However, while even the majority of these $P_i(0)$ estimates are already close to the PPV measures, the first-stage regressions underlying these results suffered from some heteroscedasticity and non-normality problems.[96] Consequently, we proceeded by trimming the sample to resolve the non-

91. For instance, the PNAD income measure for the self-employed is based on a single question that fails to distinguish between gross and net income from self-employment activities (such as farming in rural areas). It also fails to recognize that agricultural incomes accrue on a seasonal or annual rather than monthly basis. Such omissions are likely to introduce substantial distortion into the reported real living standard measures, particularly in rural areas (for example, see Ferreira, Lanjouw, and Neri—2000).

92. The approach here is still in its first stages of implementation, and standard errors have not yet been calculated for the predicted poverty rates reported here. Work on this front is in progress. A more complete description of the small-to-large sample methodology, the data sets, our econometric procedures, and estimates of other poverty measures is currently in preparation. The estimates reported here should therefore be viewed as provisional and subject to revision.

93. Some adjustments were introduced by FLN (2000) and relate essentially to adjustments for spatial price variation, and imputed rent.

94. These standard errors take into account the PPV's multi-stage sampling design.

95. See FLN (2000) for a description of the derivation of the poverty line being employed.

96. For details on the methodology, see Elbers, Lanjouw, and Lanjouw (2000).

TABLE 6.1: POVERTY HEADCOUNT MEASURES FOR THE DIFFERENT DATA SETS*

Region	Inc. PNAD $P_I(0)$	PPV $P_{ppv}(0)$	(s.e.)	Exp. PNAD(i) $P_I(0)$	Exp. PNAD(ii) $P_{ii}(0)$	$\mu(y)$
RM Fortaleza	0.263	0.185	(0.08)	0.170	0.167	192.9
RM Recife	0.277	0.221	(0.04)	0.154	0.159	189.37
RM Salvador	0.270	0.193	(0.03)	0.256	0.233	174.99
Urban NE	0.401	0.376	(0.04)	0.358	0.358	124.57
Rural NE	0.685	0.498	(0.06)	0.485	0.490	86.41
RM B. Horizonte	0.086	0.079	(0.03)	0.077	0.076	265.76
RM Rio de Janeiro	0.061	0.030	(0.006)	0.066	0.059	299.43
RM São Paulo	0.027	0.038	(0.018)	0.042	0.038	322.09
Urban SE	0.074	0.047	(0.014)	0.084	0.080	246.74
Rural SE	0.354	0.260	(0.047)	0.255	0.249	136.23

Notes: For the 10 sub-regions surveyed by the 1996 PPV only.
The poverty line is R$65.07 per person per month in 1996 São Paulo Reais (see Ferreira, Lanjouw, and Neri, 2000).
Inc. PNAD: Based on the PNAD income per capita data (adjusted for imputed rent and regionally deflated).
Exp. PNAD (i): is PNAD consumption expenditure per capita, based on an untrimmed imputation model calibrated on the PPV.
Exp. PNAD (ii): is PNAD consumption expenditure per capita, based on a trimmed imputation model (after correcting for outliers, we still used 99.5 percent of the untrimmed data set) calibrated on the PPV.
$\mu(y)$ is the mean welfare indicator (for example, average consumption expenditure).

normality issue and by adjusting the model structure for Rio, Sao Paulo, and Salvador to correct for heteroscedasticity. These final results correspond to the $P_{ii}(0)$ estimates presented in the last column. These represent our 'preferred' preliminary estimates and the poverty profile presented in subsequent sections is based on these

In Figure 6.1, for each region, the $P_{ii}(0)$ estimates are plotted against the estimated $P_{ppv}(0)$ measures and the respective $P_{ppv}(0)$ upper and lower bound standard error intervals. Firstly, observe that for six regions our estimated $P_{ii}(0)$, measures fall within one standard error deviation from the

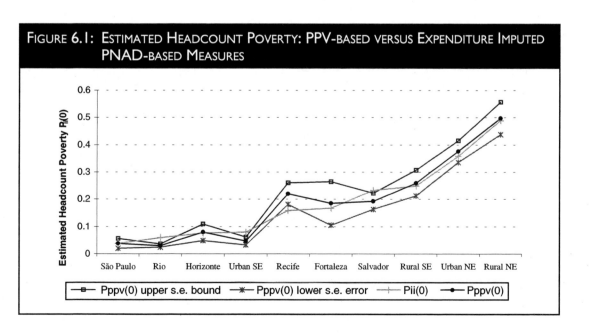

FIGURE 6.1: ESTIMATED HEADCOUNT POVERTY: PPV-BASED VERSUS EXPENDITURE IMPUTED PNAD-BASED MEASURES

TABLE 6.2: URBAN VERSUS RURAL POVERTY IN NE/SE BRAZIL

	Total Population	Population in Poverty	Population in percent Poverty
Total NE/SE	112,820,314	22,678,581	20.1 percent
Total NE/SE Urban	89,451,843	12,922,864	14.4 percent
Total NE/SE Rural	23,368,471	9,755,717	41.7 percent

$P_{ppv}(0)$ estimates.[97] Indeed, for three regions, the estimates are almost identical. Secondly, the two measures only differ substantially for 2 of the 10 regions—Recife and Rio.

When extrapolating our poverty measures using population data, we estimate that in 1996 for the NE and SE of Brazil combined, of the approximately 112.82 million people, some 20.1 percent (about 22,69 million) of the population lived in poverty.[98] Table 6.2. presents our poverty estimates when the population is categorized according to the traditional urban-rural dichotomous classification.

We see that while only 20.7 percent of the total population is rural, 41.7 percent of that rural population is below the poverty line versus only 14.4 percent of the urban population. Hence, as previous studies have reported, the incidence of poverty in rural areas appears to be much greater than in urban areas. In fact, despite the larger urban population, poverty is so widespread in rural areas that, in absolute numbers, nearly half (43 percent) of the population in poverty is actually rural. This quite clearly shows that poverty in Brazil is **not** largely an urban phenomenon.[99]

Figure 6.2 presents our poverty estimates on a regional population basis. We notice that poverty in the NE is more severe in terms of both absolute numbers of poor as well as percent of

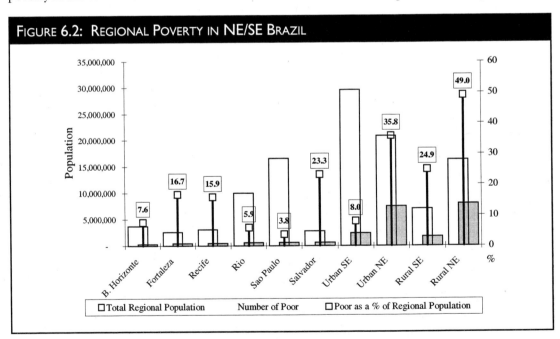

FIGURE 6.2: REGIONAL POVERTY IN NE/SE BRAZIL

97. Note that, given the preliminary nature of our analysis, we have not yet computed the standard errors associated with the $P_{ii}(0)$ poverty headcount measures. However, given the very good 'fit' of the two measures, we anticipate that $P_{ii}(0)$ standard error bounds would not considerably differ from the plotted $P_{ppv}(0)$ bounds.

98. The poverty line was set at R$65.07 in 1996 São Paulo Reais. See Ferreira, Lanjouw, and Neri (2000) for more details.

99. Note we are taking a conservative stance here. If we had employed the conventionally used income figures in the PNAD, the same conclusion would emerge much more strongly. Indeed, it is probably because PNAD income data produces such improbably high rural poverty figures that they have not tended to be used to study rural poverty questions.

population in poverty. The exceptions are the SE urban areas of Rio and Sao Paulo. In these two areas, compared to the three NE urban areas (Fortaleza, Recife, and Salvador), the incidence of poverty is low but there are large absolute numbers of poor.

Urban versus Rural Poverty: A Misleading Dichotomy?

In this section we take advantage of the PNAD questionnaire's spatial detail to examine if a richer categorization of the location spectrum ranging from rural to urban might offer a different perspective of poverty. A key question we raise is whether or not the extent of poverty is monotonically distributed across the rural-urban scale. In Figure 6.3, we present a poverty profile across seven categories that span the location spectrum from densely populated exclusively urban areas (urbana: area urbanizada) to remote exclusively rural areas (rural exclusive). The groupings can be divided as follows: *rural extensao urbana* relates to urbanized areas adjacent to the urban perimeter of municipalities (less than 1km distant) but not formally incorporated into the urban perimeter; *rural povoado* refers to agglomerations in rural areas with some permanent structures (at least one commercial establishment, and at least two of the following three structures—school, healthpost, place of worship); *rural nucleo* refers to isolated rural agglomerations with between 10 and 51 households, usually attached to some commercial entity (factory, agro-processing unit, etc.); *rural exclusive* refers to areas in rural areas which do not meet any of the criteria defining a rural agglomeration.[100] Turning to the urban categories: *urbana area urbanizada* refers to areas located within designated urban perimeters, with high population density, urban infrastructure, and multiple structures; *urbana nao urbanizadas* refers to areas within urban perimeters in which population densities remain low, agricultural actvities are still widespread, and there is relatively little urban infrastrcuture; *urbana isolada* refers to areas within the official urban perimeter though they are not directly adjacent to the center of the municipality and they are very sparsely populated.[101]

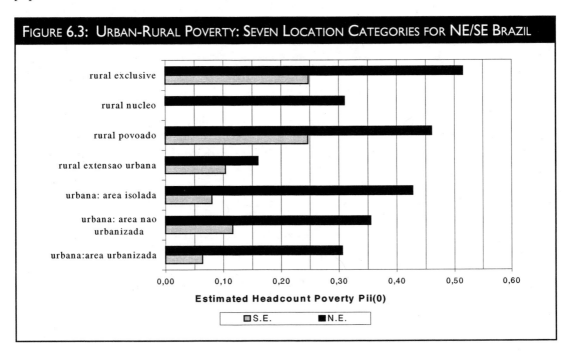

FIGURE 6.3: URBAN-RURAL POVERTY: SEVEN LOCATION CATEGORIES FOR NE/SE BRAZIL

---

100. Note that the distinction between rural and urban areas in Brazil is based on administrative as well as population density criteria.

101. The asymmetry in data between the NE and SE impede a meaningful interpretation of one location: "rural nucleo."

In terms of headcount poverty, we notice that this relationship is not monotonic. In other words, head count poverty does not monotonically decrease as we move from remote rural to heavily urbanized areas. We also observe that, regardless the location, poverty in the NE is higher than in the SE. Moreover, the gap between the NE and the SE is larger in the urban locations than in the rural locations. One exception appears to be the "*rural extensao urbana*" location. In these rural areas (presumably close to urban areas), poverty measures are the lowest across the whole NE and, for the SE they are lower compared to other SE rural areas and one of the SE urban locations.

We also note two other differences between the NE and the SE. First, unlike in the NE, in the SE there is no variation in poverty across the different rural location categories. Second, unlike in the SE, in the NE poverty is distributed monotonically across the urban location categories. The picture emerging from this categorization confirms that poverty is generally not distributed monotonically across locations, and that a simple geographical breakdown into rural and urban areas may conceal much of what is of interest.

State-Level Poverty Estimates

A major attraction with employing the PNAD data set is that its large sample size permits the disaggregation of poverty down to a level considerably lower than what is possible with the PPV survey. Based on our imputed consumption technique, we present in Table 6.3A. and Table 6.3B estimates of poverty by state, and urban/rural location in the NE and SE regions of the country, respectively. Overall, the incidence of poverty in the Northeast is estimated at 37 percent, corresponding to around 17 million persons. In rural areas the incidence is 48.8 percent, while in urban areas, the incidence is 30.7 percent. Given higher urban population figures, the headcount estimates result in roughly similar numbers of poor people in urban and rural areas of the northeast: some 8 million individuals in poverty in rural areas and 9 million in urban areas.

Poverty is estimated to be highest in the state of Maranhao, according to these provisional estimates. In the rural areas of this state, 55.8 percent of the population is estimated to be poor, (relative to 46.1 percent in urban Maranhao) representing about 1.6 million persons in rural areas and 1.1 million in urban areas. The range of poverty estimates by state in the Northeast lies between the 56 percent in Maranhao to a low of 29.5 percent in the state of Sergipe. The single largest contribution to overall poverty in the Northeast comes from the state of Bahia. Given its large population size, the overall headcount rate of 39.1 percent represents more than 5 million persons, breaking down to roughly 2.3 million in rural areas, and 2.7 million in urban areas. The biggest gap between urban and rural poverty is observed in the state of Ceara where 52 percent of the rural population is estimated to be poor, compared to half that rate in urban areas. Once again, however, because of relative population sizes, the overall numbers of poor people per region in this state are not far apart, and in fact suggest that more poor persons reside in urban areas. The overall impression is that the rural northeast is not only vast geographically and agro-ecologically, but also masks a considerable diversity of experiences regarding poverty.

We return briefly to the locational categories described above. These locational categories will prove to have some explanatory power in those models that estimate the probability of non-farm employment, so their correlation with poverty will also help to create a link between non-farm employment and poverty. We can see that in the Northeast region, the highest incidence of poverty is estimated in the *rural exclusive* areas. This is also where the bulk of the rural population resides so that the number of poor in these areas is far greater than in the other locational categories for rural areas. Rural poverty is estimated to be particularly low in the regions just adjacent to urban perimeters (*extensao urbana*) and is, in fact, estimated to be lower here than in any of the urban areas. On the other hand, poverty rate estimates in the urban areas (known as *area isolada*) are remarkably high: 41.9 percent of this population is poor. Numerically this urban category is not of great significance, however. It is useful to note that in these calculations, major metropolitan areas have been separated from the other urban areas, and that consistent with the findings of

TABLE 6.3A: POVERTY ESTIMATES IN THE RURAL NORTHEAST: INCIDENCE OF POVERTY BASED ON CONSUMPTION EXPENDITURES IMPUTED INTO THE 1996 PNAD

State/Sector	Headcount (percent)	Population Poor	# of observations in PNAD survey
Maranhao			
Urban	46.1	1,101,532	619
Rural	55.8	1,632,191	749
Total	51.4	2,731,660	1,368
Paiui			
Urban	33.5	538,160	677
Rural	50.9	589,921	489
Total	40.8	1,128,295	1,166
Ceara			
Urban	26.6	1,174,234	3,643
Rural	51.8	1,240,375	1,012
Total	35.4	2,410,372	4,655
Rio Grande do Norte			
Urban	25.2	416,489	765
Rural	43.0	418,436	387
Total	31.8	835,019	1,152
Paraiba			
Urban	25.1	547,849	998
Rural	42.9	511,519	493
Total	31.4	1,059,756	1,491
Pernambuco			
Urban	26.2	1,514,499	4,735
Rural	43.7	766,274	843
Total	30.2	2,275,274	5,578
Alagoas			
Urban	32.2	553,536	687
Rural	50.1	507,304	375
Total	38.8	1,059,876	1,062
Sergipe			
Urban	25.3	299,343	924
Rural	40.3	182,739	351
Total	29.5	482,803	1,275
Bahia			
Urban	34.0	2,749,080	5,284
Rural	47.5	2,269,218	1,890
Total	39.1	5,029,367	7,174
Rural Northeast			
Urban	30.7	8,907,297	18,332
Rural	48.8	8,120,749	6,589
Total	37.3	17,029,268	24,921
Location			
Metropolitan area	18.6	1,575,835	9,762
Other Urban: *area urbanizada*	35.7	7,375,228	8,815
Other Urban: *area nao urbanizada*	36.9	52,993	69
Other Urban: *area isolada*	41.9	18,503	21
Rural: *exensao urbana*	15.9	114,061	242
Rural: *povoado*	46.0	1,167,745	926
Rural: *nucleo*	31.8	25,468	28
Rural: *exclusive*	51.5	6,694,967	5,058

Notes: 1. Expenditures Adjusted for Spatial Price Variation (see Ferreira, Lanjouw, and Neri, 2000).
     2. Poverty Line of R$65.07 in 1996 Sao Paulo reais (see Ferreira, Lanjouw, and Neri, 2000).
Source: PNAD 1996.

TABLE 6.3B: POVERTY ESTIMATES IN THE RURAL SOUTHEAST: INCIDENCE OF POVERTY BASED ON CONSUMPTION EXPENDITURES IMPUTED INTO THE 1996 PNAD

State/Sector	Headcount (percent)	Population Poor	# of observations in PNAD survey
Minas Gerais			
Urban	9.9	1,255,831	7,787
Rural	33.4	1,310,577	1,847
Total	15.5	2,574,403	9,634
Espirito Santo			
Urban	11.1	236,402	1,091
Rural	17.6	124,914	333
Total	12.7	361,316	1,424
Rio de Janeiro			
Urban	6.2	784,583	7244
Rural	21.5	148,717	434
Total	7.0	934,240	7,678
Sao Paulo			
Urban	4.8	1,536,440	10,174
Rural	10.2	231,524	677
Total	5.1	1,767,964	10,851
Rural Southeast			
Urban	6.4	3,806,633	26,296
Rural	23.8	1,807,652	3,291
Total	8.4	5,567,128	29,587
Location			
Metropolitan area	4.9	1,461,739	13,641
Other Urban: *area urbanizada*	7.9	2,311,735	12,500
Other Urban: area *nao urbanizada*	18.2	28,156	68
Other Urban: *area isolada*	8.8	20,246	87
Rural: *exensao urbana*	9.6	40,703	162
Rural: *povoado*	24.4	135,750	268
Rural: *exclusive*	24.7	1,633,863	2,861

Notes: 1. Expenditures Adjusted for Spatial Price Variation (see Ferreira, Lanjouw, and Neri, 2000).
   2. Poverty Line of R$65.07 in 1996 Sao Paulo reais (see Ferreira, Lanjouw, and Neri, 2000).
Source: PNAD 1996.

Ferreira, Lanjouw, and Neri (2000) most of the urban poor are not estimated to reside in the large metropolitan cities.

In the Southeast, overall poverty is estimated at 8.4 percent: less than a forth of that found in the Northeast (Table 6.3B). In rural areas, the overall incidence is estimated at 23.8 percent, representing just fewer than 2 million individuals. While poverty rates in the urban Southeast are much lower than in rural areas, the overwhelmingly urban population in this region implies that the urban poor still outnumber the rural poor by a factor of 2. Poverty in general, and also rural and urban poverty separately, is estimated to be highest in the state of Minas Gerais. Just under half of the region's poor people are located in this one state, and almost three quarters of the region's rural poor are located here.

Locationally, the same patterns are observed in the Southeast as those described in the Northeast. Once again, poverty is highest and most of the rural poor pertain to the *rural exclusive* category. In urban areas, again, poverty rates are considerably higher in non-metropolitan areas, and these areas also account for the majority of the urban poor.

Non-Farm Activities in Northeast and Southeast Brazil

We now turn to an examination of the 1996 PNAD data on economic activity and occupation in order to obtain a "snapshot" overview of the non-farm sector in rural North and South Brazil during the mid-1990s.

Table 6.4A presents a breakdown of the entire economically active population in Northeast Brazil by sector of principal activity ("occupation") distinguishing between urban and rural areas. The Table does not separate wage labor from self-employment activities. In rural Northeast Brazil, 57.7 percent of the working population is engaged in agricultural activities ("cultivation"). Even in urban areas, the percentage of the working population, engaged in agricultural activities as their principal occupation, is as high as 9.3 percent. Turning to rural non-farm activities, we can see that 6.3 percent of the working population is primarily engaged in manufacturing and related activities; 3.7 percent in commerce; and 11.5 percent in various service sector activities. On the whole, about

TABLE 6.4A: PERCENTAGE OF THE WORKING POPULATION BY SECTOR OF PRIMARY OCCUPATION—NORTHEAST

	Rural Sector	Urban Sector		Rural Sector	Urban Sector
Cultivation	57.7	9.3	**3. Sales**		
Animal rearing	15.1	3.3	Wholesaling	0.1	0.1
Forest product	3.5	0.2	Food/beverage sales	1.6	5.2
Fishing	1.7	1.3	Clothing sales	0.2	1.2
1. Mining/Extraction	**0.3**	**0.3**	Street sales	1.1	5.2
2. Manufacturing			Other sales	0.7	6.4
Ceramics	0.9	0.9	**Sub-Total**	**3.7**	**18.1**
Metals	0.1	0.6	**4. Services**		
Machinery	0.0	0.3	Transport	0.7	3.9
Electronic goods	0.0	0.1	Hotel	0.1	0.4
Vehicles	0.0	0.5	Restaurant	0.7	4.1
Wooden goods	0.5	0.7	Servicing/repair	0.4	3.4
Furniture	0.1	0.8	Personal services	1.0	3.7
Paper	0.0	0.1	Own account services	2.9	10.5
Rubber	0.0	0.0	Financial services	0.1	1.1
Leather	0.0	0.0	Post/telecoms	0.1	0.5
Chemical/dyes	0.0	0.3	Arts/entertainment	0.1	0.7
Pharmaceuticals	0.0	0.1	Professional services	0.3	2.7
Cosmetics	0.0	0.1	Private organization	0.8	4.7
Plastics	0.0	0.2	Education	2.9	6.9
Textiles	0.5	0.7	Government	1.3	6.4
Clothing	0.1	0.7	Informal activity	0.1	0.6
Footwear	0.1	0.3	**Sub-Total**	**11.5**	**49.6**
Food processing	1.1	2.2	**Non-Agricultural Total (1 + 2 + 3 + 4)**	**21.8**	**85.5**
Beverages	0.1	0.2			
Tobacco products	0.0	0.0	**Total**	**100.0**	**100**
Printing	0.0	0.3			
Precision instruments	0.0	0.2	Working population (percent of total population)	7,932,229 (47.7)	11,261,726 (38.9)
Construction	2.6	6.9			
Utilities	0.2	1.3			
Sub-Total	**6.3**	**17.5**			

Source: PNAD 1996

21.8 percent of the rural working population is engaged in non-agricultural activities as their primary activity. These figures are likely to be conservative estimates of the importance of non-agricultural activities because they do not include non-farm activities, which are secondary. For example, in rural Ecuador Lanjouw (1999) finds that about 40 percent of the rural population is engaged in non-agricultural activities as either primary or secondary occupations.

In Table 6.4B we examine the breakdown of Southeast Brazil in similar terms as with Table 6.4B. In rural Southeast 41.7 percent of the working population is principally engaged in cultivation. An important related activity is livestock, accounting for 25.9 percent of the economically active population. The non-agricultural sector accounts for 31.7 percent of the economically active population, half-again as large as in the rural Northeast. In urban areas, the fraction of the population engaged in non-agricultural activities as their principal activity is about a third of what was observed in the Northeast which is consistent with the overall impression of greater levels of industrialization in urban conurbation in the south.

TABLE 6.4B: PERCENTAGE OF THE WORKING POPULATION BY SECTOR OF PRIMARY OCCUPATION—SOUTHEAST

	Rural Sector	Urban Sector		Rural Sector	Urban Sector
Cultivation	41.7	3.7	**3. Sales**		
Animal rearing	25.9	1.7	Wholesaling	0.0	0.2
Forest product	0.4	0.1	Food/beverage sales	0.9	2.7
Fishing	0.2	0.1	Clothing sales	0.1	2.3
1. Mining/Extraction	**0.5**	**0.3**	Street sales	0.7	2.3
2. Manufacturing			Other sales	1.5	8.0
Ceramics	1.1	1.0	**Sub-Total**	**3.2**	**15.5**
Metals	0.3	2.4	**4. Services**		
Machinery	0.1	1.0	Transport	1.4	4.3
Electronic goods	0.1	0.8	Hotel	0.1	0.4
Vehicles	0.3	1.4	Restaurant	1.2	4.3
Wooden goods	0.2	0.4	Servicing/repair	0.6	3.7
Furniture	0.3	0.9	Personal services	0.9	3.3
Paper	0.1	0.4	Own account services	7.9	11.2
Rubber	0.0	0.2	Financial services	0.2	2.3
Leather	0.0	0.1	Post/telecoms	0.1	0.6
Chemical/dyes	0.4	0.8	Arts/entertainment	0.2	0.8
Pharmaceuticals	0.0	0.2	Professional services	0.7	5.2
Cosmetics	0.1	0.2	Private organization	1.0	5.6
Plastics	0.1	0.4	Education	2.2	5.4
Textiles	0.1	0.8	Government	1.2	4.9
Clothing	0.4	1.3	Informal activity	0.2	0.5
Footwear	0.1	0.5	**Sub-Total**	**17.9**	**52.5**
Food processing	1.3	2.8	**Non-Agricultural Total** (1 + 2 + 3 + 4)	**31.7**	**94.2**
Beverages	0.2	0.3			
Tobacco products	0.1	0.0	**Total**	**100**	**100**
Printing	0.1	0.8			
Precision instruments	0.2	0.6	Working population (percent of total population)	3,729,313 (49.1)	25,907,114 (43.4)
Construction	4.0	7.7			
Utilities	0.5	0.9			
Sub-Total	**10.1**	**25.9**			

Source: PNAD 1996

Table 6.5 revisits the breakdowns presented above, but now focuses specifically on the non-agricultural working population in rural areas. In the rural Northeast, the important activities within the manufacturing (and related) sub-sector comprise textiles, food processing and construction. Food processing and construction are similarly important in the rural Southeast. Overall, about a third of rural non-farm employment in both the Northeast as well as the Southeast is associated with manufacturing and transformation of goods. Commercial activities in the rural Northeast account for about 17 percent of total rural non-farm activities, compared to 10 percent in the Southeast. On the other hand, self-employment activities are particularly important in the rural Southeast, accounting for about a quarter of all non-farm activities, compared to 13 percent in the rural Northeast. Employment rates in the education and government sector accounts for a considerable fraction of total non-farm employment in the rural Northeast (13 percent and 5 percent respectively) while in the rural Southeast the comparable percentages are 7 percent and 4 percent respectively. Overall, in both the rural Northeast and rural Southeast, service sector activities account for more than half of all non-farm activities. As Reardon et al (2000) point out, this observation may contradict common perceptions about the rural non-farm sector, but is actually not an uncommon feature for the non-farm sector.

TABLE 6.5: PERCENTAGE OF THE RURAL NON-AGRICULTURAL WORKING POPULATION BY SECTOR OF PRIMARY OCCUPATION

	Rural Northeast	Rural Southeast		Rural Northeast	Rural Southeast
1. Mining/Extraction	1.5	1.6	3. Sales		
2. Manufacturing			Wholesaling	0.4	0.1
Ceramics	3.9	3.4	Food/beverage sales	7.1	2.8
Metals	0.6	0.8	Clothing sales	0.8	0.3
Machinery	0.2	0.3	Street sales	5.2	2.3
Electronic goods	0.0	0.4	Other sales	3.2	4.6
Vehicles	0.0	0.9	Sub-Total	16.7	10.1
Wooden goods	2.3	0.8	4. Services		
Furniture	0.5	0.8	Transport	3.4	4.4
Paper	0.0	0.2	Hotel	0.3	0.4
Rubber	0.0	0.1	Restaurant	3.3	3.7
Leather	0.2	0.0	Servicing/repair	1.8	1.9
Chemical/dyes	0.1	1.2	Personal services	4.3	2.9
Pharmaceuticals	0.0	0.0	Own account services	13.3	24.9
Cosmetics	0.0	0.4	Financial services	0.5	0.8
Plastics	0.1	0.2	Post/telecoms	0.6	0.4
Textiles	2.3	0.5	Arts/entertainment	0.2	0.6
Clothing	0.4	1.3	Professional services	1.6	2.1
Footwear	0.3	0.2	Private organization	3.8	3.2
Food processing	5.0	4.1	Education	13.3	7.1
Beverages	0.3	0.6	Government	5.8	3.9
Tobacco products	0.1	0.0	Informal activity	0.4	0.8
Printing	0.0	0.4	Sub-Total	52.6	57.1
Precision instruments	0.4	0.5	Total	100	100
Construction	11.7	12.7			
Utilities	0.9	1.6			
Sub-Total	29.3	31.4			

Source: PNAD 1996Source: PNAD 1996

Tables 6.6A and 6.6B. scrutinize the non-farm sector against a breakdown of the rural Northeast and rural Southeast along the spatial dimension. At the bottom of Table 6.6A, we can see that although the *rural exclusive* area accounts for 82 percent of the entire rural working population, it accounts for only 59 percent of the total participation in the non-farm sector. Rural areas on the perimeter of urban municipalities (*extensao urbana*) and rural towns (*povoado*) account for a disproportionate share of employment in the non-farm sector (representing about 18 percent of the rural working population but accounting for nearly 40 percent

TABLE 6.6A: Percentage of the Rural Non-Agricultural Working Population by Location and Sector of Primary Occupation—Northeast

	Extensao Urbana[b]	Povoado[c]	Nucleo[d]	Exclusive[e]
1. Mining/Extraction	0.1	0.1	0.0	1.3
2. Manufacturing				
Ceramics	0.1	0.7	0.0	3.1
Metals	0.3	0.0	0.0	0.3
Machinery	0.0	0.1	0.0	0.0
Electronic goods	0.0	0.0	0.0	0.0
Vehicles	0.0	0.0	0.0	0.0
Wooden goods	0.1	0.3	0.0	1.9
Furniture	0.0	0.2	0.0	0.3
Paper	0.0	0.0	0.0	0.0
Rubber	0.0	0.0	0.0	0.0
Leather	0.1	0.0	0.0	0.1
Chemical/dyes	0.0	0.0	0.0	0.1
Pharmaceuticals	0.0	0.0	0.0	0.0
Cosmetics	0.0	0.0	0.0	0.0
Plastics	0.1	0.0	0.0	0.1
Textiles	0.1	0.3	0.0	1.8
Clothing	0.2	0.0	0.0	0.2
Footwear	0.0	0.2	0.0	0.1
Food processing	0.4	0.4	0.5	3.7
Beverages	0.1	0.1	0.0	0.1
Tobacco products	0.0	0.0	0.0	0.1
Printing	0.0	0.0	0.0	0.0
Precision instruments	0.0	0.1	0.0	0.2
Construction	1.1	2.8	0.0	7.8
Utilities	0.2	0.4	0.0	0.3
Sub-Total	**2.8**	**5.6**	**0.5**	**20.2**
3. Sales				
Wholesaling	0.1	0.2	0.0	0.1
Food/beverage sales	0.8	2.7	0.0	3.7
Clothing sales	0.5	0.1	0.0	0.1
Street sales	1.1	1.2	0.0	2.9
Other sales	1.1	0.5	0.0	1.6
Sub-Total	**3.6**	**4.7**	**0.0**	**8.4**
4. Services				
Transport	0.6	0.9	0.0	1.9
Hotel	0.0	0.2	0.0	0.0

(continued)

TABLE 6.6A: PERCENTAGE OF THE RURAL NON-AGRICULTURAL WORKING POPULATION BY
LOCATION AND SECTOR OF PRIMARY OCCUPATION—NORTHEAST (*CONTINUED*)

	Extensao Urbana[b]	Povoado[c]	Nucleo[d]	Exclusive[e]
Restaurant	0.4	1.6	0.0	1.2
Servicing/repair	0.5	0.5	0.1	0.7
Personal services	0.6	0.9	0.0	2.8
Own account services	2.3	2.6	0.3	8.1
Financial services	0.4	0.0	0.0	0.0
Post/telecoms	0.2	0.2	0.0	0.2
Arts/entertainment	0.0	0.0	0.0	0.2
Professional services	0.6	0.2	0.0	0.8
Private organization	1.4	0.8	0.2	1.4
Education	1.6	2.8	0.1	8.7
Government	1.4	1.5	0.0	2.9
Informal activity	0.0	0.1	0.0	0.2
Sub-Total	*10.0*	*12.1*	*0.7*	*29.1*
Total[a] (1 + 2 + 3 + 4)	**16.6**	**23.1**	**1.3**	**59.0**
Working Population (percent total Working Population)	317,289 (4.0)	1,083,146 (13.7)	23,796 (0.3)	6,504,428 (82.0)

Source: PNAD 1996
[a] Total may not equal the sum of sub-totals due to rounding.
[b] Urbanized areas adjacent to the urban perimeter of municipalities (less than 1km distant), but not formally incorporated into the urban perimeter.
[c] agglomerations in rural areas with some permanent structures: at least one commercial establishment, and at least two of the following three establishments (school, healthpost, religious establishment).
[d] Isolated rural agglomeration with between 10 and 51 households, usually attached to some commercial entity (factory, agro-processing unit, etc).
[e] Areas which do not meet any of the criteria defining an agglomeration.

of total participation in the non-farm sector). This lends credence to the notion that non-farm activities are closely linked to market centers and the basic infrastructure that supports them. The evidence does not suggest that manufacturing (and related) activities are specifically concentrated in the more urbanized rural settlements, although commercial activities do tend to be more common there.

Table 6.6B. examines the locational breakdown of non-farm activities in the rural Southeast. Here the mapping of non-farm employment patterns across locations is much closer to the mapping of the working population. While the *rural exclusive* accounts for 89 percent of the total rural working population, participation in the non-farm sector in these areas is only a somewhat lower 77 percent of all non-farm employment. In contrast, again, to the Northeast, manufacturing activities account for the bulk of non-farm employment in the rural settlements (*rural povoado*) and a significant share in the urban periphery, compared to less than a third of non-farm employment in the *rural exclusive*.

A further breakdown of the PNAD data is presented in Tables 6.7A. and 6.7B. Here we consider the participation of men and women separately. Table 6.7A. indicates that roughly the same number of men and women are active in the rural non-farm sector in Northeast Brazil. Just below 52 percent of total non-farm participation is accounted for by men as opposed to about 48 percent by women. However, because women are less involved in agricultural activities, the non-farm sector accounts for a much larger share of total economic activities carried out by women than it does for men. Nearly 30 percent of economically active women are primarily engaged in the non-farm sector, compared to 18 percent of men. Men and women are

TABLE 6.6B: PERCENTAGE OF THE RURAL NON-AGRICULTURAL WORKING POPULATION BY LOCATION AND SECTOR OF PRIMARY OCCUPATION—SOUTHEAST

	Extensao Urbana[b]	Povoado[c]	Exclusive[d]
1. Mining/Extraction	0.0	0.4	1.1
2. Manufacturing			
Ceramics	0.2	0.2	3.1
Metals	0.1	0.2	0.5
Machinery	0.1	0.0	0.3
Electronic goods	0.0	0.0	0.4
Vehicles	0.1	0.1	0.7
Wooden goods	0.0	0.1	0.7
Furniture	0.3	0.1	0.4
Paper	0.0	0.0	0.2
Rubber	0.0	0.0	
Leather	0.0	0.0	
Chemical/dyes	0.5	0.1	0.6
Pharmaceuticals	0.0	0.0	
Cosmetics	0.0	0.0	0.4
Plastics	0.0	0.0	0.1
Textiles	0.2	0.1	0.2
Clothing	0.2	0.2	0.9
Footwear	0.0	0.0	0.2
Food processing	0.3	0.5	3.3
Beverages	0.1	0.0	0.5
Tobacco products	0.0	0.0	
Printing	0.2	0.0	0.1
Precision instruments	0.1	0.1	0.3
Construction	1.2	1.9	9.6
Utilities	0.0	0.3	1.4
Sub-Total	**4.5**	**6.6**	**23.9**
3. Sales			
Wholesaling	0.0	0.0	0.0
Food/beverage sales	0.4	0.6	1.7
Clothing sales	0.1	0.0	0.1
Street sales	0.6	0.4	1.4
Other sales	0.5	0.4	3.7
Sub-Total	1.6	1.4	6.9
4. Services			
Transport	0.9	0.7	2.9
Hotel	0.1	0.0	0.3
Restaurant	0.7	0.7	2.3
Servicing/repair	0.5	0.1	1.3
Personal services	0.1	0.4	2.3
Own account services	2.4	2.2	20.3
Financial services	0.4	0.0	0.3
Post/telecoms	0.1	0.1	0.2
Arts/entertainment	0.0	0.0	0.6
Professional services	0.2	0.1	1.8

(continued)

TABLE 6.6B: PERCENTAGE OF THE RURAL NON-AGRICULTURAL WORKING POPULATION BY LOCATION AND SECTOR OF PRIMARY OCCUPATION—SOUTHEAST (CONTINUED)

	Extensao Urbana[b]	Povoado[c]	Exclusive[d]
Private organization	0.3	0.4	2.5
Education	0.3	0.6	6.2
Government	0.3	0.5	3.1
Informal activity	0.2	0.0	0.6
Sub-Total	**6.5**	**5.8**	**44.7**
Total[a] (1 + 2 + 3 + 4)	**11.9**	**11.5**	**76.6**
Working Population	188,852	228,197	3,319,089
(percent total Working Population)	(5.1)	(6.1)	(88.8)

[a]Total may not equal the sum of sub-totals due to rounding.
[b]Urbanized areas adjacent to the urban perimeter of municipalities (less than1km distant), but not formally incorporated into the urban perimeter.
[c]agglomerations in rural areas with some permanent structures: at least one commercial establishment, and at least two of the following three establishments (school, healthpost, religious establishment).
[d]Areas which do not meet any of the criteria defining an agglomeration.
Source: PNAD 1996.

also engaged in quite different activities. For example, while more than 22 percent of men who participate in the non-farm sector are involved in construction activities, only 0.2 percent of women are engaged in such activities. Other activities of importance for men include construction (22.5 percent), food/beverage sales (9.1 percent), food processing (6.7 percent), ceramic production (6.6 percent), government and administration (6.3 percent) and transport services (6.1). Women are particularly involved in education (24.9 percent) self-employment (23.4 percent), and personal services (8.4 percent).

In the rural Southeast, women are less represented among non-farm workers. While they accounted for nearly half of all non-farm employment in the Northeast, they represent only 41 percent of total non-farm employment in the Southeast. Once again, however, the non-farm sector accounts for a much larger share of total economic activities carried out by women than it does for men, because women tend to be less involved in agricultural practices than men. Considering the subsectoral breakdown for men and women separately, it appears that as in the rural Northeast, construction is of major importance for men (21.4 percent of total non-farm employment of men). Other sectors that are particularly important for men include own-account services (10.3 percent), and transport (7.3 percent). For women, self-employment for no less than 45.4 percent of non-farm employment. This is followed by education services (15.4 percent) as in the case of Northeast Brazil.

Table 6.8 presents a breakdown of broad non-farm activities by state in rural Northeast and Southeast Brazil. As a percentage of total non-farm activities in the rural Northeast, the states of Maranhao and Bahia each account for about a little over 20 percent of total non-farm employment in the region. However, while this is in fact lower than Bahia's share of the region's total rural population, the 22 percent of non-farm employment accounted for by Maranhao is somewhat higher than its regional population share of 18 percent. Much of the non-farm employment sector activity in Maranhao is associated with services (accounting for 14 percent of total non-farm employment in the region as a whole) and sales/commerce. Another state, which accounts for a larger share of regional non-farm employment than what its population share would suggest, is Rio Grande do Norte. Here, again, much of the employment is related to services, although manufacturing is also relatively significant. Manufacturing activity in the non-farm sector is also important in the states of Ceara and Bahia.

TABLE 6.7A: PERCENTAGE OF THE RURAL NON-AGRICULTURAL WORKING POPULATION BY GENDER AND SECTOR OF PRIMARY OCCUPATION—NORTHEAST

	Male	Female		Male	Female
1. Mining/Extraction	2.9	0.1	Street sales	5.3	5.1
2. Manufacturing			Other sales	4.3	2.0
Ceramics	6.6	1.0	Sub-Total	19.8	13.4
Metals	1.0	0.1	**4. Services**		
Machinery	0.2	0.1	Transport	6.1	0.4
Electronic goods	0.0	0.0	Hotel	0.4	0.3
Vehicles	0.0	0.0	Restaurant	3.6	3.0
Wooden goods	2.7	1.8	Servicing/repair	3.4	0.1
Furniture	1.0	0.0	Personal services	0.5	8.4
Paper	0.0	0.0	Own account services	3.8	23.4
Rubber	0.0	0.0	Financial services	0.4	0.6
Leather	0.2	0.1	Post/telecoms	0.6	0.5
Chemical/dyes	0.2	0.0	Arts/entertainment	0.4	0.1
Pharmaceuticals	0.1	0.0	Professional services	1.8	1.3
Cosmetics	0.0	0.0	Private organization	2.2	5.6
Plastics	0.2	0.1	Education	2.4	24.9
Textiles	1.0	3.6	Government	6.3	5.3
Clothing	0.2	0.6	Informal activity	0.5	0.3
Footwear	0.2	0.4	**Sub-Total**	**32.4**	**74.2**
Food processing	6.7	3.2		100.0	100.0
Beverages	0.4	0.2	**Non-Agricultural**	**899,220**	**841,169**
Tobacco products	0.1	0.1	**Workers (percent**	**(51.7)**	**(48.3)**
Printing	0.0	0.0	**of Total Non-**		
Precision instruments	0.2	0.5	**Agricultural**		
Construction	22.5	0.2	**Working**		
Utilities	1.1	0.6	**Population)**		
Sub-Total	**44.8**	**12.6**	**percent Share of**	**18.0**	**28.6**
3. Sales			**Total Working**		
Wholesaling	0.7	0.1	**Population**		
Food/beverage sales	9.1	5.0	**(Agriculture plus**		
Clothing sales	0.4	1.2	**Non-Agriculture)**		

Source: PNAD 1996.

In the rural Southeast, the states of Minas Gerais and Espiritu Santo both account for a smaller share of non-farm employment than what their rural population shares would suggest, while in the states of Rio de Janeiro and Sao Paulo, the opposite is true. In all Southeastern states, the relative importance of different sub-sectors is roughly constant (about one third of each state's respective overall employment share is accounted for by manufacturing, just over half is attributable to services, and so on).

We turn, finally, to a multivariate analysis of participation in non-farm activities. We estimate, in Tables 6.9A and 6.9B, a probit model of involvement in non-farm activities as the primary occupation on a range of individual, household, and geographic characteristics. We do this in turn for the rural Northeast and the rural Southeast. Rather than report the parameter estimates, which are difficult to interpret on their own, we present in Tables 6.9A and 6.9B the marginal effects associated with each explanatory variable. These can be interpreted as indicating the effect of a percentage

TABLE 6.7B: PERCENTAGE OF THE RURAL NON-AGRICULTURAL WORKING POPULATION BY GENDER AND SECTOR OF PRIMARY OCCUPATION—SOUTHEAST

	Male	Female		Male	Female
1. Mining/Extraction	2.7	0.0	Street sales	1.8	3.1
2. Manufacturing			Other sales	5.9	2.8
Ceramics	5.2	0.9	**Sub-Total**	**11.2**	**8.7**
Metals	1.2	0.3	**4. Services**		
Machinery	0.5	0.2	Transport	7.3	0.3
Electronic goods	0.6	0.2	Hotel	0.4	0.5
Vehicles	1.6	0.0	Restaurant	3.5	4.0
Wooden goods	1.2	0.2	Servicing/repair	3.2	0.0
Furniture	1.1	0.4	Personal services	0.6	6.1
Paper	0.3	0.0	Own account services	10.3	45.4
Rubber	0.1	0.0	Financial services	0.5	1.2
Leather	0.1	0.0	Post/telecoms	0.4	0.4
Chemical/dyes	2.0	0.0	Arts/entertainment	0.7	0.5
Pharmaceuticals	0.0	0.1	Professional services	2.4	1.6
Cosmetics	0.6	0.0	Private organization	1.8	5.1
Plastics	0.3	0.0	Education	1.1	15.4
Textiles	0.8	0.0	Government	5.0	2.5
Clothing	0.8	1.9	Informal activity	1.2	0.2
Footwear	0.2	0.2	**Sub-Total**	**38.4**	**83.2**
Food processing	5.2	2.5	**Total**	**100.0**	**100.0**
Beverages	1.0	0.0			
Tobacco products	0.0	0.0	**Non-Agricultural Workers (percent of Total Non-Agricultural Working Population)**	**693,038 (5.6)**	**489,882 (41.4)**
Printing	0.5	0.1			
Precision instruments	0.8	0.1			
Construction	21.4	0.3			
Utilities	2.2	0.8			
Sub-Total	**47.7**	**8.2**	**percent Share of Total Working Population (Agriculture plus Non-Agriculture)**	**27.7**	**39.9**
3. Sales					
Wholesaling	0.1	0.0			
Food/beverage sales	3.2	2.2			
Clothing sales	0.2	0.6			

Source: PNAD 1996.

change in the explanatory variable of the probability of involvement in non-farm business activities, taking all other variables in the specification at their means.[20]

From the earlier discussion regarding the non-farm sector as a source of both high-return employment as well as a "last resort" option, we go on to estimate two additional models with the same specification of regressors. However, we differentiate involvement in high return non-farm activities from low return non-farm activities. We designate non-farm sub-sectors, sectors as either high return or low return, depending on the average monthly earnings accruing to individuals whose primary occupation is in that sector. If the average monthly income accruing to particular sub-sectors of the non-farm sector is below the poverty line, the sub-sector is designated as a low return sector. All those engaged in this sub-sector are then regarded as involved in

---

20. For dummy variables, the marginal effect is calculated as the change in the dependent variable associated with a move from a value of 0 for the dummy, to 1, holding all other variables constant at mean values.

TABLE 6.8: RURAL NON-AGRICULTURAL WORKING POPULATION BY STATE AND BROAD SECTOR OF PRIMARY OCCUPATION
(As a percentage of Total Non-Agricultural Working Population in Rural Northeast and Rural Southeast Regions Respectively)

	Mining/ Extraction (1)	Manufacturing (2)	Sales (3)	Services (4)	Non-Agricultural Employment as percent of Regional Non-Agricultural Employment (1+2+3+4)[a]	Rural Population as percent of Regional Rural Population
Rural Northeast						
Maranhao	0.0	2.9	5.0	14.1	22.3	18
Piaui	0.2	2.7	0.8	3.1	6.8	7
Ceara	0.2	5.0	1.8	6.5	13.6	14
Rio Grande do Norte	0.2	3.2	1.3	5.3	10.2	6
Paraiba	0.0	1.6	0.7	4.3	6.5	7
Pernambuco	0.1	2.6	1.8	4.8	9.3	11
Alagoas	0.1	2.6	0.6	2.8	6.3	6
Sergipe	0.0	1.0	0.4	1.9	3.3	3
Bahia	0.7	6.9	4.2	9.6	21.7	28
Total	**1.5**	**28.5**	**16.6**	**52.4**	**100.0**	**100**
Rural Southeast						
Minas Gerais	1.2	11.7	3.4	23.0	39.2	52
Espiritu Santo	0.1	1.4	1.1	3.3	5.9	9
Rio de Janeiro	0.1	4.0	1.2	8.2	13.5	9
Sao Paulo	0.3	14.4	4.4	22.4	41.4	30
Total	**1.7**	**31.5**	**10.1**	**56.9**	**100.0**	**100**

[a] Total may differ slightly from sum of sub-totals due to rounding.
Source: PNAD 1996.

TABLE 6.9A: PROBIT MODEL OF NON-AGRICULTURAL EMPLOYMENT NORTHEAST

Explanatory Variables	Any Non-Agricultural Employment DF/dx (prob value)	Low-Productivity Non-Agricultural Employment dF/dx (prob value)	High-Productivity Non-Agricultural Employment dF/dx (prob value)
Male (dummy)	0.015 (0.000)	−0.025 (0.000)	0.037 (0.000)
Age in years	0.016 (0.000)	0.002 (0.000)	0.011 (0.000)
Age squared	−0.0002 (0.000)	−0.00003 (0.000)	−0.0001 (0.000)
Black (dummy)	0.0075 (0.315)	0.0057 (0.139)	0.0013 (0.810)
Mulatto (dummy)	0.001 (0.787)	0.0017 (0.303)	−0.0012 (0.660)
Asian (dummy)	0.044 (0.379)	n/a	0.051 (0.204)
Indian (dummy)	0.027 (0.495)	0.019 (0.364)	0.004 (0.889)
Household Size	−0.0005 (0.406)	0.0008 (0.006)	−0.0015 (0.001)
percent of Family involved in cultivation	−0.263 (0.000)	−0.044 (0.000)	−0.183 (0.000)
Locally-born (dummy)	−0.011 (0.003)	−0.004 (0.009)	−0.004 (0.160)
Elementary schooling Only (dummy)	0.020 (0.000)	0.009 (0.001)	0.008 (0.041)
Medio 1 (dummy)	0.059 (0.006)	0.012 (0.203)	0.036 (0.018)
Grau 1 (dummy)	0.047 (0.000)	0.017 (0.000)	0.022 (0.000)
Medio 2 (dummy)	0.233 (0.000)	0.008 (0.543)	0.173 (0.000)
Higher schooling (dummy)	0.237 (0.000)	−0.014 (0.030)	0.232 (0.000)
Extensao urbana (dummy)	0.107 (0.000)	0.019 (0.000)	0.064 (0.000)
Povoado (dummy)	0.036 (0.000)	0.004 (0.043)	0.027 (0.000)
Nucleo (dummy)	(0.098) (0.000)	0.054 (0.001)	0.047 (0.011)
Piaui (dummy)	0.010 (0.205)	−0.004 (0.198)	0.015 (0.017)
Ceara (dummy)	0.030 (0.000)	0.008 (0.017)	0.017 (0.0.001)
Rio Grande do Norte (dummy)	0.026 (0.001)	0.010 (0.008)	0.009 (0.103)
Paraiba (dummy)	0.036 (0.000)	0.002 (0.549)	0.029 (0.000)
Pernambuco (dummy)	0.007 (0.317)	0.002 (0.542)	0.002 (0.670)

(continued)

TABLE 6.9A: PROBIT MODEL OF NON-AGRICULTURAL EMPLOYMENT NORTHEAST (CONTINUED)

	Any Non-Agricultural Employment	Low-Productivity Non-Agricultural Employment	High-Productivity Non-Agricultural Employment
Alagoas (dummy)	−0.007 (0.382)	−0.012 (0.000)	0.007 (0.269)
Sergipe (dummy)	0.051 (0.000)	0.006 (0.166)	0.037 (0.000)
Bahia (dummy)	−0.008 (0.181)	−0.009 (0.001)	0.002 (0.653)
Metropolitan Area (dummy)	0.024 (0.002)	0.017 (0.000)	0.003 (0.597)
Nr. of Observations	23,631	23,598	23,631
χ^2 (27)	4,420.49	1,073.67	3,781.47
Prob > χ^2	0.0000	0.000	0.000
Pseudo R^2	0.2359	0.1490	0.2459
Log Likelihood	−7,158.84	−3,066.74	−5,797.67
Observed Probability	**0.135**	**0.035**	**0.100**
Predicted Probability	**0.071**	**0.017**	**0.043**

Source: PNAD 1996.

a low-return, last-resort activity. Conversely, if the average monthly return from a sub-sector is above the poverty line, the sub-sector is considered as high-return. In this event, it was found that the following sub-sectors could be regarded as low-return activities: cloth weaving, street and market vending, self employment services, personal services and informal activities.

Model 1 in Table 6.9A, comprising all non-farm activities in the rural Northeast combined, indicates that men are more likely to engage in the non-farm sector than women, controlling for all other variables. The likelihood of non-farm employment becomes higher with age until it reaches a turning point at around 37 years and then declines. Controlling for other characteristics, the probability of non-farm participation does not appear to be associated with race. This finding can be contrasted with the experience in other countries, where for example ethnicity, cast, religion, etc. are often associated with different participation rates, regardless of education levels, and other characteristics (see also below).

While household size does not seem to be associated with non-farm participation, the data does suggest that households that concentrate on agricultural activities (and have a high proportion of family members engaged in cultivation) are less likely to have a particular member engage in non-farm activities. This suggests that while non-farm activities may be highly sought-after by cultivating households seeking to limit their exposure to stochastic shocks through income diversification, the evidence in Brazil seems to suggest instead, that households specialize in non-farm activities or cultivation. An interesting additional finding is that individuals who were born in the same municipality as the one in which they were interviewed for the PNAD survey were (although significantly) less likely to be involved in the non-farm sector. A person (native to the area in question) has a 1-percentage-point lower probability of participating in the non-farm sector.

As has been found in other studies, the probability of involvement in the non-farm sector is positively and significantly related to education levels. Holding other variables constant at their sample means, having achieved even an elementary school education raises the probability of involvement in the non-farm sector by 2 percentage points, compared to a person with no education at all. An education level of *medio1 ciclo* raises the probability of participation in the non-farm sector by 5.9 percentage points, relative to having no education at all. If the highest education level achieved is *1 grau*, then the probability is 4.7 percentage points higher than the baseline of no edu-

TABLE 6.9B: PROBIT MODEL OF NON-AGRICULTURAL EMPLOYMENT SOUTHEAST

Explanatory Variables	Any Non-Agricultural Employment DF/dx (prob value)	Low-Productivity Non-Agricultural Employment dF/dx (prob value)	High-Productivity Non-Agricultural Employment dF/dx (prob value)
Male (dummy)	0.047 (0.000)	−0.051 (0.000)	0.083 (0.000)
Age in years	0.024 (0.000)	0.0045 (0.000)	0.016 (0.000)
Age squared	−0.0003 (0.000)	−0.00006 (0.000)	−0.0002 (0.000)
Black (dummy)	0.010 (0.340)	0.0173 (0.005)	−0.009 (0.161)
Mulatto (dummy)	−0.008 (0.266)	0.005 (0.136)	−0.013 (0.003)
Asian (dummy)	−0.092 (0.010)	n/a	−0.042 (0.055)
Household Size	−0.0006 (0.681)	−0.0007 (0.346)	−0.00002 (0.982)
percent of Family involved in cultivation	−0.387 (0.000)	−0.086 (0.000)	−0.245 (0.000)
Locally-born (dummy)	−0.005 (0.468)	−0.007 (0.047)	0.003 (0.453)
Elementary schooling Only (dummy)	0.013 (0.210)	0.016 (0.005)	−0.005 (0.413)
Medio 1 (dummy)	0.062 (0.029)	0.017 (0.266)	0.025 (0.150)
Grau 1 (dummy)	0.064 (0.000)	0.022 (0.000)	0.027 (0.000)
Medio 2 (dummy)	0.130 (0.021)	−0.029 (0.157)	0.146 (0.001)
Higher schooling (dummy)	0.192 (0.000)	−0.018 (0.169)	0.182 (0.000)
Extensao urbana (dummy)	0.049 (0.001)	0.004 (0.571)	0.031 (0.002)
Povoado (dummy)	0.098 (0.000)	0.013 (0.037)	0.066 (0.000)
Espiritu Santo (dummy)	0.026 (0.038)	0.014 (0.045)	0.009 (0.299)
Rio de Janeiro (dummy)	0.085 (0.000)	0.029 (0.000)	0.042 (0.000)
Sao Paulo (dummy)	0.062 (0.000)	0.021 (0.000)	0.030 (0.000)
Metropolitan Area (dummy)	0.153 (0.000)	0.027 (0.000)	0.091 (0.000)
Nr. of Observations	11,393	11,345	11,393
χ^2 (20)	2,707.25	699.46	2,422.58
Prob > χ^2	0.000	0.000	0.000
Pseudo R^2	0.240	0.135	0.268
Log Likelihood	−4,280.85	−2,248.0	−3,305.18
Observed Probability	0.196	0.061	0.135
Predicted Probability	0.118	0.036	0.058

Source: PNAD 1996.

cation at all. With a secondary education of *medio2 ciclo*, the probability of participation in the non-farm sector is 23 percentage points higher than the no-education baseline, while with a level of *2 grau* or higher the probability is 24 percentage points higher.

Location influences probabilities of non-farm sector participation, even after controlling for other characteristics. Relative to those residing in the *rural exclusive* regions, those residing in the *extensao urbana* areas have 11 percentage point higher probabilities of non-farm sector involvement. The other two rural settlements, *rural povoado* and *rural nucleo* are also associated with higher probabilities of non-farm sector participation, by 3.6 and 9.8 percentage points, respectively.

Relative to the state of Maranhao, probabilities of employment in the non-farm sector is higher in the states of Ceara (3 percentage points), Rio Grande do Norte (2.6 points), Paraiba (3.6 points), and Sergipe (5 points). This is after controlling for individual and household characteristics. We saw earlier that a comparison of non-controlled non-farm employment probabilities suggested that Maranhao accounted for a much larger share of total non-farm employment than its population share would have suggested.

Finally, we note that those residing in rural regions of large metropolitan areas have a 2.4 percentage point higher probability of employment in the non-farm sector than those that don't.

When we break non-farm employment activities into two types, low and high productivity, some interesting changes are observed. While men were more likely than women were to be employed in the non-farm sector in general, this finding is reversed when we focus on low remuneration non-farm activities. Here men have a 2.5 percentage point lower probability of participating in these activities. Household size is now positive and significantly related to employment in non-farm activities, suggesting that households with many family members may well need to spread their net more widely in order to make ends meet than would small households. Elementary and primary education levels are still positively associated with low-return non-farm employment participation, but at higher levels of education the statistical association disappears and even becomes negative for the highest education category. Locational effects are still positive and significant, but smaller in size. Coefficients on state dummies also tend to become smaller. While one must be very cautious with inferences based on reduced form models, as estimated here, the overall impression is that low return activities are less obviously a route out of poverty than high return activities. Low return activities may reasonably be seen as both a symptom of, and a response to, poverty.

Turning in Table 6.9B, we observe that broadly similar patterns are observed in the rural Southeast. Women are more likely to be engaged in low return activities, while men are strongly and significantly more likely to be engaged in the high return activities. In the Southeast, the Black population has a 1.7 percentage point higher probability of involvement in low return non-farm activities, while Mulattos and Asians have a 1.3 and 4.2 percentage point lower probability of involvement in high return activities, respectively, controlling for other characteristics. Education is observed to play another important role in this region as was observed in the rural Northeast, with education again being of less importance for the low return activities, and of particular importance for the high return activities. Location is once again significant, with proximity to towns of particular significance, raising the probability of participation in high return non-farm activities. High return activities are also more probable in the states of Rio de Janeiro and Sao Paulo, and in metropolitan areas.

Employment Trends in the Non-Farm Sector

A recent study carried out by Mauro Eduardo del Grossi (1999) describes the evolution of employment in the rural non-farm sector between 1981 and 1995. His analysis is based on multiple PNAD surveys and has involved painstaking work to achieve comparability of concepts, definitions, and returns over the period of study. His broad findings are mentioned briefly here.

While employment in agriculture essentially stagnated between 1981 and 1995, rural employment in non-agricultural activities in Brazil, as a whole, has grown by more than a quarter (nearly a million persons) over this time period (annual growth rate of 1.7 percent). The most rapid growth has occurred in the regions of the Southeast and Central west. Growth in the state of Sao Paulo has been particularly rapid.

Much of the growth of non-farm employment is accounted for by a 5.3 percent annual growth of self-employment (mainly domestic services). Between 1981 and 1992 the number of people working in domestic services grew from 300,000 to about 620,000. Civil construction, on the other hand, was one of the main sources of non-farm employment in 1981, but lost about 300,000 participants over the interval between 1981 and 1995 (an annualized growth rate of −4.3 percent for Brazil as a whole). The particular significance of the construction industry is worth highlighting as employment in this sector can be of great importance as regards to the poor. Particularly in regions of Brazil such as the Northeast, employment creation in civil construction projects is a well-established government response to droughts. A large decline of employment in construction between 1981 and 1995 in the Northeast (at an annualized rate of 9.0 percent per year) is likely to be, at least in part, due to relatively favorable weather conditions in the early 1990s. Other important growth sub-sectors have included education (up 3.5 percent per annum), food sales (3.4 percent), food processing (4.2 percent), restaurants (6.1 percent), public administration (9.8 percent), street selling (8.1 percent). Growth of employment in manufacturing activities (*industria transformacao*), while positive, increased at the low rate of 0.7 percent per annum.

On the whole, the evolution of employment in the non-farm sector in rural Brazil appears to be congruent with the trends observed in developing countries, more generally and particularly in Latin America (see Lanjouw and Lanjouw, 2000, and Reardon et al, 2000). The sector's growth and dynamism can be contrasted to the generally much lower growth in employment opportunities in agriculture over the same time period.

Incomes from Non-Farm Activities

How are incomes from non-farm activities distributed across households in the rural income distribution? In Tables 6.10A and 6.10B, we tabulate income shares from all sources of income against quintiles of the per capita consumption distribution, for the rural Northeast and Southeast. In Table 6.10A, we can see that in the rural Northeast, as a whole, cultivation income accounts for about 58.3 percent of the household income and agricultural labor accounts for 8.3 percent. Non-farm sources of income account for 33.4 percent of household income. These non-farm sources can be broken down to a contribution of 13.1 percent from non-farm wage income, 5.3 percent from non-farm self-employment/enterprise income, and 15 percent from other sources (remittances, transfers, pensions, etc.).

Across quintiles we can see that cultivation income is of particular importance to the higher quintiles in the population.[21] While the top quintile in the rural Northeast receives 62.3 percent of income from cultivation, on average, the poorest quintile receives only 36.3 percent from this source. For the poor, agricultural-labor income is particularly important, accounting for 39.1 percent of income, while for the richest quintile, this source of income represents only 2.1 percent of income. Non-farm labor income is distributed rather evenly across the consumption quintiles. While the lowest two quintiles receive a greater share of income from low-return non-farm activities than the average household, it is also interesting to note that households in the 4th quintile also receive a relatively large share of income from these low return labor activities. High-return labor activities are of importance to the upper quintiles, but also appear to be particularly important to the poorest quintile. Put together, high and low return non-farm labor activities account on average for 13.1 percent of household income across all quintiles, with the bottom and 4th quintiles receiving the largest shares (16.1 percent and 17.2 percent respectively).

Non-farm-enterprise income shares are much more clearly aligned with per capita consumption quintiles. Against an average share of 5.3 percent over all households, the lowest quintile receives (on average) no income from this source; the middle three quintiles receive between 1–2 percent of income from this source; and the richest quintile receives 8.6 percent. Remittance incomes are a very small fraction of overall income and tend to be concentrated in the middle consumption quintiles. The residual sources of income, accounting for an average 14.2 percent of income across all

---

21. "Cultivation" income includes income from fishing. Income from livestock ranching and other related activities were not collected in the PPV household survey.

TABLE 6.10A: INCOME SHARES BY SOURCE AND (CONSUMPTION) QUINTILE—RURAL NORTHEAST

Within-region Per capita consumption quintile	Agriculture		Non-Agricultural Income Sources						
	Cultivation Income[1] (percent)	Agricultural labor Income (percent)	Low-Return Non-farm Sector[2] Labor Income (percent)	High-Return Non-farm Sector[2] Labor Income (percent)	Total Non-Farm Labor Income (percent)	Non-farm Enterprise Income	Remittance Income	Other Income Sources	Total[3]
Bottom	36.3	39.1	1.5	14.6	16.1	0.0	0.6	7.9	100.0
2nd	50.1	23.9	2.0	8.1	10.1	1.4	1.1	13.3	100.0
3rd	62.1	6.4	1.3	13.1	14.4	1.1	2.0	14.0	100.0
4th	56.0	9.6	3.0	14.2	17.2	1.8	0.7	14.8	100.0
5th	62.3	2.1	0.6	11.9	12.5	8.6	0.5	15.0	100.0

Poor/Non-Poor (National poverty line)	Agriculture		Non-Agricultural Income Sources						
	Cultivation Income (percent)	Agricultural labor Income (percent)	Low-Return Non-farm Sector Labor Income (percent)	High-Return Non-farm Sector Labor Income (percent)	Total Non-Farm Labor Income (percent)	Non-farm Enterprise Income	Remittance Income	Other Income Sources	Total
Poor	53.4	15.9	2.1	12.6	14.7	1.8	1.1	13.3	100.0
Non-Poor	62.5	1.8	0.6	11.2	11.8	8.4	0.5	15.0	100.0

Source: PPV 1996

Notes: 1. Agricultural income shares include income from fishing. However, this component was nowhere found to represent more than 0.1 percent of total income.

2. Low and high return non-farm activities are identified on the basis of average monthly earnings associated with primary employment in different sectors of employment. Those sectors in which average monthly earnings are below the poverty line of R$132 per month are identified as low return sectors. Persons whose primary occupation is in these sectors are identified as employed in low return activities. The converse holds for high return activities. Low return activities comprise essentially: textiles (but not clothing); street and market vending; own-account services; personal services; and informal activities.

3. Row totals may not sum to 100 due to rounding.

TABLE 6.10B: INCOME SHARES BY SOURCE AND (CONSUMPTION) QUINTILE—RURAL SOUTHEAST

Within-region Per capita consumption quintile	Agriculture		Non-Agricultural Income Sources						
	Cultivation Income[1] (percent)	Agricultural labor Income (percent)	Low-Return Non-farm Sector[2] Labor Income (percent)	High-Return Non-farm Sector[2] Labor Income (percent)	Total Non-Farm Labor Income (percent)	Non-farm Enterprise Income	Remittance Income	Other Income Sources	Total[3]
Bottom	28.7	47.7	3.3	6.6	9.9	0.4	2.8	11.4	100.0
2nd	29.0	43.8	1.1	5.2	6.3	0.5	3.1	17.3	100.0
3rd	20.0	34.1	7.3	19.0	26.3	2.3	1.8	15.1	100.0
4th	21.4	28.0	1.8	16.7	18.5	7.1	2.9	22.1	100.0
5th	47.6	6.1	1.0	7.6	8.6	23.6	0.7	13.4	100.0

Poor/Non-Poor (National poverty line)	Agriculture		Non-Agricultural Income Sources						
	Cultivation Income (percent)	Agricultural labor Income (percent)	Low-Return Non-farm Sector Labor Income (percent)	High-Return Non-farm Sector Labor Income (percent)	Total Non-Farm Labor Income (percent)	Non-farm Enterprise Income	Remittance Income	Other Income Sources	Total
Poor	23.6	38.7	3.8	12.1	15.9	1.6	3.0	17.2	100.0
Non-Poor	42.6	10.6	1.3	9.7	11.0	20.5	0.9	14.5	100.0

Source: PPV 1996

Notes: 1. Agricultural income shares include income from fishing. However, this component was nowhere found to represent more than 0.1 percent of total income.
2. Low and high return non-farm activities are identified on the basis of average monthly earnings associated with primary employment in different sectors of employment. Those sectors in which average monthly earnings are below the poverty line of R$132 per month are identified as low return sectors. Persons whose primary occupation is in these sectors are identified as employed in low return activities. The converse holds for high return activities. Low return activities comprise essentially: textiles (but not clothing); street and market vending; own-account services; personal services; and informal activities.
3. Row totals may not sum to 100 due to rounding.

households, tend to be distributed regressively, with the poorest quintile receiving about 7.9 percent from this source, while the richest quintile receives 15 percent.

Rather than divide the population into quintiles which does not take into account actual consumption levels, it is also useful to divide the rural population into poor and non-poor, based on the poverty line. We can then examine income shares in the same way. This breakdown provides a rather neater picture of the importance of various income sources across the population. The poor earn, on average, just over half of their income from agriculture, compared to just under two thirds (62.5 percent) for the non-poor. Sixteen percent of income comes from agricultural labor (compared to 1.8 percent), and 14.7 percent from non-agricultural labor (compared to 11.8 percent for the non-poor). Non-agricultural-enterprise income accounts for 1.8 percent of total income (compared to 8.4 percent), remittances account for 1.1 percent (compared to 0.5 percent) and other income sources account for 13.3 percent (compared to 15 percent). In general, the poor are those who rely disproportionately on agricultural labor income, and to a much lesser extent, non-farm wage labor income, while the non-poor tend to be more concentrated on cultivation or non-farm self-employment activities.

Table 6.10B. presents the analogue for the rural Southeast. In this region, cultivation accounts for a smaller share of total income on average, and non-farm sources are much more important. Across all households, 35.4 percent of income comes from cultivation, 21.1 percent from agricultural labor, 12.8 percent from non-farm wage employment, 13.4 percent from non-farm enterprise activities, 1.7 percent from remittances, and 15.5 percent from other sources. Across quintiles, the importance of different income sources varies markedly. While the bottom quintile receives about 28.7 percent of income from non-farm sources, the top quintile receives about 47.6 percent of income from such activities. The 3rd and 4th quintiles earn the lowest shares from cultivation (20.0 percent and 21.4 percent, respectively). Agricultural labor income shares decline monotonically with consumption quintiles, from 47.4 percent of income for the poor to 6.1 percent for the top quintile. The biggest fall is between the 4th and 5th quintiles when agricultural labor shares decline from 28 percent to 6 percent.

Low-return wage labor shares are highest for the bottom quintile (3.3 percent) and the third quintile (7.3 percent), and lowest for the top quintile (1.0 percent). High-return wage labor shares are particularly high for the 3rd and 4th quintiles (19.0 and 16.7 percent respectively). Overall, non-farm wage labor shares are particularly high for the 3rd and 4th quintiles (26.3 and 18.5 percent, respectively). Non-farm self-employment/enterprise income shares are very high among the richest quintile (23.6 percent), while for the poorest two quintiles make up less than 1 percent. Remittances are least important to the richest quintile, while both the richest and poorest quintiles receive the smallest income shares from other income sources.

Breaking the population of the region into poor and non-poor, the basic picture is one of the poor with only limited involvement in cultivation, but heavy involvement in agricultural labor. Non-farm labor activities are also relatively important, compared to the non-poor. In contrast, non-farm enterprise incomes are of importance particularly to the non-poor, with the poor having almost no involvement in these activities. Remittances tend to go to the poor, as do transfers and other sources of income.

Because the distribution of landholdings in rural Brazil are often thought to closely proxy the distribution of welfare, it is of interest to examine, in a similar manner as with Tables 6.10A and 6.10B, the distribution of income shares across landholding classes. Table 6.11. produces such a breakdown for the rural Northeast and Southeast. Landholding classes have been constructed based on reported land ownership holdings. Six classes were constructed: the landless; those with 0–0.5 hectares per family member; between 0.5 and 1 hectare per person; between 1 and 3 hectares per person; 3–5 hectares per person; and 5 or more hectares per person. It would be ideal, of course, to adjust these land holdings for quality variation, but that was not readily achievable with the data at hand.

Turning first to the rural Northeast, we can see that the landless receive a non-negligible share of income from cultivation, despite being landless. The 53.1 percent of the rural population thus

Per Capita land ownership class[1]	Agriculture		Non-Agricultural Income Sources							Average land owned (ha)	Average land leased in (ha)	Average untitled land occupied (ha)	Average land other status (ha)
	Cultivation Income[2] (percent)	Agricultural labor Income (percent)	Low-Return Non-farm Sector[3] Labor Income (percent)	High-Return Non-farm Sector[3] Labor Income (percent)	Total Non-Farm Labor Income (percent)	Non-farm Enterprise Inc 85 home (percent)	Remittance Income	Other Income Sources	percent of population				
Landless	31.8	14.5	2.7	19.8	22.6	8.4	1.2	21.7	53.1	0	0.31	8.35	0.50
0–0.5 ha.	53.3	13.0	0.5	9.4	9.9	7.4	0.8	15.7	21.1	1.19	0.33	0.09	0.11
0.5–1.0 ha.	59.5	12.2	0.0	7.5	7.5	2.7	0.6	17.7	9.0	3.54	0.13	0.09	0.13
1.0–3.0 ha.	66.1	2.9	0.1	16.7	16.8	0.0	0.2	13.9	9.4	8.86	0.37	0.06	0.11
3.0–5.0 ha.	97.1	0.0	0.3	0.2	0.5	0.3	0.4	0.2	2.8	13.74	0.13	0.27	0.0
5.0+ ha	74.7	0.0	0.0	5.9	5.9	9.2	0.1	10.2	4.6	78.2	0.23	0.0	1.83

INCOME SHARES BY SOURCE AND LAND OWNERSHIP CLASS—RURAL SOUTHEAST

Per Capita land ownership class[1]	Agriculture		Non-Agricultural Income Sources							Average land owned (ha)	Average land leased in (ha)	Average untitled land occupied (ha)	Average land other status (ha)
	Cultivation Income[2] (percent)	Agricultural labor Income (percent)	Low-Return Non-farm Sector[3] Labor Income (percent)	High-Return Non-farm Sector[3] Labor Income (percent)	Total Non-Farm Labor Income (percent)	Non-farm Enterprise home (percent)	Remittance Income	Other Income Sources	percent of population				
Landless	19.6	29.0	2.7	12.8	15.5	18.8	1.9	15.0	71.8	0.00	1.07	4.83	2.16
0–0.5 ha.	21.2	14.5	6.6	17.6	24.2	6.8	2.5	30.9	9.6	0.53	0.88	0.28	0.29
0.5–1.0 ha.	36.5	19.6	0.0	3.0	3.0	0.0	0.5	40.3	2.8	3.48	5.26	0.27	0.00
1.0–3.0 ha.	48.6	14.8	1.0	4.8	5.8	1.9	2.5	26.4	6.0	6.91	1.23	0.00	0.00
3.0–5.0 ha.	63.0	4.2	2.1	13.6	15.7	1.6	2.5	9.5	3.3	16.8	0.80	0.00	0.00
5.0+ ha	83.0	1.1	0.00	3.1	3.1	3.5	0.00	9.4	6.5	107.7	0.24	2.67	1.60

Source: PPV 1996

Notes: 1. Land-ownership class is based on reported *land owned* only. The classes are defined in terms of per-capita land ownership.
2. Agricultural income shares include income from and fishing. However, this component was nowhere found to represent more than 0.1 percent of total income.
3. Low and high-return non-farm activities are identified on the basis of average monthly earnings associated with primary employment in different sectors of employment. Those sectors in which average monthly earnings are below the poverty line of R$132 per month are identified as low-return sectors. Persons whose primary occupation is in these sectors are identified as employed in low-return activities. The opposite holds for high-return activities. Low-return activities comprise essentially: textiles (but not clothing); street and market vending; self employment; personal services; and informal activities.

classified, does however, retain some access to land. This can be seen in Table 6.11 by the fact that landless households were leasing, on average, 0.31 hectares of land, plus they were observed to occupy (without title or formal property right, on average, 8.35 hectares of land. Income from cultivation thus accounts for 31.8 percent of total income to the landless. For those households that do actually own some land, cultivation shares are not surprisingly higher. Cultivation shares are highest for households with 3–5 hectares per person (97.1 percent) and somewhat lower for the largest landowning class (74.7 percent). It is possible that the largest landowning class may have a disproportionate share of non-arable land.

Agricultural labor earning is most important to the landless and marginal landowners. The landless earn about 14.5 percent of income from agricultural wage labor earnings, while those with up to 0.5 hectare of land per person receive 13 percent from this source; those between 0.5 hectare and 1 hectare receive 12.2 percent from this source. For households with more than 1 hectare of land per person, agricultural wage labor earnings are of negligible importance.

Both households that have land and those that don't carry out non-farm wage labor activities. However, Table 6.11 indicates that low-return non-farm wage income is important, essentially, with regards to the landless. This is consistent with the notion that low-return non-farm activities are viewed by households as residual activities, which they undertake alongside activities such as agricultural wage labor in order to meet subsistence needs. Households with land, it appears, would probably prefer to apply any surplus labor they may have to their land rather than hire it out to low-return non-farm activities. High return non-farm activities, on the other hand, are important not only to landless households (to whom they provide 19.8 percent of household income) but also to household with landholdings. Households with 1–3 hectares of land per person, for example, earn as much as 16.7 percent of income from high return wage labor activities. Even the largest landowning class earns 5.9 percent of income from such sources.

We saw in Tables 6.10A and 6.10B that non-farm enterprise income shares were highly correlated with consumption levels. In Table 6.11 we can see that non-farm enterprise income is important to the landless and near landless, and then to the largest landowning class (8.4 percent, 7.4 percent and 9.2 percent, respectively). This reveals that, among the landless, one is likely to find households which are not at all poor, but which are engaged in enterprise activities that are non-agricultural. As has been argued in Lanjouw (1999A), land-ownership may only be an imperfect predictor of well being in rural areas.

In the rural Southeast the general picture described above is also observed, although there are some differences. Cultivation income shares rise monotonically from the landless class to the largest landowning class, from a low of 19.6 percent among the landless to 83 percent among the largest landowning class. Agricultural labor remains of the greatest importance to the 72 percent of the population which is landless (although cultivation remains a source of income for at least some of the landless). Low-return non-farm wage employment is important to the landless and near-landless, but also to those with 3–5 hectares of land. High-return non-farm wage labor shares mirror low-return shares. Enterprise income shares are highest for the landless. In the Southeast, thus, cultivation intensity is correlated with landholding, and the landless are a heterogeneous group amongst whom some are heavily dependent on agricultural labor and low-return non-farm labor earnings, while others are likely to be well-off, with high return wage employment and/or non-farm enterprises.

We turn finally to an econometric estimation of wage earnings in rural Brazil on individual, household, sectoral and locational characteristics.[22] Table 6.12 presents results, in turn, for the

---

22. Given the findings in Tables 7.10. and 7.11., that enterprise income was associated with consumption quintiles and land-ownership classes, it would be of interest to estimate models of enterprise profits. However, the data at hand limit our ability to pursue this line of enquiry. The PPV sample includes relatively few households with non-farm enterprise incomes in rural areas. More importantly, however, the data on enterprise activities and profits is somewhat problematic, so much so that it is not obvious how far such analysis could go. It remains an option for further research.

TABLE 6.12: OLS REGRESSION MODEL OF WAGE-LABOR EARNINGS FROM PRINCIPAL OCCUPATION
(dependent variable = log monthly wages plus benefits)

Explanatory Variables	Rural Northeast Coefficient (prob value)[1]	Rural Southeast Coefficient (prob value)[1]
Household Head (dummy)	0.188	0.294
	(0.319)	(0.008)
Male (dummy)	0.423	0.305
	(0.010)	(0.003)
Age in years	0.069	0.049
	(0.001)	(0.002)
Age squared	−0.0008	−0.0005
	(0.003)	(0.003)
Black (dummy)	−0.187	0.0008
	(0.579)	(0.995)
Mulatto (dummy)	0.052	0.061
	(0.502)	(0.490)
Elementary schooling only (dummy)	0.318	−0.302
	(0.206)	(0.069)
Medio 1 (dummy)	0.411	−0.671
	(0.201)	(0.270)
Grau 1 (dummy)	0.273	−0.094
	(0.095)	(0.504)
Sup11 (dummy)	0.809	0.126
	(0.005)	(0.654)
Medio 2 (dummy)	0.685	0.265
	(0.007)	(0.131)
Supl2 (dummy)	0.654	0.424
	(0.096)	(0.060)
Superior or higher (dummy)	1.390	0.765
	(0.004)	(0.000)
Household size	0.008	0.002
	(0.655)	(0.899)
Locally born (dummy)	−0.039	−0.132
	(0.685)	(0.088)
Urban born (dummy)	0.305	0.264
	(0.000)	(0.000)
Per capita land owned	−0.078	−0.074
	(0.198)	(0.002)
Per capita land Squared	0.004	0.001
	(0.170)	(0.001)
Maranhao (dummy)	-0.189	—
	(0.419)	
Piaui (dummy)	0.885	—
	(0.009)	
Ceara (dummy)	−0.145	—
	(0.380)	

(continued)

TABLE 6.12: OLS Regression Model of Wage-Labor Earnings from Principal Occupation (CONTINUED)
(dependent variable = log monthly wages plus benefits)

Explanatory Variables	Rural Northeast Coefficient (prob value)[1]	Rural Southeast Coefficient (prob value)[1]
Rio Grande do Norte (dummy)	−0.688 (0.000)	—
Paraiba (dummy)	—	—
Pernambuco (dummy)	−0.326 (0.136)	—
Alagoas (dummy)	0.050 (0.831)	—
Sergipe (dummy)	−0.015 (0.934)	—
Minas Gerais (dummy)	—	−0.394 (0.003)
Espiritu Santo (dummy)	—	−0.530 (0.003)
Rio de Janeiro (dummy)	—	−0.102 (0.412)
Extraction industry (dummy)	1.000 (0.018)	0.301 (0.297)
Food processing (dummy)	0.207 (0.702)	0.183 (0.496)
Textiles and clothing (dummy)	—	0.069 (0.680)
Wooden goods (dummy)	—	0.442 (0.020)
Other manufacturing (dummy)	0.053 (0.829)	−0.134 (0.443)
Utilities (dummy)	1.375 (0.000)	0.585 (0.000)
Construction (dummy)	0.393 (0.052)	0.334 (0.068)
Commerce (dummy)	0.425 (0.125)	0.156 (0.480)
Restaurant/hotel (dummy)	0.063 (0.677)	0.173 (0.207)
Transport and Communications dummy)	0.605 (0.048)	0.345 (0.176)
Financial Sector (dummy)	0.849 (0.053)	—
Administration (dummy)	0.218 (0.327)	−0.123 (0.509)
Education (dummy)	−0.584 (0.008)	0.053 (0.713)
Social Services (dummy)	0.480 (0.116)	—

(continued)

	Rural Northeast	Rural Southeast
	Coefficient	Coefficient
Explanatory Variables	(prob value)[1]	(prob value)[1]
Other services (dummy)	0.002	−0.268
	(0.983)	(0.277)
Domestic Service (dummy)	0.133	−0.042
	(0.393)	(0.742)
Constant	3.055	4.404
	(0.000)	(0.000)
Nr. of Observations	362	496
R²	0.4542	0.3744
F	60537.96	869.84
Prob>F	0.0000	0.0011

TABLE 6.12: OLS REGRESSION MODEL OF WAGE-LABOR EARNINGS FROM PRINCIPAL OCCUPATION (CONTINUED)
(dependent variable = log monthly wages plus benefits)

Source: PPV 1996
Note: 1. Standard errors take into account sample design.

rural Northeast and rural Southeast. In the rural Northeast, earnings from wage labor as a principal occupation are higher for men than for women, controlling for other characteristics. A male with given characteristics could expect to earn 42 percent more than a woman does with the same characteristics, including a control for sector of employment. It is unlikely that this difference can be attributed entirely to gender discrimination. The reason is most likely due to the fact that actual occupations of men and women are quite different even within a particular sub-sector of employment. In agriculture, for example, men and women often carry out quite different tasks, and the differential in remuneration observed here may simply reflect such differences.

Earnings rise with age up to a turning point of around 48 years after which they start falling. There are no significant differences in earnings between whites and individuals of other races, once educational and other characteristics are controlled for. Earnings rise significantly with education levels, once one looks beyond the lower levels of education. An individual with a level of education of grau 1 would expect to earn 27 percent more than a person with no education at all would. At higher levels of education the returns become very substantial: an individual with superior education or higher earns about 138 percent more than an individual with no education.

An individual who was born in an urban municipality but now works in wage employment in the rural sector can expect to earn about 30 percent more than someone who was born in rural areas. This probably captures the fact that the more remunerative non-farm jobs often originate in urban areas (government jobs or teachers, for example) and that these vacancies are not necessarily filled by local residents.

Relative to the state of Bahia, labor earnings are generally lower in the state of Piaui and Rio Grande do Norte. No states stand out as offering returns to labor that are significantly higher than what is offered in the state of Bahia. Relative to the not-included agricultural labor sector, wage employment in non-farm sector appears to be particularly high in the extraction industry (mining, etc.), utilities, construction, transport and communications and finance. Interestingly, it can be seen that earnings in educational services tend to be lower even than agricultural wage labor.

In the rural Southeast, wages are higher if the individual employed is the head of the household (a return of 29 percent). Once again earnings are higher for males but with a slightly lower premium (30 percent). Earnings rise with age, with a turning point around 49 years of age.

Once again, race does not seem to influence wage earnings separately from other factors. Interestingly, very low levels of education are associated with *lower* earnings than is no education at all (although this is significant only for those with no more than elementary schooling). However, once again, returns to higher levels of education are pronounced and highly significant. An individual with superior or higher education would expect to earn 76 percent more than would a person with no education. Once again, if an individual was born in urban areas, he could expect to earn a substantial premium (26 percent) over an individual born in rural areas. Moreover, if the individual currently resides in the same municipality where he was born, he can expect to earn 13 percent less than a person born elsewhere does (although this is significant only at the 10 percent level).

In the rural Northeast, landholdings did not influence a person's wage earnings. In the southeast, the larger a person's landholdings, the lower the returns from wage labor. This is consistent with cultivation increasing in intensity as with land-ownership, so much so that an individual is unlikely to work in remunerated wage labor for the same duration if he comes from large landholding households. Interestingly, the relationship between labor earnings and landholding is not linear—for households with more than 41 hectares, non-farm wage earnings rise with landholding. This indicates, most presumably, that a person from such a landholding household would be less likely to consider taking up paid employment unless the remuneration was particularly high.

Relative to the state of Sao Paulo, earnings in Minas Gerais and Espiritu Santo are significantly lower. In Rio de Janeiro, the difference is not statistically significant. Relative to agricultural labor, wages are significantly higher in the wooden product manufacturing sectors, utilities, and construction. No other sector appears to offer significantly higher returns than agricultural labor does, once other characteristics are controlled for.

Concluding Comments

Rural poverty remains an important part of the poverty story in Brazil as a whole. Brazil is a largely urbanized country, but poverty in rural parts of the country is so widespread and persistent that about two fifths of the country's poor are still found in the countryside. In addition, urban poverty itself appears to be concentrated in the smaller conurbation areas (and, therefore, likely to be more closely linked to the surrounding rural sector), and it seems clear that the rural economy must remain a central focal point for policy makers aiming to combat poverty.

Land reform is a high profile and widely debated element in the poverty reduction agenda. However, land reform is difficult to implement on a large scale; it is expensive; time consuming; and is unlikely to suffice to eliminate poverty. There is growing interest in Brazil, and Latin America more broadly, to ascertain whether, and to what extent, the rural non-farm sector can provide an additional entry point into efforts to address poverty.

Experience in Latin America, and the developing world more broadly, indicates that the non-farm sector is often surprisingly large in size and often more dynamic than the agricultural sector. However, the sector is generally found to encompass an enormous variety of activities, not all of which can be regarded as very productive and likely to offer great prospects for upward economic mobility. It is often observed the vulnerable segments of the population, such as women, minority groups, and the poor in general, tend to be concentrated precisely in those rural non-farm activities, which do not contribute much to household income. However, such an observation is not sufficient to warrant the conclusion that the non-farm sector is of only limited relevance to poverty reduction efforts. First of all, it is possible that appropriate policy intervention could influence the degree to which the poor are excluded from the more remunerative non-farm activities. Second, a growing non-farm economy can generate second-round effects (such as wage rates in agriculture) which may indirectly benefit the poor in a substantial way. Third, even the low returns that accrue to the poor in their relatively unproductive non-farm activities can play a critical role in preventing them from falling even further into poverty.

What are some of the dimensions of the non-farm sector in rural Brazil? In this paper we focus on the Northeast and Southeast regions of the country only. Non-farm activities are found to represent up to a third of primary occupations in rural areas of these regions. These activities tend to be more common in the rural Southeast of the country, but even in the Northeast, more than a fifth of the economically active rural population has as principal occupation a non-farm sector job. These figures understate the full size of the rural non-farm sector because many are likely to combine agricultural activities with non-farm activities, and as such, would record non-farm activities as secondary rather than primary occupations.

Scrutiny of the sub-sectoral breakdown of non-farm activities in rural Brazil reveals the importance of service sector activities, particularly own-account services (such as domestic service). Construction, food processing, commerce, education, and general administration activities are also numerically important. While a wide range of manufacturing activities can be discerned, they do not dominate the non-farm landscape.

Non-farm activities are disproportionately represented in those rural areas, which are better connected, to the broader economy. They are concentrated periurban areas or in rural towns, even though the bulk of the rural population, and in particular the rural poor, are found in more remote rural areas.

As has been observed in other countries, women are well represented in the non-farm sector. As a percentage of the overall labor force, non-farm activities account for a much larger share of employment of women than of men. Women tend to be concentrated in two sub-sectors: self-employment, and education.

A state breakdown reveals that in the Northeast, Maranhao, Bahia, and to a lesser extent Rio Grande do Norte and Ceara account for a large share of total non-farm activities. The two states of Maranhao and Rio Grande do Norte are significant in that in these two states, their share of the region's non-farm activities is greater than their share of the region's population. In the Southeast, the two states of Rio de Janeiro and Sao Paulo are particularly well represented.

Multivariate analysis, examining the correlation of non-farm employment in rural Brazil reveals the importance of education in determining the probability of employment in non-farm activities. In both the Northeast and Southeast, there is strong evidence that the educated, particularly those with secondary education or higher, have better prospects in the non-farm sector. This is emphasized when non-farm activities are divided into low-return and high-return activities. Education is a particularly important determinant of employment in high remunerative non-farm activities. Breaking the non-farm sector into two types of activities also reveals that men and women tend to concentrate in different non-farm sectors: the women in low-return activities and the men in high-return activities. The patterns are broadly similar for both the rural Northeast and Southeast, except that in the Southeast, there is also some suggestion that, controlling for individual and household characteristics, whites enjoy some advantage in obtaining high return non-farm jobs over non-whites.

Over time, the non-farm sector in Brazil appears to have been growing. Between 1981 and 1995, non-farm sector employment grew at an annual rate of around 1.7 percent per year. This masks considerable variety across sub-sectors. Employment in construction has been declining at a rate of around 4.3 percent per year, while domestic service and municipal administration has been growing at rates of 5.3 percent and 9.8 percent per year. Overall, employment growth in the non-farm sector has been more rapid during recent years than employment growth in agriculture.

Non-farm income shares tend to rise with overall consumption levels, although the relationship is rather flat. The composition of non-farm income also changes markedly. The lower quintiles of the consumption distribution tend to earn a larger share of their non-farm incomes from wage labor activities. For the poorest population, low-return wage labor activities tend to be more important, while high-return activities are spread rather evenly over the consumption distribution. What is striking is that non-farm enterprise income rises very sharply with consumption quintiles: income shares from self-employment/enterprise activities are concentrated among the richer quintiles.

Non-farm income shares are distributed in an interesting way within landholding classes. The landless, unsurprisingly, receive a large share of their income from non-farm activities. These non-farm incomes also include self-employment/enterprise incomes, and as such this indicates that the landless are not uniformly poor. In the rural Northeast, the very largest landholding classes also receive a sizeable share of income from non-farm sources, while in the Southeast, large landowners tend to concentrated on agricultural activities.

Non-farm earnings are related, in a way similar to employment probabilities, to education levels, gender, and region. The better educated earn considerable returns on their education, with the premium being particularly high in the rural Northeast. Women tend to earn less, controlling for their education and other characteristics. In both regions, it seems that an individual, who was born in urban areas rather than in his/her current rural place of residence, enjoys higher earnings from non-farm activities than a rural born person. This may indicate that at least some of the rural occupations, particularly those associated with higher ranks, may be recruited out of urban areas rather than locally. Earnings tend to be highest in regions such as the state of Sao Paulo, where the rural sector is small and the urban economy is most vibrant.

What might be some of the emerging policy considerations that arise out of this analysis? The general patterns, which have emerged out of the preceding discussion, suggest that governments may wish to pay particular attention to the construction and education sectors in rural areas. Employment levels in the construction sector have been declining in recent years. The sector is an important source of employment (particularly to men) and appears to offer good returns. It is typically well targeted to the poor as it does not generally demand high educational qualifications and the nature of the work is such that those with alternative options typically choose those alternatives. It also has a well-recognized function as a counter-cyclical means of employment generation, particularly in the drought prone Northeast of the country. It is not clear as to what extent the decline in employment levels in construction has been due to favorable weather conditions, which have reduced the need for employment generation. It is also not clear from the data at hand to what extent the decline in construction sector employment is due to a decline in public spending as opposed to reduced private investment in construction activities. The analysis here can, at best, highlight the significance of this sub-sector of the non-farm sector. Further analysis is required to spell out what, if any, options exist for policies directed at the construction sector.

The education sub-sector also deserves consideration. First of all, one of the more robust findings from the analysis is that education has an important influence on opportunities and earnings in the non-farm sector. The education sector also happens to be an important non-farm sector source of employment, particularly for women. Expansion of the provision of education would thus have the joint benefit of improving the prospects of the younger generations in the non-farm sector, while providing, at the same time, an important source of employment to a segment of the rural population which appears to be relatively poorly placed where earning significant non-farm incomes is concerned.

The non-farm sector in Brazil has been found to be closely linked to location. In particular, there seems to be clear evidence that the non-farm sector is more vibrant in those areas which are well connected to markets and which enjoy certain minimum standards of infrastructure. This connection between the non-farm sector and infrastructure is not new. It poses, however, important challenges to policy makers. There is a strong movement to incorporate the participation of the private sector in the provision of infrastructure in many Latin American countries. What remains to be determined is to what extent these initiatives are able to secure the kind of rural infrastructure provision which is most necessary to promote the non-farm sector.

While the non-farm sector in rural Brazil appears to offer some opportunities to address rural poverty, the analysis in this paper does suggest that a sense of perspective be maintained. The rural poor tend to be concentrated in the most remote rural areas. They typically possess the lowest levels of human capital. The non-farm sector, on the other hand, particularly the high-return activities, which are most directly able to lift people out of poverty, tends to be concentrated in the more urbanized rural areas, and to employ persons with secondary and higher levels of education. It is unclear exactly how much one can expect from the non-farm sector, in terms of rural poverty reduction, in the short run.

References

De Janvry, A., and E. Sadoulet. 1993. "Rural Development in Latin America: Relinking Poverty Reduction to Growth" in Lipton, M. and van der Gaag, J. (eds) *Including the Poor* (Washington D.C.: the World Bank).

Del Grossi, M. 1999. "Evolucao das Ocupaciones Nao-Agricolas No Meio Rural Brasileiro: 1981–1995," Ph.D. dissertation, Instituto de Economia, Universidade Estadual de Campinas, Brazil.

Elbers, C., and P. Lanjouw. 2000. "Inequality and the Non-Farm Sector in Rural Ecuador: Evidence at the Household and Community Level," mimeo, Free University Amsterdam and World Bank.

Elbers, C., Lanjouw, J. O., and P. Lanjouw. 2000. "Welfare in Villages and Towns: Micro-Estimation of Poverty and Inequality," mimeo, Free University of Amsterdam and World Bank.

Fafchamps, M. and F. Shilpi. 2000. "The Spatial Division of Labor in Nepal," mimeo, World Bank.

Ferreira, F., Lanjouw, P., and M. Neri. 2000. "A New Poverty Profile for Brazil Using PPV, PNAD and Census Data," mimeo, IPEA/PUC/World Bank.

Jolliffe, D. 1998. "Skills, Schooling and Household Income in Ghana," *World Bank Economic Review*, 12(1), 81–104.

Klein, E. 1992. "El Empleo Rural no Agricola en America Latina' Documento de Trabajo" No. 364. Programa Regional de Empleo para America Latina y El Caribe. Santiago, Chile.

Lanjouw, P. 1999a. "Rural Non-Agricultural Employment and Poverty in Ecuador" *Economic Development and Cultural Change,* 48 (1), October.

Lanjouw, P. 1999. "Poverty and the Non-Farm Economy in Mexico's Ejidos: 1994–1997," mimeo, World Bank, Washington D.C.

Lanjouw, P., J. Quizon, and R. Sparrow. 2000. "Non-Agricultrual Earnings in Periurban Areas of Tanzania: Evidence from Household Survey Data," mimeo, World Bank.

Lanjouw, J. O. and P. Lanjouw. 2000. "Rural Non-Farm Employment: an Update," forthcoming *Agricultural Economics.*

Lanjouw, P. and A Sharriff. 2000. "Rural Non-Farm Employment and Poverty in India," mimeo, World Bank.

Morley, S. 1994 *Poverty and Inequality in Latin America: Past Evidence, Future Prospects,* Policy Essay No. 13, Overseas Development Council, Washington D.C.

Lopez, R. and A. Valdes. 2000. *Rural Poverty in Latin America: Analytics, New Empirical Evidence and Policy,* Macmillan (UK) and St Martin's Press (New York).

Reardon, T., J. Berdegue, and G. Escobar. 2001. "Rural Non-farm Employment and Incomes in Latin America: Overview and Policy Implications," World Development.

Van de Walle, D. 2000. "Is the Emerging Non-Farm Market Economy the Route Out of Poverty in Vietnam?" mimeo, World Bank and University of Toulouse.

CHAPTER 7

RURAL EDUCATION

Introduction[102]

As stated elsewhere in this report, two facts about income distribution in Brazil stand out strongly. First, that education is the single most important determinant of poverty, no matter the poverty line or concept being used. Second, that the country's rural areas concentrate a disproportionate amount of poor people. This makes the study of rural education an important part of any study on rural poverty. The links between rural poverty and education have been examined elsewhere in this report. The objective of this section is to provide a brief diagnosis of the educational situation in rural areas and the Federal government's role in it.

The analysis is divided into two main sections. The first section takes an observant look into the situation of schools. This section compares inputs and outputs for rural and urban schools such as enrollment and approval rates, human resources, and physical inputs and tracks their recent evolution. The second section takes a look at the policies of the Federal Government for rural education and assesses their impact. Sources of rural education data used in this study include: the Education Census, an annual school-level census of Brazilian schools, and the PNAD (*Pesquisa Nacional por Amostragem de Domicílios*), a household survey consisting of 100 thousand households that are sampled every year. For the analysis of subject matter content, the SAEB standardized tests will be used.

What is the Situation Regarding Rural Education?

When looking at an educational system, two aspects are very important: results and inputs. Results can be defined as the objectives to be achieved and the reason for the existence of schools in the first place—and the inputs are determined by the immediate means for achieving them. Following this logic, the next two sections of this report will focus on educational results and inputs. Ideally, the relationship between results and inputs should also be looked at but this is a nontrivial endeavor involving estimation of educational production functions, which is beyond the scope of

---

102. This paper was prepared by Sergei Soares, Jorge Abrahão de Castro, and Adriana Fernandes Lima (IPEA).

this report. What we will do here, in addition to summarizing educational results and inputs in rural and urban areas, is speculate about possible causal connections.

If someone is to be educated in a graded system, three kinds of results are relevant: access, promotion, and content. Children must have access to schools. If they do not even begin to go to school because there are no schools where they live, all else is useless. Access is no longer a problem in Brazil as a whole, as net enrollment rates are now above 95 percent, but it is possible that the problem still exists in certain parts of the country, such as the rural North and Northeast.

After entering the school system, children must progress. There is no point for a child to spend many years in school if he or she does nothing but repeat first grade many times. This is *the* most important issue in Brazilian education. An immense work volume[103] has shown that repetition is responsible for Brazil's dismal performance in terms of grade level achieved, that it is ultimately responsible for dropping out, and more recent work shows that it is the strongest predictor of poor standardized test performance, given grade level. There is, however, little statistical work on the specific impact of repetition on rural education.

Finally, one of the ultimate goals of education is learning content.[104] Amongst other things, children go to school to learn subject matter. Fortunately, Brazil has an excellent nationwide standardized testing system, the SAEB, that can track learning, both across regions and over time. We will use SAEB data to compare rural and urban content mastery.

An important comment that must be made before we turn to school access is the definition of urban and rural. Rural schools are those classified as such by their respective school secretariats. Rural households are those classified as such by the Brazilian Geographical and Statistical Institute (IBGE). Children studying in schools classified as rural do not necessarily live in households classified by the IBGE as rural. Unfortunately, the solution to this problem would involve a detailed nationwide GIS system covering both census tracts and schools, and this is quite beyond the means of the Brazilian government at this time. Having no other solution, the problem will be ignored for now.

Access to Schools (Enrollment)

Before going into access itself, we will begin with a quick description of rural enrollment. As Tables 7.1 to 7.3 show rural education is essentially a 1st to 4th grade affair. In 1998, 27 percent 1st to 4th graders studied in rural schools, but only 6 percent of 5th to 8th grade children and 1 percent of secondary school students were enrolled in rural schools. Conversely, 85 percent of children enrolled in rural schools were 1st to 4th graders, as opposed to 50 percent for the nation as a whole.

The weight of rural enrollment is not, however, geographically homogeneous and varies quite a bit by region. The regions with the highest percentage of children in rural schools are the North and Northeast, and the lowest is the Southwest. A notable phenomenon is the reduction in 1st to 4th grade rural enrollment in the Southern Region. This is a result of a school consolidation policy by states in the South, whereby small rural schools are being closed down and their students transferred to larger, often urban, schools. Such school consolidation policies have been subject to much debate, but there is no consensus on their desirability.

It is true that rural education is becoming less and less a 1st to 4th-grade phenomenon. In 1991, 92 percent of rural enrollment was 1st to 4th grade, as opposed to 85 percent in 1998. Also, the largest growth rates in rural enrollment are those corresponding to grades from 5th to 8th and secondary education, albeit from very low baselines. Notwithstanding these trends, when we speak of rural education, we are speaking about 1st to 4th grade education. Therefore, from now on we will concentrate our analysis on these grade levels.

Finally, Table 7.5. shows the evolution of urban and rural net enrollment rates. Two things are quite apparent. First, net enrollment has increased from 1991 to 1998. In urban areas the improve-

---

103. Klein, Cost Ribeiro, Fletcher.

104. It is not the only ultimate goal, as socialization and learning behavioral norms may be at least as important as subject matter content. There is, however, no existing measure of these other goals as of today.

TABLE 7.1: ENROLLMENT BY TYPE OF LOCALITY, YEAR AND REGION (in 1.000 students)

Urban	1st to 4th grades			5th to 8th grades			Secondary Education		
	1991	1996	1998	1991	1996	1998	1991	1996	1998
North	1,027	1,253	1,352	545	799	881	196	360	437
Northeast	3,649	4,325	4,820	2,204	2,962	3,480	802	1,158	1,457
Southwest	5,773	6,229	6,154	4,454	5,798	6,143	1,789	2,706	3,259
South	1,976	1,987	2,031	1,466	1,856	1,951	544	844	1,008
Center-West	975	1,173	1,217	751	1,006	1,100	251	401	483
Brazil	**13,399**	**14,967**	**15,574**	**9,419**	**12,420**	**13,555**	**3,582**	**5,468**	**6,645**

Rural	1st to 4th grades			5th to 8th grades			Secondary Education		
	1991	1996	1998	1991	1996	1998	1991	1996	1998
North	616	702	882	30	67	92	2	6	8
Northeast	2,638	2,920	3,532	129	269	379	13	21	30
Southwest	770	786	757	94	146	196	16	20	26
South	636	471	402	122	161	175	7	10	11
Center-West	233	181	186	23	41	62	3	5	9
Brazil	**4,894**	**5,060**	**5,759**	**398**	**684**	**905**	**40**	**61**	**84**

Source: Educational Census microdata.

ment from 91 percent to 96 percent was reasonable, but in rural areas, the improvement from 75 percent to 91 percent was considerable.

Secondly, although the average enrollment rate is quite high, there is still room for improvement in many areas, mainly the rural Northeast. For example in the urban South, Southeast, and Center-West enrollment is at 97 percent. Although this means almost half a million children are out of school and all efforts should be made to reach 100 percent, there is not much room for

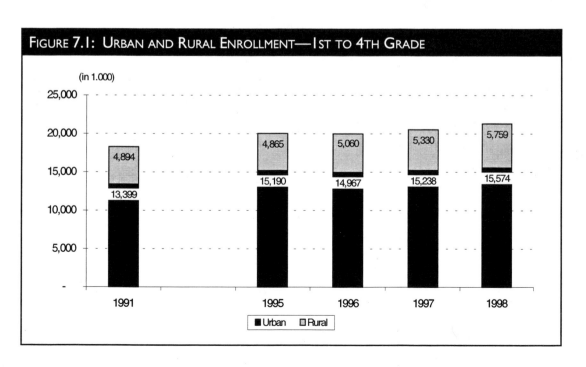

FIGURE 7.1: URBAN AND RURAL ENROLLMENT—1ST TO 4TH GRADE

TABLE 7.2: RURAL ENROLLMENT AS A PERCENTAGE OF TOTAL ENROLLMENT PERCENT RURAL

percent Rural	1st to 4th grades			5th to 8th grades			Secondary Education		
	1991	1996	1998	1991	1996	1998	1991	1996	1998
North	38 percent	36 percent	39 percent	5 percent	8 percent	9 percent	1 percent	2 percent	2 percent
Northeast	42 percent	40 percent	42 percent	6 percent	8 percent	10 percent	2 percent	2 percent	2 percent
Southwest	12 percent	11 percent	11 percent	2 percent	2 percent	3 percent	1 percent	1 percent	1 percent
South	24 percent	19 percent	17 percent	8 percent	8 percent	8 percent	1 percent	1 percent	1 percent
Center-West	19 percent	13 percent	13 percent	3 percent	4 percent	5 percent	1 percent	1 percent	2 percent
Brazil	27 percent	25 percent	27 percent	4 percent	5 percent	6 percent	1 percent	1 percent	1 percent

Source: Educational Census microdata.

improvement. On the other hand, in the rural Northeast alone, there are almost 400 thousand children out of school that account for 10 percent of the school-age population. Even in the rural Southeast, there are about 300 thousand children out of school—8 percent of all school-age children. In other words, there is still considerable room for improvement in rural enrollment rates.

Figure 7.2 above shows the trends in net rural enrollment. The convergence between Northeast and Southwest is quite clear, particularly in 1997 and 1998. We will show below that this may be a direct consequence of the Federal education policy.

Student Flow in Rural and Urban Schools

If almost all children in Brazil have access to schools, then why are educational outcomes so dismal? The reason is that they begin school, but do not finish, and they do not finish because of repetition. Up to the beginning of the 1990's, for every year successfully completed in school, on average, one was repeated. For children in poor areas or from disadvantaged backgrounds, the probabilities of repetition are much higher and children that have repeated the same grade four or five times are not uncommon. To these children, progressing from grade to grade was (and is) an almost insurmountable obstacle and their rational decision in the face of such difficult odds was to drop out with almost no education. The situation has much improved during the 1990's but remains the single most important issue in education in Brazil.

Table 7.5 and Figure 7.3 show how approval rates have evolved from 1991 to 1997. Three pieces of information can be extracted from the Table. First, approval rates are still very low. The average urban approval rate for Brazil in 1997 was 81.7 percent. This may not seem so low but it still means that an average student has a 55 percent probability of repeating at least one grade before finishing 4th grade.

Second, approval rates have been climbing at a steady but low rate. From 1991 to 1997, urban approval rates increased 7 percent and rural rates increased 6 percent. The fact that these rates appear to be climbing at a faster rate gives us even more grounds for optimism.

Finally, approval rates are much lower in rural areas, particularly in the North and Northeast (exactly where rural enrollment rates are highest). The difference between the average urban and rural rates in 1997 was 16 percent. Once again, this may not appear to be much, but it means that the probability of getting to 4th grade without repeating falls from 44 percent to 18 percent.

It is important to remember that these are average rates. For the children from less advantaged backgrounds in any of these areas, the specific approval rates are much lower and their chances of going through school plagued by multiple repetitions, and finally dropping out, are much higher.

TABLE 7.3: 1ST TO 4TH GRADE ENROLLMENT AS A PERCENTAGE OF TOTAL ENROLLMENT

	Rural			Brazil		
	1991	1996	1998	1991	1996	1998
North	95 percent	91 percent	90 percent	68 percent	61 percent	61 percent
Northeast	95 percent	91 percent	90 percent	67 percent	62 percent	61 percent
Southwest	88 percent	83 percent	77 percent	51 percent	45 percent	42 percent
South	83 percent	73 percent	68 percent	55 percent	46 percent	44 percent
Center-West	90 percent	80 percent	72 percent	54 percent	48 percent	46 percent
Brazil	**92 percent**	**87 percent**	**85 percent**	**58 percent**	**52 percent**	**50 percent**

Source: Educational Census microdata.

TABLE 7.4: RURAL ENROLLMENT AVERAGE YEARLY GROWTH RATES

	1st to 4th Grade		5th to 8th Grade		Secondary Education	
	91–96	96–98	91–96	96–98	91–96	96–98
North	3 percent	13 percent	31 percent	19 percent	32 percent	23 percent
Northeast	3 percent	10 percent	27 percent	20 percent	18 percent	20 percent
Southwest	1 percent	−2 percent	14 percent	17 percent	7 percent	13 percent
South	−7 percent	−7 percent	8 percent	4 percent	11 percent	10 percent
Center-West	−6 percent	1 percent	19 percent	26 percent	17 percent	46 percent
Brazil	**1 percent**	**7 percent**	**18 percent**	**16 percent**	**13 percent**	**18 percent**

Source: Educational Census microdata.

TABLE 7.5: NET ENROLLMENT RATES

Urban	1992	1993	1995	1996	1997	1998
North	89 percent	91 percent	92 percent	92 percent	92 percent	95 percent
Northeast	86 percent	88 percent	89 percent	91 percent	92 percent	94 percent
Southwest	93 percent	94 percent	95 percent	95 percent	96 percent	97 percent
South	91 percent	93 percent	93 percent	95 percent	96 percent	97 percent
Center-West	92 percent	92 percent	94 percent	95 percent	95 percent	97 percent
Brazil	**91 percent**	**92 percent**	**93 percent**	**94 percent**	**95 percent**	**96 percent**
Rural	1992	1993	1995	1996	1997	1998
North	—	—	—	—	—	—
Northeast	71 percent	77 percent	80 percent	80 percent	86 percent	90 percent
Southwest	79 percent	82 percent	87 percent	86 percent	91 percent	92 percent
South	80 percent	82 percent	87 percent	90 percent	93 percent	92 percent
Center-West	77 percent	78 percent	81 percent	86 percent	84 percent	92 percent
Brazil	**75 percent**	**79 percent**	**82 percent**	**83 percent**	**88 percent**	**91 percent**

Source: PNAD microdata. The PNAD does not sample the rural North

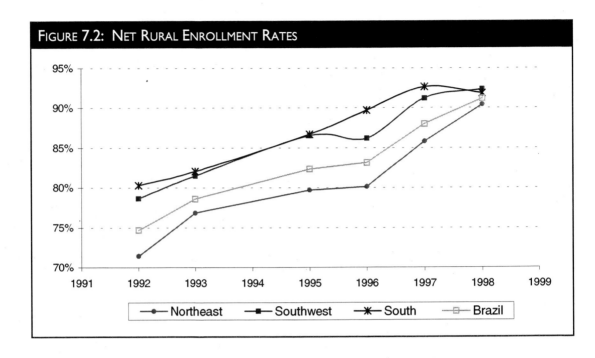

FIGURE 7.2: NET RURAL ENROLLMENT RATES

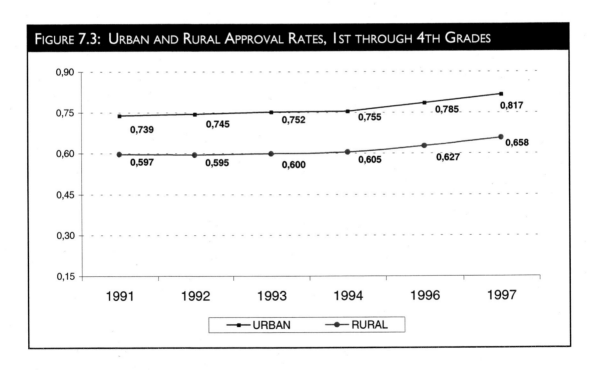

FIGURE 7.3: URBAN AND RURAL APPROVAL RATES, 1ST THROUGH 4TH GRADES

TABLE 7.6: AVERAGE APPROVAL RATES FOR 1ST TO 4TH GRADES

Urban	1991	1992	1993	1994	1996	1997
North	67.1 percent	67.2 percent	67.5 percent	66.7 percent	68.8 percent	71.2 percent
Northeast	63.9 percent	64.3 percent	65.5 percent	66.6 percent	68.4 percent	70.9 percent
Southwest	79.6 percent	80.7 percent	81.4 percent	82.1 percent	86.7 percent	90.9 percent
South	78.4 percent	79.1 percent	80.0 percent	80.1 percent	82.0 percent	85.1 percent
Center-West	71.8 percent	71.9 percent	73.3 percent	73.2 percent	76.6 percent	79.6 percent
Brazil	**73.9 percent**	**74.5 percent**	**75.2 percent**	**75.5 percent**	**78.5 percent**	**81.7 percent**
Rural	**1991**	**1992**	**1993**	**1994**	**1996**	**1997**
North	56.1 percent	55.2 percent	56.2 percent	55.6 percent	57.0 percent	58.3 percent
Northeast	54.3 percent	53.9 percent	54.7 percent	55.8 percent	57.2 percent	61.6 percent
Southwest	65.7 percent	66.7 percent	68.8 percent	71.0 percent	74.3 percent	79.9 percent
South	75.7 percent	76.5 percent	76.7 percent	77.0 percent	79.4 percent	81.7 percent
Center-West	63.1 percent	62.9 percent	63.8 percent	64.2 percent	68.6 percent	70.1 percent
Brazil	**59.7 percent**	**59.5 percent**	**60.0 percent**	**60.5 percent**	**62.7 percent**	**65.8 percent**

Source: Educational Census microdata.

TABLE 7.7: DIFFERENCE BETWEEN URBAN AND RURAL APPROVAL RATES FOR 1ST TO 4TH GRADES

	1991	1992	1993	1994	1996	1997
North	11 percent	12 percent	11 percent	11 percent	12 percent	13 percent
Northeast	10 percent	10 percent	11 percent	11 percent	11 percent	9 percent
Southwest	14 percent	14 percent	13 percent	11 percent	12 percent	11 percent
South	3 percent	3 percent	3 percent	3 percent	3 percent	3 percent
Center-West	9 percent	9 percent	10 percent	9 percent	8 percent	9 percent
Brazil	**14 percent**	**15 percent**	**15 percent**	**15 percent**	**16 percent**	**16 percent**

Source: Educational Census microdata.

It is interesting to note that rural education in one region, the South, does not appear to lag behind urban education. Further on we will see that this may, in part, be explained by the availability of educational inputs, but that they do not tell the whole story.

Scores on Standardized Tests in Rural and Urban Areas— Using the SAEB Data

Brazil has an excellent standardized test system, the SAEB, which is made up of questions that are comparable both between moments in time and grade levels. While we will not use this comparability in this study, we will use the fact that great effort has gone into formulating questions that adequately reflect the curriculum that students are supposed to follow.

The scores on the SAEB tests are ordinal and not cardinal so that averages are meaningless. Some points on the scale have, however, been interpreted so that they carry special meaning. These points are 100, 175, and 250 for the Portuguese language tests and 175 and 250 for mathematics tests. The percentages of children in rural and urban fourth grade achieving at least a given content level equivalent to these interpreted points in Portuguese and mathematics are shown on Tables 7.8 and 7.9.

The tables are to be interpreted as follows: in the Northeast, 82 percent of urban students achieved scores of at least Grade 100; 76 percent of rural students in the same region achieved or surpassed this same grade level.

TABLE 7.8: 4TH GRADE STANDARDIZED TEST SCORES FOR PORTUGUESE LANGUAGE SKILLS

	Urban Students			Rural Students		
	100	175	250	100	175	250
North	82 percent	28 percent	3 percent			
Northeast	82 percent	34 percent	7 percent	76 percent	21 percent	1 percent
Southeast	89 percent	51 percent	12 percent	75 percent	29 percent	9 percent
South	91 percent	48 percent	9 percent	80 percent	34 percent	1 percent
Center-West	87 percent	38 percent	6 percent	74 percent	14 percent	1 percent
Brazil	87 percent	43 percent	9 percent	76 percent	25 percent	4 percent

Source: SAEB microdata.

TABLE 7.9: 4TH GRADE STANDARDIZED TEST SCORES FOR MATHEMATICS SKILLS

	Urban Students		Rural Students	
	175	250	175	250
North	41 percent	3 percent		
Northeast	49 percent	8 percent	32 percent	3 percent
Southeast	62 percent	15 percent	42 percent	4 percent
South	65 percent	11 percent	54 percent	7 percent
Center-West	55 percent	9 percent	36 percent	2 percent
Brazil	**57 percent**	**11 percent**	**39 percent**	**4 percent**

Source: SAEB microdata.
Note: these points correspond to the following skills:

    100 in Portuguese — Identification of a single piece of information in a text, identification of punctuation.

    175 in Portuguese — Identification of central themes in short notes, relation of information in different texts, identification of characters from their way of speaking.

    250 in Portuguese — Recognition of the context for text interpretation, identification of the structure of a text

    175 in Mathematics — Recognition of value of coins and bills, simple addition and subtraction with natural numbers, recognition of elementary geometric shapes, reading the time on digital and analog clocks.

    250 in Mathematics — Recognition of polygons, interpretation of simple graphs, geometric description of movement, solution of mathematical operations involving more than one step.

The Tables show clearly the gap between urban and rural content mastery. In all regions, rural students have less (and in some regions, much less) content mastery than urban ones. Once again, the region where rural students are best placed, both in relation to their urban counterparts and in absolute terms, is the South. Once again, the region where rural students perform the worst is the Northeast.

School Inputs

Many factors are important in the determination of school success or failure. Family background, in particular the education of the student's mother, is of paramount importance. Community variables, such as the cultural value attributed to education, are also relevant. Many studies have also shown the importance of school inputs, particularly teachers, in determining school success.[105]

In this section we will look at the availability of these inputs both in urban and rural areas. Inputs can be classified into at least three categories: human resources (teachers), physical and

---

105. Many studies, such as the famous Coleman Report, find that inputs, even teachers, have little impact. However, most of these studies do not look at value added in the school year and thus measure stock variables as if they were flow variables.

TABLE 7.10: TEACHER QUALIFICATION OVER TIME							
Urban	**1991**	**1992**	**1993**	**1994**	**1995**	**1996**	**1998**
Incomplete Primary	1 percent	1 percent	1 percent	1 percent	1 percent	1 percent	0 percent
Complete Primary	3 percent	3 percent	4 percent	4 percent	2 percent	3 percent	2 percent
Secondary	66 percent	63 percent	70 percent	66 percent	52 percent	70 percent	69 percent
Higher Education	30 percent	33 percent	25 percent	29 percent	45 percent	27 percent	28 percent
Rural	**1991**	**1992**	**1993**	**1994**	**1995**	**1996**	**1998**
Incomplete Primary	28 percent	26 percent	31 percent	27 percent	26 percent	26 percent	18 percent
Complete Primary	20 percent	20 percent	20 percent	20 percent	19 percent	18 percent	16 percent
Secondary	47 percent	47 percent	44 percent	46 percent	48 percent	52 percent	61 percent
Higher Education	6 percent	7 percent	6 percent	7 percent	8 percent	4 percent	5 percent

Source: Educational Census microdata.

infrastructure inputs (buildings, installations, furniture), and pedagogical inputs (books, teaching materials). We will treat each one in turn.

Teachers. Teachers are perhaps the most important educational input and a good teacher can make all the difference between success and failure. In Brazil, there are various sources of data about teachers: the Educational Census, the Ministry of Labor, and even household surveys, but only the Educational Census allows us to identify the school in which the teacher works. The Educational Census also provides information on teacher qualification and we can thus compare the quality of this fundamental input in rural and urban areas.

The results are striking. Figures 7.3 and 7.4 show the distribution of urban and rural teachers by qualification and show quite clearly the gap between teachers in the two areas. Individuals

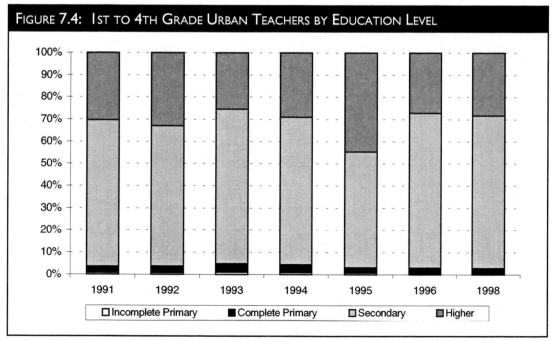

FIGURE 7.4: 1ST TO 4TH GRADE URBAN TEACHERS BY EDUCATION LEVEL

☐ Incomplete Primary   ■ Complete Primary   ☐ Secondary   ▨ Higher

Source: Educational Census microdata.

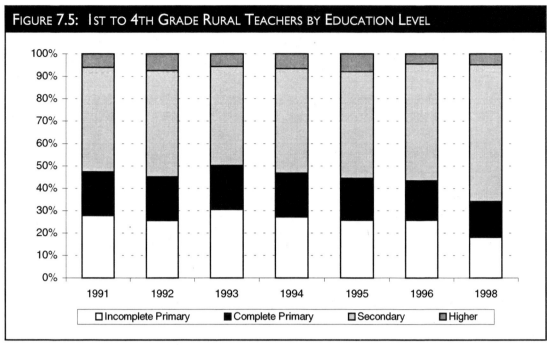

FIGURE 7.5: 1ST TO 4TH GRADE RURAL TEACHERS BY EDUCATION LEVEL

Source: Educational Census microdata.

with *incomplete primary* education make up, essentially, zero percent of the urban teaching corps but have varied between 18 percent and 30 percent of rural teachers. At the other extreme, individuals with a college education make up around 5 percent of rural and 30 percent of urban teachers.

Teacher qualification, however, varies immensely by region. Table 7.11 shows that 90 percent of the 41 thousand rural teachers with incomplete primary education are found in the North and

TABLE 7.11. TEACHER QUALIFICATION BY REGION IN 1998

	Incomplete Primary	Complete Primary	Secondary	Higher Education
Urban				
North	1 percent	5 percent	89 percent	5 percent
Northeast	1 percent	5 percent	80 percent	13 percent
Southwest	0 percent	1 percent	62 percent	37 percent
South	0 percent	1 percent	57 percent	42 percent
Center-West	0 percent	2 percent	63 percent	34 percent
Brazil	**0 percent**	**2 percent**	**69 percent**	**28 percent**
Rural				
North	27 percent	30 percent	42 percent	1 percent
Northeast	23 percent	17 percent	58 percent	2 percent
Southwest	4 percent	4 percent	80 percent	12 percent
South	4 percent	10 percent	71 percent	15 percent
Center-West	17 percent	18 percent	58 percent	7 percent
Brazil	**18 percent**	**16 percent**	**61 percent**	**5 percent**

Source: Educational Census microdata.

Northeast regions and a full 24 percent of rural teachers in these areas have such poor qualifications. On the other hand, 92 percent of rural teachers in the Southeast have at least a complete secondary education and 12 percent of them have college degrees (often a two-year teaching degree, but college degrees, nonetheless).

The data shows clearly that rural schools are very heterogeneous. Rural schools in the North and Northeast are one thing, rural schools in the South and Southwest quite another.

Physical Infrastructure (buildings). Figure 7.6 shows that the same gap that exists in teacher training also exists in physical infrastructure. Table 7.12 and Figure 7.6 show the percentage of urban and rural students studying in schools endowed with teacher's rooms (where they prepare class), bathrooms, sanitation (being linked to a sewage pipe or other adequate method of disposal), and having and adequate water supply. Although in urban areas the presence of bathrooms, adequate sanitation, and an adequate water supply is essentially universal (the data refers to 1998), in rural areas only 82 percent, 73 percent, and 88 percent of students studied in schools provided with these facilities. The one physical infrastructure item that is less essential and less widespread in urban areas, the presence of teacher's rooms, also show a very large difference: while 75 percent of urban students study in schools that have them, this is true of only 14 percent of rural students.

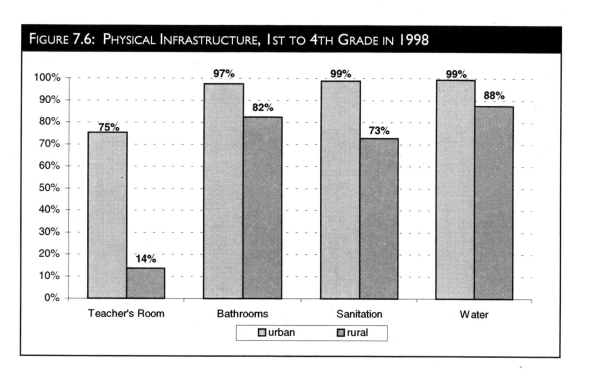

FIGURE 7.6: PHYSICAL INFRASTRUCTURE, 1ST TO 4TH GRADE IN 1998

When the data is disaggregated by region, the same pattern that was visible for teacher qualification emerges: in the South and Southwest, rural students are almost as well served as urban ones. This is only not true of teacher's rooms, of which there are relatively few even in the urban area in the North and Northeast.

Although no studies have found that physical infrastructure is as important as teachers in the determination of academic success, the same pattern emerges. Rural education is severely hampered in the North and Northeast, but less so in the rest of the Nation.

TABLE 7.12: PHYSICAL INFRASTRUCTURE BY REGION IN 1998

	Teacher's Rooms	Bathrooms	Sanitation	Adequate Water
Urban				
North	76 percent	97 percent	98 percent	99 percent
Northeast	51 percent	97 percent	98 percent	99 percent
Southwest	88 percent	98 percent	99 percent	100 percent
South	86 percent	98 percent	99 percent	100 percent
Center-West	86 percent	98 percent	99 percent	100 percent
Brazil	**75 percent**	**97 percent**	**99 percent**	**99 percent**
Rural				
North	11 percent	76 percent	42 percent	81 percent
Northeast	9 percent	80 percent	74 percent	86 percent
Southwest	27 percent	93 percent	89 percent	95 percent
South	26 percent	94 percent	95 percent	99 percent
Center-West	35 percent	88 percent	78 percent	98 percent
Brazil	**14 percent**	**82 percent**	**73 percent**	**88 percent**

Source: Educational Census microdata.

Pedagogical infrastructure. Finally, the educational census provides some information on pedagogical inputs, such as the presence of libraries, computers, and audiovisual equipment. Once again, what is shown is the number of urban and rural students studying in schools in which these inputs exist. We have no information on their usage or even their availability within the school, and accounts of computers or videos being locked up by overly zealous principals are relatively frequent. Thus, the percentages shown provide an upper limit to the availability of these pedagogical instruments for students.

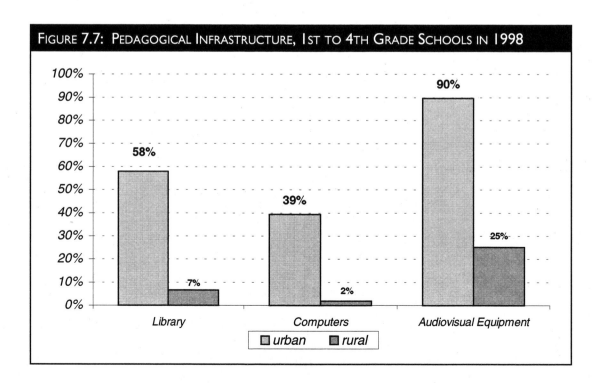

FIGURE 7.7: PEDAGOGICAL INFRASTRUCTURE, 1ST TO 4TH GRADE SCHOOLS IN 1998

	Library	Computers	Audiovisual
TABLE 7.13: Pedagogical Infrastructure by Region in 1998			
Urban			
North	45 percent	23 percent	89 percent
Northeast	33 percent	14 percent	80 percent
Southwest	73 percent	67 percent	96 percent
South	81 percent	64 percent	96 percent
Center-West	53 percent	38 percent	94 percent
Brazil	**58 percent**	**44 percent**	**91 percent**
Rural			
North	4 percent	1 percent	19 percent
Northeast	3 percent	1 percent	22 percent
Southwest	16 percent	8 percent	45 percent
South	27 percent	13 percent	47 percent
Center-West	15 percent	7 percent	44 percent
Brazil	**7 percent**	**3 percent**	**27 percent**

In the case of libraries, computers and audiovisual equipment, the regional differentiation picture that emerges is quite different from the two previous types of inputs. Rural schools everywhere are poorly endowed with libraries or computers. Somewhat less than half of the rural students in the South and Southwest study in schools that provide access to audiovisual equipment, but almost all urban students in these regions study in schools so endowed.

In the North and Northeast, availability of libraries or computers is less than half for urban students and virtually nonexistent for rural ones. In the case of audiovisual equipment, the correct terms would be less than universal for urban and rare for rural schools.

In Brazil, as whole, rural schools both present results that are considerably worse than those in urban schools and are provided with human resources and physical and pedagogical inputs that are much worse. However, when we look by region, we see that this picture is not homogeneous. In the South, rural school results are almost as good as urban ones. In both the South and Southeast, rural school inputs, except for pedagogical ones, are almost as good as the urban.

A comparison between rural and urban results and inputs presents a somewhat paradoxical picture. On the one hand, urban schools are much more generously endowed with human and physical inputs only in the North and Northeast. On the other, in the Southwest and Center-West, the difference in rural and urban approval rates is as large as in the North and Northeast. Only in the South do rural schools present approval rates close to those in urban schools.

It is clear that this difference and the issue of whether rural education is in some fundamental way qualitatively different from urban education requires more study. One extreme position, held by many experts, is that rural schools are not pedagogically viable and thus are doomed to extinction, their students being bussed to nearby urban schools in a rural to urban consolidation effort. The Ministry's present position is that rural education does not present any fundamental differences with regard to urban education and that rural schools should be treated the same as their urban counterparts. This position has direct consequences in terms of policy, as we shall see below.

MEC policies for Rural Education and the impact of MEC Universal Policies on Rural Education

The objective of this part of the chapter is to analyze the main programs of the Ministry of Education (MEC) and their impact on rural education. This is a limitation because the levels of government closest to rural schools are the state and local administrations. We do not go into state and local programs, not because they are not important, but because we have little or no information on them.

The Federal Government does not really have a rural education policy. This does not mean that there are no Federal actions focused on rural education. There are several such actions, ranging from the Fundescola Project's *Ecola Ativa* program to TV and video programs made specifically for the rural areas. It only means that there is no group of major programs orchestrated with one another for the benefit of rural schools. This follows from MECs epistemological position that there is no fundamental difference between the two types of schools. According to Ministry policy, once rural schools have access to the same inputs as urban ones, they will perform just as well.

Whether or not there should be a specific rural education policy is an open issue, but the Federal Government sees rural education as education as a whole and not just rural. All the major Federal programs benefit rural schools but none are specifically designed for them. Nevertheless, many Federal programs have had a profound and positive impact upon rural schools and their students and these policies will be analyzed.

Since 1994, MEC has targeted primary education as its number one priority. Since primary education supply is a responsibility of state and local governments, the Ministry has concentrated on normative, redistributional, and supplementary actions. Special emphasis has been given to reforming the historically centralized nature of educational program management. Centralized management has historically led to administrative inefficiency, massive corruption in the distribution of resources according to clientelistic principles, and very inequitable distribution of resources.

The Ministry's actions have been led according to the following principles:

- Equity in allocation of resources. Almost all MEC's programs are today distributed according to formulae. This is in strong opposition to the traditional pork barrel distribution of resources that has, of course, favored the states and municipalities with the most political clout. Today MEC programs are either distributionally neutral or they channel more money to the poor, as in the case of the *Fundo de Manutenção e Desenvolvimento do Ensino Fundamental e Valorização do Magistério* (Fundef).
- Decentralization. Almost all MEC programs today are highly decentralized with funds going either to municipalities and states, such as the *Programa Nacional de Alimentação Escolar* (Pnae), or even individual schools, as in the *Programa de Dinheiro Direto na Escola* (Pdde). The one large program that remains centralized is the textbook program due to the massive returns to scale in publishing.
- Support for technological innovation. The TV-Escola and Programa Nacional de Informática na Educação (Proinfo) have attempted to push schools towards new technologies. While programs focusing on technological modernization are, in quantitative terms, not as important as most other programs, they have remained a guideline for the MEC policy during the past six years.

The above are the guiding principles for the Ministry of Education that are the groundwork for all Federal Programs. But, as there is a variety of different programs with different objectives, we shall classify them into four groups: (i) the Fundef is so important it deserves a group of its own; (ii) the programs targeted on students; (iii) the programs targeted on schools; and (iv) the programs supporting technological innovation. We now turn to the analysis of these policies and their immediate impact upon rural education.

The Education Maintenance and Development Fund—FUNDEF

Coherent with the allocation priority to primary education and MEC's redistributive role, perhaps the most important action of the Ministry of Education during the past six years has been the creation of a Fund whose resources would be earmarked for education. The Federal Government proposed to the Congress a Constitutional amendment that would create the Education Maintenance and Development Fund (Fundo de Manutenção e Desenvolvimento do Ensino Fundamental e Valorização do Magistério—Fundef).

The Fundef is a Fund composed of 15 percent of all Value Added Tax and 7.5 percent of all Income and Industrial Taxes collected in Brazil. This money is to be used only in primary education, distributed within each state, proportional to enrollment. At least 60 percent of it must be used for paying wages of teaching and support staff.

The Fund is composed at the state level. In other words, all school systems within a state receive the same per student values. However, given the large differences in wealth between states, the Federal Government is responsible for complementing the Fund, up to a minimum-per-student level in states whose tax base is considered insufficient.

In short, the Fundef could be considered to be a kind or Robin Hood Fund. It takes a fixed proportion of resources from state and municipal governments and redistributes it within each state, proportional to enrollment, so that all municipal school systems and the state school system receive the same amount. The Federal Government complements the Fund in those states whose tax base is too weak to allow for a minimum level of resources. This minimum level was established at R$ 315 per student per year in 1998.

Although it was implemented in three states in 1997 (Goiás, Espirito Santo, and Pará), the Fundef was established on a nationwide basis in 1998. As has been said, the minimum value was established at R$ 315 per student. In 1998, the Federal Government transferred R$ 424.95 million reais to eight states[106] in order to bring their per capita values up to the minimum. The transfers between systems within each state were much larger. Some 2–3 billion reais will be exchanging hands, and most of it will be lost by state and capital city systems to be transferred to smaller rural municipalities.

It is impossible to estimate exactly what rural schools have gained in terms of resources from the Fundef. To do so, we would need information on intra-system allocation of resources, which does not exist. But this does not mean that the Fund's impacts cannot be measured.

Given the fact that the structure of education finance differs greatly from state to state, it is to be expected that the Fundef has different impacts on enrollment by state. This gives us the possibility of testing its impact. The idea is to use the heterogeneity of states to estimate a fixed effects model and see what impact, if any, the Fundef has upon enrollment. The procedure used was the following:

1) The net enrollment rates from 1992 to 1998 were calculated for urban and rural areas.
2) A fixed effects model with a linear time trend was estimated separately for rural and urban areas. Two estimation strategies were adopted: the first was to estimate the Northeast and North on the one hand, and the rest of the country on the other; as a check, we estimated the effect for the whole country as well. In both cases, rural and urban schools were separately estimated.
3) The rural and urban populations of each state were used as weights in the equation.
4) A dummy was added for the year in which the Fundef began (1998).
5) The value of this dummy is the effect of the Fundef upon net enrollment.

The table below shows the impact of this change in financing. It is interesting that there a positive and significant effect exists only for the rural Northeast and North. According to our estimates, the Fundef significantly increased enrollment in this area by 5.5 percent.

This is probably due to two factors. First, the other areas of the country already had very high net enrollment rates and, thus, had little space for improvement. Secondly, it was precisely the school systems of the small municipalities in the Northeast and North that profited the most from Fundef's redistribution.

The value of the time trend is also interesting. In urban areas, enrollment increased close to 1 percent per year—slightly more in the North and Northeast, slightly less in the rest of the country. In rural areas, the increase was larger—about 2 percent per year.

---

106. The states were Alagoas, Bahia, Ceará, Maranhão, Pará, Paraiba, Pernambuco and Piaui.

			MODEL			
	Rural North and Northeast	Urban North And Northeast	Rural South, Southwest and Center-West	Urban South, Southwest and Center-West	All Rural	All Urban
FUNDEF	5.5 percent	1.7 percent	0.6 percent	0.5 percent	2.9 percent	1.2 percent
p-value	0 percent	16 percent	64 percent	20 percent	1 percent	9 percent
Time trend	2.8 percent	1.1 percent	2.1 percent	0.7 percent	2.5 percent	1.0 percent
p-value	0 percent	0 percent	0 percent	0 percent	0 percent	0 percent

TABLE 7.14: ESTIMATION OF FUNDEF IMPACT: VALUE OF THE 1998 DUMMY AND OF THE LINEAR TIME TREND

Programs Focusing on Students

Programs focusing on students are those whose objective is to finance or provide services used directly by students, such as school lunches, transportation, and textbooks. The goods and services are, of course, always provided to the students through schools or school systems, but the focus of the program is the student. These programs are usually distributed on a per-student basis and account for most of the Federal Government's expenditures in education.

The School Lunch Program—PNAE: The School Lunch (*Programa Nacional de Alimentação Escolar*—Pnae) is one of the most important Federal programs. The objective is to provide one healthy meal per school day to each student. The target population is pre and primary school children of the public and non-profit private schools in Brazil. The program's objective is to assure supplementary nutrition so as to improve school attendance and learning.

The program's operation is simple: it transfers either to the states or the municipalities 0.13 reais per child per school day. The states and municipalities then either buy the food and distribute it to the schools or pass down the funds so that the schools themselves can provide the meals.

In 1997, the Federal Government spent R$ 687 million reais on the Pnae. In 1998 R$ 903 million were budgeted but due to fiscal restrictions, only R$ 785 were actually spent. These figures make the School Lunch the single most important Federal Program in education.

The coverage rates can be seen in Table 7.15. The table may be slightly confusing and since identical tables will be used from here until the conclusion of this report, a little explanation is worthwhile.

The first four lines represent the coverage rates—in other words, the percentage of state, municipal, and all students, urban and rural, in 1997 and 1998—that studied in schools in which the program existed. For example, 96 percent (last column, second row) is the percent of 1st to 4th children enrolled in municipal, rural schools in 1998 whose schools were covered by the program.

TABLE 7.15: COVERAGE RATES OF THE SCHOOL LUNCH PROGRAM 1997–1998

		1997			1998		
		Total	State	Municipal	Total	State	Municipal
Coverage Rates							
1st to 4th	Urban	88 percent	85 percent	93 percent	89 percent	85 percent	93 percent
	Rural	95 percent	89 percent	97 percent	95 percent	88 percent	96 percent
5th to 8th	Urban	86 percent	84 percent	93 percent	86 percent	84 percent	92 percent
	Rural	92 percent	88 percent	96 percent	93 percent	88 percent	96 percent
percent Rural		20 percent	—	—	22 percent		
Rural 1st to 4th		29 percent	10 percent	45 percent	31 percent	8 percent	44 percent
Rural 5th to 8th		6 percent	4 percent	14 percent	7 percent	4 percent	17 percent

Source: MEC/INEP—Educational Census

The last three lines show the percentage of covered children that study in rural schools. For example, 44 percent (last column, sixth row) is the percentage of 1st to 4th children studying in 1998 in schools covered by the school lunch program, whose schools were rural. Table 7.2 shows that 27 percent of 1st to 4th students are enrolled in rural schools. If a greater percentage than this receives the program, it means the program is more focused on rural schools; if the percentage is smaller, it is urban-focused. Table 7.15 shows in column 4, line 6, that 31 percent of rural children was covered by School Lunch. In other words, school lunch is rural-focused and this is coherent with the fact that the coverage rates are 89 percent in urban and 95 percent in rural schools.

The data shows that, with this program, rural schools are better covered than urban schools. The table shows that while 95 percent of rural students were enrolled in schools covered by the program, only 89 percent of urban students benefited by it. Since rural enrollment is a fraction of urban enrollment, only 22 percent of beneficiary students were rural.

Since the School Lunch program is supposedly a universal program, it is surprising that only 89 percent of urban students were enrolled in schools served by the program. The answer to this paradox is that in the state of São Paulo, where there is a large number of urban schools, the program works differently and many school principals may have misinterpreted the question on the Educational Census.

The School Health Program—PNSE: This is a small program to provide health coverage in very few selected schools. Only 670 of the more than 5.000 municipalities were covered. The only reason we include this measly program in this text is because it has been, for the most part, a rural program.

Table 7.16 shows that coverage rates are from four to eight times higher in rural areas than they are in urban areas, but these rates are so low that it is an almost nonexistent program.

TABLE 7.16: COVERAGE RATES OF THE SCHOOL HEALTH PROGRAM, 1997–1998

		1997 Total	State	Municipal	1998 Total	State	Municipal
Coverage Rates							
1st to 4th	Urban	2 percent	1 percent	3 percent	2 percent	1 percent	3 percent
	Rural	8 percent	2 percent	9 percent	8 percent	2 percent	9 percent
5th to 8th	Urban	1 percent	1 percent	2 percent	1 percent	0 percent	2 percent
	Rural	4 percent	1 percent	8 percent	5 percent	1 percent	8 percent
percent Rural		59 percent	—	—	60 percent	—	—
Rural 1st to 4th		66 percent	25 percent	75 percent	66 percent	19 percent	70 percent
Rural 5th to 8th		25 percent	9 percent	36 percent	31 percent	9 percent	42 percent

The School Transportation Program—PNTE: This is as "rural education" a program as will be found. In the cities students wearing school uniforms are given free transportation on public buses and trains, resulting in little need for children living in urban areas to use school buses. But rural children often live very far from their schools, making school buses very important for these children.

The Federal Government provides 60 to 70 thousand reais to states and municipalities for acquisition of transportation. The amount does not vary with demand and this is a serious limitation in the design of the program. In 1997, 1,5 million reais were spent and 120 vehicles were purchased; in 1998 this total increased to 80 million reais granted to 1.558 municipalities.

Table 7.17 shows that this is, for the most part, a rural program. Not only are students studying in rural schools much more likely to benefit from this program, but many of the students studying in urban schools may actually be rural inhabitants bussed to urban schools.

It is also a predominantly 5th to 8th grade program and the coverage is only really significant for 5th to 8th grade rural children—35 percent. This is to be expected, given the larger school size, and thus, greater bussing needs of this level of education.

TABLE 7.17: COVERAGE RATES OF THE SCHOOL TRANSPORTATION PROGRAM, 1997–1998							
		1997			1998		
		Total	**State**	**Municipal**	**Total**	**State**	**Municipal**
Coverage Rates							
1st to 4th	**Urban**	12 percent	10 percent	15 percent	12 percent	10 percent	15 percent
	Rural	13 percent	14 percent	12 percent	13 percent	15 percent	12 percent
			13 percent	16 percent	14 percent	13 percent	16 percent
5th to 8th	**Urban**	14 percent	34 percent	37 percent	35 percent	33 percent	37 percent
	Rural	35 percent	—	—	24 percent	—	—
percent Rural		22 percent	13 percent	39 percent	30 percent	12 percent	39 percent
Rural 1st to 4th		28 percent	9 percent	27 percent	16 percent	9 percent	30 percent
Rural 5th to 8th		14 percent					

The Textbook Acquisition Program—PNLD: This is another heavyweight Federal Program. The Textbook Acquisition Program (*Programa Nacional do Livro Didático*—Pnld) has spent about R$ 100 million reais per year in the past few years. Its objective is to provide schools with timely delivery of quality textbooks every year. The Textbook Acquisition Program is the only MEC program whose execution is centralized. Because of large economies of scale, all textbooks are bought centrally by the Federal Government and then distributed directly to the schools. The exact operation is as follows:

- First, a commission of educators and specialists meets to judge all textbooks presented by publishers. This commission reads and comments on the books, and finally classifies them as acceptable or not.
- The list of acceptable books, together with the commission's comments, is handed to schools. The schools then choose which books they wish to buy. They are given a virtual budget, proportional to their enrollment, that they use to buy textbooks for the coming school year.
- Once the schools decide which books they want, the Federal Government orders the books from the publishers and, through the mail, distributes them directly to the schools. The textbooks are assumed to last four years, although this is being revised to allow for regional variation.

Table 7.18 shows that the textbook program is truly universal. Ninety-six percent of urban and 97 percent of rural students study in schools that receive textbooks, which, together with their timely delivery, make textbook acquisition one of the more successful Federal Programs.

TABLE 7.18: COVERAGE RATES OF THE PNAE, 1997–1998							
		1997			1998		
		Total	**State**	**Municipal**	**Total**	**State**	**Municipal**
Coverage Rates							
1st to 4th	**Urban**	96 percent	97 percent	96 percent	96 percent	97 percent	95 percent
	Rural	97 percent	95 percent	98 percent	97 percent	93 percent	98 percent
5th to 8th	**Urban**	95 percent	95 percent	95 percent	95 percent	95 percent	95 percent
	Rural	95 percent	93 percent	97 percent	94 percent	91 percent	96 percent
percent Rural		19 percent			21 percent		
Rural 1st to 4th		27 percent	9 percent	44 percent	30 percent	8 percent	44 percent
Rural 5th to 8th		6 percent	4 percent	14 percent	7 percent	4 percent	17 percent

Source: MEC/INEP—School Census

Programs Focusing on Schools

Decentralization has been a hallmark of Federal Education Policy for the last six years. The programs focusing on schools are those passing funds to schools so they can better provide educational services for their students. While the client of the program is the same—schools or school districts—as in the programs centering on students, the focus is different.

The Programa de Dinheiro Direto na Escola (Pdde): The Pdde is MECs most decentralized program. It sends money directly to schools to spend as they see fit. The funds are distributed to schools according to formula-driven transfers. This is in stark contrast with previous transfers that were almost always negotiated politically.

Not all schools are eligible. The program requires that the schools: (i) have a Bank account in which the funds can be deposited (it is not acceptable for the education secretariat to centralize the funds and spend them on the schools' behalf); and (ii) have a school council to oversee the use the school director gives them.

In 1997 only schools with 200 students or more were eligible, the number being reduced to 150 in 1998. All schools receive a minimum of R$ 500 which increases in discrete steps to a maximum of $15,000 as enrollment rises.

The idea of the program is not only to provide schools with resources but also to empower the community to better spend them. By requiring that schools actually spend the money and that they have school councils to do so, the project attempts to shift power from the education secretariats to the community.

Table 7.19 shows that the Pdde is an overwhelmingly urban program. While 78 percent of urban students studied in schools with Pdde, only 33 percent of rural students did so. This is to be expected, owing to the fact that few rural schools have 150 students or more. Even so, the coverage rates, given the various demands made of schools before they are eligible to receive the funds, are surprisingly high.

TABLE 7.19: COVERAGE RATES OF THE PDDE, 1997–1998

		1997			1998		
		Total	**State**	**Municipal**	**Total**	**State**	**Municipal**
Coverage Rates							
1st to 4th	**Urban**	81 percent	89 percent	70 percent	78 percent	88 percent	68 percent
	Rural	35 percent	75 percent	27 percent	33 percent	73 percent	28 percent
5th to 8th	**Urban**	85 percent	88 percent	74 percent	84 percent	87 percent	73 percent
	Rural	71 percent	87 percent	56 percent	68 percent	87 percent	54 percent
percent Rural		10 percent		–	11 percent	–	–
Rural 1st to 4th		14 percent	8 percent	23 percent	15 percent	7 percent	24 percent
Rural 5th to 8th		5 percent	4 percent	11 percent	6 percent	4 percent	13 percent

Source: MEC/INEP—School Census.

Programa de Trabalho Anual (Pta): The Pta is the pork barrel equivalent of the formula-driven Pdde. There is a demand-driven mechanism according to which education secretariats demand money for projects and MEC decides who will get money and who will not. Traditionally, the Pta is a way of getting money easily to one's political allies. It used to account for almost all of MEC's financial relations with states and municipalities. Fortunately, the Pta today is an almost nonexistent dinosaur.

TABLE 7.20: COVERAGE RATES OF THE PTA, 1997–1998

			1997			1998	
		Total	State	Municipal	Total	State	Municipal
Coverage Rates							
1st to 4th	Urban	5 percent	3 percent	8 percent	5 percent	2 percent	7 percent
	Rural	4 percent	1 percent	5 percent	4 percent	1 percent	5 percent
5th to 8th	Urban	4 percent	3 percent	10 percent	4 percent	3 percent	9 percent
	Rural	4 percent	1 percent	6 percent	4 percent	2 percent	5 percent
percent Rural		18 percent			19 percent		
Rural 1ª to 4ª		25 percent	5 percent	32 percent	27 percent	4 percent	33 percent
Rural 5ª to 8ª		5 percent	2 percent	9 percent	6 percent	2 percent	10 percent

Source: MEC/INEP—Educational Census.

The Table above shows the small extent of Pta coverage. The probabilities of a rural or urban school receiving money through this channel are both low and about the same.

Support for Technological Innovation

The programs described above would all be adequate for a nineteenth-century school system—they focus on good management, equity, and decentralization. However, the 21st Century poses new dilemmas and challenges. To prepare Brazil's education system for these new challenges, the Federal Government has created programs to push for the adoption of new technologies. As we will see below, coverage of these programs is woefully inadequate and many also argue that these programs are implemented in ways that are friendlier to high-tech vendors than they are to schools, but it is important that steps be taken to ensure that Brazil is not left too far behind in the technological information revolution.

TV Escola: The TV Escola program is the oldest of the two large Federal programs in support of technological innovation. Its objective is to provide as many schools as possible with television sets, VCRs and satellite dishes in order to enhance their pedagogical instruments.

The Ministry also works on program production by making and broadcasting educational programs. In 1996, 2.460 hours of programming were broadcast, although their quality has never been adequately tested.

The program has received much criticism in that many of the schools were ill prepared to use this new technology, and there were horror stories of boxes of VCRs and satellite dishes never hav-

TABLE 7.21: COVERAGE RATES FOR TV ESCOLA 1997–1998

			1997			1998	
		Total	State	Municipal	Total	State	Municipal
Coverage Rates							
1st to 4th	Urban	74 percent	82 percent	62 percent	71 percent	82 percent	59 percent
	Rural	20 percent	47 percent	14 percent	18 percent	47 percent	14 percent
5th to 8th	Urban	81 percent	85 percent	65 percent	80 percent	84 percent	64 percent
	Rural	61 percent	73 percent	49 percent	58 percent	72 percent	48 percent
percent Rural		7 percent			7 percent		
Rural 1st to 4th		9 percent	5 percent	15 percent	9 percent	5 percent	16 percent
Rural 5th to 8th		5 percent	3 percent	11 percent	5 percent	3 percent	13 percent

Source: MEC/INEP—Educational Census.

ing been opened. Although adequate surveys were never carried out, preliminary work suggests that many schools had trouble getting the equipment to work, mostly due to lack of specialized personnel to operate it. This same work shows, however, that 80 percent of students that actually watched the programs were satisfied with them. The program, therefore, shows mixed results.

The table above shows that TV Escola is basically an urban affair. For 1st to 4th grade schools where the immense majority of rural enrollment is concentrated, the probability of studying in a TV Escola school was three to four times higher in urban areas than it was in rural areas. This is to be expected as few rural schools have the required installations or personnel qualified to receive VCRs or satellite dishes.

Whether expected or not, this anti-rural bias is particularly distressing given the fact that distance learning is one of the better ways to overcome the dearth in qualified teachers in rural schools. If you can have the best math teacher in the nation on VCR, the fact that the local math teacher is not very good becomes less serious. However, Table 20 shows that only 18 percent of children study in schools that have been contemplated by the program. Given this reality, it is not surprising that only 27 percent rural children study in schools that have any kind of audiovisual equipment.

PROINFO: The other large technological innovation program is the PROINFO. This program has as its objective the massive introduction of computers into education, both as a management tool and as a pedagogical instrument. The original objective of the program was to buy 100 thousand computers for 6 thousand schools. In addition, 26 thousand teachers and 6 thousand computer- technicians were to be trained.

As usual, what was actually achieved thus far has been somewhat short of this. Although 22 thousand teachers were trained, neither the quality of their training nor their performance thereafter have been adequately observed. In terms of hardware, the Federal Government bought only 37 thousand computers by the end of 1998. The program was continued and we should expect the targets to be better met in 1999.

TABLE 7.22: COVERAGE RATES FOR PROINFO, 1997–1998

| | | 1997 | | | 1998 | | |
		Total	State	Municipal	Total	State	Municipal
Coverage Rates							
1st to 4th	Urban	13 percent	17 percent	7 percent	12 percent	18 percent	6 percent
	Rural	1 percent	3 percent	1 percent	1 percent	3 percent	1 percent
5th to 8th	Urban	22 percent	25 percent	11 percent	21 percent	24 percent	10 percent
	Rural	4 percent	7 percent	2 percent	4 percent	8 percent	2 percent
percent Rural		2 percent			2 percent		
Rural 1ª to 4ª		3 percent	2 percent	6 percent	3 percent	1 percent	6 percent
Rural 5ª to 8ª		1 percent	1 percent	2 percent	1 percent	1 percent	3 percent

Source: MEC/INEP—Educational Census

Nevertheless, the table below shows that a reasonable amount of schools received either the training or the computers. However, the PROINFO, is almost exclusively an urban program, even more so than TV Escola: only 2 percent of students studying in PROINFO schools are rural.

Conclusion

The picture painted in the first part of this report is not new. The deficiencies of rural education have not become an issue overnight in Brazil. Rural schools in Brazil have always lagged behind urban ones. Their results are much worse than those of urban schools, both in terms of progression and learning of contents. The physical, pedagogic, and human resources they have at their disposal are far behind those of their urban counterparts. The quality of their students, coming from poorer and less educated agricultural families, is also worse.

This, however, should not be interpreted with pessimism implying that improving rural schools is a hopeless endeavor and that rural children are forever condemned to lag behind urban children. The strong regional variation in inputs, but most of all in results, shows that it is possible for rural schools to approach urban ones. If so, it may be possible for them to eventually become equivalent to the schools in the cities.

The situation of rural education is in part due to natural difficulties posed by rurality—small schools, large distances, and poorer agricultural families—but it also comes from decades of neglect. In the past, Federal Funds were channeled disproportionately to higher education and, through clientelistic education policy, within primary education, to schools in the systems with the most political influence.

We have seen that remedying this neglect has direct influence on both inputs and results. The Fundef has had a statistically significant effect upon rural enrollment. We have also seen that the change from pork barrel education policy to universal formula-driven programs has greatly increased the access to Federal Programs on the part of rural schools. This change, however, is incomplete—while most of MEC's funds today run on formula-driven allocation, many smaller programs such as PTAs, School Health, and School Transportation still follow the pork barrel logic.

Obviously, much remains to be done. In the field of research, more work on the kind of pedagogical approach that may work in rural schools is highly necessary. As we have seen, whether rural schools require special treatment or only fair treatment, is an issue that has direct implications on policies adopted.

In terms of immediate policy initiatives, faster and better way to expose rural (and also urban) children to new technologies are very important in a rapidly evolving world, as is the extinction or modification of those programs that still follow the pork barrel approach. If a conclusion is to be had, it is that using Federal funds in universal programs driven by formulae and not constant political negotiation produces benefits for everyone, especially for those most neglected in the past, such as rural schools.

CHAPTER 8

SOCIAL INSURANCE OR SOCIAL ASSISTANCE FOR BRAZIL'S RURAL POOR?

Introduction[107]

There has been a substantial increase in the coverage of social security in Brazil in the last decade. The 1988 Federal Constitution established the universal right to social security and instituted special eligibility conditions for rural workers under the *Regime Geral da Previdência Social* (RGPS), Brazil's public pension system for workers in the private sector.[108] However, these new conditions—which increased both the accessibility and generosity of RGPS benefits— were not effectively extended to rural areas until implementing legislation was passed by Congress in 1991.[109] Social security benefits paid to rural households as income support for workers in old age, for the surviving spouses and children of deceased workers, and for the temporarily injured and permanently disabled, have grown steadily in number and size ever since.

Recent analysis based on the 1996–1997 *Pesquisa sobre Padrões de Vida* (PPV) survey, found that the proportion of rural households receiving pensions from public institutions averages 30 percent in Brazil's poorer Northeast, and 24 percent in the Southeast. In 1999 the National Social Security Institute (INSS)—an arm of the Ministry of Social Security and Social Assistance

---

107. This paper was prepared by Truman Packard.

108. Brazil has a long history of government-organized social security. The current system has its roots in legislation first passed in 1923, and has since taken on various institutional forms. Social security for rural workers was first formalized in 1955 with the creation of the *Serviço Social Rural*, made effective in 1963 with the creation of the *Fundo de Assistência e Previdência do Trabalhador Rural* (FUNRURAL), complemented in 1971 with the *Programa de Assistência ao Trabalhador Rural* (Pro-Rural), and unified with the first national system (*Sistema Nacional de Previdência e Assistência Social*—SINPAS) in 1977. For a complete legislative and institutional history of Brazil's social security system, and the evolution of special benefits for rural workers, see Beltrao et al (1999)

109. The 1988 Constitution (i) granted equal eligibility rights to households headed by men and women; (ii) lowered the age at which rural workers could receive benefits; and (iii) raised the minimum RGPS benefit to 100 percent of the legal minimum wage from 50 percent prior to 1988. The new parameters for rural workers came into full effect at the start of 1992.

(MPAS)—paid R$10.8 billion in benefits to 6.3 million rural beneficiaries—three times as many benefits paid prior to the implementation of the new eligibility rules in 1991.[110] Benefits to rural households made up over 18 percent of total RGPS benefits paid by INSS in 1999.

This note will focus on the impact of social security on rural poverty. It reviews the structure of RGPS benefits and the special eligibility parameters available to rural workers, as well as provides a breakdown of benefits paid in 1999. Then, it examines the role that social security plays in reducing rural poverty, and finds that while public pensions are an increasing share of total household income in rural areas and have contributed to a lower incidence of rural poverty, there is no evidence that the positive impact of social security can be attributed to the successful implementation of contributory social insurance, or simply to the expansion and increased generosity of non-contributory social assistance transfers. Then, it argues that while rural pensions play a valuable role and should be protected, for the sake of fiscal transparency and efficiency the program should be restructured as social assistance and financed out of general revenues, rather than maintained as social insurance financed with payroll contributions from workers and employers. Finally, this note explains the implications of recent reforms to the RGPS on the pension benefits received by rural households, and concludes.

RGPS Benefits for Rural Households

A short review of the various benefits offered under the RGPS will be useful to understand the contribution of social security to the incomes of rural households, the different social insurance options available to rural and urban workers, as well as the incentive structure faced by workers in rural areas.[111] A short description of each benefit option is provided in Box 8.1.

To avoid loosing the reader in the complex maze of benefits and eligibility requirements in the Brazilian social security system, a simplifying generalization can be made: of the two contributory retirement benefits paid by the RGPS—the *Length of Service* pension and the *Old Age* pension—recipients of the Old Age benefit are typically rural households, often headed by elderly male agricultural workers or by widowed women. The typical recipients of length of service pensions, on the other hand, are the once formally employed, urban workers. In 1999 over 70 percent of RGPS Old Age pensions were paid to rural workers, while 99 percent of Length of Service pensions were paid to urban workers

The special contribution and benefit parameters for rural workers introduced in the 1988 Constitution and implemented in 1991, make the old age pension more attractive and more likely to be taken up by farmers, the self employed, and workers in small rural enterprises. Rural workers are allowed to receive an old age pension five years earlier than workers in the private sector workers in urban areas—at age 60 for men and 55 for women. For those retiring prior to 1991, only five years of contributions were needed to qualify for old age pensions. Recent legislation has increased the minimum vesting period so that it reaches 15 years by 2011. Figure 8.1 shows how the total amount paid by RGPS to rural households was distributed between the various social security benefit programs in 1999.

The Old Age retirement benefit is paid as 70 percent of a worker's average earning in the last three years (36 months) before retirement, plus an accrual of 1 percent of average earnings for every year the worker actually contributed to the system. As it is difficult for MPAS/INSS to verify the earnings and contribution histories of workers in rural areas, and since many rural workers earn incomes below the legal minimum wage, rural recipients of Old Age pensions on average receive a "top up" from RGPS—either a default, 100 percent replacement of their last declared wage, or the legal minimum benefit in the RGPS (equal to the minimum wage), whichever amount is higher. As

---

110. Beltrao et al (1999) find that the 1988 Constitution had huge impact on benefit take up. In 1996 three times as many women, and 2.5 times as many men received pension benefits as did in 1988.

111. For a fuller review of the RGPS as well as of the other branches of Brazil's social security system, see World Bank 2000.

Box 8.1: RGPS Benefits

Old Age retirement benefits are paid to both rural and urban workers. The age of retirement is 65 years for men and 60 years for women working in the urban sector. Presently, rural workers can retire 5 years earlier than their urban counterparts. In 1998, the minimum period of contribution to be eligible was about 102 months and is scheduled to increase at 6 months per year until the end of 2011. The replacement rate is 70 percent of the wage base—the average of the last 3 years' salaries subject to contribution, adjusted for inflation—for reaching the retirement age subject to the minimum vesting period plus an additional 1 percent per year of service, up to a limit of 100 percent or about 10 minimum wages.

Length of Service retirement benefits were paid to workers after they met a required number of years of service, irrespective of age. Before constitutional reform in 1998 and the introduction of the new RGPS benefit formula in November 1999, the minimum vesting periods were 30 years for men and 25 years for women, for individuals to receive 70 percent of their reference wage as "reduced" pensions. The annual accrual rate for additional years of service was 6 percent, which implied that a man could receive 100 percent replacement rates after 35 years of service while a woman could retire with the price-indexed average of her last three years of wages after 30 years of contribution. The reference wage—the average of the last 36 months—was the same as that for Old-Age pensions, as are the maximum and minimum level of benefits. Since 1994, pensions have been adjusted to inflation and the minimum benefit has increased in real terms.

Special Length of Service can be claimed by individuals working in sectors considered to be arduous after 15, 20 or 25 years of service depending on the nature of the activity. The replacement rate for this category of service is 85 percent with an additional 1 percent for each year of service in addition to the stipulated minimum vesting period. Eligibility for this benefit has been significantly restricted under recent reforms.

Disability Pensions are paid to those individuals certified by an INSS doctor as permanently handicapped and unable to exercise any economic occupation. The minimum qualification period for this kind of pension is only 12 months. The reference wage is the average of the individual's actual wages up to the last three years of service if applicable. Replacement rates are at 80 percent of the reference wage with the accrual rates for additional years of service at 1 percent. A separate, more generous workmen's compensation benefit is offered for disabling injuries on the job.

Survivors and orphans of deceased pensioners receive 100 percent of the pensions due to the deceased contributor. Such benefits are paid even if the contributor had only a single day of recorded work. The replacement rate is based on an average of the wages actually received by the individual if the individual's work history does not reflect three years of work. If the deceased individual were already receiving benefits, these are transferred to the survivors or orphans.

Workmen's compensation is paid to any individual's suffering from a work-related, permanent disability. The benefit is 100 percent of the wages on the day the individual was rendered disabled.

Figure 8.1: Distribution of RGPS Benefits to Rural Households, 1999
(MPAS/INSS, January 2000)

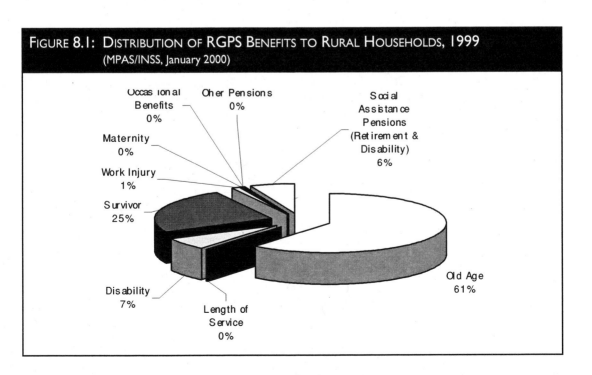

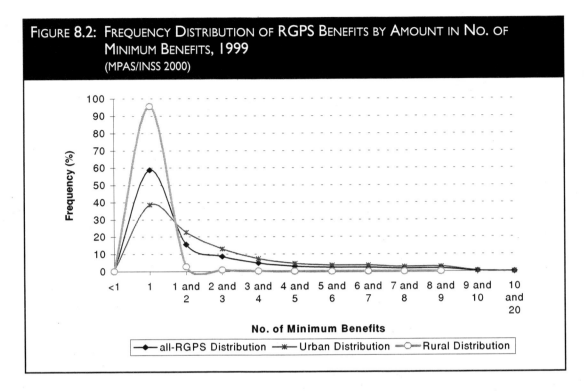

FIGURE 8.2: FREQUENCY DISTRIBUTION OF RGPS BENEFITS BY AMOUNT IN NO. OF MINIMUM BENEFITS, 1999
(MPAS/INSS 2000)

is shown in the frequency distribution of RGPS benefits in Figure 8.2, most rural beneficiaries receive the minimum pension, equal to the minimum wage since the 1988 Constitution.

In addition to contributory pensions (*length of service* and *old age*), the RGPS pays a non-contributory social assistance benefit for old age and disability to poor workers without a documented work/contribution history (to avoid confusion this benefit will be referred to as the "*social assistance pension*"). Workers can receive the social assistance pension upon reaching 70 years of age, or if they become disabled. Almost 20 percent of social assistance pensions for retirement and disability are paid to rural households. While the amount of the social assistance pension and that of the average old age pension received by rural beneficiaries is almost identical (see Figure 8.3), the average old age pension paid to urban beneficiaries is 65 percent *greater* than the average social assistance pension.

The Impact of Rural Pensions on Poverty and Welfare

Does the Brazilian social security system help or hurt the rural poor? This is a particularly important question for researchers to address, especially in evaluating the impact of the large expansion in coverage to rural areas since the 1988 Constitution, and in charting the present course of reforms to the social security system. This section will employ two different approaches to answer the question above: (i) analysis of the benefit structure of the contributory old age pension; and (ii) review of empirical findings from studies using household level data.

Most social security systems in developing countries that operate on a pay-as-you-go (PAYGO) basis—where the contributions of current workers pay the pensions of current beneficiaries—can be regressive (intentionally and unintentionally) in a number of ways (World Bank, 1994).

- First, PAYGO pensions are typically financed with a flat tax on covered wages up to a maximum taxable income, with no exemptions for workers earning lower wages.
- Second, pension benefits are based on earnings rather than on need, and are often calculated to favor better educated workers with rising age-earnings profiles.
- Third, contributions from poorer workers with higher average mortality often subsidize the pensions of longer-lived, higher income workers.

FIGURE 8.3: AVERAGE BENEFIT AMOUNT, RURAL AND URBAN, BY BENEFIT CATEGORY, (1999—MPAS/INSS 2000)

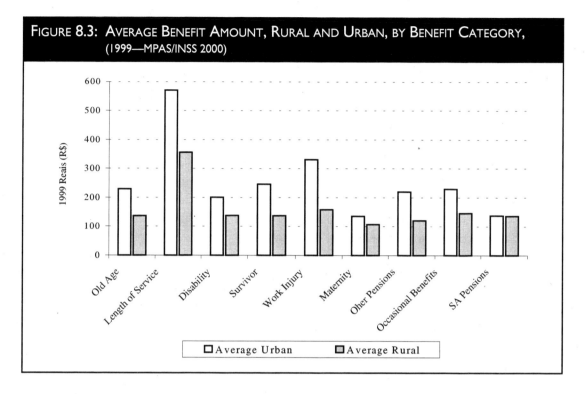

- Fourth, and related the above, poorer workers tend to begin working and contributing earlier than those who are better off—often the poor contribute longer during their active lives, for a shorter stream of benefits in retirement.
- Fifth, formal sector workers or workers in larger enterprises usually enjoy better access to pensions coverage.
- Finally, the unfunded pension liabilities of a privileged few, who enjoy coverage and the deficits of fiscally unbalanced systems, are often passed on to the broader, uncovered population in the form of distorting taxes today or crippling debt in the future.

Both the length of service and old age pension programs fall into the PAYGO category, and suffer from many of the regressive features listed above. Having said this, the two contributory benefits are intended to carry out different social functions. The length of service pension is (at least) intended to be an actuarially fair social insurance system that ties benefits closely to contributions and efficiently transfers participants' income from their working lives to when they can no longer work—especially since the reforms passed in 1998 and 1999. The old age pension, on the other hand, is meant to act as a contributory safety net or back-stop to prevent workers with shorter or irregular work histories from sliding into poverty in retirement. The special eligibility and benefit parameters of the old age pension program for rural workers correct several of the usual regressive structural biases seen in PAYGO systems in the Region.

- Earlier access to benefits partially corrects the bias against poorer rural workers with higher average mortality, lengthening the stream of benefits they receive when they can no longer work
- A shorter minimum contribution period shifts the cross subsidy away from higher earning workers who enter the labor market later in life, toward workers from poorer households who often have to start working earlier
- The minimum pension guarantee explicitly redistributes income to many rural workers whose earnings fall below the minimum wage

■ The incidence of pension and survivor benefits is highest among rural households headed by women (Beltrao, et al, 1999), indicating another positive redistribution of income to workers who often face wage discrimination on the labor market

Despite these positive features, the old age pension system still suffers from several of the regressive features of a PAYGO scheme. To the extent that some rural workers receive less than an actuarially fair return on their contributions to the RGPS while others receive higher than market returns, the scheme may not benefit the poorest households and still may impose a cross subsidy from the relatively less well off to the better off. In terms of the contribution of RGPS pensions to household income, preliminary results suggest a regressive profile. As shown in Figure 8.4, the importance of pensions (as share of income), increases with income. Readers should note that most household

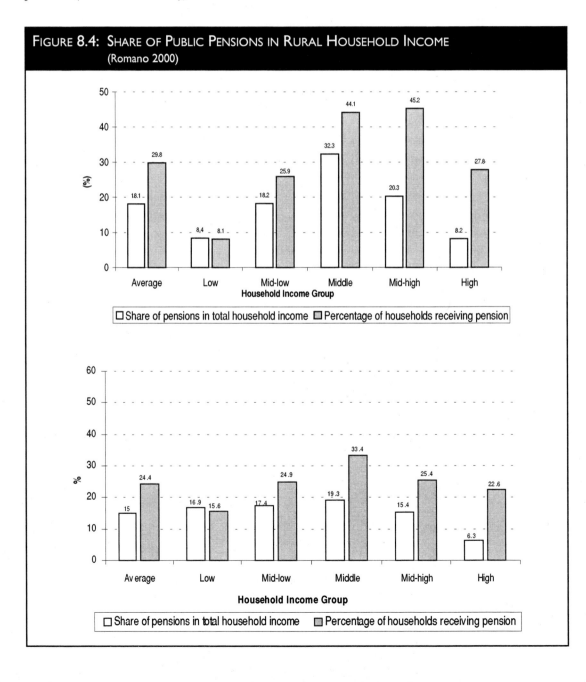

FIGURE 8.4: SHARE OF PUBLIC PENSIONS IN RURAL HOUSEHOLD INCOME
(Romano 2000)

level data in Brazil do not allow separate analysis of contributory old age and length of service benefits, from non-contributory social assistance pensions. Thus while the incidence of contributory pensions and survivor benefits may be regressive, the social assistance pensions may not be.

A recent study by IPEA sheds light on the incidence of pension benefits and their impact on income distribution in rural areas. Beltrao, et al. (1999) test whether the greater incidence of pension benefits in rural areas since 1988 is merely due to the aging of the population and the greater number of elderly in rural households, or if it can be attributed to the new special eligibility conditions for rural workers. The study found that the increased share of pensions in the income of rural households was due to both factors, but that the doubling of benefits with the establishment of the minimum pension and easier eligibility conditions had a dominant effect.

Beltrão et al, go on to find that while the population over 60 years of age in rural households rose from 7 percent in 1988 to 9 percent in 1996, over the same time period the population over 60 in households with lower incomes *fell* from 2.7 percent to 1.6 percent, and in higher income households the share of elderly *rose* from 8.6 percent to 15.7 percent. To the extent that the members of wealthier households in rural areas live longer, the cross subsidies structured into old age pension scheme will increasingly flow toward the better off. Thus, the incidence of pension benefits may be regressive since there are on average a larger share of elderly in richer households to take advantage of higher benefits and easier eligibility conditions passed in the 1988 Constitution.

Two other studies of the impact of pensions on rural poverty paint a more positive picture. Delgado (1999) finds strong evidence that implementation of the 1988 eligibility and benefit criteria have been effective in lowering the incidence of poverty among rural households. Using data from a survey of rural households headed by retired workers or widows in the Northeast and the South of Brazil, the study found that pension benefits represent 41.5 percent and 70.8 percent of household income in each region, respectively.

A similar study using data from the PNAD survey finds that 13 percent of rural households across the country receive over half of their income in the form of retirement and survivor pensions from the government (David, et all, 1999). The study shows that the incomes of three million rural workers, or 10 percent of the rural population, were significantly increased by receipt of retirement or survivor benefits, raising their household income above the poverty line. The authors' evidence of the incidence of poverty in rural areas when pensions are included and omitted from total household income, are tabulated below. As mentioned above, efforts to separate the poverty impact of the contributory old age pension and the non-contributory social assistance pension, are frustrated by the lack of separate data on the incidence of each benefit.

Both studies expand their focus to include the impact of pension and survivor benefits on household welfare—measured by quality of family residence and access to consumer durables.

TABLE 8.1: PERCENTAGE OF RURAL POOR**, BY REGION (PERCENT) WHEN SOCIAL SECURITY IS INCLUDED & OMITTED FROM HOUSEHOLD INCOME

	1992	1995	1996	1997
Northeast, pensions included	59.82	41.19	43.12	43.95
Northeast, pensions omitted	59.92	53.65	56.17	57.13
Southeast, pensions included	33.75	20.64	19.61	18.85
Southeast, pensions omitted	33.82	27.82	27.84	26.42
South, pensions included	26.96	15.75	16.29	14.38
South, pensions omitted	27.04	22.92	24.72	22.23
Center West, included	32.82	24.3	18.69	17.84
Center West, omitted	32.82	29.02	23.68	21.77

Source: David et al (1999), with data from IBGE—PNADs 1992–1997
**Authors define poverty line at 1/4 the minimum wage in 1997

Delgado finds that 27 percent of rural households in the South reported moving to a better residence (better access to utilities and infrastructure) upon receiving pensions. The 72 percent of responding benefit recipients that did not report changing residence, reported making improvements to their homes. David et al. find a similar positive impact on welfare with steady improvements in the living conditions of rural benefit recipients from 1992 to 1997, relative to households not receiving benefits. Both studies found that households receiving pension benefits had increased their holdings of consumer durables.[112]

Additionally, the benefits of expanding social security payments to rural areas may extend beyond the household and into the productive sector. The majority of rural households receiving a pension are involved in family agriculture as their primary work activity. Although an unintended outcome of the increase in coverage of social security, RGPS pensions may have become the indirect insurance for family farming in Brazil (David, et al, 1999). The guarantee of a stable minimum income considerably reduces the risks inherent in agricultural activity, allowing farmers to make production decisions with greater protection and confidence (Holzmann and Jorgensen, 1999). Studies show that 44 percent of rural households in the South and 34 percent in the Northeast report using pension income as working capital for their farming and non-farming activities (Delgado, 1999).

Since the expansion of coverage and the increase in the minimum RGPS benefit, studies show that publicly provided pensions are an *increasing share of total household incomes* in rural areas; that benefits have *contributed to lower incidence of rural poverty;* and that there are measurable *improvements in the welfare of rural households* that receive benefits. Furthermore, there is evidence that rural pensions and survivor benefits *play an important insurance role,* especially for family farmers and rural employers—an unintended outcome of the measures taken in 1988/1991, but one that is entirely consistent with poverty alleviation.

However, the findings presented do not provide a clear answer to the question posed at the start of this section. The evidence provided indicates that the Brazilian social security system helps the rural poor. However, there is no evidence as to whether the positive impact of rural pensions can be attributed to the successful implementation of contributory social insurance for rural workers, or simply to the expansion and increased generosity of non-contributory social assistance transfers.

Should Rural Old Age Pensions be Replaced with Social Assistance?

A critical feature of the RGPS is the de facto combination of social insurance and social assistance systems for the elderly under the single regime. This feature is especially important to note when analyzing the impact of public pensions on the welfare of rural households in Brazil.

As cited in section II, in rural areas the average amount of the contributory old age pension and the non-contributory social assistance benefit is almost identical. The only statutory difference between the two benefit programs is that the former is *exclusive*—requiring that beneficiaries contribute to qualify for benefits—while the latter is *universally available* to any worker who reaches the age of 70. Whether the current benefit structure for rural workers should be maintained as an exclusive social insurance system financed with payroll contributions, or restructured into a universal social assistance benefit financed out of general tax revenues, is an argument that must be made on the related counts: (i) the efficiency of the contributory pension scheme as an actuarially and fiscally balanced mechanism for smoothing consumption over the life-cycle; (ii) the administrative costs of social insurance versus that of targeted social assistance; and (iii) the implications of maintaining the rural old age program along side other contributory programs offered by the RGPS, in light of recent reforms.

To start it is helpful to review how contributory social insurance is different from social assistance. Social insurance systems rely on earmarked taxes levied on payroll, tie individual claims or

---

112. David, et al, try to take their analysis of externalities a step further. The authors attempt to determine the impact of pension income on investment in rural businesses, crossing data from the PNAD survey with a national survey of rural firms. The study finds that while pension income contributes to well over 50 percent of the total incomes of self employed farmers and employers, especially in the poorer Northeast, that impact is limited since the largest business expenditure of self employed and rural employers was on hired labor and rented farm land, rather than investment in new technology.

acquired rights to benefit payments, relate benefits to contributions and/or earnings, and maintain accounts that are usually separated from general revenues. Social assistance operates on explicit taxes and transfers, is financed from general revenues rather than earmarked taxes, does not operate on the concept of acquired rights, relates benefits strictly to need, and is universally accessible (Cohen and Friedman, 1972). In evaluating the actuarial efficiency of a contributory pension system, it is common to equate contribution with similar long term investments, and to compare the rates of return from the pension "investment" with the market rate of interest. Actuarially balanced systems should deliver a rate of return on a worker's investment roughly in line with the market rate of interest. All the retirement programs in place previous to the 1998/1999 reforms gave rates of return that were considerably higher than market rates. Since it has remained largely unaffected by recent reforms the returns from the average Old age pension remain the same. Above-market rates imply that the pension programs—intentionally or otherwise—redistribute wealth from younger to older generations of Brazilians, and to the extent that benefits are unfunded and taxes are borne by the lower income workers, from the poor to the non-poor (World Bank, 2000).

The individual cases selected in Table 8.2 below, profile retiring men and women under normal Length of Service (LoS) vesting parameters, and men and women retiring under the Old Age program with 5, 8 and 15 years of contributions.

TABLE 8.2: INTERNAL RATES OF RETURN IN RGPS CONTRIBUTORY PENSION PROGRAMS

Individual—(years of contributions[1])	IRRs (percent) Pre-Reforms	
Men		
Unreduced LoS[2]—100 percent Replacement (35)	9	
Reduced LoS—70 percent Replacement (30)	9	
Special (teacher) Unreduced	10	
Special Reduced LoS (25)	10	
	rural[4]	**urban**
Old Age (5)	41	34
Old Age (8)	26	25
Old Age (15)	15	14
Women		
Unreduced LoS—100 percent Replacement (30)	10	
Reduced LoS—70 percent Replacement (25)	10	
Special (teacher) Unreduced (25)	12	
Special Unreduced LoS (20)	12	
	rural	**urban**
Old Age (5)	41	41
Old Age (8)	27	26
Old Age (15)	16	16

Source: World Bank Report No. 19541-BR, Brazil: Critical Issues in Social Security
1. Before 1998 eligibility was by *years-of-service,* but we assume no evasion and that years of service equal years of contribution. We assume that individuals meet the full vesting requirements (no gaps in employment) of each benefit category.
2. LoS—Length of Service pension benefits.
3. Calculation assumes worker earning legal minimum wage, no difference in rate of earnings growth between men and women, workers entering formal employment at 20 for LoS pension, inflation at 5 percent, market interest 4 percent
4. Differing assumptions on earnings, growth in earnings and mortality between urban and rural workers, have been avoided. This is likely to understate the differential between returns of the system to rural and urban workers. The only difference in the calculations between IRRs for rural and urban recipients of Old Age benefit, is that rural workers begin receiving pensions 5 years earlier.

Within the RGPS contributory pension schemes, the Old Age program is the most generous in terms of the returns to the contributions made by rural workers. Although the inequity between returns to the Old Age and the Length of Service retirement benefits is clear, as mentioned in the first section most recipients of the Old Age pension program are poor rural workers, while those who benefit from the early retirement, Length of Service pensions are urban, middle/upper class workers. However, while redistribution between these groups may be justifiable, the old age program is clearly inefficient when judged on purely actuarial criteria.

In fiscal terms, the program fares little better. The RGPS as a whole went from a current surplus of 0.3 percent of GDP in 1991, to a deficit of 0.9 percent of GDP in 1999. Since the doubling of the minimum RGPS benefit in 1988 and the expansion of coverage to rural areas in 1992, the current PAYGO deficit of the old age scheme has jumped dramatically. MPAS/INSS have managed to collect roughly half of the contribution revenue needed to pay for current pension and survivor benefits.

Furthermore, retaining the old age benefit as contributory social insurance along side the reformed length of service program, may provide workers with strong incentives to strategically abuse the RGPS. Recent reforms to the length of service parameters, discussed in World Bank 2000, dramatically tighten pension benefits to contributions, and cut the generous replacement rates that drove the RGPS into deficit. Current length of service contributors have an incentive to opt for the now relatively generous benefits of the old age program, which could undermine the fiscal sustainability of the reforms. By restricting reforms of the RGPS to the length of service pension, the Government laudably intended to protect the incomes of poorer households, however, the lenient eligibility requirements for an old age pension extended to rural workers increase the potential for strategic abuse.

While it might be argued that the old age program should not be judged on the grounds of fiscal and actuarial efficiency, or that a social program that redistributes from urban to rural workers should not be expected to be self-financing, (David, et al. 1999) current actuarial and fiscal imbalances call into question the sustainability of contributory social insurance for poor rural households.

- First, as discussed in the previous section, when an income subsidy program intended to redistribute from the wealthy to the poor is combined with social insurance that aims to relate benefits with contributions, unintended redistribution can result.
- Second, although redistribution to poorer rural areas is probably justified in a country like Brazil with one of the worst rates of income inequality in the world, one might ask why RGPS affiliates in the urban private sector should bear the brunt of this redistribution alone. Currently, workers and employers in the informal sector that easily evade pay-roll taxes, civil servants in federal and local government, the police and the armed forces are exempt from this responsibility.
- Third, as policy makers take further steps toward actuarial balance between contributions and benefits in the RGPS with the 1998/1999 reforms, the magnitude of redistribution between the length of service and old age programs becomes increasingly inconsistent, may increase the perception of RGPS benefits as "unfair", and provide further incentives for workers to evade or abuse public pensions programs.

Furthermore, separating the social insurance system from the social assistance function might be beneficial even if both continue to be administered by the same agency, preventing cross-subsidies from one to the other, and allowing the government to target poverty relief at one group with fewer disincentives for the other. There is evidence that length of service pensioners after beginning to collect length of service pensions, continue to contribute and are able to collect old age pensions (World Bank, 2000). In order for recent reforms to succeed, MPAS/INSS will have to improve their information systems both to prevent this "double dipping" and to increase collection efficiency. The resources currently spent by MPAS/INSS on collecting pension contributions from the workers in rural areas, might be better spent on more efficient means of targeting a social assistance pension and on preventing leakage to households already receiving length of service pensions, thus ensuring that public benefits truly reach the poorest. Whether there are efficiency gains to be had from restructuring MPAS/INSS contributory programs into targeted social transfers, lies outside the scope of this note, but is a question worthy of consideration.

From a political perspective the arguments on both sides are less clear cut. By laying the burden of income redistribution to rural households solely on the shoulders of workers and employers in the private sector (especially as reforms shift the RGPS away from redistribution and towards actuarially fair public pensions), policy makers risk providing workers with additional motives to evade participation. On the other hand, by locking the public pensions received by rural households, contributive and non-contributive alike, firmly within a system benefiting a large constituency of poor and non poor, policy makers may effectively insulate a critical poverty alleviation program from careless budget cuts. This said, a new institution of "protected" social protection programs has recently emerged from the fiscal crisis of 1998/1999. If there were significant savings and efficiency gains to be had from restructuring the pension and survivor benefits for the rural poor as targeted social assistance, future governments in Brazil would probably find it very difficult to cut an effective poverty reducing social program from the federal budget.

There is reason to believe that the poverty impact and welfare benefits cited in the previous section would be attained, and perhaps increased if the current contributory old age pensions program were restructured as social assistance with a more secure, more broadly based source of revenue. As a social insurance system the old age pension system largely fails both on actuarial and fiscal grounds, and while it succeeds in redistributing income from urban to rural workers, the redistributive effect between rural households and the net impact on income distribution in rural areas is ambiguous—largely because the incidence of contributory social insurance and non-contributory social assistance cannot be analyzed separately.

Conclusions

There are several good arguments to support replacing the contributory pensions received by rural households with targeted social assistance. The poverty impact and welfare benefits cited in this note would be attained, and perhaps increased if the current contributory old age pensions program were a social assistance program with a more secure, more broadly based source of revenue. As a social insurance system the old age pension system fails both on actuarial and fiscal grounds, and while it succeeds in redistributing income from urban to rural workers, the net impact on income distribution in rural areas is ambiguous—largely because the incidence of contributory social insurance and non-contributory social assistance cannot be analyzed separately.

Additionally, retaining the old age benefit as contributory social assistance may provide workers with strong incentives to strategically abuse the RGPS. Recent reforms to the length of service program, dramatically tighten pension benefits to contributions, and cut generous replacement rates. Current length of service contributors have an incentive to opt for benefits under the old age system, undermining the fiscal sustainability of the reforms. The lenient eligibility requirements for an old age pension extended to rural workers increase the potential for strategic abuse. Separating the social insurance system from the social assistance function might be beneficial even if both continue to be administered by the same agency, preventing cross-subsidies from one to the other, and allowing the government to target poverty relief at one group with fewer disincentives for the other.

On the opposite side of the argument, separating the public pensions received by rural households from the mainstream social security regime, may leave the program without a political constituency to defend it, and lay public benefits for the rural elderly vulnerable to budget cuts by future governments seeking quick fiscal gains in a crisis. Additionally, eliminating the contributory component of the old age pension benefit—however symbolic or nominal this may be—might trap poorer workers in a marginalized social program with no mechanisms for eventually graduating them into the general pension system.

Since the expansion of coverage and the increase in the minimum RGPS benefit, studies show that publicly provided pensions are an increasing share of total household incomes in rural areas; that benefits have contributed to lower incidence of rural poverty; and that there are measurable improvements in the welfare of rural households that receive benefits. Furthermore, there is evidence that rural pensions and survivor benefits play an important insurance role, especially for family farmers and rural employers—an unintended outcome of the measures taken in 1988/1991, but one that is entirely consistent with poverty alleviation. However, the findings presented do not provide a clear answer as to whether the positive impact of rural pensions can be attributed to the *successful implementation of contributory social insurance for rural workers,* or simply to the *expansion and increased generosity of non-contributory social assistance transfers.* Further work is needed to determine whether there would be significant efficiency gains from restructuring the current contributory program into better targeted social assistance.

References

Beltrão, Kaizô Iwakami, Sonoê Sugahara Pinheiro and Francisco Eduardo Barreto de Oliveira. 1999. *A População Rural E A Previdência Social No Brasil: Uma Análise Com Ênfase Nas Mudanças Constitucionai.* IPEA. mimeo

Cohen, Wilbur J. and Milton Friedman. 1972. *Social Security: Universal or Selective.* American Enterprise Institute, Washington D.C.

David, Mauricio Dias, Antoni Carlos de A. David, Monica dos Santos Rodríguez and Paula de Andrade Rollo. 1999. "Previdência Rural no Brasil: Uma Analise de seu Impacto e Erficaia como Instrumento de Combate a Pobreza Rural", paper delivered at CEPAL/FAO Workshop Experiências Exitosas de Combate a Pobreza Rural: Lições para Reorientacao de Políticas, held at Valle Nevado, Chile, January 2000.

Delgado, Guilherme Costa. 1999. "Caso Brasil: Sistema de Previdência Social Rural", paper delivered at CEPAL/FAO Workshop Experiências Exitosas de Combate a Pobreza Rural: Lições para Reorientacao de Políticas, held at Valle Nevado, Chile, January 2000.

Holzmann, Robert & Steen Jorgensen. 1999. "Social Protection as Social Risk Management: Conceptual Underpinnings for the Social Protection Strategy Paper." Social Protection Discussion Paper No. 9904.

World Bank. 1994. *Averting the Old Age Crisis: Policies to Protect the Poor and Promote Growth,* Oxford University Press.

World Bank. 2000. *Brazil: Critical Issues in Social Security* Report No. 19641-BR, Washington D.C.

CHAPTER 9

PUBLIC POLICIES TO REDUCE RURAL POVERTY A SELECTIVE ASSESSMENT

Introduction[113]

In 1996, Brazil's rural population was 31.8 million, 16.6 million (52 percent) of which resided in the poorest Northeast Region. With an average of 4.1 people per household, there were 7.76 million rural households in Brazil.

Using a food-only poverty line (extreme poverty) of R$65 per capita in the São Paulo Metropolitan Area prices, analysis based on the PPV 1996–7 and the 1996 PNAD suggests that the headcount poverty rate for Northeast and Southeast Brazil together was 20.1 percent (14.4 percent in urban areas and 41.7 percent in rural areas) (Ferreira, Lanjouw, and Neri 1998 and Lanjouw, 2000). The poverty rate was 49.0 percent in the rural Northeast and 24.9 percent in the rural Southeast. Assuming that the national rural poverty rates were the same as the rural poverty rate for the Southeast and Northeast together (41.7 percent), there would have been 13.3 million poor in rural Brazil in approximately 2.8 million households. 8.1 million (61 percent) of these poor lived in 1.6 million households in the Northeast, and 1.9 million (14 percent) lived in 0.4 million households in the Southeast.

Based on the PNAD 1996, the aggregate annual income of Brazil's rural poor was approximately R$5.3 billion, or less than 1 percent of the income of all households (urban and rural poor and non-poor). The aggregate income gap of Brazil's rural poor was R$5.1billion. This is the amount theoretically needed to bring all of Brazil's rural poor up to the poverty line for one year (assuming perfect targeting, no administration costs, and no negative incentive effects). If poverty

---

113. This paper was prepared by Joachim von Amsberg, Lead Economist at the World Bank, Brazil Country Management Unit, Email: jvonamsberg@worldbank.org. The views expressed in this paper are those of the author and should not be attributed to the World Bank or its Board of Executive Directors. The paper incorporates substantive contributions from Jacob Yaron (rural credit), Martin Ravallion (drought relief), Johan Van Zyl, Loretta Sonn and Alberto Costa (Rural Poverty Alleviation Projects). Peter Lanjouw and Claudia Romero provided special tabulations from the PPV/LSMS. Alexandre Moreira Baltar provided compilations of data from the federal budget. Edward Bresnyan and Leo Feler provided editorial support.

were defined as insufficient income alone, the task of ending extreme poverty would be to transfer the annual amount of R$5.1 billion to the poor. Given the aggregate resources available to Brazil and its governments, or even just considering total spending of the Federal Government in rural areas, this task seems achievable.

In fact, the elimination of extreme income poverty in rural areas would be no small accomplishment. However, the task is more complicated and more costly than suggested above since perfect targeting is not feasible, program administration is costly, and well-targeted means-tested programs exert a significant negative incentive effect on the efforts of the targeted population. Also, the task at hand is bigger than the elimination of extreme income poverty. First, an income level of R$65 per month will permit satisfaction of basic nutritional requirements but will not likely meet many other basic requirements. Therefore, perspectives need to be created beyond reaching this extreme poverty line. Second, there is broad consensus that poverty is not just insufficiency of income but unacceptable human deprivation. This definition of poverty includes insufficient income and consumption, unsatisfied basic needs such as basic education, health, nutrition and housing, insecurity and risk, as well as voicelessness and powerlessness. This paper focuses on the income dimension of poverty; however, the broader understanding of poverty has to be present in any discussion of overall poverty reduction strategies.

This report uses data from the *Pesquisa Sobre Padrões de Vida* (PPV), a household survey conducted in 1996–97 by Brazil's national statistics agency, IBGE, and modeled after the Living Standard Measurement Surveys, to assess the coverage and poverty targeting of government social spending in rural Brazil. Of the five geographic regions of Brazil, the PPV covers the Northeast and the Southeast regions, which together account for 73 percent of the population and 80 percent of the poor in Brazil. Findings presented in this paper are based on analysis of these two regions only.

The distributional analysis in this paper is based on national expenditure quintiles (Northeast and Southeast regions). Using these "national quintiles," the distributional impact of most programs differs quite significantly between areas (rural versus urban areas and different regions of the country). In particular, in the richer areas (urban areas or Southeast), the incidence appears much more regressive than in the poorer areas. The simple reason underlying this observation is that there are very few people in the richer areas (such as São Paulo) that belong to the bottom quintile of the national distribution, and there are very few people in the poor areas (such as the rural Northeast) that belong to the top quintile (see Figure 9.1). As a result, most programs in the poor areas are well targeted from a national perspective even though they may benefit the relatively better off within the rural Northeast. Figure 9.2. shows the composition of the population of the rural Northeast and Southeast in terms of quintiles of the national distribution. Approximately 50 percent of the population of the rural Northeast and approximately 25 percent of the population of the rural Southeast come from the bottom quintile of the national distribution and are poor by the standards applied for this report.

Incidence analysis on the basis of the national distribution is useful for national policy making. Targeting of social spending would indeed improve if resources were shifted from wealthier to poorer parts of the country. From the national perspective, a program with more than 20 percent of the benefits accruing to the poorest 20 percent of the population would be considered progressive. There is, however, another equally valid point of view. From the perspective of a local policy maker who decides on the allocation of local revenues, the choice is not to spend in different parts of the country but in different programs within the same region. From this perspective, it is instructive to compare the incidence of spending across spatial units based on the distribution of a single region. From the local perspective of the rural Northeast, a program would only be considered progressive if at least 49 percent of a program's benefits accrued to that part of the local population that forms part of the bottom 20 percent of the national income distribution (this part is exactly 49 percent of the local population). For the rural Southeast, the bottom 20 percent of the national distribution is comprised of 25 percent of the local distribution. Hence, a progressive program would distribute benefits to at least 25 percent of the local population in the rural Southeast.

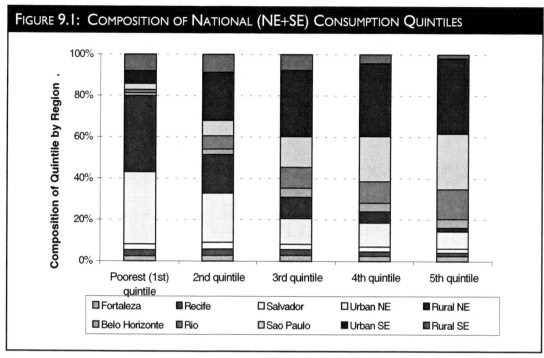

FIGURE 9.1: COMPOSITION OF NATIONAL (NE+SE) CONSUMPTION QUINTILES

Source: IBG E-PPV.

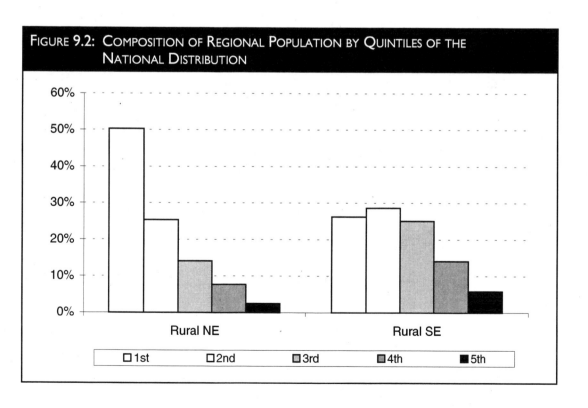

FIGURE 9.2: COMPOSITION OF REGIONAL POPULATION BY QUINTILES OF THE NATIONAL DISTRIBUTION

This paper analyzes selected social programs in two dimensions. First, the coverage by consumption quintile shows the share of the population (or a subgroup of the population) in each quintile that receives a given service. The share of the uncovered poor population can be referred to as the error of exclusion (poor people excluded from the program).[114]

Second, the targeting ratio refers to the share of program beneficiaries that come from the poorest quintile. The share of participants from the other four quintiles can be referred to as the error of inclusion (non-poor people included in the program).

Each program has particular characteristics that complicate the analysis of both coverage and targeting. The extent to which these complications have or have not been appropriately addressed through the chosen methodology is briefly discussed in the context of each program.

The applied methodology has some limitations that apply across most programs. In particular, conclusions regarding benefit or spending incidence can only be drawn from the presented beneficiary incidence if it is assumed that the quality of the service received is the same for individuals from all quintiles and that spending on beneficiaries from all quintiles is the same. Almost universally, these assumptions are violated in that the poor usually receive less valuable or less costly services. For example, the spending on and quality of schools and health care in poor areas is typically lower, and water services to poor areas are often intermittent. These differences introduce a systematic bias in the estimates that follow. The incidence of services to the poor should therefore be interpreted as a lower bound on the incidence of benefits or spending received by the poor.

Important policy changes have occurred since the PPV survey, especially in the areas of health and education funding. This analysis obviously reflects none of the changes that occurred after 1996–97, many of which are likely to have been positive in terms of their impact on the distribution of program incidence.[115]

Government Policies and Spending Related to Rural Poverty, Targeting, and Impact

Overview

This section includes a partial assessment of main government programs affecting rural areas and rural poverty in particular. Only the main spending items at the federal level, very few spending items at the sub-national level, and rural credit are included in this assessment. Depending on the availability of data and information, detailed coverage of programs differs considerably without necessarily reflecting priorities.

The main elements of rural policies include: rural credit (R$10.3 billion lending, including debt rollover); rural pensions (R$10.8 billion); spending of the Ministry of Agriculture (R$3.7 billion) mostly related to programs to stimulate overall agricultural development, land reform (R$1.9 billion); education and health spending in rural areas (estimated at about R$4.5 billion); infrastructure investments (including water resource investments accounting for R$0.7 billion); and drought relief programs (accounting for approximately R$1 billion in drought years). Total selected rural spending analyzed in this report (excluding credit, programs that cannot be easily assigned to rural or urban areas, and many sub-national spending programs) amounts to approximately R$24 billion (see Table 9.1).

Land Reform

Background: Brazil has one of the most unequal distributions of land ownership in the world [Deininger and Squire 1998]. Limited access to land and extreme inequality in land ownership are

---

114. Strictly speaking, incomplete coverage over a specific population can only be interpreted as exclusion if the entire population is supposed to receive the benefit. In this paper coverage often refers to the entire population even though the target group of the program is much smaller. The target group for unemployment insurance, for example, is the group of all unemployed rather than the entire population, and low coverage among the population does not necessarily indicate exclusion.

115. For a description of some of these recent reforms, see World Bank 2001.

central factors contributing to rural poverty in Brazil. Moreover, studies undertaken in Northeast Brazil and confirmed by the 1995–6 Agriculture Census have shown that, on average, family farms are more efficient and labor-intensive than large farms, thus demonstrating that the skewed land distribution limits agricultural productivity and employment. This finding is consistent with studies in other rural labor surplus economies that show significant efficiency gains in family farms compared to large estates. Access to credit for small landholders is often limited by lack of secure land titles, creating a further bias in favor of large farms. Rental and sharecropping arrangements are not particularly common (see Table 9.2). Without security of tenancy and access to credit, they do not provide the same benefits as land ownership.

The 1996 Agriculture Census shows 4.5 million rural households that do not own land or are considered smallholders (Table 9.2). More than half of these are smallholders (*minifundiarios*). While this data does not imply a direct relationship, most of the 13.3 million rural poor are likely to be found among the 4.5 million rural households with little or no land, and the majority is found in the small landholder category.

Historically, land reform in Brazil has focused on Government-administered approaches through expropriation with compensation. These approaches experienced limited success due to long delays, high costs, the possibility for abuse, and political conflict. Also, repayment for the cost of land expropriation and complementary investments by those resettled almost never occurred. However, the speed and effectiveness of the expropriation process has been greatly improved. The Cardoso administration has greatly accelerated the pace of land reform in Brazil. From 1995 through the end of

TABLE 9.1: SUMMARY OF SELECTED RURAL SPENDING

Program/Area	Total Spending 1998 in R$ billions
Ministry of Agriculture	
Rural Electrification	0.04
Product Classification and Normalization	0.039
Agriculture Technology	0.082
Product Acquisitions	0.823
Basic Food Commercialization	0.089
Rubber Commercialization	0.056
Agricultural Development	0.045
Total Ministry of Agriculture	*3.689*
Ministry of Agrarian Policy (Land Reform)	
Beneficiary Credit	0.446
Settlements	0.218
Land	0.793
Total Ministry of Agrarian Policy (Land Reform)	*1.95*
Ministry of Environment	
Irrigation Projects	0.45
Water Resource Projects	0.30
Total Ministry of Environment	*1.69*
Ministry of Health (1999)	
FNS—Rural Water Supply	0.41
Health Services (SUS), rural	1.98
Total Ministry of Health (1999)	*20.1*
Education	
Ensino Fundamental	2.08
Ensino Médio	0.09
Social Security (1999)	
Rural Pensions	10.8
Social Assistance and Others	
Sub-national RPAPs	0.09
Drought Relief	
Northeast Drought Workfare	0.558
Emergency Food Distribution	0.221
Emergency Credit Program (1999)	0.459
Total of Quantified Rural Programs in Budget Spending	**24.02**
Rural Credit Programs	
PRONAF and PROCERA	1.5
PROGER	0.4
Other (mostly controlled resources, including debt rollover)	8.4
Total	**10.3**

TABLE 9.2: Rural Households in Brazil, by Land Tenure Status, 1996

Number of Households	Small land Holder	Renter	Sharecropper	Occupant	Worker	Total
North	217,036	2,726	5,236	69,354	53,999	348,351
Northeast	1,201,739	150,441	180,116	472,289	344,720	2,349,305
Center-West	98,873	4,801	2,014	14,023	97,247	216,958
Southeast	448,138	23,499	32,148	33,867	291,314	828,966
South	488,698	46,776	48,254	58,088	130,415	772,231
Total	**2,454,484**	**228,243**	**267,768**	**647,621**	**917,695**	**4,515,811**

1999, approximately 372,500 families were resettled, by far exceeding combined resettlements under the previous three administrations since 1985. Land reform can make a quantitatively important contribution to a rural poverty reduction strategy. At the recent rate of 100,000 families settled per year, land reform can reach 2.5 million people or 15 percent of Brazil's rural poor in five years.

In 1998, the Land Reform budget of the Federal Government was nearly R$2 billion. This amount has been reduced to R$1.4 billion in the 1999 budget under the Government's drastic fiscal adjustment program. Given the fact that 100,000 families received land reform benefits in 1998, this spending amount suggests an aggregate cost of R$20,000 per family. However, this calculation is excessively simplistic. First, the land reform budget contains extraneous activities. Second, given the slow pace of "graduating" land reform beneficiaries from continuing public support, expenditures for new beneficiaries extend over several years. As the number of beneficiaries has been rising rapidly, it would be expected that future budgets would have to increase substantially to fully attend to the requirements of beneficiaries already in the system. Several more thorough studies of the per-beneficiary cost of land reform have been undertaken. They produce results in the range of R$15,000–50,000 per family depending on the region.

Considering the fact that land reform creates a sustainable source of income for the beneficiaries, the cost of land reform at the lower end of the range quoted above can compare favorably with alternative strategies. The cost of simple urban housing with basic public services in a mid-sized Northeastern city would typically be R$8,000–10,000. The investment cost per industrial employment has been above R$30,000. Due to its productive and economically viable nature, land reform can also be attractive compared to the alternative of investments into a stronger rural safety net. If the cost of about R$15,000 per family were converted into a perpetual income support (using a discount rate of 16 percent), this would be insufficient to achieve the same household income gains expected through well-implemented land reform.

Economic changes over recent years have made land reform an investment that can be cost-effective in reducing poverty and inequality while, at the same time, improving the efficiency of the rural economy. Many of the economic distortions that have historically contributed to land concentration have been alleviated. Agricultural credit subsidies have been cut drastically, and inflation is at a historic low. The rural land tax (ITR) has been modified to significantly raise taxation on unproductive land. These changes have reduced the financial attractiveness of land holdings for non-productive purposes and have consequently increased the supply of land and reduced its price. Particularly in the Northeast, large tracts of land are available for sale at low prices by owners and banks that hold land as collateral for defaulted farm debt. With labor-intensive production systems (partly subsistence and partly market-oriented), small farmers can significantly increase production on these lands and thus both increase their family income and repay the cost of the land.

In the South, higher land prices, higher wage levels, and a higher levels of sophistication of production systems necessary for financial viability create somewhat different economic conditions, although there are still significant areas available where land reform can increase both efficiency and family farm income. From the perspective of the Federal Government, it seems clearly less desirable to finance land reform for a less poor family in the South at a cost of up to R$50,000 than for a poorer family in the Northeast at a cost of R$15,000. At the same time, states of the wealthier Southern part of the country may want to assume some of these financing activities with their own resources.

Community-Based Land Reform: The challenges associated with the traditional approach to land reform encouraged the Government to explore complementary approaches to improve land access. For example, INCRA launched a public land auction in Rio Grande do Sul that seeks to reduce the costs of land acquisition and expedite the creation of new settlements. Also, *Projeto Casulo* has already benefited 1,300 families in the North and Northeast by providing land for commercial agricultural purposes in peri-urban areas. Finally, a community-based approach to land reform has been piloted—first under the Ceará Rural Poverty Alleviation Project and more recently under the *Cédula da Terra* project—where beneficiaries negotiate the purchase of land directly with owners. By creating new options for land access through credit provision, community-based land reform increases the menu of available options for agrarian policy and the scope of land reform.

The community-based land reform approach was initially piloted under the Bank-financed Ceará Rural Poverty Alleviation Project in 1996–97 at a total cost of R$4.1 million for land purchases and R$3.9 million for complementary investments. Families financed land purchases for over 15 years, with five years of grace, at the Government established long-term interest rate (TJLP) plus one percent with funds from the state government. The complementary investments were financed on a matching grant basis with a 10 percent beneficiary contribution either in cash or in kind. Under this pilot, 44 community associations, with a total of 688 families, acquired a total of 23,377 hectares of land, at a per-family cost of R$6,083 and a per hectare cost of R$179. With average complementary investments of R$5,574 per family, total per family costs were R$11,657.

Given the promising results of community-based land reform under the Ceará Rural Poverty Alleviation Project (both in terms of administrative and cost efficiency), the Brazilian Government initiated the *Cédula da Terra* Project in five Northeastern States (Bahia, Ceará, Maranhão, Minas Gerais, and Pernambuco). *Cédula da Terra* combines a community-based approach to land acquisition with a matching grant mechanism to finance complementary investments toward increasing land productivity and the incomes of small land holders. Under the *Cédula da Terra* project, rural families come together to form community associations with the objective of identifying suitable land for purchase and then negotiating the sale of land with willing land owners. Following title clearance from the STU/State Land Institute, these associations are eligible for loans for land purchases. Communities then determine internally the allocation of land among participating families, and the corresponding payment obligations.

Following the land purchase, community associations are eligible to present proposals for on-land complementary investments, under grant-financing from Federal, State, and Bank sources, including a beneficiary contribution of at least 10 percent of subproject cost, in cash or in-kind. Technical assistance and community support are also financed through the pilot project, as well as a comprehensive impact evaluation that seeks to draw important lessons concerning the targeting and cost effectiveness of the community-based approach to land reform.

The pilot project with total funding of US$150 million sought to resettle some 15,000 families over a three-year period following its implementation on September 12, 1997. For the first 9,000 families, about 225,000 hectares were purchased through negotiations between community associations and willing landowners, with implementation strongest in Bahía, Ceará, and Maranhão (Table 9.3). Cost per beneficiary family averaged R$4,759 and average land cost per hectare was R$193. In total, approximately 23,000 families are expected to benefit under the project with purchases of about 617,000 hectares. An average of R$4,114 has been available for each family resettled for the purpose of complementary subproject investments.

Results from the various evaluation studies and from Bank supervision reveal that the *Cédula da Terra* project is achieving its objective of expediting land access to the rural poor. The evaluation

TABLE 9.3: LAND REFORM PILOT PROJECT, IMPLEMENTATION SUMMARY FOR THE FIRST 9,000 FAMILIES

State	Number of Families	Total Land Area (Hectares)	Hectares per Family	Total Value (R$ million)	R$ per Hectare	R$ per Family
Bahia	2,429	44,986	18.5	10.58	235.1	4,355
Ceará	2,597	84,945	32.7	12.72	149.7	4,897
Maranhão	1,588	43,483	27.4	5.34	124.8	3,419
Minas Gerais	1,044	25,260	24.2	5.13	203.0	4,913
Pernambuco	1,435	25,996	18.1	9.51	365.8	6,627
Total	9,093	224,670	24.7	40.36	192.6	4,759

Source: NEAD, INCRA.

confirms that the innovative community approach is working and producing effective results. Given the innovative nature of this pilot project, the evaluation shows results as favorable as they could possibly be expected at this stage, lending strong support to the continuation and expansion of the approach. As detailed below, land quality is adequate, land prices are lower than under more traditional approaches, self-selection is quite satisfactory and newly acquired farms show favorable expectations for financial and economic viability. Equally important, beneficiaries should be able to generate sufficient earnings to service their debt obligations and significantly raise both incomes and living standards. The following are summary assessments of implementation progress and impact to date, as well as modifications both introduced to the current project and slated for introduction in the a proposed national follow up project:

a) *The project has created an agile and effective method of settling landless rural families:* A central message from many organizations and the beneficiaries themselves is that the target population wants land access in a rapid, participatory, and less conflictive manner, even though they know the land must be purchased. The huge demand for the purchase of land, which reached about 40,000 families by the end of the first year of project implementation, serves as proof of the beneficiaries' desire to participate even though the land purchase must be repaid. The community-based approach expedites the settlement of landless rural families with the process of land acquisition, from identification to purchase, which typically takes less than 90 days (as long as funds are available).

b) *Self-selection of the landless rural poor is working well:* Results of the preliminary evaluations demonstrate that the project is attracting families with the social and economic profile of the intended target group (poor families in rural areas) [Buainain et al. 1999a and 1999b]. The average beneficiary household monthly income was R$92, or about 73 percent of the national minimum wage. About one-half of this income was generated off-farm. Approximately 32 percent of beneficiaries were illiterate, while another 47 percent had completed no more than four years of education. Discriminate analysis of the data reveals that *Cédula da Terra* beneficiaries have lower overall asset ownership, larger household density, and poorer quality housing, relative to comparisons with a control group of households with similar socioeconomic standing (Filho, et al., 2000). Leakage to non-poor beneficiaries is minimal and would not justify a more structured targeting mechanism. Most beneficiaries are previous tenants or sharecroppers, often on the same lands purchased under the project. Practically, all participants have some previous farming experience, with 90 percent having worked in the rural sector prior to becoming project beneficiaries. The requirement for active participation of beneficiaries leads to a desirable self-selection of "entrepreneurial poor" who are more likely to be successful as farmers than are the average rural poor.

c) *Most settlements under the pilot project have been small relative to traditional land reform settlements:* It has been observed that groups should have a minimum of 10 families and a maximum of 30 to 35 for optimal performance. Community associations under the pilot project tend to range in size from 15 to 30 families. Groups with less than 10 families are likely to have difficulty forming an association board, which is a condition of eligibility for land. The resources available to a very small group are likely to be insufficient for certain investments, either due to cost (as in the case of rural electrification) or to under-utilization of purchased equipment (in the case of a tractor). For groups with over 50 families, experience shows that management of a rural property by a large group can be difficult. The tendency, demonstrated in traditional land reform settlement, where 100, 200, or more families are settled, has been for such groups to ultimately be sub-divided into smaller groups of around 50 families that then create their own associations.

d) *Land quality is generally adequate and representative of the predominant conditions in each state:* Most purchased land shows good productive potential including adequate water supply or irrigation. In fact, beneficiaries have often made excellent choices for their land. Typical examples include the purchase of banana, coconut, and cacao plantations that were previously underutilized by their owners because of high labor and labor supervision requirements but were then made productive and profitable again after purchase through the program. This result is, in fact, quite striking given the often-low quality of agricultural lands in the Northeast and the tendency of past land reform programs to focus on low quality lands. Buainain, et al. (1999b) analyzed the prevailing geography in each state, comparing it with the characteristics of the purchased lands under the project, and found the *Cédula da Terra* projects to be well distributed among the meso-regions in the participating states. In line with overall agro-climatic conditions in the region, some areas are prone to periodic droughts and require access to water or irrigation investments to ensure sustainable production. In drought-prone areas, the pilot project is focusing on ensuring sufficient access to water resources, particularly through TA available for production, productive investment planning, and complementary investment in irrigation. Also, STUs will avoid approving land purchases in drought-prone areas where irrigation either does not exist or cannot be rapidly put into place.

e) *Land prices are very favorable:* Land prices under *Cédula da Terra* are about 22 percent lower per hectare and 28 percent lower per family than the present value of initial INCRA expropriation prices in the Northeast (in many cases expropriated owners later obtain additional compensation through judicial actions that can increase the final cost of expropriated lands to as much as three times the initial compensation amount). Under the pilot project, land has been acquired at an average cost of R$193 per hectare and R$4,759 per family.

f) *Project implementation through community associations has been successful overall:* The success of community associations in mobilizing members, selecting land for purchase, and designing and implementing a productive subproject is remarkable given the constraints they face. The design of the project gives control to beneficiaries, and success depends entirely on active participation in all stages of the project cycle. Experience to date has been very positive at the community level, with the associations (many of them pre-dating the project) showing strong interest, initiative, and active participation. Experience has shown that several more recent associations can lack a set of agreed principles to guide interpersonal relationships between the formed groups. Moreover, these associations often lack an understanding of public policies and basic notions of planning that are needed to make sustainable settlements. The key challenge is to provide support to these associations while encouraging and fostering their autonomy. Recommendations have been adopted for the proper training of settlers to efficiently implement settlement activities and create the foundations for the settlement's sustainability. This model for building human and social capital will also be a feature of the proposed project.

g) *The subprojects demonstrate the expectation for financial and economic viability:* Simulations based on actual properties purchased and conditions faced by beneficiaries show that the

great majority of production systems under the project have the capacity to generate sufficient income to lift families out of poverty and enable them to repay their loans (Buainain
et al., 1999b). In the more favorable agro-climatic regions, financial returns are likely to be
very high (Box 9.1). In the semi-arid *Sertão,* financial viability is very likely where adequate
access to water is available. In the least advantageous regions, however, principally the semi-
arid region, which is subject to periodic droughts, some families might have found it difficult
to fulfill their repayment obligations under the originally envisaged terms. As a result of this
analysis, financing conditions have been changed to a fixed real interest rate of 4 percent per
annum and a repayment period of 20 years. These new charges and terms will apply retro-
actively. Under these conditions, financial and economic viability in all areas is highly likely.

h) *State Technical Units and CSOs play an important role in supporting community associations
in the identification and negotiation of land purchase opportunities:* Lack of information and
some tendency toward purchasing the land, previously utilized by share-croppers, have
inhibited many beneficiary associations from comparing a broader range of properties available for sale and actively negotiating the purchase price with the previous owners. Frequently,
state agencies have assisted in land identification and subsequent negotiations, thus ensuring that land quality and purchase prices are consistent with prevailing market conditions.
In other cases, NGOs, churches, and other organizations have provided useful support to
community associations in the identification and negotiation processes. As local capacity is
strengthened, the role of state agencies in helping communities during the land negotiation
process is expected to diminish. The follow-up project will include several modifications
to provide additional support to beneficiary associations in selecting and negotiating land
for purchase. In particular, beneficiary associations can contract technical assistance for the
preparation of their project proposal. This technical aid includes assistance in land selection
and negotiations. Subproject applications would include information on other properties
previously considered for purchase and rejected.

BOX 9.1: FINANCIAL VIABILITY OF FARMS REPRESENTATIVE OF *CÉDULA DA TERRA* PROJECTS

Northern Coast of Bahia: Typical production systems include coconut, fruits, and livestock, and net family
incomes are expected to reach R$3,000 after four years and R$5,000 after ten years, leaving no doubt as to
capacity to repay land purchase loans.

Cacao Region of Bahia: Annual net family incomes will range from R$2,500 to R$2,800 in Year 7 and R$3,700
to R$4,000 in Year 10, depending on climatic conditions. Expected financial outcomes in the extreme south of
Bahia are similar or marginally better than those in the cacao region.

Semi-arid Region of Bahia: Production systems are similar to those in the semi-arid zone of Ceará (beans,
corn, manioc, and livestock), although access to irrigation is much better. Net family incomes are expected to
reach R$4,000 in years of normal rainfall, while drought years will yield net incomes substantially lower, thus
making debt repayment questionable and again highlighting the importance of evaluating irrigation potential on
prospective land purchases.

Semi-arid Zone of Ceará: This is the most difficult area, typically with subsistence production systems (beans,
corn, manioc), some livestock (goats, cattle), and some higher value crops in relatively small irrigated areas. Under
rain-fed conditions in normal years, net family incomes could reach R$1,300 in Year 4 and R$2,000 in Year 10, but
a significant share of this income is in the form of on-farm consumption. Drought years in the rain-fed areas would
make loan repayment extremely doubtful, while irrigated areas in drought years would be expected to have net
family incomes in the range of R$888 to R$2,000. Irrigation in normal years would yield net incomes in the order
of R$1,600 to R$3,400.

Maranhão: Cattle production, beans, rice, maize, and cassava (possibly using animal traction) would yield net
family incomes of R$2,000 in Year 4 and R$3,500 by Year 10.

***Zona de Mata* of Pernambuco:** Drawing on an existing *Cédula da Terra* property should yield net family
incomes of about R$5,500 by Year 4.

i) *Technical assistance (TA), in conjunction with land purchase and subsequent productive activities, is crucial to realize and sustain project benefits:* Under the pilot project, community associations have access to technical assistance for their specific investment projects. The extent and quality of broader technical assistance has differed with the availability and quality of local public extension services (EMATER) or different private institutions. Studies and observations during the first year of project implementation indicated that official TA has fallen short of expectations in both quality and timeliness. The Project calls for TA funding for the preparation and implementation of community investment subprojects. However, communities need more effective and efficient TA in planning family farming activities, especially in the production, processing, storage, and marketing of crops.

j) *In some states, there have been significant and unnecessary delays in the approval of investment subprojects after land acquisition:* Bureaucratic bottlenecks and a slowdown of the flow of funds at the Federal level hindered the implementation of complementary investments to the newly acquired lands. Such delays slow the establishment of productive farm operations in the critical first year and need to be avoided. Experience with land reform over many decades shows that to avoid out-migration, families must establish themselves in the area immediately after land is acquired.

Overall, the results have been very encouraging. Of course, it is still too early to fully evaluate the lasting impact of this new land reform approach. While the decentralized approach to negotiated land reform has been criticized for, among other things, indebtedness of beneficiaries with loans they cannot repay and for trying to replace expropriate land reform, the revisions to the approach discussed above have sought to address these and other concerns.

Targeting and Coverage of Land Reform: In order to assess the targeting of the community-based land reform program, the pilot evaluation study (Buainain, et al., 1999a) was used as the primary information source. Income was determined based on a detailed questionnaire for the 222 sampled households. The income concept includes all sources of monetary income (including remittances, pensions, and other transfer payments) but does not include own farming products consumed by the household. While a direct link to the poverty concept used for the programs with PPV data is impossible, a family income of R$3,000 annually was considered comparable to the poverty line used for the PPV analysis. Approximately 85 percent of *Cédula da Terra* beneficiaries were below this line.

Since no detailed assessment of overall land reform beneficiary income is available, this targeting rate is assumed to be applicable to the land reform program overall. This approach does not account for benefits to parties other than the settlers. In particular, past practices under the government-administered land reform programs are alleged to have transferred significant resources to expropriated landowners who often have received compensation exceeded market values of expropriated lands by a multiple. While reliable quantifications are not available, it is clear that the actual share of public spending that has reached the poor in such cases would have been much lower than the 85 percent targeting rate used here.

Based on the current rate of 100,000 beneficiary families per year and a targeting rate of 85 percent, 85,000 poor families, or 3.8 percent of all poor rural families in Brazil would be benefited each year. The 372,000 land reform beneficiary families from 1995–99 would include 316,000 poor families, accounting for about 12 percent of Brazil's rural poor.

Northeast Rural Poverty Alleviation Projects[116]
Since the 1970s, the Federal Government and the World Bank have implemented a range of targeted rural development initiatives. These earlier rural development programs coalesced around two themes: (i) drought relief and discrete sectoral projects; and (ii) the integrated development of

---

116. This section is extracted from Van Zyl, Sonn, and Costa (2000)

selected areas. The first approach mainly employed emergency relief programs or projects to increase the productivity of scarce water resources. The second approach included two generations of integrated sub-regional development programs. These programs evolved into classic-style integrated rural development (IRD) projects designed to improve agricultural efficiency, raise rural incomes, improve social services, and increase employment.

Analysis undertaken in the early 1990s of these rural development programs indicated that they suffered from many of the generic problems identified in the general critiques of integrated rural development. The Northeast projects foundered due to faulty poverty targeting mechanisms that resulted in benefits not going to intended project beneficiaries; intractable problems of land tenure, which undermined many project initiatives; institutional deficiencies reflected in the costliness and inefficiency of development agencies and the favoring of larger producers; political manipulation associated with entrenched patron-client relationships; the uncontrolled expansion of federal and state bureaucracies; and repeated macroeconomic and fiscal crises.

The difficulties encountered in the earlier projects led to comprehensive reformulation in 1993. Lessons learned from schemes elsewhere in Latin America, particularly in the Mexican *Solidaridad* program, and some elements of World Bank-supported emergency social funds were also incorporated into the reformulated program. These schemes shared two important common features: they were based on participatory, community-driven initiatives, and decision-making was decentralized to community-level government and non-government institutions. Subsequently, efforts to encourage and facilitate rural development in Northeast Brazil have been based on decentralized and participatory approaches. The old projects were reformulated in 1993 to include decentralization and community participation. The main change involved shifting the execution of project investments away from state agencies in favor of project implementation by beneficiary community associations. In addition, the projects shifted away from an almost exclusive focus on agriculture to permit the inclusion of non-farm-related activities. A new generation of projects (the Rural Poverty Alleviation Projects—RPAPs) focused exclusively on this approach was implemented.

Two different delivery mechanisms for screening, approving, and implementing community subprojects were adopted. First, under state community schemes such as *Programa de Apoio Comunitário* (PAC), rural communities submitted subproject investment proposals directly to their own state project technical unit, the STU. The agency screened, approved, and released funds for subprojects, interacting directly with the beneficiaries. Second, there were the municipal community schemes such as *Fundo Municipal de Apoio Comunitário* (FUMAC), under which subprojects identified and prepared by rural communities were presented to project Municipal Councils for approval. The Councils are intended to encourage local-level consensus building on priority needs.

The RPAPs involve three components: (a) Community Subprojects (90 percent of total cost), which support small-scale investments selected and subsequently operated and maintained by the beneficiaries themselves; (b) Institutional Development (6 percent of total cost), which provides all implementing entities and communities with technical assistance and training to increase their capacity and improve project implementation; and (c) Project Administration, Supervision, Monitoring, and Evaluation (4 percent of total cost), which finances project coordination and activities to provide feedback on project performance and impact. The RPAPs provide matching grants to rural community associations to finance small-scale subprojects (up to US$50,000 each) identified by these groups as priority investments for improving community well being. Subproject types are diverse, broadly classified as infrastructure, productive, and social. Selection is demand-driven and reflects community preferences; for example, the beneficiary rural communities themselves identify, prepare, and implement all subprojects. There is a negative list of subproject types ineligible for financing and productive subprojects. In particular, there are additional and rigorous eligibility criteria. Finally, subproject proposals observe standard documentation and technical, economic, environmental, and sustainability criteria established in a detailed Project Operational Manual.

Findings from various evaluations of these programs suggest that more participatory approaches encouraging the involvement of civil society organizations and greater decentralization of decision-making power over financial resources, can result in positive outcomes for poor rural communities, with more of their priority needs being met. The early findings from the reformulated program are now confirmed by results obtained from the RPAP.

The aggregate socio-economic benefits of the older reformulated projects and the RPAPs are significant: at a total project cost of about US$800 million, more than 44,000 subprojects in over 1,400 municipalities (77 percent infrastructure, 20 percent productive, and 3 percent social) were completed, benefiting about 2.5 million families (or around 1.7 million without repetition). For a sample of 8,123 subprojects funded in 1995 and 1997–98 it was found that at least 7,244, or 89 percent, were fully operational to date, demonstrating the sustainability of the investments chosen, executed, operated, and maintained by the beneficiaries. These investments generated almost 100,000 additional permanent jobs and increased the area cultivated by more than 80,000 hectares. These investments generated additional sustainable annual income or savings of more than US$200 million. Implementation of productive subprojects and rural water supply works under these programs enabled families to take fuller advantage of available productive resources than families not participating. For a summary of subprojects funded and their estimated impact, see Table 9.25, Table 9.26, and Table 9.27.

Institutional analysis reveals important achievements in social capital formation as a result of actually turning control of resource allocation over to beneficiary communities. Not only are these groups interacting to carry out subprojects, but they are also beginning to exercise considerable influence over decision-making within their municipalities. Of the almost 1,000 project Municipal Councils, about 30 percent have moved on from making decisions only on the subprojects to engaging also in municipal planning and allocation of non-project resources. In addition, approximately 25 percent of community associations are leveraging social capital acquired under the Program to access other non-RPAP investment financing not available to them before. Although intangible and difficult to quantify, there is a palpable difference in self-respect and confidence in many RPAP communities.

The creation of social capital was analyzed using a representative sample of 225 community associations (56 of which were already visited during similar studies conducted in 1993 and 1994). Community Participation Indices (CPI) were developed to analyze the evolution and increase in social capital as a result of the program. The composite CPI improved by 36 percent due to the program, but particularly noticeable was that formation of social capital remained constant for the PAC approach, though it increased some 64 percent for FUMAC, and rose by 90 percent for FUMAC-P (a further evolution of the FUMAC scheme, under which Municipal Councils not only approve but themselves allocate resources to subprojects).

In summary, the RPAPs are achieving the expected objectives and targets. The projects generate social capital by promoting community organization, reinforcing popular confidence in collective action to solve local problems in lieu of dependence on the public domain, and encouraging the exchange of experiences between communities. The creation of FUMAC and FUMAC-P Municipal Councils has both generated and elevated social capital at the municipal level. The most telling transformation is the gradual shift in the nature and functions of those Councils. From initially being mere arenas for discussing the legitimacy of investment proposals and prioritizing them for funding, the Councils have increasingly become full-fledged forums of popular participation, with a wider sense of responsibility for municipal development. While the PAC strategy has been less successful due to its inherent vulnerability to both local and state level interference, FUMAC and FUMAC-P have clearly demonstrated that empowerment of communities through devolution of decision-making and even financial management responsibilities, leads to more effective and truly demand-driven rural development. Indeed, one of the most subtle feats of the RPAP has been to gradually convince the states of the superiority of FUMAC over PAC. The potential of FUMAC-P should be fully exploited by giving the Councils much greater autonomy to manage subproject funds while simultaneously being accountable for them.

To extend these concepts, the next generation of rural poverty projects for the Northeast should incorporate several additional features:

a) *Expand the community-based FUMAC approach into a municipal fund program* based on the successful FUMAC-P component. A true municipal fund approach gives responsibility for the management of fiscal resources and project implementation to municipalities and communities, thus further promoting decentralization of decision-making, and encouraging greater municipal cost-sharing of subprojects.

b) *Limit the PAC approach to a minimum,* particularly since the FUMAC component performed significantly better and shows clear advantages with respect to targeting, sustainability and building social capital in poor rural communities.

c) *Revisit the issue of productive subprojects,* particularly the relationship between these kinds of investments and proper targeting, graduation, and co-financing. The high financial returns on productive investments obtained indicate that productive investment could be financed through loans at market interest rates rather than through grants.

The evaluation study shows that, depending on the state, between 70 percent and 90 percent of the beneficiary families have a family income of less than two minimum salaries (about R$300 per month in 1999). The methodology is not directly comparable with the one used for analyzing the targeting of other social programs. Specifically, beneficiary income is probably underestimated compared to the more detailed income calculation derived from the PPV. It may thus be reasonable to assume based on an average household size of 5 in the poor rural Northeast, that 70 percent of the benefits accrue to those considered poor for the purposes of this report (with a per capita income of less than R$65 per month).

From 1993 to 2000, about 32,000 subprojects were completed at a total cost of about US$800 million. Per year, about 4,600 projects were completed at a total cost of about US$115 million (or about R$205 million at the current exchange rate). Per year, 275,000 families were benefited at a per-family cost of US$412. With targeting of 70 percent, the project would reach 192,000 poor families in the rural Northeast each year. This compares to a total of 1.6 million poor families in the rural Northeast. The project therefore reaches about one eighth of the poor families in the rural Northeast each year. Over seven years, projects for 1.9 million households were completed. Adjusting for repeated projects for the same household and the targeting rate of 70 percent, about 905,000 households (56 percent) of the 1.6 million poor households in the rural Northeast may have been covered. This means that about 34 percent of all rural poor in Brazil would have been covered.

Drought Relief [117]

Current Approaches: The 1998–9 drought in Northeast Brazil was reckoned to be the worst in 15 years and to have affected more than 10 million people in eight Northeastern states. As with previous droughts, a massive relief effort was undertaken. The three main components of the relief effort were targeted food handouts, a workfare program, in which participants must work or attend training to obtain benefits, and a subsidized credit scheme.

Emergency food distribution involves basically an expansion of the existing food distribution system, under the *Comunidade Solidaria* program, which is permanently in place in poor municipalities. The coverage has been extended to include all designated drought affected municipalities. Temporary Municipal Councils set up specifically for the drought decide who should receive the food handouts in drought-affected municipalities. No data is available for assessing the targeting of food handouts, though there is nothing to suggest a serious misallocation. The handouts are composed

---

117. This section was prepared by Martin Ravallion based on a mission by Martin Ravallion, Antonio Magalhaes, and Joachim von Amsberg to Northeast Brazil in the first week of September 1998, at the invitation of SUDENE.

of basic necessities and unprocessed or prepared meals, which are unlikely to be of much appeal to the non-poor. The program covered about three million people during the 1998–9 drought.

The Municipal Councils are crucial to the success of the drought relief operation and were introduced (initially in Ceara in the 1987 drought) to attempt to get around past problems of corruption in drought relief, whereby some local mayors and large landowners were known to be diverting resources. The composition of the Municipal Council is stipulated by central regulations that severely limit a mayor's ability to exert influence or manipulate Municipal Council members. The broad membership of the Municipal Councils provides a very important check on the many ways in which funds for drought relief could otherwise be mistargeted. This check on funding is reinforced by public information and disclosure practices.

The workfare component provides work on various community projects and training. Until September 1998, 1.2 million people were employed on the workfare component, at a cost of R$110 million per month. While the Municipal Councils propose the projects, selection of projects amongst those proposed is done by state coordinating committees. In previous droughts the emphasis was on water-related projects, but this has now broadened to include a wider range of community projects and training. Examples of projects covered include underground dams and similar small-scale irrigation projects, water and sanitation projects, building and maintaining community facilities (such as schools, health clinics, and parks), rural road construction, and training projects. The latter entails a combination of basic literacy skills and knowledge about droughts and how to dampen their impact.

The choice of the wage rate is critical to the success of workfare programs. The wage rate determines who wants to participate, and (with the budget allocation) how many can actually be accommodated in the program. A good rule of thumb is that the daily wage rate should be no higher than the market wage for similar work at normal times. This helps the program reach the poor by both assuring that a higher proportion of those participating are amongst the poor and by assuring wider coverage of the poor. A lower wage rate will also protect work incentives by reducing dependency on the scheme, in that workfare should not be more attractive than regular work when it becomes available.

In the case of the relief work provided during Brazil's drought, the Federal Government pays the bulk of the wages plus a contribution to the non-wage costs. The Federal Government's contribution to the wage is R$65 per month for a 27-hour working week. The Federal Government also pays 20 percent of this amount for non-wage costs (tools and materials), representing R$15.6 per person per month. State governments complement the resources. For the wage bill, this amounts to an extra R$15 in most states. The exceptions are the states of Ceará, which pays an extra R$25 to bring the wage up to R$90, and Piaui, which pays nothing extra. The states also contribute R$3.12 per month per worker to non-wage costs.

The daily equivalent of the average workfare wage is roughly the same as the average wage rate for casual wage labor in a normal year, which is about R$5 per day in Northeast Brazil. The statutory minimum wage is R$130 per month for a 5.5 day week, or about R$5.50 per day which is also close to the implicit daily wage on workfare. Allowing for the training component, workfare is more likely preferred over the wage work available in a normal year.

The workfare wage is probably well above the shadow wage rate during the drought, implying sizable transfer benefits to participating families. In the drought-affected municipalities, current wages for unskilled manual labor (when available) were reported to be 30–50 percent below their level in the pre-drought year.

Given the available budget, workfare jobs have to be rationed at the wage rate paid. Municipal Councils select beneficiaries based on their incomes and losses due to the drought. Only one participant is allowed per family (though an extra participant is often allowed for large families), and the family can have no other income source (though it is unclear how well the latter criterion can be implemented). State and local governments retain power over the geographic allocation. Drought-affected municipalities are identified on the basis of rainfall data. The program is confined to rural areas.

In 1998 workfare appeared to cover 60–70 percent of the number of workers in drought-affected areas who wanted work at the offered wage rate. Some of the unmet demand is found in small towns and the urban periphery, where a non-negligible number of farm workers live. This unmet demand is also found among large poor families that require more than one income earner for subsistence. No doubt there are also families with one wage job for which the earnings are too low to make ends meet, particularly since the wage rates for the work that is available appear to have fallen sharply during the drought. In terms of the overall efficacy of the drought-relief operation, there is a strong case for relaxing the current restrictions on eligibility and the geographic targeting, to assure wider coverage of those needing help.

The average labor intensity (share of wages in cost) is a key factor in the cost-effectiveness of workfare programs relative to alternative transfer schemes using the same gross budget. The labor intensity of the workfare projects is claimed to be 81 percent. This is very high even for a workfare scheme. However, the calculation is deceptive since it was clear from interviews with a number of local mayors that the municipalities help finance the non-wage costs to allow a wider range of projects consistent with their development plans in the area. It is not possible with the current information system to calculate the actual labor intensity. With a full accounting of non-wage costs, the share of wages in the projects visited would probably be about 75 percent.

The Bank of the Northeast (BNB) operates the credit program in response to the drought under policy guidelines developed by the Government. Approximately 100,000 families received subsidized credit amounting to about R$450 million. Drought loans operate under similar rules as those applied for general loans, which continue during the drought. The main difference is that the drought loans have more favorable terms. The interest rate is well below the market rate. For investments in farm capital, the normal interest rate is 8 percent or 9 percent; for the drought loans it is 6 percent. For working capital, the drought loans are at an interest rate of 3 percent, as compared to 6.5 percent for other similar BNB loans. The repayment period is about the same for the drought loans. However, there is a grace period of up to 4 years (2 years for working capital) to reflect the impact of the drought on farm revenues. Also there is a 50 percent rebate on principle and interest for drought loans. The Federal Government covers the rebate.

BNB's drought relief operation was clearly under-funded given the demand. An expansion in aggregate credit availability would be of much assistance. At the same time, the program is not sufficiently focused on reaching the small land holders in most pressing need, nor is it sufficiently linked to the drought relief operations more generally. BNB reports that 60 percent of the drought loans go to "family farms." A family farm, as defined by BNB, has no more than two employees, no more than four times the land area needed for subsistence and no more than R$27,000 annual gross revenue. It is clearly implausible that all "family farms," as defined above, are poor, and very few of those amongst the other 40 percent of borrowers are likely to be considered poor. This would not be a concern if the loans were not so heavily subsidized; but given the subsidy, one should ask whether it is reaching the poor. It might be argued that second round employment gains to the poor would accrue from loans to relatively well off landowners. However, this will take time, and is not of obvious relevance for short-term drought relief. BNB offices have no formal contact with the Municipal Councils for drought relief, though they do consult with Municipal Credit Commissions.

Recognizing the limitations of credit as a drought relief instrument, a re-orientation and re-design of drought relief loans should be considered. A better allocation of credit for drought relief would be possible by putting a ceiling on the loans. Another step would be to lower the grant component. Together with an expansion of lending volume, these steps could help BNB meet the demand for credit during a drought.

Implications for the Future: While the 1998 drought relief effort has been exemplary in a number of respects, and has undoubtedly saved many families in the Northeast from destitution, there are three main areas where the relief effort could be improved. The first area concerns preparedness and speed of response. This aspect is often a weak point of drought relief efforts, and the 1998 drought was no exception. The federal funding response was slow, civic meetings to mobilize action were held as early as August 1997 in one state (Pernambuco), and the signals were clear from about the beginning of 1998, yet it was not until May 1998 that the relief effort became active. Ceará is the only exception where relief programs began in December 1997.

The second area concerns coverage of the affected population. The overall coverage of the 1998 drought relief effort was less than ideal. A reduction in the wage rate would permit larger reach without higher spending. In the aggregate, a higher funding level is also needed. There is also scope for improving efficiency in reaching those in greatest need.

The third problem area concerns coordination of drought relief efforts with anti-poverty policy in normal (non-drought) years. There have been some attempts to coordinate the drought relief efforts with other pre-existing programs (in Ceará, for example, a World Bank poverty alleviation program was accelerated in response to the drought). However, these efforts have been ad hoc and partial. More systematic coordination efforts must start from the realization that droughts are intimately connected to the problems of rural development more generally: high risk, credit and insurance market failures, under-investment in local public goods, and often-weak local institutions.

A permanent safety net program in the Northeast could help deal with all three of these problems. This safety net would extend the coverage of the workfare component of the current drought relief effort to include non-drought periods (at which demand would be much lower but still existent). A permanent safety net should also relax the current eligibility restrictions on relief work. Such a social safety program could thus combine the best features of a low-wage employment guarantee scheme with current social funds for supporting labor-intensive community projects in poor rural areas.

Under such an employment program, the Federal Government could offer to finance 15 days per month of work on community projects and training for any adult. To assure that the work reaches those in need and protects incentives to resume regular work when available, the wage rate should be set no higher than the local wage rate for unskilled agricultural labor in a normal year. In the case of training, the wage rate should be lower than the unskilled agricultural labor wage. The work scheme should apply to a technically feasible project proposed by a *bona fide* Municipal Council. As in the present drought relief program, the Federal Government could pay a small amount extra for non-wage costs, though this will often be inadequate and further funding of the non-wage costs may have to be secured from other public programs, or by cost-recovery from non-poor beneficiaries. Market-based insurance schemes could complement such a safety net program.

The current drought relief Municipal Councils should become a permanent institution dealing simultaneously with droughts and the problems of poverty, risk, and rural underdevelopment in non-drought years. The Municipal Councils should maintain a shelf of useful projects in the community. With wide public knowledge of the existence of a federal employment guarantee on community work, and the permanent Municipal Councils ready with a shelf of such projects, the basis for a rapid response would be generated from the bottom up, rather than relying on administrative discretion from the top down.

Pensions

Pensions paid under the public sector system for private sector workers (RGPS), special rural pensions, and special social pensions (LOAS) administered by INSS constitute the most important and largest program for the reduction of rural poverty in Brazil. The basic rural pension scheme pays one minimum salary to rural workers who can prove a certain minimum length of rural activity without requiring proof of contribution to the INSS.[118] LOAS special pensions (BPC—*Benefício de Prestação Continuada*) are also one minimum salary for the elderly or disabled in households with a per capita income of less than one-quarter minimum salary.

Total pensions paid under the rural pension scheme amount to almost R$11 billion annually. There are more than 6 million recipients of rural pensions (compared to less than 8 million rural households in total).

---

118. For a detailed discussion of the special rural pension regime, see Delgado (2000).

The PPV permits analysis of pension receipts by households residing in rural areas. Pension receipts in rural areas may differ from receipts under the rural pension scheme in important ways. First, rural residents may receive non-rural pensions under either the private or public sector pension regimes. Second, recipients of rural pensions may reside in non-rural areas, especially in small towns that are nevertheless classified as urban. All following statements regarding rural pensions, thus, refer to pension receipts by rural residents rather than rural pensions as a special program under the overall government pension system.

Among the rural poor, only 6 percent of the population receives a pension, compared to rates between 10 and 20 percent for higher income groups. Roughly 28 percent of households include at least one member who receives a pension; however, this coverage rate is lower for the poorest.

Incidence analysis from the PPV suggests that 13 percent of rural pension receipts accrue to the poor (10.5 percent within the rural Southeast and 14 percent within the rural Northeast). These values compare favorably to the national benefit incidence of only 3.7 percent of pension receipts accruing to the poor. Based on these estimates, Brazil's rural poor receive about R$1.4 billion annually in pension benefits, which is roughly a quarter of their total aggregate income of R$5.3 billion.[119] One particularly striking finding on the targeting of pension receipts in the Northeast is that the 3 percent of the rural Northeast population that are part of the top quintile of the national distribution appear to receive 43 percent of the pension receipts within the rural Northeast.

One important aspect of cash transfer programs, such as pensions, is that they themselves change the income distribution. This means that many pension recipients who are not classified as poor in this analysis would have been poor without pension receipts. All pensions imply a payment of one minimum salary (R$130 per month in 1997), and in fact, most rural pensions are exactly one minimum salary. This means that with one pension receipt alone, two people would reach the poverty line used in this report. In other words, one pension constitutes 50 percent of the income necessary to lift a family of four out of poverty. It is therefore not surprising that there are few poor pension recipients. However, pension benefit incidence is concentrated in the third to fifth quintiles, which are comprised of households that would not have been poor even without pensions.

A recent study analyzes the effect of pensions on poverty rates, measured at a much lower poverty line than the one used in this report [Rocha 1998]. That study shows that the national rural poverty rate would be 45 percent higher, and the Northeast rural poverty rate would be 42 percent higher in the absence of pension benefits. This analysis is based on the PNAD, which is likely to underestimate pension receipts. From these numbers, the relative impact of urban pensions appears to be more important for poverty reduction. However, given the much higher poverty rates in rural areas, the absolute effect is expected to be higher in rural areas.

In summary, pensions for rural residents are extremely important for the poor. They are biased toward the non-poor (on average, a non-poor individual receives higher benefits than a poor individual) but they improve the overall income distribution (the distribution of rural pension receipts is less unequal than the overall income distribution). Most rural pensions are non-contributory at the individual level,[120] but more detailed analysis is needed to determine the net-incidence of the rural pension system, taking contributions into account. Also, further work should differentiate the impact of pension receipts from different pension regimes to permit more specific policy recommendations. Without doubt, and despite their regressivity, rural pensions are an extremely important source of income for Brazil's rural poor and near poor. Any reforms need to protect these important benefits to the poor or those who would into poverty in the absence of the program.

---

119. Disaggregation of derived income estimated in the PPV yields a lower share of pensions in total income (about 17 percent for the entire rural population), suggesting the possibility of underreporting of pensions in the survey.

120. Partial contributions are now collected through sectoral taxation (FUNRURAL).

TABLE 9.4: COVERAGE WITH PENSIONS: PERCENT POPULATION THAT RECEIVES PENSION

Region	National Consumption Quintile				
	1	2	3	4	5
Rural Northeast	0.063	0.117	0.224	0.179	0.141
Rural Southeast	0.061	0.085	0.089	0.146	0.180
Rural and Urban	0.073	0.099	0.127	0.140	0.181

TABLE 9.5: INCIDENCE OF PENSIONS

Region		National Expenditure Quintile				
		1	2	3	4	5
Rural Northeast	Beneficiaries	0.252	0.268	0.307	0.134	0.039
	Benefits	0.139	0.152	0.203	0.076	0.430
Rural Southeast	Beneficiaries	0.149	0.255	0.234	0.234	0.128
	Benefits	0.105	0.211	0.211	0.263	0.211
Rural and Urban	Beneficiaries	0.099	0.148	0.205	0.232	0.315
	Benefits	0.037	0.060	0.100	0.159	0.643

Water and Sanitation

In the rural Northeast, most poor get their water from on-site or off-site wells or other presumably precarious sources. Coverage with water distribution systems is minimal. Even coverage with water trucks is minimal (this coverage is probably higher in drought years). Water networks almost exclusively cover the small share of the population in the top three quintiles of the national distribution. Access to drinking water clearly remains a major issue in the rural Northeast.

TABLE 9.6: COVERAGE WITH WATER SERVICES ACCESS

Region	Source of Water[121]	National Expenditure Quintile				
		1	2	3	4	5
Rural Northeast	Piped water	0.032	0.130	0.311	0.499	0.606
	General Network	0.052	0.157	0.311	0.499	0.606
	Well in own house	0.238	0.225	0.209	0.223	0.235
	Well off house	0.313	0.239	0.185	0.000	0.000
	Stand pipe	0.020	0.016	0.013	0.055	0.000
	Truck	0.005	0.037	0.020	0.000	0.050
Rural Southeast	Piped water	0.102	0.148	0.245	0.272	0.206
	General Network	0.184	0.167	0.262	0.272	0.206
	Well in own house	0.390	0.448	0.426	0.577	0.556
	Well off house	0.072	0.088	0.076	0.011	0.026
	Stand pipe	0.000	0.000	0.000	0.000	0.000
	Truck	0.000	0.000	0.000	0.000	0.000
Rural and Urban	Piped water	0.361	0.594	0.779	0.886	0.958
	General Network	0.447	0.634	0.792	0.893	0.960
	Well in own house	0.139	0.139	0.101	0.063	0.029
	Well off house	0.149	0.079	0.032	0.007	0.001
	Stand pipe	0.034	0.011	0.010	0.006	0.000
	Truck	0.140	0.014	0.004	0.002	0.001

---

121. Multiple answers are possible. The response "other sources" has been omitted.

TABLE 9.7: INCIDENCE OF SANITATION SERVICES (SEWER SYSTEMS)					
	National Expenditure Quintile				
Region	**1**	**2**	**3**	**4**	**5**
Rural Northeast	0.250	0.000	0.125	0.250	0.375
Rural Southeast	0.091	0.364	0.273	0.182	0.091
Rural and Urban	0.040	0.135	0.220	0.280	0.324

In the rural Northeast, the incidence of water trucking services is heavily concentrated in 25 percent of the local population that is in the second quintile of the national distribution (and above the poverty line). This population receives 59 percent of the water service. The 50 percent of the region's population that constitute the poor receive only 16 percent of this service.

In the rural Southeast, almost 20 percent of the poor have access to the water network. This share rises only a little for the higher income groups. The rest of the population depends on on-site wells and other sources. Given more favorable overall water availability, access to drinking water is clearly less precarious than in the Northeast.

In the rural Northeast, coverage with sanitation services is extremely low, especially among the poor. Less than one-quarter of the poor have access to any kind of sanitation system whether septic tanks, latrines, or ditches. In the rural Southeast, more than one-third of the poor population has at least some access to rudimentary septic tanks.

TABLE 9.8: COVERAGE OF SANITATION SERVICES						
		National Expenditure Quintile				
Region	**Energy Source**	**1**	**2**	**3**	**4**	**5**
Rural Northeast	Sewer system	0.017	0.000	0.029	0.077	0.346
	Septic 'fossa'	0.014	0.172	0.189	0.354	0.434
	Rud. 'fossa'	0.132	0.242	0.360	0.349	0.203
	Ditch	0.009	0.025	0.010	0.104	0.000
	Other	0.063	0.091	0.035	0.000	0.016
Rural Southeast	Sewer system	0.034	0.109	0.114	0.118	0.079
	Septic 'fossa'	0.000	0.006	0.063	0.168	0.168
	Rud. 'fossa'	0.353	0.457	0.597	0.579	0.579
	Ditch	0.157	0.075	0.061	0.061	0.000
	Other	0.080	0.200	0.120	0.172	0.165
Rural and Urban	Sewer system	0.10	0.35	0.57	0.73	0.84
	Septic 'fossa'	0.050	0.141	0.140	0.106	0.083
	Rud. 'fossa'	0.266	0.273	0.181	0.116	0.059
	Ditch	0.056	0.041	0.037	0.025	0.001
	Other	0.078	0.056	0.026	0.013	0.001

Transport

The rural poor typically walk and rarely use other modes of transport. They simply cannot afford to use paid transport as a means of getting to work. Consequently, the poor usually live on or near the land on which they work. Lack of motorized transport often impedes the poor from reaching medical facilities in case of need and constrains the sale and marketing of farm produce. Table 9.9 describes the coverage of transport modes among the different expenditure quintiles.

TABLE 9.9: COVERAGE OF TRANSPORT MODES

Region	Type of Transportation	National Expenditure Quintile				
		1	2	3	4	5
Rural Northeast	Public transport	0.022	0.061	0.071	0.097	0.174
	Foot	0.679	0.616	0.558	0.419	0.209
	Vehicle	0.004	0.010	0.060	0.082	0.319
	Other	0.010	0.033	0.115	0.091	0.059
Rural Southeast	Public transport	0.003	0.015	0.191	0.049	0.057
	Foot	0.746	0.698	0.501	0.551	0.341
	Vehicle	0.007	0.018	0.063	0.064	0.112
	Other	0.087	0.143	0.191	0.080	0.209
Rural and Urban	Public transport	0.122	0.189	0.286	0.299	0.231
	Foot	0.586	0.473	0.336	0.249	0.138
	Vehicle	0.017	0.017	0.065	0.143	0.353
	Other	0.066	0.103	0.132	0.073	0.047

Energy

Only 37 percent of the poor in the rural Northeast and 56 percent of the poor in the rural Southeast have access to the electricity network. The remainder almost exclusively uses kerosene lamps. This coverage rate contrasts with the coverage of the wealthiest income groups where 90 percent have electricity access in both the Northeast and Southeast regions. Table 9.10. describes electricity coverage among the expenditure quintiles.

TABLE 9.10: COVERAGE WITH ENERGY SERVICES

Region	Type of Energy	National Expenditure Quintile				
		1	2	3	4	5
Rural Northeast	Electricity	0.37	0.49	0.69	0.84	0.95
	Generator	0.00	0.00	0.00	0.00	0.00
	Lantern	0.60	0.49	0.30	0.15	0.05
	Candle	0.03	0.01	0.01	0.01	0.00
Rural Southeast	Electricity	0.56	0.81	0.89	0.93	0.93
	Generator	0.01	0.00	0.01	0.01	0.00
	Lantern	0.43	0.16	0.09	0.06	0.05
	Candle	0.00	0.03	0.00	0.01	0.02
Rural and Urban	Electricity	0.714	0.860	0.952	0.987	0.997
	Generator	0.001	0.000	0.001	0.000	0.001
	Lantern	0.275	0.129	0.046	0.012	0.002
	Candle	0.009	0.010	0.001	0.001	0.000

According to the 1996 PNAD, 66 percent of rural households are served with electricity. This share is 52 percent for the rural poor. The absence of modern energy for almost half of the rural poor directly reduces the quality of life and constrains educational and income earning opportunities (no lighting for reading, writing, and no power for pumps or other small machinery).

Education

In Brazil, rural illiteracy above 15 years of age is still at 32 percent. In the Northeast, this rate reaches 46 percent, drastically limiting the options of nearly half of the rural population to find employment in the urban or modern rural sectors of the economy.

TABLE 9.11: INCIDENCE OF PUBLIC EDUCATION USE

Region	Level of education	National Expenditure Quintile				
		1	2	3	4	5
Rural Northeast	Day Care	0.72	0.28	0.00	0.00	0.00
	Kindergarten	0.68	0.22	0.06	0.04	0
	Primary school	0.50	0.26	0.16	0.06	0.01
	Secondary school	0.37	0.17	0.20	0.24	0.02
	University	0	0	0.24	0.38	0.38
	Adult education	0.33	0.67	0	0	0
Rural Southeast	Day Care	0.50	0.34	0.16	0.00	0.00
	Kindergarten	0.34	0.17	0.25	0.18	0.06
	Primary school	0.32	0.32	0.23	0.10	0.03
	Secondary school	0.04	0.29	0.40	0.20	0.06
	University	—	—	—	—	—
	Adult education	—	—	—	—	—
Rural and Urban	Day Care	0.24	0.33	0.14	0.23	0.07
	Kindergarten	0.24	0.33	0.14	0.23	0.07
	Primary school	0.26	0.27	0.23	0.16	0.15
	Secondary school	0.07	0.12	0.28	0.33	0.19
	University	0	0	0.03	0.22	0.76
	Adult education	0.24	0.13	0.29	0.19	0.15

Primary school enrollment has now reached 88 percent of 7–14 year olds in the rural areas. Even in the Northeast, this rate has now reached 86 percent, suggesting that the focus now needs to shift from additional coverage to better quality of education.

The PPV survey suggests a more cautious assessment even on basic coverage. The survey suggests that 45 percent of 7–14 year old poor children in the Northeast do not attend primary school. This figure is 17 percent for the rural Southeast. There are two lessons. First, aggregate enrollment data hide much worse indicators for the lowest income groups. Second, more research and analysis is needed to reconcile higher enrollment rates reported by the education system with lower attendance rates reported by the households.

Less than 5 percent of the poor attend secondary school in both the rural Northeast and Southeast. More than 10 percent coverage is reached only for the top two quintiles in the Northeast and the top three quintiles in the Southeast.

Targeting ratios are highest for public daycare and kindergarten and decline with education level. Up to the primary level, targeting is highly progressive from a national perspective and moderately progressive from a local perspective. Table 9.11. describes the incidence of public education usage and Table 9.12 describes the coverage of education services across the different expenditure quintiles.

Rural expenditure on education is estimated by multiplying the number of students at the primary level with the mandated FUNDEFF spending floor of R$315 per student per year. While urban areas in the South typically have much higher spending levels, the floor seems to be an appropriate estimate for rural areas. At this spending floor, the fiscal costs of rural primary education are R$2.1 billion. Rural education spending at higher levels is essentially negligible. Approximately 45 percent of the primary school enrollment in rural areas comes from the poorest quintile. Thus, approximately R$1 billion is spent on public education for the rural poor.

Health

Spending on rural health is estimated by apportioning total federal spending on SUS maintenance (R$11.1 billion) for the share of public health users from rural areas (17.8 percent). Average spend-

TABLE 9.12: COVERAGE OF EDUCATION SERVICES						
Region and Level of Education	**Type of education**	**National Expenditure Quintile**				
		1	**2**	**3**	**4**	**5**
Rural Northeast						
Day Care	Public	0.014	0.000	0.000	0.000	0.000
	Private	0.000	0.000	0.000	0.000	0.501
	Not Attending	0.986	1.000	1.000	1.000	0.499
Kindergarten	Public	0.243	0.411	0.465	0.408	0.000
	Private	0.039	0.118	0.000	0.228	1.000
	Not attending	0.719	0.471	0.535	0.364	0.000
Primary school	Public	0.546	0.746	0.747	0.789	0.230
	Private	0.000	0.023	0.048	0.123	0.430
	Not attending	0.454	0.231	0.205	0.087	0.340
Secondary school	Public	0.040	0.052	0.072	0.081	0.030
	Private	0.006	0.000	0.000	0.119	0.342
	Not attending	0.954	0.948	0.928	0.800	0.628
University	Public	0.000	0.000	0.032	0.000	0.156
	Private	0.000	0.000	0.000	0.014	0.030
	Not attending	1.000	1.000	0.968	0.986	0.813
Adult education	Public	0.002	0.004	0.000	0.000	0.000
	Private	0.000	0.000	0.000	0.000	0.000
	Not attending	0.998	0.996	1.000	1.000	1.000
Rural Southeast						
Day Care	Public	0.045	0.030	0.000	0.000	0.000
	Private	0.000	0.000	0.021	0.000	0.000
	Not Attending	0.955	0.970	0.979	1.000	1.000
Kindergarten	Public	0.106	0.124	0.284	0.476	0.410
	Private	0.000	0.000	0.000	0.000	0.153
	Not attending	0.894	0.876	0.716	0.524	0.437
Primary school	Public	0.835	0.843	0.900	0.937	0.878
	Private	0.000	0.000	0.010	0.037	0.122
	Not attending	0.165	0.157	0.090	0.026	0.000
Secondary school	Public	0.020	0.081	0.184	0.159	0.120
	Private	0.000	0.000	0.000	0.000	0.000
	Not attending	0.980	0.919	0.816	0.841	0.880
University	Public	0.000	0.000	0.000	0.000	0.000
	Private	0.000	0.000	0.000	0.000	0.000
	Not attending	1.000	1.000	1.000	1.000	1.000
Adult education	Public	0.000	0.000	0.000	0.000	0.000
	Private	0.000	0.000	0.000	0.000	0.000
	Not attending	1.000	1.000	1.000	1.000	1.000
Rural and Urban						
Day Care	Public	0.008	0.023	0.015	0.027	0.000
	Private	0.001	0.014	0.005	0.014	0.197
	Not Attending	0.992	0.964	0.980	0.959	0.803
Kindergarten	Public	0.008	0.023	0.015	0.027	0.000
	Private	0.001	0.014	0.005	0.014	0.197
	Not attending	0.992	0.964	0.980	0.959	0.803

(continued)

TABLE 9.12: COVERAGE OF EDUCATION SERVICES (CONTINUED)

Region and Level of Education	Type of education	National Expenditure Quintile				
		1	2	3	4	5
Primary school	Public	0.683	0.816	0.846	0.716	0.415
	Private	0.005	0.055	0.062	0.215	0.511
	Not attending	0.312	0.129	0.093	0.069	0.074
Secondary school	Public	0.051	0.098	0.206	0.277	0.224
	Private	0.002	0.000	0.031	0.100	0.280
	Not attending	0.947	0.902	0.763	0.623	0.496
University	Public	0.000	0.000	0.005	0.032	0.136
	Private	0.000	0.001	0.000	0.021	0.193
	Not attending	1.000	0.999	0.995	0.946	0.671
Adult education	Public	0.006	0.003	0.005	0.003	0.003
	Private	0.000	0.003	0.001	0.002	0.002
	Not attending	0.994	0.995	0.993	0.995	0.995

TABLE 9.13: INCIDENCE OF PUBLIC HEALTH SERVICES

Region	National Expenditure Quintile				
	1	2	3	4	5
Rural Northeast	0.350	0.317	0.158	0.125	0.050
Rural Southeast	0.220	0.203	0.271	0.254	0.051
Rural and Urban	0.163	0.195	0.222	0.233	0.186

TABLE 9.14: COVERAGE OF HEALTH SERVICES

Region		National Expenditure Quintile				
		1	2	3	4	5
Rural Northeast	Public	0.058	0.102	0.093	0.139	0.149
	Private	0.022	0.008	0.017	0.024	0.005
	No use	0.920	0.890	0.890	0.837	0.846
Rural Southeast	Public	0.082	0.071	0.105	0.179	0.080
	Private	0.003	0.014	0.041	0.042	0.112
	No use	0.915	0.915	0.854	0.779	0.808
Rural and Urban	Public	0.084	0.099	0.059	0.067	0.073
	Private	0.010	0.009	0.072	0.089	0.103
	No use	0.906	0.892	0.869	0.844	0.824

ing per user in rural areas is R$250. This amount is likely to overestimate spending on health for rural residents since rural residents are likely to use less costly procedures than urban residents are.

The rural poor depend predominantly on public health care and make very limited use of private health services. Thirty-one percent of public rural health care users are poor. The data suggests that rural health spending is progressive from a national point of view but mildly regressive from a local perspective. Overall, the data suggests that the Federal Government spends approximately R$600 million on health care for rural poor residents.

Nutrition

Nutrition programs have considerable reach among Brazil's poor. Free milk distribution reaches 18 percent of the poor in the rural Northeast and 30 percent of the poor in the rural Southeast. Coverage is highest among those from the second quintile of the national distribution.

TABLE 9.15: COVERAGE OF MILK PROGRAMS

Region	National Expenditure Quintile				
	1	2	3	4	5
Rural Northeast	0.177	0.250	0.120	0.269	0.018
Rural Southeast	0.303	0.352	0.319	0.237	0.165
Rural and Urban	0.130	0.145	0.080	0.059	0.029

Most children who go to school receive free school lunch. In line with the progressive distribution of public school enrollment, school lunches up to the primary level constitute highly progressive spending from the national and moderately progressive spending from the local perspective.

TABLE 9.16: INCIDENCE OF SCHOOL LUNCHES

Region	Grade	National Expenditure Quintile				
		1	2	3	4	5
Rural Northeast	All	0.521	0.236	0.146	0.083	0.014
	Kindergarten	0.560	0.259	0.112	0.069	0.000
	Primary	0.504	0.237	0.165	0.079	0.014
	Secondary	0.143	0.229	0.114	0.486	0.029
Rural Southeast	All	0.293	0.320	0.240	0.107	0.040
	Kindergarten	0.333	0.167	0.250	0.187	0.063
	Primary	0.300	0.337	0.237	0.100	0.025
	Secondary	0.045	0.299	0.373	0.209	0.075
Rural and Urban	All	0.244	0.246	0.233	0.182	0.094
	Kindergarten	0.369	0.242	0.189	0.133	0.067
	Primary	0.245	0.257	0.239	0.171	0.087
	Secondary	0.052	0.137	0.274	0.362	0.175

TABLE 9.17: COVERAGE OF SCHOOL LUNCHES

Region	Grade	National Expenditure Quintile				
		1	2	3	4	5
Rural Northeast	All	0.62	0.59	0.67	0.65	0.20
	Kindergarten	0.42	0.56	1.00	0.62	0.0
	Primary	0.71	0.60	0.67	0.74	0.41
	Secondary	0.10	0.42	0.20	0.41	0.07
Rural Southeast	All	0.88	0.97	0.91	0.91	0.79
	Kindergarten	1.000	1.000	1.000	1.000	0.73
	Primary	0.86	0.94	0.96	0.89	0.84
	Secondary	1.000	1.000	1.000	1.00	1.000
Rural and Urban	All	0.726	0.706	0.690	0.563	0.273
	Kindergarten	0.636	0.591	0.592	0.429	0.200
	Primary	0.763	0.744	0.778	0.680	0.447
	Secondary	0.314	0.489	0.392	0.391	0.177

Agricultural Credit[122]

Agriculture credit has been an important element of overall rural policies. In addition to general rural credit from the mandatory allocation of savings deposits, rural credit also includes specific programs, such as PRONAF (a program directed at family agriculture) that are funded mostly from special constitutional funds and FAT. An-depth analysis of the multiple complex issues related to rural credit is beyond the scope of this paper. In particular, the adequate role of a public credit policy in the existing environment in which there is only very limited private sector lending, is not adequately discussed here. Only some very basic issues are touched upon in this section.

Overall Agriculture Credit: Like many other developing countries, Brazil provides directed loans and concession terms of credit to agriculture. The level of agricultural credit as a share of agricultural GDP varied enormously during the last decades and oscillated between a high of 22 percent in 1987 and a low of 6 percent in 1996, reflecting in part the substantial changes in monetary and fiscal policies that took place during this period. There is no indication that increases in agricultural credit as a share of agricultural GDP affected production. On the contrary, there are convincing findings indicating that, in many instances, credit was in demand precisely because the concession terms eventually generated diversion and substitution of funds (substitution of own funds or non-subsidized borrowed funds for concession agricultural credit funding).

Since the late 1980s, there has been a substantial reduction in subsidies through subsidized agricultural credit. In particular, the grant element embedded in the directed credit to agriculture has been markedly reduced in recent years. As the agricultural finance system becomes more market oriented, the availability of rural finance services will further diminish and the creditworthiness of clients will become the main criteria for gaining access to credit.

Treasury resources now play a much smaller role in providing funding for the agricultural sector. Resources have been substituted instead by mandatory usage of funds from private banks. Estimates indicate that in 1998 the flow of formal agricultural credit reached US$8.8 billion and that informal credit ranged between US$2.5 to $4.0 billion. Self-financing has been rising too, reflecting the improved terms of trade and enhanced efficiency in production. Table 9.18 shows that the total level of rural credit in 1998 was similar to the level in 1985, significantly less than the level in 1980, but almost twice the level of 1996. These numbers need to be interpreted with care as a significant share reflects the rescheduling and refinancing of old debt and do not represent new loans.

TABLE 9.18: TOTAL AGRICULTURAL CREDIT IN BRAZIL
(US$ Millions)

1980	1985	1990	1995	1996	1997	1998
19,508	8,340	8,445	6,022	4,915	6,692	8,766

Source: Guimaraes, 1999.

The main resources used to finance agricultural loans are generated now from the mandatory lending of 25 percent and 10 percent of the volume of sight and savings accounts, respectively. In 1998, the mandatory use of these resources accounted for 37 percent of the total resources lent to the agricultural sector. In contrast, only 4 percent of the total financial resources to agriculture was lent voluntarily. The difference between compulsory and voluntary lending rates indicates the level of administrative control under which agricultural lending takes place in Brazil.

---

122. This sub-section is extracted from notes by Jacob Yaron prepared in January 2000 and May 2000.

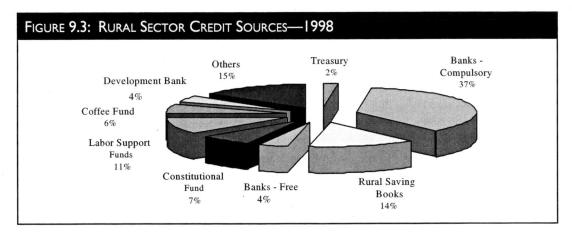

FIGURE 9.3: RURAL SECTOR CREDIT SOURCES—1998

Private banks have to decide whether to deposit the value of 25 percent of their sight deposits in the Central Bank with no remuneration or to lend these funds to agriculture. Lending to agriculture faces ceiling lending interest rates of between 5.75 percent and 8.75 percent per annum, depending on the program. These controlled interest rates compare to the annualized overnight interest rate that has not fallen below 18.5 percent and has substantially exceeded this level since 1994.

Only a small share of farming households has access to general rural credit. Subsequently, it is clear that the majority of the agricultural sector is not benefiting from the subsidy involved in directed credit. The minority of the agricultural sector that benefits from directed credit does so in proportion to the size of the loan received. In addition, it is very likely that ultimate borrowers would face no difficulties in obtaining credit even if loans were not subsidized and if lending were not mandatory. Clearly, there is no justification for subsidizing the cost of funds by penalizing the rest of the users of financial sector services. In view of the past distribution of loans, the contribution of the subsidized credit system to a more equitable income distribution is questionable at best.

There is a substantial element of additional indirect subsidization that supports the agricultural sector through the credit system. This indirect subsidization involves mainly the non-recovery of agricultural loans and their re-negotiation, whereby more favorable borrowing terms are introduced including reduced lending interest rates, extended loan maturities, and grace periods.

Commercial farmers, who are financially sound and would otherwise have met the borrowing prerequisites from private banks, still face difficulties in gaining access to credit because the overhanging and not-fully-settled agricultural debt, calling for political intervention. Political intervention has resulted in frequent debt forgiveness and re-negotiation of loans on more favorable borrowing terms. Consequently, private banks continue to be "crowded out" and have become increasingly reluctant to engage in agricultural lending, preferring non-agricultural clients whose indebtedness is much less susceptible to political intervention and debt forgiveness.

Debt rescheduling and forgiveness have also generated regressive income distribution, since the grant element embedded in the debt forgiveness and concession borrowing terms was proportional to the loan's size and highly correlated with wealth (although not necessarily agricultural wealth). Maintenance of these policies has generated fiscal deficit, accelerated inflation, and increased reliance on state banks, many of which have been performing as subsidized credit disbursement windows, rather than as efficient financial intermediaries. The involvement of state banks also results in the crowding-out of private, for-profit banks. This crowding out trend is well demonstrated in Figure 9.3, which indicates the share of controlled resources in financing the agricultural sector.

Family Farm Credit (PRONAF) and Microcredit: PRONAF benefits agricultural producers who rely on family labor in their operations and has characteristics markedly different from the general agricultural credit described above. PRONAF allows agricultural producers to borrow funds at a fixed nominal interest rate of 5.75 percent per annum (which, as the result of a spike in inflation, was negative in real terms in 1999). The maximum loan amounts under this program are R$5,000 for working capital and R$15,000 for investments in fixed assets. The program grew in its volume of lending and accounted for about 16.3 percent of total agricultural lending in 1999, compared to about 13.1 percent in 1998. *Banco do Brasil* is the main implementing agency of PRONAF and has approximately R$0.87 billion in 1999, benefiting about 450,000 families with loans that averaged R$2,000 each. The Ministry of Finance covers the difference between the actual cost and the low lending interest paid by the borrowers. In 1999 PROCERA, a special credit program for land reform beneficiaries was absorbed by PRONAF as a separate category with more favorable financing conditions.

PRONAF started operations only in 1995 and, according to *Banco do Brasil*, its loan collection performance is about 98 percent. With these high repayment rates, PRONAF is considered extremely successful in an environment that has become used to poor financial discipline and low loan recovery rates. The low lending interest rate should be, however, a matter of concern. When the majority of the farming households have neither access to formal credit nor a chance to obtain it in the foreseeable future, priority should be given to increased coverage rather than low rates. Setting the lending rate higher would allow the expansion of lending to this clientele as the accumulation of interest revenue will make the program more financially independent and less susceptible to reductions in budgetary allocations needed to continue the program.

In contrast to lending with controlled resources, Banco do Nordeste recently initiated the CrediAmigo program that is targeting low-income entrepreneurs by providing them with much smaller loans and charging monthly interest rates of 5 percent, only slightly below what PRONAF charges annually. Even recognizing the different conditions of small-scale agricultural lending, the successful CrediAmigo program demonstrates an important lesson for all lending: financially sustainable rates can lead to larger coverage and generate large benefits for the poor.

Overall Assessment and Recommendations: Overall, un-targeted, subsidized credit is not a cost-effective instrument for assisting the agriculture sector, and even less to address rural poverty. Given Brazil's high concentration of land ownership, the incidence of subsidies embedded in general rural credit is likely to be highly regressive.

Information on the coverage and incidence of agricultural credit from the PPV is very limited due to the small sample size. However, available data suggests that access to agricultural credit rises with income level. Interestingly, targeting in the Northeast does not seem regressive. This information appears doubtful. If the result is correct, it could be due to the large amount of PRONAF resources applied in the Northeast and directed to poorer farmers.

TABLE 9.19: INCIDENCE OF SUBSIDIZED FINANCING FOR AGRICULTURAL ACTIVITIES (Farmers only)

Region	National Expenditure Quintile				
	1	2	3	4	5
Rural Northeast	0.545	0.091	0	0.182	0.182
Rural Southeast	0	0	0	0.500	0.500
All Rural	0.400	0.067	0	0.267	0.267

TABLE 9.20: COVERAGE OF SUBSIDIZED FINANCING FOR AGRICULTURAL ACTIVITIES (Farmers only)

Region	National Expenditure Quintile				
	1	2	3	4	5
Rural Northeast	0.029	0.010	0	0.105	0.333
Rural Southeast	0	0	0	0.065	0.125
All Rural	0.022	0.007	0	0.080	0.182

Recognizing the still very limited role of private financial markets, in particular on long-term lending, the role of the state in supporting rural financial markets should be to create an enabling environment, conducive to the promotion of rural financial markets. In the Brazilian context, improving agricultural finance involves several reforms:

a) *Introduce major improvements in the legal, regulatory, and enforcement systems, in particular with respect to the removal of debtor biases.* Effort should be exerted to improve the performance of registries and the issuance of warehouse receipts. The Government should also seek to expand the types of collateral accepted as payment guarantees and reduce the expenses associated with foreclosures. Improvements in these areas should be initiated without delay, as they are independent from other actions that aim to reduce overall lending interest rates and spreads.

b) *Reduce interest-rate subsidies for directed credit systems.* Moreover, the Government should attempt to increase uniformity and establish a "level playing field," thereby eliminating a situation in which eventually the Treasury assumes much of the expenditures associated with implementing subsidized and directed loans.

c) *Introduce annual performance assessments of the various programs of interventions in agricultural and rural finance, based on two primary criteria: outreach to target clientele and self-sustainability.* As long as the system of rural credit is subsidized, the Government should adopt policies that create a "level playing field" between state-owned and private banks.

d) *Eliminate or at least minimize debt forgiveness.* Debt forgiveness only breeds further expectations for moratoriums, inflating land prices, generating misallocation of resources, and creating artificial demand for agricultural loans.

e) *Enhance the volume of business, and particularly the access of small-scale farmers and rural businesses to unsubsidized price and yield hedging mechanisms.* The purpose of such a policy is to diversify risk and allow rural clients to climb up the income ladder by adopting high-yield technologies that foster their specialization along their comparative advantage.

f) *Encourage voluntary lending of the financial sector while reducing the share of mandatory lending.* The share of private, for-profit banks in financing the agricultural sector should increase while the share of state-owned banks decreases.

g) *Eliminate the ceiling lending interest rates that are presently imposed on "free cost" resources lent to agriculture.* This policy of forcing banks to lend to agriculture or receive no remuneration on deposits at the Central Bank is counterproductive. Moreover, this policy impedes the development of a market for risk in the agricultural sector. Instead of assisting the poor, this policy results in an unwarranted transfer of resources and subsidies to banks and their better-off and financially sound clients.

h) *Support rural microfinance institutions and programs.* The experiences of other countries in implementing microfinance operations should serve as a useful guide. Key lessons to adapt include setting interest rates that fully cover the long-term costs (including unsubsidized financial resources), introducing appropriate spreads, and integrating client and staff incentives that ensure appropriate screening and monitoring of credit risks as well as high rates of loan recovery. Microfinance support should ensure an enabling environment, removal of legal and regulatory barriers, and initial financial support, if necessary, which is both capped and phased out over time in pursuit of self-sustainability and expanded outreach to target clientele.

i) *Gather more uniform and meaningful data.* The data used for this analysis included information submitted to the authors by the Central Bank, *Banco do Brasil,* the Ministry of Agriculture, the Ministry of Finance, and other salient banks and prominent agro-business corporations. The database on rural finance, as a whole, could substantially benefit from a concerted effort to provide more uniform and meaningful information on salient variables pertinent to the Brazilian rural finance system.

Comparing the Effectiveness of Different Programs

Table 9.21 compares the effectiveness of different public programs to transfer resources (either directly in cash, by means of services, or in the form of future services or income streams) to the rural poor. Indicators listed for each program include the coverage of the poor among the target population, the targeting rate (incidence) to the poor, the size of benefits and spending accruing to each participating household, an assumption regarding the benefit cost ratio of the program, and an indicator of cost-effectiveness in transferring resources to the poor: how many *Reais* from the budget does it take to transfer one *Real* of benefits to the poor through the program as it is currently structured. The basic assumptions used to compile this table are summarized in Table 9.28.

Table 9.21 shows that of total spending estimated at near R$20 billion, R$5.7 billion reaches the poor as benefits either as monetary income or as in-kind benefits. It is instructive to compare these amounts to the aggregate income gap of Brazil's rural poor of R$5.1 billion. Abstracting from measurement errors, this is the remaining income gap taking cash transfers (but not in-kind transfer) from government into account. Without suggesting simplistic and unrealistic policy solutions based on transfer programs only, the comparison shows that, in orders of magnitude, public policies already are very significant compared to the scale of the rural poverty problem and would be able, with further significant effort over the medium-term, to address most of the remaining income gap of the poor (using an admittedly low poverty line).

The information contained in Table 9.21 is reproduced in several forms to draw attention to different aspects of rural social spending. Figure 9.4 graphically compares programs along three dimensions: each bubble represents one spending program; the size of each bubble is proportional to annual per household spending (annualized in the case of investment programs) showing the relative importance of the program to beneficiaries; the horizontal position of the bubble shows the level of targeting of the program to the bottom quintile; the vertical position of the bubble shows the reach (coverage) of the program among the bottom quintile. Programs in the lower left corner are poorly targeted and do not reach many of the poor (pensions, urban services, secondary education, and credit). Programs in the bottom right-hand corner are those well-targeted, but only reaching a small share of the poor (land reform). Programs near the top left are universal (basic health, education, and school lunches). The "ideal" social program is located in the top right-hand corner. These "ideal" social programs are well targeted and reach a large share of the poor. For reference, the impact of distributionally neutral annual growth of 4 percent is shown in the top left-hand corner.

Figure 9.4 suggests a trade-off between targeting and reach among the poor. The more complete the reach to the poor, the more difficult it is to control leakage. This is the challenge faced in up-scaling small and well-targeted social development programs. The challenge is to either reallocate funds from programs with inadequate reach and targeting to programs further away from the top left-hand corner, or to redesign existing programs such that they move toward the top right corner, representing better targeting and wider reach among the poor. A second trade-off suggested is one between benefit size and coverage. Expensive programs, like land reform, reach only a small number of the poor, while cheaper programs, such as the RPAP or workfare can afford larger coverage.

Figure 9.5 shows the ranking of the evaluated social programs in terms of budgetary cost per total benefit to the poor. This indicator is calculated as the inverse of the benefit cost ratio times the targeting ratio. As a reference, Figure 9.5 also includes two benchmarks that are hypothetical and do not refer to actual social programs. The first benchmark is a hypothetical universal transfer program that would distribute an equal cash amount to every Brazilian (poor or non-poor) at an administrative cost of 20 percent. Since Brazil's poverty rate is roughly 20 percent, the indicator is equal to 6. The second benchmark is a hypothetical universal transfer program only for the rural population. Given the higher poverty rate in rural areas, the latter is significantly more cost effective. It is instructive that some social programs (including mostly non-contributory rural pensions) do not appear to meet the cost-effectiveness test against untargeted transfers.

TABLE 9.21: COMPARISON OF RURAL SOCIAL SPENDING PROGRAMS

Program/Area	Total Spending 1998 in R$bn	Million beneficiary Household	Coverage of Poor Potential Beneficiaries	Benefit per Beneficiary Household R$	Incidence to the Poor	Receipt by Poor R$bn	Benefit-Cost Ratio	Budget Outlay per Benefit to the Poor
PRONAF	1.65	0.72	6 percent	1242	25 percent	0.41	1	4.0
Rural Electrification	0.04	5.10	40 percent	112	18 percent	0.01	1	5.5
Land Reform	1.90	0.37	11 percent	4000	85 percent	1.62	1	1.2
NE Drought Workfare	0.56	1.20	56 percent	700	75 percent	0.42	0.7	1.9
Food Distribution	0.22	3.00	66 percent	40	41 percent	0.09	0.8	3.0
Piped Water Supply	0.41	3.40	7 percent	80	15 percent	0.06	1	6.7
Health Services	1.98	6.60	75 percent	299	31 percent	0.61	1	3.2
Ensino Fundamental	2.08	6.60	60 percent	315	45 percent	0.94	1	2.2
Ensino Médio	0.09	0.62	3 percent	315	17 percent	0.01	1	5.9
Rural Pensions	10.80	6.30	28 percent	1714	13 percent	1.40	0.9	8.5
RPAPs	0.21	1.30	57 percent	112	70 percent	0.14	1	1.4
Total of Listed Programs	19.92					5.71		

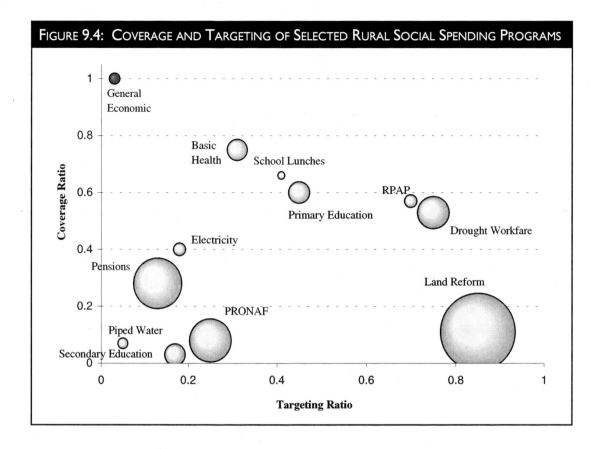

FIGURE 9.4: COVERAGE AND TARGETING OF SELECTED RURAL SOCIAL SPENDING PROGRAMS

Finally, Table 9.22 compares the physical benefits that could be obtained from the alternative use of R$1 million in different social programs. This approach avoids the use of benefit-cost ratios and is thus more appropriate for the comparison of those programs whose benefits are not exclusively or predominantly monetary or easily evaluated in monetary terms. For example, a policy maker who can spend an additional R$ 1 million on social programs in rural areas can chose between including another 40 families (34 of which are poor) in the community-based land reform program; bringing school lunches to another 25,000 children (10,250 of which are poor) for one year; or connecting another 2,000 households (300 of which are poor) to piped water.

The preceding analysis of the cost effectiveness between different rural social programs requires several rather strong assumptions to fill data gaps and make different programs comparable. The analysis should be understood as highly tentative. It should provide stimulation for more detailed investigation along the lines proposed rather than be taken as a definitive judgment about the incidence and effectiveness of social rural spending in Brazil.

The analysis presented here is instructive and permits the quantitative comparison of a wide range of very diverse social programs. However, several limitations need to be considered before drawing simplistic and premature policy conclusions from this analysis. These limitations imply that the analysis cannot be used as a direct guide to resource allocation but should serve as a departure point for further in-depth analysis.

a) The analysis ranks programs by their effectiveness to transfer resources to the poor. However, many of the analyzed programs have additional objectives that need to be considered in a more comprehensive evaluation. For example, programs, such as social security and unemployment insurance, have an insurance function regardless their social objectives. Many investment programs also have a growth objective. Thus, low effectiveness in trans-

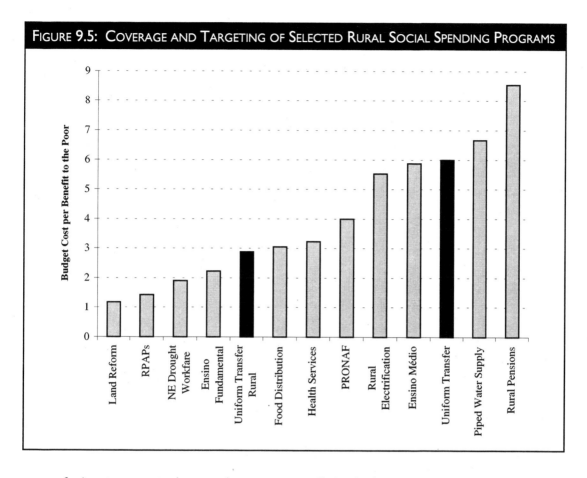

FIGURE 9.5: COVERAGE AND TARGETING OF SELECTED RURAL SOCIAL SPENDING PROGRAMS

ferring resources to the poor does not necessarily imply that a program should be abandoned. However, low effectiveness does imply that a program should not be a priority for the reduction of rural poverty and should not be justified on such grounds.

b) For several programs, non-monetary benefits for the poor are difficult to measure. Therefore, the assumed benefit-cost ratio may well underestimate the benefits of several programs.

TABLE 9.22: BENEFITS FROM R$1 MILLION SPENDING IN DIFFERENT PROGRAMS

Benefit for R$1 million Budget Spending	Total Beneficiaries	Poor Beneficiaries
Households in Community-Based Land Reform Program	40	34
Households with RPAP	1429	1000
Temporary Drought Workfare Jobs	1429	1071
Children in Primary School	3175	1429
Children with School Lunch	25000	10250
Households Covered with Basic Health	3344	1037
PRONAF Loans	435	109
Households Connected to Electricity	1429	259
Children in Secondary School	3175	540
Households Connected to Piped Water	2000	300
Pension Recipients	583	76

c) Targeting typically refers to average spending in the recent past. New and additional spending may, however, have a different incidence. For example, the average targeting of sewage investments in the past has been very regressive. However, as coverage of the better-off population increases, additional investment may be better targeted.

d) As discussed before, some types of resource leakage are not reflected in these calculations. This includes the transfer of resources to expropriated landowners through compensation above market value of their land. The comparison for land reform program presented here is only valid to the extent that such leakage can be prevented, for example through community-based schemes.

e) Some programs have limited objectives and a specific target group (drought relief workfare, for example). While they may be well suited to effectively obtain their objective and reach their target group, these programs cannot reach other objectives or other poor groups. It would thus be mistaken to substitute them for programs with broader objectives and target groups, such as basic education or basic health services.

Priorities for Policy Reform

Overall, rural social spending is very progressive compared to total social spending in Brazil. Simply because the poverty rate is so much higher in rural areas, a less intensive targeting effort is necessary for bringing a larger share of the benefits to the poor. Rural social spending has a larger poverty reducing effect than social spending overall. This would suggest, on the margin, that increasing rural social spending more than urban social spending would have a greater effect on poverty reduction.

Given tight fiscal constraints, however, a more selective and specific approach to rural social spending is indicated. This selective approach requires a more specific look at the different groups of rural poor and the appropriate policy instruments for helping these different groups escape from poverty. This section attempts to assess the changes that are necessary to provide better support for the different poverty escape paths.

Five strategies to overcome rural poverty are identified. Each of these strategies is suitable for a different segment of the rural poor population:

1. First, especially in the Northeast, there are many opportunities for economically viable small-farm activities, typically comprising a combination of subsistence and market production. Capitalization, physical investments, and services for family farmers can increase labor productivity and incomes and reduce migration pressures. These programs include intensification through small-scale irrigation projects, community-based land reform, and small infrastructure investments such as access roads. Where such investments are efficient and where the underlying economic activity is viable, they should be supported. Family farm investments can be efficient and can reduce poverty even though they typically do not contribute significantly to the growth of the overall economy.

2. Second, a revitalized commercial agriculture sector can absorb wage labor and thus increase employment and reduce rural poverty. For example, efficient, market-driven expansion of irrigated areas in the Northeast will create new opportunities. Critical for growth and increased employment in the sector are improvements in the workings of the factor markets, labor, water, land, and capital. From the perspective of the poor, better education levels will increase the chances of finding employment in the commercial agriculture sector.

3. Third, rural non-farm activities are promising to increase rural employment, especially in the food processing and service sectors, and thus reduce poverty. Critical ingredients to a vibrant rural non-farm economy are better education levels and good basic infrastructure.

4. Fourth, further migration into urban areas seems inevitable and even desirable, considering the high incidence of rural poverty, the very large absolute number of very small farms, and

the relatively low agricultural growth potential in non-irrigated areas of the Northeast. More training and educational opportunities for the rural poor appear to be the most critical policy variable for facilitating this absorption into other sectors of the economy. An important preoccupation of policy makers is to maintain migration to urban areas at a level that can be managed in the receiving areas. Thus, the simultaneous pursuit of the other strategies that are directed at increasing the income of the rural poor within the rural areas can avoid excessive migration.

5. Fifth, there is a group of rural poor who will not be able to benefit from opportunities in commercial agriculture, from small-scale intensification, or from migration. Members of this group are typically older, often widows, and occasionally farm workers in poorly endowed areas. This group is "trapped" in extreme poverty with no viable future in agriculture. Members of this group face considerable barriers in finding off-farm employment. For this group, a social safety net is critical to ensure a basic decent living standard.

From this discussion follows an emphasis on five policy instruments to be simultaneously applied for the reduction of rural poverty in Brazil, in tentative order of priority. Each of these five policy instruments facilitates one or more of the five escape strategies from rural poverty (see Table 9.23).

First, more and better education for the rural population should be the top priority. Better education not only increases employment opportunities but also facilitates opportunity-driven migration. Opportunity-driven migration should be an additional reason for rural education even though it is sometimes stated as a reason against rural education. However, the externalities related to education of migrants may suggest that municipalities should not be left alone in the struggle for better rural education.

Second, capital, services, and basic infrastructure for economically viable family farms are often cost-effective for the reduction of poverty. The Northeast RPAPs have established a methodology for effectively delivering such services, including the extension to community based land reform. The capital, services, and infrastructure approach can be further expanded and refined, with a perspective toward improved access to credit for advancing communities.

Third, regulatory reform for land, labor, capital, and water markets is critical for a revitalization of commercial agriculture. Land market reform needs to increase effective tenure security and facilitate the development of more effective land rental markets. Labor market reform needs to address the artificial inflexibility of labor contracts that is likely to depress farm employment. Reforms of land and labor regulation should facilitate efficient land rental contracts with adequate land tenure security. Capital market reform overall (not just for the rural sector) needs to increase the level of financial intermediation, reduce the cost of intermediation, and develop unsubsidized term lending. Finally, water market reforms need to create incentives for private investment into water resource infrastructure and security over water rights.

Fourth, given the large outlays for rural pensions and drought emergency relief, a significant social safety net is in place. Targeting of non-contributory rural pensions requires further analysis and improvements. Drought relief could be improved and integrated with more continuous income support through a community-based workfare program. This community based workfare program could use the methodology of the RPAPs for the implementation of small-scale local work. The low wage rate paid by the workfare program would ensure that the program automatically expands and contracts with the climatic conditions and subsequent fluctuations in excess labor supply.

Finally, there are still significant infrastructure gaps in rural areas. In particular, lack of electricity in poor rural areas and difficult road access to remote locations complicate dynamic development of family or commercial agriculture as well as non-farm activities.

TABLE 9.23: STRATEGIES FOR POVERTY REDUCTION AND POLICY INSTRUMENTS

Policy Instruments	Strategy for Escape from Poverty				
	Family Agriculture	Commercial Agriculture	Rural Non-Farm Sector	Urban Migration	Social Safety Net
Education and Health	Moderate effect of education on farm productivity	Moderate effect of education on farm productivity	Education essential to enable non-farm activities	Essential to enable opportunity-driven migration	Reduces number of those dependent on safety net
Capitalization of Small Farmers, Agriculture Credit, Extension	Critical to enable small scale and economically viable activities	Commercial agriculture typically not dependent on public services		Reduces migration pressure	Reduces number of those dependent on safety net
Making factor markets work (water, land, labor, and capital)		Critical for commercial farm productivity and employment		Reduces migration pressure	Reduces number of those dependent on safety net
Transfer Programs				Reduces migration pressure	Group depends on transfer programs
Basic Infrastructure	Critical to improve productivity and market access	Critical to improve productivity and market access	Critical to improve productivity and market access	Reduces migration pressure	Reduces number of those dependent on safety net

Legend:

Core Policy for this Strategy	Important Policy for this Strategy	Policy that Reduces Pressure on this Strategy

References

Buainain, Antônio Márcio, et al. 1999a. "Avalia Preliminar do Programa Cédula da Terra." Brasília. UNICAMP. mimeo.

Buainain, Antônio Márcio, et al. 1999b. "Community-Based Land Reform Implemantation in Brazil: A new way of reaching out the marginalized?" mimeo.

Buainain, Antônio Márcio, J. M. F. J. Silveira, and Edson Teófilo (2000). "O Programa Cédula da Terra no contexto das novas políticas de reforma agrária, desenvolvimento e participação: uma discussão das transformações necessárias e possíveis." in MDA/NEAD, *Reforma Agrária e Desenvolvimento Sustentável*. Brasília, 1a. ed., Ed. Paralelo 15., 380p:157–175.

Delgado, Guillerme. 2000. *A Universalização de Direitos Sociais no Brasil: A Previdência Rural nos Anos 90.*

Deininger, Klaus and Lyn Squire. 1998. "New Ways of Looking at old Issues: Asset Inequality and Growth." Mimeo. Brasília.

Ferreira, Francisco H. G., Peter Lanjouw and Neri, Marcelo. 1998. "The Urban Poor in Brazil in 1996: A New Poverty Profile Using PPV, PNAD and Census Data" mimeo.

Filho, Hildo Meirelles de Souza, Antônio Márcio Buainain, Carolina Junqueira Homem de Mello, José Maria da Silveira, Marcelo M. Magalhães. 2000. "Does community-based self-selection of land reform beneficiaries work? An assessment of the Brazilian Cedula da Terra Pilot Program." mimeo. UNICAMP.

Rocha, Sonia. 1998. "Pobreza e Condições de Vida no Ceará." mimeo.

World Bank. 2001. "Attacking Brazil's Poverty." Report No. 20475. Washington DC.

Zyl, Johan Van, Loretta Sonn and Costa, Alberto. 2000. "Decentralized Rural Development, Enhanced Community Participation And Local Government Performance: Evidence From Northeast Brazil." Mimeo.

Appendix

TABLE 9.24: SOURCES OF FUNDING FOR RURAL CREDIT PROGRAMS 1998—PRELIMINARY
(in R$ and percentages of column total)

	Cost	%	Investment	%	Trade	%	Pronaf
	\multicolumn{6}{c}{Credit operations not connected to special programs}						
National Treasury	1 591 243	0.03	35 881	0.00	178 503 592	14.23	
Mandatory Resources	2 398 436 612	46.06	310 178 739	19.19	964 572 021	76.88	157 788 170
BNDES	22 175	0.00	249 319 145	15.42			
Finame			198 477 074	12.28			
Incra							
FAT							1 058 566 855
FAT with subsidy							44 304 427
FAT without subsidy	84 778 065	1.63	149 650 269	9.26	68 056	0.01	
Commodities	4 817 000	0.09	553 798	0.03	465 000	0.04	
Foreign Markets with subsidy	124 062 936	2.38					
Rural Savings with Conditionalities	1 432 161 756	27.51	258 737	0.02			
Rural Savings without Conditionalities	1 879 637	0.04	1 659 640	0.10			
Rural Savings at free interest rates	196 312	0.00					
Free resources	256 787 586	4.93	61 411 351	3.80	81 534 243	6.50	
State Government	7 298 091	0.14	12 574 841	0.78			
External Sources - Resolution No. 63	232 083 634	4.46	58 834 909	3.64	23 911 668	1.91	
Funcafé	617 311 966	11.86	11 412	0.00			
Fundo Constitucional do Nordeste (FNE)	15 249 135	0.29	194 351 727	12.02	581 478	0.05	81 494 183
Fundo Constitucional do Norte (FNO)	15 263 660	0.29	121 557 847	7.52			
Fundo Constitucional do Centro-Oeste (FCO)	56 280	0.00	253 022 355	15.65			480 706
Others	14 698 361	0.28	4 861 942	0.30	5 056 268	0.40	
Total	**5 206 694 451**	**100.00**	**1 616 759 667**	**100.00**	**1 254 692 326**	**100.00**	**1 342 634 341**
Share of total		**50.63**		**15.72**		**12.20**	

[1]Including resources allocated to Prodecer (I and II), to Proest, to Proinap and to Cocoa Farming

Source: Banco Central—Department of Registration

%	Procera	%	Proger	%	Others[1]	%	Total	%
	18 678	0.01			4 875 274	1.91	185 024 682	1.80
11.75							3 830 975 696	37.25
					29 174 113	11.41	278 515 448	2.71
							198 477 087	1.93
	127 301 159	69.57					127 301 229	1.24
78.84	4 098	0.00			55 666 143	21.77	1 114 237 175	10.84
3.30			423 939 613	100.00			468 244 144	4.55
							234 496 402	2.28
							5 835 798	0.06
							124 062 938	1.21
							1 432 420 520	13.93
							3 539 277	0.03
							196 312	0.00
							399 733 195	3.89
							19 872 933	0.19
							314 830 222	3.06
							617 323 390	6.00
6.07	55 670 193	30.42			124 937 245	48.86	472 284 010	4.59
							136 821 515	1.33
0.04					41 039 495	16.05	294 598 851	2.86
							24 616 572	0.24
100.00	182 994 127	100.00	423 939 613	100.00	255 692 270	100.00	10 283 407 395	100.00
13.06		1.78		4.12		2.49		

TABLE 9.25: ECONOMIC BENEFITS OF RPAP SUBPROJECTS BY MAIN SUBPROJECT TYPE

Project Type	Total No. of Sub-projects Completed	No of Beneficiary Families per Subproject	Cost per Sub-project (US$)	Net No. of Jobs Created per Sub-project[1]	Net Annual Incremental Income/savings per Subproject (US$)	Incremental Crop Area Cultivated per Sub-project (hectares)[2]	Cost Effectiveness			
							Economic Internal Rate of Return (percent)	Total Investment per Beneficiary Family (US$)	Total Investment per Job Created (US$)	Economic Benefit-Cost Ratio[3]
Infrastructure:										
Rural water supply	4,025	71	30,149	—	12,369	1.4	—	425	—	—
Rural electrification	4,080	49	22,400	—	1,942	1.6	—	457	—	—
Small bridges	538	139	26,350	—	1,040	2.3	—	190	—	—
Community telephones	435	140	22,944	—	422	0	—	164	—	—
Productive: Manioc mills	412	68	18,451	10.8	17,148	16.3	>30	271	1,708	>2.0
Tractors for communal use	573	95	30,870	29.3	28,137	22.6	>30	325	1,054	>2.0
Small-scale livestock	110	40	16,354	2.5	6,214	2.8	>30	409	6,542	>2.0
Small-scale irrigation	146	36	25,158	25.4	23,800	37.9	>30	699	990	>2.0
Social:										
Road paving and rehabilitation	675	82	31,930	—	242	1.7	—	389	—	—
Sanitation systems	171	72	29,727	—	0	0	—	413	—	—

Note: 1. Many jobs created by the infrastructure and social subprojects come from additional economic activities made possible by the investments, but not directly involved with the project after its construction/establishment.

2. The incremental crop areas associated with infrastructure and social subprojects come from the cultivation of additional areas which was made possible by the projects.

3. Obtained by using a real rate of 10 percent for the opportunity cost of capital.

TABLE 9.26: AGGREGATE ECONOMIC BENEFITS OF RPAP SUBPROJECTS BY MAIN SUBPROJECT TYPE

Project Type	Total No. of Subprojects Completed	Total Cost for all Subprojects (US$ million)	Total number of beneficiary families	Aggregate Benefits[1]		
				Total Net No. of Permanent Jobs Created	Total Net Annual Incremental Income/savings (US$ million)	Total Incremental Crop Area Cultivated (hectares)
Infrastructure:						
Rural water supply	4,025	121.349	257,198	6,521	44.807	5,072
Rural electrification	4,080	91.392	179,928	8,813	7.131	5,875
Small bridges	538	14.176	67,304	1,355	0.504	1,113
Community telephones	435	9.981	54,810	823	0.166	0
Productive: Manioc mills	412	7.602	16,810	2,670	4.239	4,030
Tractors for communal use	573	17.689	32,661	10,073	9.674	7,770
Small-scale livestock	110	1.799	2,640	165	0.410	185
Small-scale irrigation	146	3.673	3,154	2,225	2.085	3,320
Social:						
Road paving and rehabilitation	675	21.553	49,815	972	0.147	1,033
Sanitation systems	171	5.083	11,081	15	0	0
Aggregate for all RPAPs[2]	**13,784**	**362.271**	**833,831**	**41,521**	**85.387**	**35,059**

Note: 1. The aggregate benefits were derived by scaling up typical subproject results. Important assumptions were made with regards to subproject types not analyzed and sustainability of major subproject categories. It was assumed that, sustainability levels of infrastructure, productive and social subprojects are 89 percent, 60 percent and 88 percent, respectively. Fiscal benefits were not included.

2. The aggregate impact also include estimates for those types of sub-projects not included in the analysis. The totals therefore do not add up.

3. It should be taken into account that some families benefit from more than one subproject. Without repetition, the number of beneficiary families amounts to 661,314 if all projects are considered sustainable. However, if the assumptions with respect to sustainability are applied, 578,133 households eventually benefit from the RPAPs (without repetition).

TABLE 9.27: COMBINED ECONOMIC BENEFITS FROM THE R-NRDP AND RPAP, 1993–2000

Program	Total No. of Subprojects Completed	Total Cost for all Subprojects (US$ million)	Total number of beneficiary families	Total Net No. of Permanent Jobs Created	Total Net Annual Incremental Income/savings (US$ million)	Total Incremental Crop Area Cultivated (hectares)
				Aggregate Benefits[1]		
Aggregate for the reformulated RDP[1].	17,860	430.390	1,088,427	55,938	117.911	46,339
Aggregate for the RPAP	13,784	362.271	833,831	41,521	85.387	35,059
Aggregate for NRDP and RPAP	31,644	792.661	1,922,258	97,459	203.298	81,348

Note: 1. The benefits for the R-NRDP were calculated in exactly the same manner as for the RPAP.
2. Some families benefited from both the R-NRDP and the RPAP. This data is not available. Also, some families benefit from more than one subproject with the R-NRDP and RPAP.

TABLE 9.28: ASSUMPTIONS UNDERLYING PROGRAM COST-EFFECTIVENESS COMPARISONS

Assumptions and Calculations	Total spending 1998 in R$bn	Million beneficiary households	Coverage of potential beneficiaries	Benefit per beneficiary household R$	Incidence
PRONAF and PROCERA		Administrative data	Assumption based on interviews and eligibility criteria	Assumed subsidy of 54 percent on average loan size of R$2300	Assumption based on interviews and eligibility criteria
Rural Electrification		PAND Data	PNAD Data	Annualized household connection costs of R$700 (only local grid connection)	PPV Data
Land Reform		Beneficiary households 1995–99	2.8 million poor rural households	R$25000 annualized at 16 percent	Estimate from Cédula da Terra. Excludes leakage through excessive compensation of expropriated landowners
NE Drought Workfare		SUDENE	1.6 million poor rural households in NE	Program design data	Assumption based on RPAP experience
Food Distribution		Coverage of school lunches	Coverage of students with school lunches, from PPV	200 meals at R$0.20 per meal	Incidence of all School Lunches, from PPV
Rural Water Supply		PNAD Data	PNAD Data	Assuming R$500 per household investment cost, annualized	PPV Data
Health Services		Assumed 85 percent of total rural households	Assumption based on PPV responses citing supply reasons for non-treatment	Per household with access rather than per household that used health service	PPV Data
Ensino Fundamental		Assumed 85 percent of total rural households, based on actual attendance rate	Share of 7–14 year olds attending primary school (PPV)	Spending floor for basic education	PPV Data
Ensino Médio		Coverage Data	PPV Data	Spending floor for basic education	PPV Data
Rural Pensions		Administrative data	PPV: Poor households with at least one pension recipient	One minimum salary	PPV Data
RPAPs		Beneficiary households 1993–99, without repeater projects	1.6 million poor rural households in NE	R$700 annualized at 16 percent	From evaluation study